IT WAS ALL A DREAM

IT WAS ALL A DREAM

BIGGIE AND THE WORLD THAT MADE HIM

JUSTIN TINSLEY

Abrams Press, New York

ABRAMS The Art of Books
195 Broadway, New York, NY 10007
abramsbooks.com

To my mother, Karen, and my grandmother, Clemmie, who dealt with me during those days when I was really trying to figure life out. I wasn't easy to live with then, but you loved me unconditionally. Thank you. For everything.

TABLE OF CONTENTS

INTRODUCTION

FOR THE PAST QUARTER CENTURY, A QUOTE FROM CHRISTO-
PHER WALLACE HAS RESONATED WITH ME. It's from an interview
filmed just two weeks before his murder, and it's haunting because at its
core lives an innocence, a sort of pure, unfiltered honesty that we all want to
believe about the purity in ourselves despite the mistakes we've made. And
Wallace, known the world over and immortalized in history as the Notorious B.I.G. (short for Business Instead of Game) or Biggie Smalls or Big, was
far from perfect, in many ways, as this book will establish. Yet as we'll also
come to discover, Biggie carried with him a soul so genuine that those who
knew him still laugh, cry, and speak with deep reverence at the mention of
his name. It's inspiring, if we're being real.

Every life ends with two dates on its tombstone—the day of arrival and
the day of transition. But as the life and times of Christopher Wallace attest,
it's not the dates that matter. Well, I take that back: They absolutely matter. But
it's the hyphen separating them that matters more than anything. That dash
represents the entirety of our lives. The inspirations, the defeats, the highs,
the lows, the joys, the pain. All within the context of the world we were raised
in and, in Biggie's case, oftentimes battled to insist that our lives were actually worth a damn. That dash means everything. The mistakes we made and
the lessons we learned—the pitfalls we couldn't avoid and the legacy we leave

behind. The first day Christopher took his breath in Brooklyn, New York, and the early morning hours of Los Angeles, California, when he took his last, will be deeply examined. They have to be. But it's that dash where this story lives.

So much of Big's life story lives in that aforementioned interview. He sat in a California parking lot with *Rap City* host Joe Clair as he filmed the video for "Hypnotize," the lone video he'd be in from his forthcoming *Life After Death* double album. The date was February 24, 1997. Two and a half years had passed since his first album, *Ready to Die*, one of the most impressive debuts in rap history, had lyrically detonated shelves nationwide. It was only five years removed from when he and his fellow Brooklynite DJ Mister Cee (Calvin LeBrun) had sat in the office of an up-and-coming music executive named Sean "Puffy" Combs, and that executive had made him a promise.

"I can have a record out on you by summer," Puffy had said, leaning over his desk.

"Yo, whatever Cee say, man," a still-very-shy Big had answered.

The interview was only six or seven or so years from when Wallace was selling crack on the streets of New York and Raleigh, North Carolina. Less than a decade before the interview, he had dropped out of high school to hustle. Over the course of the 1990s, Christopher Wallace's life changed dramatically in such a ridiculously short amount of time. Now, here he was, the most popular rapper in the game, but also one of the most criticized, analyzed, and, true to his name, notorious. There were the hit records that became instant smashes, like the socioeconomic advancement anthem "Juicy," the undeniably addictive remix to "One More Chance," or Junior M.A.F.I.A.'s "Player's Anthem." He was an evolving actor given appearances on *Martin* and *New York Undercover*. And though he played himself in both, there was an unavoidable radiance that glistened off the ebony skin that he once described as "ugly as ever." Anyone who got close to Big felt his charisma. They knew he had the gift of gab that could make men want to be him and women want to be with him. His presence, well over six feet tall and more than three hundred pounds, intimidated people. And if anyone listened to his music, Big gave more than enough reasons to fear him. Yet in reality, he was as affable a superstar as there's ever been. From the moment he opened his mouth, he disarmed you. Whatever fear he first struck into people instantly morphed into a ghetto tranquility.

"He swear he's the best drink maker. He wanna make all the drinks in the studio," said Big's former stylist, Groovey Lew, reflecting on countless studio sessions. "Like, 'What you drinkin', homie? What you drinking, baby?' Mixing, shaking ice—just being happy serving people. He was the best when he came to that. Then he wanna watch you drink it, and you tell him how you like it. He'd just be happy off doing that."

Yet as much as success seemed to naturally gravitate toward him like bees to nectar, adversity never seemed to leave his side either. The previous year, 1996, was a tumultuous one for Big. His marriage to R&B star Faith Evans seemed to dissolve almost as quickly as it came together. He was arrested several times for reasons running from an assault on two autograph seekers to weapons and marijuana possession. And a September car accident had broken his leg, leaving him with limited mobility for months and a cane he'd use until the very end of his life. And then there was the trouble he never truly wanted to be part of from his falling-out with former friend Tupac Shakur. At the time of his *Rap City* interview, Shakur's September 1996 murder in Las Vegas was still fresh in the rap world's consciousness. Not that it's gone anywhere in the quarter century since.

Something I've learned over the years is that people get so obsessed with how these two rap icons were taken from us that it overshadows the magic, nuance, and complexities that made up their brief, young lives. It's deeper than them being Gemini twins separated by eleven months. In this book, we'll connect the dots that trace back to the 1960s and '70s and how legislation, systemic racism, and America's evolving fear of the Black body transformed a generation's worth of lives. As bodies floating through the universe and this thing called life, we're all connected in ways we could never imagine. So yes, we'll get to Biggie and Tupac eventually. How the two rap supernovas initially met, how there was so much love between the two, how their falling-out—really, more so, Tupac's falling out with Biggie—affected so many, and the extent to which it is still felt today. How the two never had a chance to reconcile and mend a friendship that should've never been dismantled to begin with. And we'll briefly examine the conspiracies that surround their tragic murders a quarter century later. Speaking of one without the other is impossible. But it is important to remember they're two larger-than-life figures whose work should speak for itself.

"Christopher and Tupac were just so big. They were just such iconic and unique people, and offered so much not only by their lives, but through their music and other creative works," said Greg Kading, the former Los Angeles Police Department detective who was assigned to lead a special task force into the Wallace murder. "The hardest thing is that people just can't really digest the idea that two people that are so influential and so important can die just by some simple, random bullshit violence."

The interview on the set of the "Hypnotize" video, a month and a day out from the release of *Life After Death*, proved expansive. It had to be. Biggie had so many different pockets in his life, and he addressed much of it. He had no issue with discussing the past, but he was more focused on what the future held. He was finally at a place in his life where peace seemed to outweigh chaos. He was a man his mother could be proud of, and a father his young kids could grow to cherish.

Toward the end of the interview, Biggie said the words that have stuck with me for all the years since.

"Get to know me, man," he said with a smirk, lounging slightly in the director's chair. "To know me is to love me."

Biggie had been in Los Angeles for weeks. He enjoyed Cali and all of its fruits—as he put it in "Going Back to Cali," on *Life After Death*: "the weather / women, and the weed, sticky green." This isn't to say there wasn't more than the occasional side-eye from Los Angelenos. There was still very much a visceral animosity toward his label, Bad Boy Records, in early 1997. He'd heard "West Side!" yelled at him many times and seen people throw up the "W" hand gesture. Many inside and outside the industry openly wondered why he'd be so public with his West Coast excursions given the culture's temperature.

But Biggie wasn't entertaining any negative energy because he'd committed himself to positivity, just like he wasn't tripping on the boos that showered down when he attended a Los Angeles Clippers and Philadelphia 76ers game on February 25. The cheers outnumbered the boos, but the boos could still be heard. Following the game, he told the then rookie Allen Iverson that he was looking for a house to purchase in L.A. Biggie was done running from death. He'd looked the Reaper in the eyes so many times he could tell you their color. But not anymore. The future was bright, and Biggie Smalls, the superstar, was nowhere near his peak. He was ready to live.

Big already knew the first date on his tombstone: May 21, 1972. And as far as he knew then, his dash still had decades to unfurl itself. That's the beautiful thing about his final weeks—Christopher Wallace was happy, genuinely happy, for what felt like the first time in his adult life. Fourteen days after the interview taped, in the early morning hours of Los Angeles on March 9, 1997, that happiness would be cut short.

Three days later, that *Rap City* interview aired on BET.

When my editor initially approached me to write this book a few years ago, I nearly deleted the email—I thought it was spam. I never thought I'd be linked to something like Biggie Smalls's legacy in a way as direct as writing a biography of his life. It's beyond daunting. Intimidating, and, in ways, it felt damn near like a setup. What the hell could I say about the Notorious B.I.G. that hadn't already been said? That people were willing to speak about? And then to be on that journey during a pandemic made it even more petrifying. But even in moments when I'd hit a brick wall and wonder what the hell I'd gotten myself into, there was Biggie. There was that quote that stuck with me.

"Get to know me, man. To know me is to love me."

To say those words didn't haunt me throughout the process of writing this book would be like saying the remix to "One More Chance" was just an average song. Biggie lived just under twenty-five years, and he's been gone a quarter century, and yet there are still generations of fans who adore his music, many of whom never walked the Earth at the same time as Christopher Wallace or breathed the same air that he did. People love him, no question. People cling to him. They think they know him, too. That's because in life the man born Christopher Wallace was a magnet. In death, that magnetic force still lives in who he was, what he represented, and the joy his music brought to an entire generation that was more than willing to pass it down. Biggie's life has been covered in books and articles and podcasts and documentaries and a Hollywood biopic. But beyond the music his fans listen to, beyond some inspirational quote from him they post on their Instagram, there was a man. A man who was more than just the biggest and most controversial moments of his life. There was a man behind the man. And there was a clear distinction between the two.

"Biggie is an entertainer," he once said, speaking in the third person. "He makes music and he makes videos. That's Biggie Smalls, but Christopher Wallace is the person. That's the one that has to take care of the family. The daughter, the wife—all of that. That's Christopher. That's the real person. I leave all that Biggie stuff alone. We don't blend too much."

I thought I knew so much about Biggie Smalls. And in a way, I always did. What I came to understand, both deeply and quickly, is that the more people I spoke to, the more I grew weary of just calling him by his stage name. That was him, but it wasn't all of him. Long before he became an international supernova, Christopher Wallace was one of the most definitive code-switchers. As the legendary journalist Rob Marriott told me, this first-generation American kid *became* American through Brooklyn. And because of that, he spawned into this superhero-like Brooklyn figure. He's Brooklyn incarnate. When you hear the name "Brooklyn," the man who once proudly proclaimed that he "repped BK to the fullest" is either at the top of the list or near the very top. The borough of Brooklyn is greatly responsible for such a significant portion of hip-hop culture, and for Big to represent so much of that in one body is both awe-inspiring and tragic.

"Get to know me, man. To know me is to love me."

How well do we really know Biggie Smalls? Sure, we could rap his entire verse on "Mo' Money, Mo' Problems" — but could we recite what it was like growing up on Fulton Street and St. James Place, or how it felt to evolve from an innocent mama's boy to a naturally curious and inquisitive adolescent who saw peers hustling on the corner and wanted a taste of that life? Sure, we can talk about why he and Tupac fell out—but do we really know the ghetto love stories of how they'd perform at concerts together and 'Pac would pull up in Brooklyn and smoke weed on the corner with Biggie and his people? And sure, we know Biggie was a ladies' man—but do we really know the mountain of complexities that brought into his life?

The answer is that many do, but even more don't. So while it is daunting, it's even more of an honor to chronicle the good, the bad, the indifferent, and everything in between that led to the corner where he hustled at Fulton and St. James to be renamed "Christopher 'Notorious B.I.G.' Wallace

Way," and which led to him being part of the 2020 induction class in the Rock & Roll Hall of Fame.

A quarter century later, so many who loved the Notorious B.I.G. and actually knew Christopher Wallace are still struggling to come to terms without him. They've moved on but never moved past him.

"Over the years, whenever Biggie would call me and leave a voice message, he'd leave a rhyme," said Drew Dixon, a friend of Biggie's and a former music industry executive. She lived a few Brooklyn blocks away from Biggie in the early nineties. Their journeys in the music industry ran parallel in many ways, Dixon remembered during our interview, hers on the business side and his on the artistic side. "It'd be like, 'Drew, eyes blue . . . whatcha gonna do? Call me back!' I didn't save those. I just never thought to save them. I never thought Biggie wouldn't be here forever."

"It was almost more than a friendship to me. For me, [my bond with Biggie] was such a huge part of everything that's happened to me in my life," said Matteo "Matty C" Capoluongo, whose Unsigned Hype column on Biggie in *The Source* propelled him into the national spotlight. "It's so much more than friendship."

Very few words exist that elicit more pain than "what if." Envisioning a world where Christopher Wallace turns fifty years old in May 2022 is almost as difficult as it is to realize that the memories of Biggie Smalls are actually older than the man himself. I'm thirty-six years old, making me from the generation that was alive when Biggie was around, but not quite old enough to live with his music at that time. Yet I was old enough to understand that his death was more than just a one-day story on the evening news.

Biggie, like Tupac, seemed so much older at the time of his death. Being twenty-four might as well have been forty years old in my eyes, in the eyes of my peers. Biggie seemed so much older because that's how he carried himself. Yet unlike Biggie, my generation aged. We graduated from high school. We went to the military. We graduated from college. We became doctors, teachers, lawyers, journalists. Some, like Biggie before the music, went into hustling. Some never made it out. Some will never see the outside world again. Some, like Biggie, left the streets before their luck ran out.

Yet by the time we became twenty-four, we all realized that twenty-four wasn't old at all. Being twenty-four means your life has hardly begun. Being twenty-four means you're still trying to figure out whatever the hell life is really about. Being twenty-four means there are way more mistakes in the future, and if you play your cards right, the blessings to come from those mistakes are wilder than your wildest dreams. Biggie was a star by the time he was twenty-three and dead just two months before turning twenty-five.

People ask me all the time what I hope readers will get from a book about someone so well known. The answer is simple. There is no bombshell revelation about a secret life in these pages. Nor does this book confirm who pulled the triggers on Biggie or Tupac Shakur. Do enough digging on the internet, watch the right documentaries and read the right books, and that truth, or at least the closest version of the truth that the world will likely ever know, is out there. It's been hiding in plain sight for years. And by now, the suspected triggermen are long dead.

To those of you who grew up with Biggie Smalls, who make his music part of your life's official soundtrack, perhaps this is a nostalgic trip down memory lane. Maybe it's a chance to reconnect with a different part of your life that's a quarter century in your rear view. But it'll take you back to those house parties, cookouts, marathon smoking sessions, Freakniks, or Atlanta Greek Picnics when the Notorious B.I.G. held court. And maybe it's a way to view how different your life has been in the twenty-five years since we all felt part of our innocence leave with Biggie.

And for the generations that followed Big, consider this part of the curriculum when trying to understand who Christopher Wallace was and who Biggie Smalls still is. How the world around him influenced his decisions, his mistakes, and his triumphs. How he was a natural comedian and a fun-loving and debonair young man who also grew up in a world of toxic masculinity. How in the final years and months of his life he was so desperately trying to evolve into a better person—forget rapper. He already had that mastered. And why, from the moment the first bullet burst out of the assassin's gun and connected with Biggie's torso at the corner of Fairfax Avenue and Wilshire Boulevard in Los Angeles on March 9, 1997, rap has tried—is still trying—to pay homage to his legacy.

"Get to know me, man. To know me is to love me."

He always did have a way with words.

01

COMING TO AMERICA

FOR VOLETTA WALLACE, THE VISION WAS CLEAR. It was all she could think about. She was smitten. Not with a man. Not yet, at least. The feeling in the pit of her stomach centered on a country, a place that seemed so luxurious, exotic, and effortlessly sublime. And, most importantly, it wasn't Jamaica. All that mattered to Voletta, just sixteen at the time, was seeing, touching, smelling this place—calling it, the United States of America, home.

Voletta was born in Trelawny, Jamaica, in 1953. The rustic parish, later home to the world's fastest man, Usain Bolt, rests on the northern coast, east of Montego Bay. Voletta was the fourth of ten children, though in her 2005 memoir, *Biggie: Voletta Wallace Remembers Her Son, Christopher Wallace, aka Notorious B.I.G.*, she admitted feeling like "an only child."

Despite her son rhyming about living in a "one-room shack" years later, it was Voletta who grew up in such conditions.

"The room had a table, a bed, and three little chairs," she reflected. "Thinking back on it, the house was not really a house where one could live and enjoy . . . Most of our living took place outside the house and in the yard."

When Voletta turned seven, her father moved the family into a larger house built on a farm with a copious amount of land. Voletta learned the importance of family from her mother, the value of work ethic from her father, and the importance of religious discipline from her whole family. Jamaica wasn't close to being in the company of the wealthiest countries in the world, and Voletta's family wasn't anywhere near the model of wealth on the island, but she didn't go without love or the basic necessities. She was a daydreamer, a daddy's girl—as her older siblings teased her of being—who would follow her father into the fields where he worked, sit under a tree, and allow her mind to wander until it was time for lunch. Those trips with her father proved transformational for Voletta as she saw firsthand the value a powerful male figure in her life could bring. She never forgot this value, either.

By the time she turned she turned sixteen, Voletta received her first experience of life outside Trelawny. She moved to a suburb outside Kingston to live with the aunt of one of her cousins. The partnership proved immediately fruitful. Voletta helped her aunt, who was pregnant at the time, and got a chance to attend school in Kingston and work part-time. Education in Jamaica wasn't free after the sixth grade, and many students—those who didn't receive a scholarship or have parents who could foot the bill themselves—had their academic careers come to an early close.

Still, Voletta never stopped daydreaming. In Kingston, her part-time job was at a travel agency, and there, all the brochures and colorful magazines around the office captured her imagination. They made the United States seem like a utopia that was only a body of water away. Everything was bigger, shinier, and more opulent there. Voletta wanted that good life, and as far as she knew, America was more than willing to offer it to her. The only problem was that she had to find a way to get there.

Voletta never finished high school in Jamaica. And not because she was a lackluster student. The night her aunt went into labor, she awoke to her aunt's husband in her bedroom touching her body. To make the experience even more repugnant, his son lay asleep on the other side of the room. However long it took to process for Voletta, she wouldn't allow the unforgivable breach of trust to advance any further.

"I swung at his face—intending to take his eyes out," she later wrote.

Her aunt's husband immediately knew that what he intended to happen would never happen, and his embarrassment and fear were visible in the pitch-blackness of night. His apologies did nothing to quell Voletta's anger or fear, and by the next day she was gone.

The trauma from that experience fueled her decision. It was time to go. Time for fresh air in fresh surroundings. The opportunity to travel to America came in the form of an invitation from, as Voletta remembered it, Jules Georgeson, House of Fashion. Voletta had once ordered a watch through the mail from the company, and a friend convinced her that with the invitation she could persuade the American embassy that she was a model. That was her ticket to America, and that was all that mattered to her in the moment. What she'd do once she got there wasn't so clear.

"Here I was, actually going to a place that I had already visited a million times in my head," she said.

Voletta had family in London. Her aunt Ethel had been trying to get her to visit for years, but Voletta never jumped at the opportunity. The thought of overcast skies, perpetual rain showers, and cobblestone streets didn't excite her. American swagger was something else, something she needed to experience firsthand. She confirmed lodging logistics with a family friend in New York. From there, all that was left was packing a suitcase and boarding a plane for the first time in her life.

Jamaica had gotten its independence in 1962. Voletta found her own seven years later. Charting the course of her own life was important to Voletta. From the moment she moved back home after the traumatic experience with her aunt's husband, she made a promise to herself. No one would dictate her actions. If she was going to live a good life, it would be because she, Voletta Wallace, had manifested it. And if she failed in her great American experiment, she'd have no one else to blame.

"I always daydreamed of being a filthy rich lady. A lady of great means and three children," Voletta said in the 2021 Netflix documentary *Biggie: I Got a Story to Tell*. "I would have a beautiful home on the hill. I did not see that in the country for me. That was not my life."

Dreams and reality rarely start out eye-to-eye. In some cases, they never do. The view of New York as her plane descended toward John F. Kennedy International Airport looked similar to the images from those travel agency brochures. And there were people for as far as her eyes could see. But Voletta's "Welcome to America" moment didn't take long, either.

Before she even got into a cab to her temporary home in the Bronx, she saw a taxi driver yell at a policeman, "You motherfucker! You better get out my face, motherfucker!" The reality was that America and Voletta were both in a state of massive transition. America just conveniently forgot to include that on those travel brochures.

———

By the time Voletta arrived in America in 1969, the country she convinced herself was a dream was, in many ways, closing a decade defined by its nightmares. For Black folks, there had been prideful moments on which to hang their hats, like Muhammad Ali shaking up the world with his 1964 victory over Sonny Liston, Berry Gordy's Motown becoming the sound of young America, and landmark pieces of legislation like the Civil Rights Act of 1964 and Voting Rights Act of 1965.

But it was also a decade of death and despair. Within a five-month span in 1963, civil rights activist Medgar Evers and President John F. Kennedy were assassinated, and white supremacists detonated a bomb at the 16th Street Baptist Church in Birmingham, Alabama. Underneath the rubble in a restroom lay the bodies of four Black girls, Addie Mae Collins, Cynthia Wesley, Carole Robertson, and Denise McNair. The Freedom Summer murders of James Chaney, Andrew Goodman, and Michael Schwerner by a Mississippi Ku Klux Klan mob happened a year later.

Malcolm X and Martin Luther King Jr., the decade's two most beloved and stalked civil rights champions, were assassinated, as were the Black Panthers Fred Hampton, Mark Clark, Bunchy Carter, and John Huggins. Black blood on pavements across America didn't have time to dry before more saturated it. Black death and anger worked in tandem. And in April of 1969, thirteen members of the Black Panther Party were arrested and charged with a conspiracy to kill multiple police officers and destroy several New York City buildings.

But if a domestic racial crisis awaited Voletta in the land of the free and the home of the brave, riding shotgun was international chaos. The United States entered the Vietnam War on March 8, 1965, when the first marines landed in Da Nang, and over the next four years, tens of thousands of

American lives were lost in Vietnam. A day earlier, an entire country watched in horror as Alabama state troopers brutally attacked more than six hundred marchers, led by the late John Lewis, who walked across the Edmund Pettus Bridge in Selma demanding racial equality.

In a new country by herself, Voletta didn't have time to be scared by the harsh contrast between fantasy and reality. She had to figure out her new life on the fly.

Her first place of residence was with a family friend at 111 Tudor Place in the Bronx, a stone's throw from Grand Concourse and a few blocks north of Yankee Stadium. Voletta lived in a basement-level studio apartment, sharing both a kitchen and a bathroom with other residents in the building. The city felt grimy. The streets were dirty. And to be quite honest, she thought the people in New York City were rude.

"I was disappointed, but still hopeful," Voletta wrote. "I knew there had to be more in this big country. I just needed time, money, and a plan."

Voletta didn't mind working for her own. She came to America with the expectation that she'd have to hustle for the life she wanted. Within six months, she had already begun to level up, moving to a small studio in Brooklyn off Franklin Avenue. Her rent increased nearly threefold, to $35 a week, but most importantly, it was hers alone. And she came up a five-year plan, vowing to save as much money as she could, and if, at the end of that time, she didn't want to stay in America, she'd return to Jamaica and build a house on her parents' land.

She held a multitude of jobs in those days. She worked at a psychiatrist's office, and she picked up babysitting gigs to make sure she covered her rent. She may have been petite in size—ninety-eight pounds when she first arrived in the States—but her work ethic was nothing short of Olympian. She didn't realize it at the time, but the hustle-and-bustle mentality that New York inevitably breeds had rubbed off on her. Voletta was making do on her own. *Work. School. Home. Babysit.* Five days a week, this was Voletta's life. She was content with that. There was a powerful sense of tranquility and belonging in that routine. America damn sure wasn't perfect. She could watch the nightly news or turn on the radio and understand that much. But neither was Trelawny, and neither was England, where part of her family resided. She was already here, so why not make it work?

"Two years into my plan, I decided to stay in America," she wrote. "This was going to be my permanent home."

That's the thing about a comfortable routine, though. Without knowing, at some point, you let your guard down. Voletta met Selwyn George Latore through a mutual friend. Though he was nearly twenty years her senior, the two Jamaican expats instantly hit it off. Maybe it was the perceived sense of maturity or the role of protector, but Voletta liked older men. She was a homebody, and Selwyn helped bring her out of her shell. They spoke on the phone all the time, and much of the conversation stemmed around Selwyn telling her she worked too much.

A welder by trade, Selwyn had relocated from London. He was a handsome man, tall, with attractive features from his nose to his eyes, and his smile was comforting. He had a sense of humor, and the gift of gab, too. The good times Voletta and Selwyn shared were incredible. He put her on to a new side of life, one that didn't involve textbooks and long work hours. They went to new restaurants, new places around the city she'd never been. Selwyn took Voletta to see her first movie in America, *Shaft*, the Gordon Parks–directed 1971 classic starring Richard Roundtree.

"He brought spontaneity into my life and it felt good," Voletta wrote in her memoir.

Yet as Voletta's life was in a romantic whirlwind, the world around her remained in a constant state of transition, so much of which would impact her life in ways she wouldn't understand until years later.

By the spring of 1971, some 1,800 miles away from Brooklyn in Estes Park, Colorado, a conference was taking place that would redirect the course of American history. The meeting was the result of an appointment by President Richard Nixon. On December 5, 1969, while Voletta was still gathering her bearings in her new country, Nixon appointed Stephen Hess as the national chairman of the White House Conference on Children and Youth. Hess's task was to "listen well to the voices of young Americans—in the universities, on the farms, the assembly lines, the street corners." By talking with these young people, the Nixon administration hoped to gain a glimpse into what Americans thought of the country's affairs at home and abroad.

Hess appointed nearly 1,500 delegates nationwide to meet in Estes Park from April 18 to 22, 1971, for the youth portion of the conference. There they discussed issues that young Americans deemed most critical: the draft and the Vietnam War, employment and the economy, education, the environment, poverty, and, what would become the most infamous of them all, drugs. The task force on drugs consisted of eight youths and four adults. Their take on drug usage in America was that it primarily stemmed from an "individual's inability to cope with his immediate personal environment," and that a person's desire to turn to drugs only increased due to the pitfalls society placed in front of them. "If the administration is sincere in its concern with drug abuse," the task force strongly advised, "it must deal aggressively with the root causes as well as implement the recommendations contained herein." Those included a recommendation "that persons who possess drugs for their personal use no longer be subject to the criminal law." Criminalization of drug use, the task force argued, "has proved too costly to the individual who is criminalized, degraded and outlawed by the process" as well as too costly to the law enforcement system, and too costly to the courts.

Nixon heard those words, but he didn't adhere to them. On July 17, 1971, Nixon declared drug abuse public enemy number one. "In order to fight and defeat this enemy," he said, "it is necessary to wage a new all-out offense." The war on drugs had been officially declared, and millions of Black and brown Americans, including a Jamaican immigrant named Voletta Wallace, would soon be caught up in it.

Black America in 1971 was on full tilt. Over a three-year stretch beginning in 1967, Muhammad Ali would lose the prime years of his boxing career in battling the United States government over his refusal to report to Vietnam, citing religious beliefs. This decision made him and Martin Luther King Jr. the two most hated antiwar activists in America. But in just his third fight back, in March 1971, the Louisville Lip suffered his first career loss to Joe Frazier in the "Fight of the Century"—the first of three clashes that would cement theirs as one of the greatest—and most taxing—rivalries in sports history. Meanwhile, Marvin Gaye's *What's Going On* carried elements that were rooted in Ali's defiant stance. In less than forty minutes, Gaye, much to the initial chagrin of Motown's Berry Gordy, who opposed his artists tackling such societal subjects, captured the elixir of hopelessness, anger, and the demand for social, racial, and economic equity. Black America was sick and tired of being sick and tired. And if it was disgusted with one uphill battle after another, the wins felt few and far between, but all the more reason to celebrate. In New York, thirteen Black Panthers were unanimously acquitted on charges of conspiring to bomb department stores and police stations and murder cops in what history has come to call the Panther 21 Trial.

One of those thirteen was an eight-months-pregnant woman born Alice Faye Williams, known now as Afeni Shakur. She decided to represent herself throughout the trial after reading Fidel Castro's *History Will Absolve Me*, and as a three-hundred-year prison sentence hung over her head, Shakur spent eleven months in prison before being acquitted. A month into her newfound freedom, she gave birth to a baby boy, Lesane Parish Crooks, on June 16, 1971. Soon Afeni changed his name to Tupac Amaru Shakur.

At the time, though, it was not as if Voletta could really concern herself with an American freedom fighter and her infant child. She had her own issues to deal with. The infatuation phase with Selwyn was over. She was still reporting to work and school on time, but now she was tired and sick often. That's when her doctor delivered the news.

"You're pregnant."

It's paralyzing how two words can forever alter your future in a second. Sitting in that doctor's office, Voletta knew her life wasn't just about herself anymore. Sure, she wanted to have kids, but she didn't envision it like this. She still had more to accomplish professionally. She wanted to get married, move into a big house, and then think about babies. Initially, Voletta was disappointed in herself. That five-year plan hadn't included childbirth.

The conversation with Selwyn didn't go any better. After Voletta gave him the news, he responded with a sarcastic "Oh, great!" as if he was annoyed that he now had this new responsibility. In her memoir, Voletta remembered the conversation as a masterclass in manipulation. Selwyn didn't sound excited to have a child, but he also took offense that Voletta may not want to have *his* child. Which one was it, Voletta wondered? In the end, she bet on who she had always bet on: herself. She told Selwyn all she needed help with was care until the child was born. He readily agreed.

As if Voletta's situation wasn't already complex enough, she later found out that Selwyn was married. She had been used. Here he was, this older man living some sort of fantasy with a young Jamaican girl still trying to find her way in America. She hated feeling manipulated. She hated Selwyn for manipulating her. The first man she really had a chance to know in America had only been out for himself. Whatever romantic relationship had existed before was now eternally extinguished. She felt she had seen who he really was. "I may have been the last one to know, but I finally knew," Voletta wrote. But regardless of her feelings about the father, growing inside her was a life that she knew would be solely her responsibility. Voletta grew more and more into the idea of motherhood. She was a natural caregiver, and her child would never worry about being loved.

On May 21, 1972, it was go time. Selwyn was still playing mind games with Voletta. She needed to go to the hospital, but he didn't show up—he said later he didn't understand that she was in labor, and she wouldn't see him for another fifteen hours. Voletta's water eventually broke. Her doctor advised a cesarean section. Her pelvis was small, and the child inside her was robust, eight pounds and twenty-two inches long. By the time she woke up from the anesthesia, Voletta and her baby boy locked eyes for the very first time. Now that he was finally here, all Voletta wanted to do was give him her world. Christopher George Latore Wallace was still years away from being Big, but he was damn sure a big boy. And without question, he was Voletta's heartbeat in human form.

02

VOLETTA, CHRISTOPHER, AND BROOKLYN

TO SAY VOLETTA WAS OBSESSED WITH CHRISTOPHER WOULD BE AN UNDERSTATEMENT. She had come to America in search of her own purpose, and career-wise, she hadn't totally figured it out, but with Christopher, she couldn't just think about a five-year plan. Every facet of her life took on more importance. That's the funny thing about life. While there are benefits to being organized, to being prepared, it's just as important to be able to adjust on the fly.

Looking Christopher in the eye confirmed one thing for Voletta: her past relationship with Selwyn wasn't love. It may have been fun in the moment and good for her when things were at their best. At the root, though, it wasn't a bond built on trust or longevity. Looking at her infant son's infectious smile, hearing his coos, and feeling the way he nestled perfectly on her when she held him—that was love. That's what made her eyes glisten and heart flutter. It wasn't going to be easy, but Voletta and Christopher had each other.

During the first few months of Christopher's life, Selwyn was around. He'd bring supplies like diapers and formula, but that routine didn't last long. Before Christopher was three, the visits stopped.

Years later, Christopher would say of his father, "I don't even remember that cat," laughing as he spoke. Within that laughter, though, lived anger, sadness, and the looming mystery of why his pops ducked out to begin with. "I wouldn't even wanna see this nigga. It's like, what could I have to say to him? What could he have to say to me? I don't need that cocksucker for nothing. I don't need him for shit . . . My moms is straight."

In June 1972, Voletta and her son moved into apartment 3L at 226 St. James Place in Brooklyn. Four decades later, an apartment at that same address, then a cultural landmark, would be listed for north of $4,000 per month. Though her son would later become singularly synonymous with Bedford-Stuyvesant, their apartment was actually to the west of that neighborhood in Clinton Hill. Nevertheless, all of Voletta's time was devoted to her child. She wished he could stay a baby forever, one who'd always reach for her from his crib, who'd crawl around the apartment perfectly content staying within those four walls. She missed him every second of every day when she was at work. All she wanted was peace for Christopher. "I never wanted him to experience a moment of discomfort," she later wrote.

Being a young single parent came with tremendous stresses, but if it did anything for Voletta, it simply poured gasoline on the fire that had led her away from Jamaica in the first place. Where once she might have been happy with a GED, she began to fine-tune her focus. "I knew that I needed a profession, not just a job, to give my son the best," she reflected. The last thing she wanted was for her and Christopher to live on government assistance. She didn't need Selwyn, and she damn sure wasn't going to depend on Uncle Sam.

Voletta enrolled at a Brooklyn training center to become a nurse when Christopher was still a baby. The motivation was simple. It wasn't like she had a calling toward the field, and the thought of being around blood and death all day wasn't exactly enticing. But nurses made good money, and Voletta was on her own paper chase—a motivation her still-infant child would eventually become consumed by. Her first, second, and third priorities were making the best life possible for her son. Yet the routine of traveling from Brooklyn to Queens and all around the city day in and day out became taxing.

A conversation with a professor led to a career change. Voletta had always loved kids, and she had a natural warmth that made them gravitate toward her. She wouldn't just talk to kids, she'd stoop down and look them in their eyes. Voletta was a natural. She switched studies to early-childhood education and enrolled in Kingsborough Community College.

Not long after beginning classes, Voletta was offered a job working with young children. Professors saw natural teaching abilities in Voletta that couldn't necessarily be taught in a classroom. She took the gig, and, in her own words, "It was the most incredible thing to happen to me," because everything seemed to be falling into place. Voletta had a new career she loved and a child she loved even more. She was proud of herself—and she had every right to be.

If Voletta's job was allowing her to pay all the bills and take care of her baby boy, she was doing so in spite of a foundering American economy.

By the mid-seventies, the stock market was in shambles, dropping nearly 50 percent over a twenty-month period. And if that weren't enough, the inflation rate was rising, as was the unemployment rate. New York City in particular faced dire circumstances. In May 1975, in an absolute act of desperation, the city's mayor, Abraham Beame, and the New York governor, Hugh Carey, visited President Gerald Ford at the White House. The city was short on cash, they told the president. And if help wasn't provided soon, the city could slip into chaos, not just financially but on the streets as well. Ford thought the proposal over for twenty-four hours before coming back to Beame and Carey to say there was nothing the federal government could do. New York City was on its own.

"The message was clear," Ford said in a speech at the National Press Club. "The responsibility for New York's financial problems is being left on the front doorstep of the federal government—unwanted and abandoned by its real parents."

For the bulk of the year, New York was robbing Peter to pay Paul. For every gap closed, two more would open. The city's fiscal crisis had been years in the making for anyone who cared to pay close enough attention. There was the problem of the city's falling tax receipts, and the combination of the loss of manufacturing jobs and white flight dealt significant body blows. No matter how bad it looked, though, most city leaders figured the economy would eventually heal itself. Because a city like New York couldn't actually go broke—until it did. By the spring and summer of 1975, straits had become so dire that banks told the city the bond market was no longer open for its business. New York City didn't have any credit.

In December, Congress passed and Ford signed into law legislation that extended billions of dollars in federal loans to the city. The city repaid them all with interest. Total disaster may have been averted, but damage was done.

Even before Ford's change of heart, some of the city's most important cultural resources were casualties of budget cuts. Music education was deemed nonessential, and thousands of arts teachers lost their jobs. The responsibility for carrying the torch fell on community groups or exclusive programs at private institutions—great if a family could afford to send their kids there, but for the majority of the city's working class, who lived check-to-check, it was yet another systemic disadvantage handed to them.

With so much economic uncertainty, it's no surprise that Black music mirrored the times. Dating back to a song like Billie Holiday's "Strange Fruit," Curtis Mayfield's "People Get Ready," or Louis Armstrong's ironically titled "What a Wonderful World," Black music was then and remains an essential record of American history. The music reflected not only the times, but also the wide swath of emotions Black people carried on a day-to-day basis in a society that historically conspired against them. The seventies were a fertile ground for transformative Black music, featuring the likes of Aretha Franklin, Diana Ross, the rise of disco, the Jackson 5 and later Michael Jackson's solo career, the soulful tragedy that was Donny Hathaway, and everything from Marvin Gaye's social awakening to his sexual dynamo peak. Not to mention the greatest album run in music history with Stevie Wonder's *Music of My Mind*, *Talking Book*, *Innervisions*, *Fulfillingness' First Finale*, and *Songs in the Key of Life*. So much of this music, including the country music Voletta adored growing up in Trelawny, reverberated through the walls of 226 St. James Place, apartment 3L, outside on the street corners, and at neighborhood block parties. Christopher Wallace's first DJs, in essence, and whether he realized or not at the time, were his mother and his neighborhood.

As Voletta carefully curated the music in her apartment for her and her still-baby boy, what she didn't realize was that just outside her door, an infant genre was being raised by the streets of New York City. And that one day soon, that infant would single-handedly turn that genre on its head.

Hip-hop was born in perhaps the most innocent of settings: at a back-to-school party in the Bronx. From graffiti, to DJing and MCing, facets of the culture had been in existence in some form prior to the party. The music represented an amalgamation of styles that came before it, from the blues, jazz, and old Negro spirituals all the way back to the call and dance routines from Africa. But on August 11, 1973—some fifteen months after Christopher was born—it was officially given a birth date. Clive Campbell, known locally as DJ Kool Herc, was throwing a birthday party for his sister at 1520 Sedgwick Avenue in the Bronx. Herc had been spinning for a few years, and he always got a kick out of how the crowd would react to various records. He'd become a recognizable figure behind the turntables, and his sister's party would be his biggest crowd to date. Around the neighborhood, Herc had earned a reputation as a master showman and a local celebrity. One of his calling cards was stretching out specific sections of records that would have those in attendance losing their minds. Those sections became known as "breakbeats." The trick was that he wouldn't do this in private and then present it to the crowd with a fully finished product. He'd create the breakbeat in the moment. Partygoers were stunned, but they couldn't stop dancing, either. They didn't exactly know what was going on or what was spawning in front of their eyes. They just knew they liked it, and they wanted more of it. What Herc did that fateful day in the Bronx is what he always did. The major difference this time was the size of the crowd. At that very moment, Herc planted some seeds that changed the world. Especially the world of one young Black boy from Brooklyn.

———

It's nearly impossible to imagine now, but there was once a time when New York was, in essence, closed off from the rest of the world. In the 1920s, immigration quotas handed down by the federal government vastly decreased the number of immigrants allowed into the country. New York had been a prime landing spot for generations of immigrants, but by the 1950s, north of 80 percent of New Yorkers were locally born.

This all began to change by the mid-1960s with the passage of the Hart-Cellar Act. The legislation loosened the vice grip on the city's demographics. More Black and brown folks began moving into the city. More white people began flocking to the suburbs. In the 1970s, over 800,000 immigrants came to New York City, and by the '80s, it was more than a million. In the blink of a generation, New York City looked nearly completely different.

People from all over the world were flocking to the Big Apple for many of the same reasons Voletta came. Everyone yearned for freedom, whether financial, religious, or personal. And, by and large, New York embodied all of that—from the outside looking in, at least. It was only once they arrived in America that these immigrants came to understand how much of a rat race it was. This is why many of rap's first generation of stars and influential names were, in fact, first-generation Americans themselves. Kool Herc, born in Jamaica, was part of a generation of Caribbean children that helped create hip-hop. They included figures like Afrika Bambaataa (born in the Bronx to immigrants from Jamaica and Barbados), Grandmaster Flash (born in Barbados), Slick Rick (born in England to Jamaican parents), and the Jamaican Shabba Ranks. And others with Caribbean ties, like Heavy D, Busta Rhymes, Jacques "Haitian Jack" Agnant, James "Jimmy Henchman" Rosemond, and Randy "Stretch" Walker, would later play roles of varying degrees in Christopher's life story.

The irony in immigrants transitioning to America and establishing new lives there was that many of the same problems seemed to follow them. In the 1980s, there was a huge crackdown in Jamaica on gangs—which had significant ties to the two leading political parties—and it led to an exodus to the States, where the gangs took root. The Jamaican gangs took on a larger role in illegal drug operations, transshipping cocaine from South America through Jamaica and bringing in potent Jamaican weed. In 1988, the *New York Times* cited a claim by federal authorities that Jamaican gangs were involved in 1,400 drug-related killings in the previous three years, and stated that "today, the Jamaican posses are one of the most vicious criminal forces in America."

But the great majority of Caribbean immigrants were much like Voletta Wallace. All she wanted was a better life—not to cause havoc in anyone else's.

There was always value to be found in the community, especially in a new country. When Voletta initially moved from Trelawny to New York, it was a family friend who took her in. And it was a friend who ultimately introduced her to her son's father, Selwyn. And it was a friend from Jamaica she lived with while she was pregnant. And now one of Christopher's first friends was, like him, a first-generation American. Voletta and Joyceleen Deflorimonte, who was originally from Guyana but now lived on nearby Quincy and Lexington, were both hardworking single mothers. The two became good friends based off similar life experiences and responsibilities. But it would be their sons, Christopher and Hubert Sam, who met in kindergarten and were pretty much inseparable from day one.

"He was the first official friend of my life. I have a whole space for him," said Sam. "I don't have no brothers or sisters that live with me, period. He's the first person I remember meeting after my moms."

By almost any metric, Christopher Wallace was a normal kid. He was bigger than everyone even then, but it wasn't like he used his size to intimidate. During his early years, Christopher never had to want for much thanks to his mother. Voletta felt that if she could give him whatever he wanted, she could keep him off the streets for as long as possible. Action figures? Chris had them. Video games? Those, too. But there was also an eclectic side of young Chris.

"Even from a young age, I'd catch him watching stuff that was way advanced. He'd bring back information to school that we weren't really privy to," said Sam. "Stuff like science fiction, classic dramas. He absorbed the classics of the culture. Like *The Warriors*. Things that as a kid maybe your parents might watch. I don't know if his moms would sit him down and watch stuff with her, but he'd bring back classic music from the fifties and sixties and be singing it in elementary."

Chris, Sam said, had this "strange side of him, and he actually listened to country music as a kid." That was Voletta's influence. That was music she grew up on and held close even in adulthood. She savored the storytelling aspect of country music. For Chris, who grew up basically on his mother's hip, Sam says, "He didn't just stay in the cartoon zone."

He really didn't. His interests were all over the place—even when they got the best of him. When Christopher was ten years old, Voletta sent him to bed one night. He wasn't in trouble, but as they sat on the couch watching *Ten Little Indians*, the 1965 film adaptation of Agatha Christie's novel, Voletta realized that her child shouldn't be watching people get murdered. Hours later, Voletta was awoken by her son, out of breath, asking if he could stay in her room that night. Christopher had gone to his room, but he hadn't exactly gone to sleep. He'd turned the television on in there and watched the rest of the movie and now he couldn't sleep.

———

Voletta valued education. That much was a given. She had enrolled in night school almost immediately after landing on American soil, and she understood how education could open up the world. And an education, too, was one of the rare gifts that once obtained could never be stripped away. It was hers—for life. Voletta wanted the exact same for her son.

"One day I was reading Christopher a story," Voletta recalled in a 1997 *SPIN* feature, "and he said, 'You know what I want? I want you to be my husband.' I asked him what a husband was and he looked me in the eye and said, 'Someone who loves you and kisses you and brings you flowers and looks at you nicely.' I said, 'I can't be your husband, but I will always love you.'"

The thing about Christopher was that he was naturally loyal. Naturally smart, with a strong ability to retain information, too. As an elementary student at St. Peter Claver School in Brooklyn (now the Brooklyn Waldorf School), he was a model student who consistently made the honor roll. At the end of the day, Christopher loved making his mother happy, and seeing him do well in school put a huge smile on her face—like the day he brought home his very first award, a tiny fireman with a hose in his hand given for delivering a report on fire prevention. In his heart, though, Christopher's attitude toward school, at least around his closest friends, was lackadaisical.

"His grades were so stellar that you'd start to think doctor, lawyer—he could choose whatever he wanted to," said Sam. Nearly forty years later, that astonishment still lives in his voice. "He wasn't impressed with getting good grades. It was a little confusing because he didn't act like he was aspiring to be anything, to be honest. But you would think he had the skills to be whatever he wanted."

At St. Peter Claver, Chris's two best friends were Sam and Michael Bynum. They were all American-born children of West Indian immigrants, and all lived within walking distance of one another. The trio would walk to school together, and though maybe their mothers didn't completely grasp how difficult that could be, with their uniforms—yellow shirts and plaid ties—making them a target for bullies, the boys knew all too well. Nothing life-threatening, but still enough for Chris, Hubert, and Michael to know they had to have each other's back. There was no breaking that code. Chris wasn't an instigator, but he wouldn't back down either. None of them did.

"In Catholic school, regular kids pick on you. We got picked on every day," said Bynum in the 2007 documentary *Notorious B.I.G.: Bigger Than Life*.

Such was life growing up in Brooklyn in the early eighties. You fought. If you took a loss, you took a loss, but you didn't back down. That's how it became for Chris, Hubert, and Michael—don't get it twisted, they dished out their share of Ws, too.

Leadership looks different on everyone. For young Chris, it was subtle. He wasn't the in-your-face type of leader. He was always big in terms of height and weight, and his natural gravitas and creative knack made his presence loom even larger. Chris became the leader of their little crew, and it felt right. There was even discipline and structure, a financial secretary to make sure they had money for things like pizza or arcade runs, and even a sergeant at arms (though none of them had guns). But for the Hawks, as they called themselves, to be truly official, they needed gear. Chris, Hubert, and Michael all got custom hats with hawks on them. They even had their own theme song.

> *Everybody talkin' bout the Hawks 'cause they're nice*
>
> *Heartbroken Hubert, Captain Chris and Master Mike*
>
> *Big Bad Barry, Scooty Scott and Dizzy Don*
>
> *We are the best all over town*
>
> *If you mess with the Hawks*
>
> *You are pressing your luck*
>
> *Why is everybody always fuckin' with us?*

They were just kids finding their way around Brooklyn, inspired by a growing cultural phenomenon that influenced the way they dressed, walked, and talked. It was innocent and creative. The Hawks' routine after school was simple. Snatch that damn tie off, play video games, eat pizza, and laugh and joke until their stomachs hurt or one of their mothers came looking for them. Whatever came first. This is what friendship looked like for young Black Brooklyn boys. And if this was how it felt to have a brother, then all they wanted to do was continue to live in that moment.

On any given trip outside for the Hawks, they could hear it. By the early-to-mid-eighties, hip-hop was really coming into form. Chris was famous for singing songs from artists like Frankie Avalon and Frank Sinatra—Voletta would play them around the house, and Chris's excellent memory did its job from there—but it was hip-hop that won him over.

"I remember him writing 'Rapper's Delight' by the Sugarhill Gang and the whole song was out," said Sam. "It was like a test because you ain't hip-hop if you can't write the whole song and know all the lyrics. I remember him doing that and it was amazing. I tried, of course, and I ain't finish. He just really started submersing himself in the music and really study it."

Chris recalled later, "When my moms got me a radio for Christmas, she got me a Fat Boys tape and a Run-DMC tape. That's all I had." For Voletta, hip-hop was just noise. For her son, it was becoming a way of life.

Growing up in the neighborhood with the restrictions he had, like being unable to leave his stoop and having an early curfew, Chris wasn't always the most street savvy. Hip-hop became a bridge between creativity and authenticity. That's when the rhymebooks started to pop up—as far back as elementary school—as did the new personas he'd create for himself. This is pretty much the start of Christopher Wallace the entertainer. That's when Hubert realized his friend could rhyme, at about ten or eleven years old. With hip-hop itself being so young, the culture was in flux—rules were being written in real time. Though music was always its most recognizable facet, hip-hop culture was more expansive than that. Some rapped and others DJed. Then there was breakdancing and graffiti.

"So during that era, you really gravitated to what called you spiritually. Some people didn't do nothing," said Sam. "They just listened to the music and that was okay."

And there was a ton of music on the streets. The genre already had its first crop of superstars in names like Grandmaster Flash and the Furious Five, Run-DMC, and Melle Mel. Records like Kurtis Blow's "Basketball" or LL Cool J's *Radio* album were game changers. In 1984, MTV aired the first rap video in Run-DMC's "Rock Box" (and four years later launched *Yo! MTV Raps*). The culture was growing by the minute, and there was a young Christopher Wallace devouring everything it had to offer.

When Hubert was eleven, he received a pair of turntables. He and Chris would write rhymes together, but Chris would leave the wheels of steel to his friend.

"How the hell you do that?" a fascinated Chris would ask whenever Hubert would do something amazing on the turntables.

But if Chris was impressed by Hubert's DJ skills, Hubert was blown away by his friend's wordplay. They weren't attending the same school anymore. Hubert was attending New Bedford-Stuyvesant Catholic Junior High School. Chris was set to go there as well, but ended up transferring to Queen of All Saints for middle school off Lafayette Avenue, walking distance from his apartment. While there, Chris's creative writing skills won him multiple awards. He was calling himself MC C.W.E.S.T. Hubert can't remember what the acronym was for, but he does remember seeing the name a few times in his friend's early rhymebooks. Hubert was DJ Spinback, and along with Bynum, they became the Techniques.

While attending Queen of All Saints, Chris's friend circle began to expand even more. Some elements of his personality were universal, like his sense of humor.

"He was one of the funniest guys I've ever met," said Dr. Moises Smart of Stanford University, who attended middle school with Chris and considered him one of his best friends then. "I mean, he was very chubby, so when he would do break dancing moves and all that stuff, it was funny. He took it all as a joke."

Chris earned quality grades, but it wasn't like he was ever invested in academic notoriety. Copying homework was a norm, and so was cheating on tests. But when he wanted to, Chris could study right before an exam and pass with flying colors. It was all a matter of how Chris was feeling that day.

The teachers at Queen of All Saints saw promise in Chris. He could be the smartest in the class—but he never cared to earn that title.

Smart remembers that one teacher in particular, Ms. Cohen, would be particularly hard on Chris for not applying himself. In middle school, Smart saw it as a teacher being too difficult on his friend for no reason. As the years passed, though, Smart began to view her tough love from a different perspective.

"Chris was gifted. I wasn't. I mean, I had a talent for math and science," Smart said. "But he had a talent for words and for writing. And drawing. We used to have these drawing battles between him and myself."

He may not have cared much about school, but one item he always kept on him was a rhymebook. Chris would constantly write in it—his own lyrics and lyrics to songs on the radio. Whenever he'd get a chance, he'd show those rhymes off in battles. Aside from that, Chris's middle school years were that of a typical preadolescent boy. When school ended, Chris, Smart, and their group of friends would end up at one of their houses. On the occasional instance they'd camp out at Chris's house, Voletta was never there. But he always talked about his mother and about how great a relationship they had. At Smart's house, where they ended up more times than not, video games were normally the preferred choice of entertainment. That included Smart's younger sister, Jessica, who'd often try to hang out with Smart, Chris, and their friends.

"I was in my brother's room, and he wasn't there. I thought he was going to be out with his friends for longer. I memorized the code to play the game. So when he wasn't home, I would play on it. But he caught me several times," Jessica Chong laughed. "One of those times he had Christopher Wallace with him. We used to have to say his whole name because there was two Chrises in the group. He's yelling at me like, 'Get out of my room! I better not see you in here!' And Christopher Wallace was like, 'Yo, she's a genius. She remembered all them codes.' And I'm just like thank you, Chris, because my brother doesn't see the silver lining! I am smart!"

Smart and Chong's great-grandmother lived with them then. She was the old-school Dominican type who would start cooking early, and dinner would be ready by 2:00 P.M., so by the time Smart, Chris, and the gang arrived at the house after school, there was an entire spread waiting for them, much to the appeasement of Chris, who loved the plantains she'd make.

They were middle school boys, talking about topics middle school boys do and getting into hijinks middle school boys did. They talked about how they could avoid the Decepticons, a local gang forming at the time that would frequently come down from Brooklyn Technical High School into their neighborhood. And when they weren't devising plans to avoid getting into fights, they had a stash of *Playboy* magazines they'd look at from time to time.

"Someone brought out a porn movie once," Smart said, laughing at the memory, "and that was the first time we all saw a porn. We were all like, 'Oh shit! I can't believe this exists!' But it was all innocent fun."

Smart knew Chris had other friends outside their friend group. It never affected them, but he also knew his friend had another life outside their *Playboy*-browsing, video-game-binging sessions. "He always kept me away from most of them," Smart recalled. "He had like a separate . . . double life. I can say that."

Chris was a curious kid. And there was nothing anyone could do to curb the natural curiosity that burned inside him.

―――――

The older Chris became, the more intrigued he was by the world around him—in particular, the neighborhood around him. And that's what Voletta feared the most. She could control things as long as her son was within her eyesight, which is why she showered him with gifts and items that any child would love. After a while, though, there's only so much that video games or action figures can do to blunt that curiosity. Chris planted himself on the stoop of 226 St. James for hours and people watched. It was there his small world began to expose its realities to him. Chris would witness a lot of things, illegal and legal, funny and sad, and fascinating and eye-popping. Voletta may have been able to keep him on the stoop, but she couldn't control what he saw.

There was one person who caught his attention: a young Black guy always carrying a horn with him. His name was Donald Harrison. A New

Orleans–born jazz artist who moved to the East Coast to attend the Berklee College of Music in Boston, Harrison had come to hang out in New York, and by the time he was nineteen years old in 1980, he was playing with jazz drumming savant Roy Haynes. Two years later, he was the newest member of Art Blakey's band, the Jazz Messengers. Harrison lived by a Charlie Parker quote: "If you don't live it, it won't come out of your horn." Living in Clinton Hill at 218 St. James, Harrison remembers seeing a young kid sitting on the stoop a few doors down.

Chris lived near the corner of St. James and Fulton, and the contrast between the two was striking. St. James wasn't all that bad, but Fulton Street—known around the neighborhood as "the Ave."—was a war zone full of drugs and fast tracks to a precinct or a morgue. One turn onto Fulton Street and the entire mood changed. Fulton was where the hustlers resided, where the dope fiends converged, and where everything Chris was being shielded from was taking place. It was also where all the money resided. On any given day on the Ave., Mercedes-Benzes, Jeeps, and all sorts of luxury vehicles were the norm. And there was enough jewelry around the necks of the power brokers on the block that Chris could've believed they'd robbed the exhibition of King Tut's tomb. But on any given day, seeing dozens of addicts walk around like zombies plotting on their next hit was commonplace, too.

For a while, Harrison and Chris didn't say anything to each other. Then one day, the shy Chris finally built up the courage to introduce himself.

"Yo, what do you do?" he asked. "I always see you with the horn and the ladies? What's going on?"

"I play music," Harrison responded.

"I love music, too," Chris replied.

Harrison noticed early on that the young kid who stopped him to talk was extremely mature. From that moment, a mentor/mentee relationship was born. Whenever Donald would walk by and Chris was on the stoop, the two would stop and chat about music. Chris was thrilled. He knew a real-life musician, and he rushed to tell two people. One was Hubert, because now they could learn music with real instruments. The other was his mother, though she was dubious. A young man in his twenties wanting to mentor her son in music? But Voletta was put at ease by meeting Harrison. And if nothing else, if her son was with him learning about music, at least he was off the streets. That's what she wanted more than anything.

Initially, when Chris came over, Harrison had visions of him becoming a jazz musician. But it was the teenage Chris who made it clear that what he wanted to do was hip-hop. Harrison's generation were the original creators of hip-hop, so he was eager to help his young musical apprentice. Plus, he was just an all-around lover of music, so whatever was being made was going to be fine with Harrison. Both Chris and Donald soon came to realize that many of the same principles that went into making a great jazz artist applied to hip-hop as well. Storytelling, breath control, counting bars, standing back from the mic, and cadence—all the pieces mattered.

"We started working on some jazz ideas and hip-hop and how to make him stand out and move the idea of hip-hop into another kind of way of dealing with it," Harrison said. Then he paused, almost as if to understand the totality of what his next thought would portray. "I think . . . well, I know some aspects [he'd incorporate in his career later] were what we were doing."

"I used to fuck with Donald all the time. He got my ears turned to jazz music," Biggie was quoted as saying in the 2003 biography *Unbelievable: The Life, Death, and Afterlife of the Notorious B.I.G.* "He put me on to Herbie Hancock and Terence Blanchard."

The mentoring relationship was pure and stretched beyond music. They went to the movies and the Museum of Modern Art in Midtown Manhattan. Through Harrison, Chris was learning of an entirely new world far beyond Brooklyn. Music, by proxy, was taking Chris places he had never imagined. Harrison remembers times when Chris would have him and all his friends keeling over in laughter impersonating Pee Wee Herman or his famous "word of the day" schtick. He'd pick a word and spend the rest of the day cracking jokes about said word all day. Chris, to Donald, was always joking about something, and even at such a young age he had a way of putting people at ease. It was always about balance, though. If he could make everyone around him believe he had the comedic timing of an Eddie Murphy or Richard Pryor, it always came back down to the music.

Harrison thoroughly enjoyed passing his wisdom down to the next generation, and Chris wanted nothing more than to learn everything he could, soaking up any knowledge Donald was willing to pass down. Through

Donald, he was exposed to artists like the hard bop saxophonist Cannonball Adderley and the soul, jazz, and R&B singer Nancy Wilson. Chris was dedicated to learning more, to getting better, though he had no clue what sort of musical career, if any, lay ahead.

"If you a hip-hop artist and you try to sing a Cannonball Adderley solo, you'll realize how hard that is. He was super intelligent to figure that out with no formal training," said Harrison. The jazz musician would have the young hip-hop aspirant in the studio listening to singers like Marvin Gaye to understand why ad-libs mattered, as well as enunciation. "Then," Harrison reasoned, "even people who don't like hip-hop will understand what you're saying. They'll put it in another space."

Chris always brought the Techniques with him when he went to Harrison's. Neither side quite came out and said they appreciated the other's presence, but the sentiment hovered in the air.

"Donald poured a lot into us in a short few years," Sam recalled. "I was there when Donald opened up the horizon for us. Donald was really hipping us on how to take hip-hop to a higher arc and that we could blend all the music that came before."

Harrison learned to see these young kids on his block as dreamers. Despite the violence, drugs, and potential pitfalls on every street corner, they all wanted something bigger for themselves. They taught him empathy, even more than he already had. And for Chris Wallace, Hubert Sam, and Michael Bynum, Harrison expanded their musical horizons.

Music, for Chris, had graduated from a love to an obsession. He didn't just want to listen to music and learn about it. He wanted to make it, and use the lessons Harrison had poured into him. When he, Sam, and other friends were around fourteen, they pooled their allowance money to purchase time at a studio in downtown Brooklyn called Funky Slice. There, Wallace and crew used the instrumental from Toto's 1982 single "Africa." Chris, of course, came up with his own lyrics but also, even more impressively, the direction and content for the song, which centered around a teenager's love letter.

But relationships, no matter how fruitful, sometimes run their course. By the time Chris was sixteen, the at-home music education lessons began to differ. Sam was focusing on his high school football career at Thomas Jefferson High School—and also coping with the passing of his mother when he was only sixteen. Meanwhile, Chris was still into music, but he was also interested in another game. One that Donald hoped his musical tutelage would steer him away from.

In Chris, he saw an immensely talented young man heading down a path that no music equipment or magazines in his house could compete with. That innocence, now, was no more.

"He couldn't keep those two parts of his life separate because it was right on the corner," Harrison said. "Fulton Street."

03

A WHOLE NEW WORLD

CHICO DEL VEC REMEMBERS THE QUIET KID SITTING ON THE STOOP WATCHING HIM COUNT HIS MONEY. They'd see each other all the time, but they never spoke. Chico also never knew that the kid's mom was watching him from their nearby apartment window. At most, all Chico and the kid did was offer a head nod toward each other and keep moving.

The kid, who Chico would soon come to learn was named Chris, would always see Chico on the block. Their apartment buildings were connected. In the front, Chico and all the other kids their age would play stickball, football or kickball. There was a playground outside P.S. 11 close by, but the nearest park was a dozen blocks away, so they stuck close to home, going down to the basement to shoot skelly (a bottlecap shooting street game). Sitting on the stoop allowed Chris to see damn near everything that happened in his neighborhood. Chico was all up and down the block hustling—or, in more explicit terms, he was selling crack.

"He'd just watch," Chico says.

Both were still in school at the time. Chico would come outside in his normal gear, and there was Wallace in his Catholic school uniform.

"He was really, like really, uncomfortable," Chico says of Chris's aversion to his mandated wardrobe at the time.

At the time, Chris didn't really interact with a lot of kids on the block. He had to be in the house by 8:30 at night, whereas many of the kids in his neighborhood seemingly made their own hours. Outside his close friends, few of his peers knew how creative and musically gifted he was. Chris was that big quiet kid with the incredibly overprotective mom. But what Chico had is what Chris really coveted: *money*.

Voletta was a schoolteacher, so it's not like she was making a salary that would get her interviewed by Robin Leach anytime soon. But she spoiled her only child, giving him everything she could to deter him from a life she couldn't control. Still, there was nothing Voletta could've done to stop her son's curiosity. He wasn't a learn-by-example kid. The only way he ever learned something was by trying it himself. Anyone as naturally inquisitive as Chris was eventually going to venture out beyond his stoop.

———

Connect the dots throughout history and an undeniable trend emerges. Wars are remembered for the carnage they carry, the lives they claim, and the legacies they leave behind. But no war starts with the first battle or the first shots fired. Animosity doesn't magically appear out of thin air. There's always a chain of events. Ask a historian about World War II and they'll hammer home the importance of the Treaty of Versailles. Ask them about the Civil War and all roads lead back to the first Africans captured and brought to America in 1619 and the purposeful protection of human bondage in the Constitution. Even ask about of mass incarceration and a historian will discuss its direct ties to continuation of slavery through the Fifteenth Amendment.

Just beyond Chris's Brooklyn stoop raged a war that didn't just appear randomly. The roots of it dated back at least a generation, even before Chris was born. What young Christopher never realized was that the world he was inching closer and closer toward was a byproduct of years of discrimination, legislation, and overpolicing. Nothing ever really happens by coincidence in America, especially not when it involves racism. And in America, it's possible to trace nearly every societal discussion back to race. What Christopher saw as a paper chase in what Chico and other hustlers in the neighborhood were doing was really a war. They were all soldiers in a war they inherited.

Every detail is critical when discussing the socioeconomic disparities in both Christopher's neighborhood and other primarily Black and brown communities across the country during this time. The paper trail speaks for itself. The Federal Highway Act of 1956 redirected roads through these communities, many times purposefully, setting up literal barriers so that those in real estate could label affluent and subpar neighborhoods. Neighborhoods were stripped of homes, churches, and schools and even had property seized under the government policy of eminent domain.

A century after the end of the Civil War, the Civil Rights Act of 1964 and the Voting Rights Act of 1965 were passed. These acts, in the most simplest of descriptions, argued that Black people deserved the most basic of human rights that America said its citizens were guaranteed in the Constitution. Both were devised with the intention of expanding Black political power, in particular in the South, where the legacy of Jim Crow was still the desired way of life by white segregationists. In what felt like the blink of an eye, Black voter registration rates skyrocketed. For example, despite numbers still lagging considerably behind their white counterparts, Mississippi catapulted from 6.7 percent of Black voters registered in 1965 to 59.8 percent in 1967, according to the U.S. Commission on Civil Rights. And the Fair Housing Act in 1968 did little to live up to its name as private developers gamed the system not only to discriminate racially against potential homeowners, but also to get federal funding in the process.

In the 1970s, the decade Christopher Wallace (and hip-hop) was born, New York's unemployment rate skyrocketed, causing many families, the majority of them white, to flee to the suburbs in an exodus known as white flight. More than 820,000 people left the city during this time in search of jobs, but in doing so, took valuable economic and financial resources with them. In turn, crime rates began to escalate dramatically as social services like employment benefits and governmental financial support were slashed.

Added to all of that was the ending of the Vietnam War in the 1970s. When veterans had returned home from World War II some three decades earlier, they were treated as American heroes. They, to this day, still boast the tag of America's "greatest generation." Vietnam veterans received the opposite reaction. The war had been drawn out, seemed unwinnable, and had grown increasingly unpopular in America; that unpopularity fueled by anger over the draft and outrage over news of American atrocities.

The challenges for returning Vietnam veterans were compounded by America's unwillingness to properly address its drug issue. In May 1971—the same month an eight-months-pregnant Afeni Shakur was acquitted and released from prison—the *New York Times* reported that heroin usage by American troops in Vietnam "had reached epidemic proportions."

"Tens of thousands of soldiers are going back as walking time bombs," an officer was reported as saying. "And the sad thing is there is no real program under way, despite what my superiors say, to salvage these guys."

They were returning from a war they were hated for to a country unwilling or unable to help them with their addictions. This was particularly hard for Black veterans, and the armed forces had a disproportionately high percentage of Black service members. Back in 1965, approximately 11 percent of the population was Black, but a quarter of Americans who died in combat in Vietnam were Black, and in 1967, 23 percent of combat troops were Black. And back home, resources and tax dollars were being stripped from densely populated areas where the Black population was high. The quality of the schools and neighborhoods diminished. And rather than answering drug use with treatment, as the Estes Park, Colorado, conference advised, the approach was based on punishment. Two months after the *Times* article came out, President Nixon declared drug abuse the country's top ill.

In 1973, New York governor Nelson Rockefeller signed into law the Rockefeller Drug Laws, which mandated harsh minimum sentences of fifteen years for the sale or possession of even small amounts of marijuana, cocaine, or heroin. Years later, statistics would show that almost 90 percent of those convicted under these laws were either Black or Latino. And throughout the 1970s, Black folks were twice as likely as white people to be arrested on drug-related offenses. By the eighties, when the young Christopher Wallace was sitting on the stoop, that number ballooned to five times as likely.

Under Ronald Reagan's administration in the 1980s, the war on drugs intensified, fueled not just by domestic policy, but by foreign entanglements as well. The Reagan administration funneled money to right-wing paramilitaries in Central and South America, offering protection to cocaine traffickers like Nicaragua's Manuel Noriega. Drugs flowed into the country in more ways than anyone could count; the 1980s were called the "crack era" for a reason. On October 14, 1982, less than a month before Republicans would suffer an embarrassing showing in the midterm elections, Reagan declared a new front in the war on drugs—establishing a dozen task forces under the direction of the attorney general "to mount an intensive and coordinated campaign against international and domestic drug trafficking and other organized criminal enterprises."

But three years later, Reagan called the Contras, who were seeking to overthrow the Nicaraguan government, "our brothers" and "freedom fighters" who were "more equal of our Founding Fathers." They were also, as National Security Council Lieutenant Colonel Oliver North knew, protecting traffickers and running cocaine themselves.

"We permitted narcotics," then-U.S. senator John Kerry said at a 1988 subcommittee hearing on drugs, terrorism, and international operations. "We were complicitous as a country in narcotics traffic at the same time as we're spending countless dollars in this country to try to get rid of this problem. It's mind-boggling."

"I don't know if we've got the worst intelligence system in the world," Kerry blasted. "I don't know if we've got the best, and they knew it all and just overlooked it. But no matter how you look at it, something's wrong. Something is really wrong out there."

By January 1983, in the midst of a recession, Black unemployment had reached an astounding 21.2 percent. While American history frequently chooses to romanticize him, there was perhaps no bigger antagonist to Black Americans, legislatively at least, than President Ronald Reagan. His economic agenda, better known as "Reaganomics," disproportionately harmed lower-income Black communities. Reagan cut funding for the Equal Employment Opportunity Commission and the civil rights division of the Department of Justice, and his emphasis on "trickle-down" economics was starving Black communities. The former Hollywood-actor-turned-California-governor-turned-American-president understood the value of crippling Black lives. It was both politically beneficial and fell in line with his core values—he once referred to people from African countries as "monkeys" and chastised them for being "uncomfortable wearing shoes" in a taped 1971 conversation with then president Richard Nixon. Reagan, the first presidential candidate to run under the phrase "Make America Great Again," is historically remembered, among many things, for enforcing the stereotype of Black women being "welfare queens" who manipulated government assistance programs. During Reagan's last year in office in 1988, the poverty rate for Black Americans stood at 31.6 percent compared to 10.1 percent of whites. And he made deep cuts in funding for school services including unemployment, childcare, school lunches, and job training. "It's like a jungle," Grandmaster Flash said on "The Message," released in July 1982, "sometimes it makes me wonder how I keep from going under."

All of this was happening while a young Christopher Wallace was running with his crew, the Hawks, just enjoying the innocence of being young Black boys in Brooklyn. They had no clue of the extent of the war that would eventually come looking for them.

In 1986, shortly after Chris's fourteenth birthday, came a moment that would permanently alter drug enforcement polices moving forward. On June 19, just two days after being selected second overall by the defending champion Boston Celtics, Len Bias died from an overdose, and the world stopped. Bias was a basketball superhero. He had dominated college basketball at the University of Maryland with a combination of force, beauty, grace, and destruction that made him a true one-of-one. In joining the Celtics, he was pinned to become Michael Jordan's greatest rival (the two had phenomenal duels in college) and prolong the dynasty in Boston, where Larry Bird had led the team to three titles in the last six years.

Rumors spread in the press that Bias died after smoking crack. Cocaine, usually associated with lavish white communities and those living in the lap of luxury, was seen as an addiction. But crack was a crime. The drug, far cheaper than powder cocaine, was largely associated with Black communities and was being held significantly responsible for the erosion of society's moral fabric. *Time* magazine dubbed crack the "issue of the year," while NBC News labeled the rock "America's drug of choice." In September, CBS News and Dan Rather produced a two-hour special program called "48 Hours on Crack Street," a "message of utter hopelessness" according to the *Chicago Tribune*. Meanwhile, First Lady Nancy Reagan peddled her "Just Say

No" crusade, which in hindsight we can see spread more fear and disinformation than it actually quelled drug usage. Rock was cheaper and seen as more addictive and more dangerous than coke. And Bias, in many ways, became a face for that fear.

In reality, Bias died from sniffing cocaine. Almost immediately, amid an avalanche of media attention of Bias's death, Congress passed the Anti-Drug Abuse Act of 1986.

It was signed so quickly that no one really took the time to understand its long-term ramifications, of which there many.

"It was a real low point and dark chapter in the war on drugs," Michael Collins, deputy director of the Drug Policy Alliance's Office of National Affairs, said on the thirtieth anniversary of Bias's death in 2016. "It was a point where hysteria dominated over evidence, and it was really the catalyst for a lot of the prison problems we are trying to reform today."

There was an all-out assault on drugs in America, but in practice, that meant there was an all-out assault on Black communities. For young Black folks just trying to make it in neighborhoods gutted by abandonment and disinvestment, drug dealing was about money and a lack of other opportunities. Hustling was appealing because one could walk out their door and have money in their pocket by the end of the day. Of course, the drug game is way more complex than that, but for many, it beat filling out endless applications for minimum-wage jobs they'd have to be lucky to get.

While all of this was going on in America, all the economic and physical destruction, there was a young Christopher Wallace just sitting on his stoop at St. James and Fulton watching money exchange hands almost quicker than he could keep up.

"I heard about crack on the news and I was like, 'That's what niggas must be doing,'" Chris would say later in life. "I knew they were fly as hell—they had $150 Ballys and bubblegoose jackets and sheepskins. I was like, 'Oh shit. These niggas are doing it.'"

━━━━━━━━━━

Chris was the one who finally broke the ice. One day Chico was counting his money after pulling a shift working the block. He had to know.

"Yo," he said. "Wassup? What you do?"

"I hustle," Chico responded.

Chris was asking out of genuine curiosity. He was as green as the money Chico held in his hand. He thought Chico was a stickup kid, which in all fairness, was a popular line of illegal employment in the eighties—especially in Brooklyn. Chico was more comfortable not bringing attention to himself, making his deals and counting his money on the stoop. And now actually holding a conversation with the big kid he'd always see and nod to.

"Yo, man, I wanna get some of that money," Chris told him.

Chico thought about it for a moment.

"You know what? I'ma take you around the block with me," he said. "I'm gonna show you some things if you up to it."

Chris was up to it for sure—but he also wasn't up to it. He knew he wasn't supposed to leave that stoop for anything. In fact, Voletta was watching him through the window at that moment. Because he was a kid who needed to learn everything through his own experiences, Chris followed Chico around the block to a nearby sandwich shop. It was like an entirely new world. Loud music, pickups and drop-offs, people whizzing by at even faster than the normal New York pace. He was introduced to hustlers with names like Cheese and Tony Rome, whom most everyone knew if they spent any time on the block. And Chico, as young as he was, moved around like a savvy veteran. It was almost balletic, something out of an Alvin Ailey production, except in the hood. The rush of excitement and fear was almost too much for Chris.

"Hurry up with your food!" he pleaded. "I gotta get home!"

Chico laughed at the memory nearly forty years later. He tried to get Chris to hold some drugs for him, but he wouldn't. Chris had to get back home.

"He was just so paranoid. He was scared, you know what I'm saying," said Chico. "When I went in the store, I came back out and he was gone!"

Chico went back around the corner and there was Chris, out of breath, trying to fend off an asthma attack.

"Nah, I can't do that. Nah, son," he panted. "That's too much for me, man. I can't be running."

Perhaps because it sounds good in music or feels immediate in movies or documentaries, the concept of "jumping off the stoop" is popularized, but it was neither glamorous nor expeditious. Hubert would walk to Chris's stoop on many days. When they weren't working on music either by themselves or with Donald Harrison, they'd just sit there, crack jokes, and people watch. There was a point when, under inflexible orders from his mother, Chris couldn't even walk to the next St. James block. But the stoop provided a court-side view to any- and everything.

"Even sitting on the stoop, you're exposed. You're listening to things. You're watching," Sam says. "His mom didn't even realize just being on the stoop what we saw. It's things we would see right across the street that was our early educations to the streets."

This gradual process occurred roughly between the ages of twelve and fifteen for Wallace. It was never an instant realization but more a slow-footed slide toward getting money in the streets. Each year, young boys—not just Wallace and his childhood best friend Hubert Sam, but more like an entire class—moved closer and closer toward that life. A generation earlier, they may have been drafted and shipped off to Vietnam, but now it was the crack game that needed soldiers, and the primary target was young Black boys who, if they were lucky, grew to be men. For Chris and Hubert, life was different because their mothers were so strict. Over time, though, in particular for Chris, who grew more and more enamored with the life his mother desperately tried to keep him from, it became an irresistible force meeting an immovable object scenario. As each summer passed, he began to stray closer and closer to that world.

"I was a sweet little boy," he would later say. But he added, "I was a sneaky nigga, man. I was *real* bad, you know? And you know what made shit worse? Mothafuckas would tell Moms that I did something, but she just wouldn't believe them. She'd be like, 'Not *my* Christopher.'"

It wasn't just because Voletta kept a short leash on him that her only child kept his distance from the streets as long as he did. He was reticent, and there lived in him a deep love, respect, and fear for his mother. She might have been naive to most of what was happening on the corner, but she was not a pushover.

"She's a little lady, but she has such a big presence. The Jamaican spirit in her is definitely strong," said Sam. "She was very direct with us. She was trying to understand what Chris was going through. I could relate to it because my mom was kinda like that way with me, but I don't think I pushed my moms as much as Chris did with her."

As her son grew older and older, the two began to clash more and more. Not in a way that would diminish their love for each other—in a way, that was all they had—but Chris wanted to march to the beat of his own drum. Such was a near-impossible task as long as he lived under his mother's roof. Voletta has always said that when her son was young, she didn't understand why he was so fixated on rap music. She just heard it as loud noise. She didn't connect that noise to what was happening right outside her front door. Honestly, how could she?

"I could definitely remember times with her just dealing with the growing pains of raising a son in this society she didn't really understand," said Sam.

Her priority was protecting her son. All around Brooklyn, Jamaicans had developed a reputation as people not to be messed with or taken lightly, whether on the streets or in the living room. And at all times, Voletta commanded respect.

"I was really on my Ps and Qs when it came down to his moms. I was always like, 'How you doing, Miss Wallace?'" recalled Chico Del Vec, who by that time had become another one of her son's closest friends. "Like really respectable. I ain't want no problems with that lady."

One way to maintain some semblance of control over her son was making sure he knew where he came from. Chico didn't even know Chris was Jamaican until he heard Voletta speak.

"Wait," Chico said, befuddled. "You're Jamaican?"

"Yeah, man," Chris responded with a chuckle.

One day, Chris invited Chico up to eat dinner with him. One thing about Voletta is that she kept her son well-fed, and one thing about Chris is that he had a wait problem—not "weight," but "wait"; he could never wait to eat. Whether it be on the block with hero sandwiches or the neighborhood chicken or Chinese spots, he was always eating. But there was no better chef than Voletta. Chico was treated to an immaculate spread of fried chicken, macaroni, curry goat, jerk chicken, and more. He had never seen anything like it. Their friendship continued to evolve and deepen. And Chris would open up more and more about his Jamaican heritage.

For much of his childhood, and even into his preadolescent years, it was an annual tradition for Chris and Voletta to take summer pilgrimages back to her native Jamaica. In Brooklyn, the hustle and bustle of the big city didn't split mother and son up, but Voletta's responsibilities to take care of her son revolved around a myriad of arenas from school, work, bills, and more. In Jamaica, on vacation to visit family, she could focus on her son. Whatever temptations he was experiencing as a child and later as a young teenager in New York, Voletta could temporarily eliminate them. They could get back to what they both had earlier in America: each other. She was keeping her boy close—a pledge she made from the moment she first laid eyes on him. Taking trips to Jamaica, too, was her way of making sure he knew his uncles, aunts, grandparents, and the overall way of life in her home country.

In Jamaica, Chris loved spending time with his uncle Dave, his mother's brother. Back in Brooklyn, his father, Selwyn, wasn't around, so Uncle Dave filled a role Chris needed in his life. He was charismatic and affectionate, and they shared a common bond through music. Chris would follow his uncle to events around the Trelawny parish where he'd perform. It was one thing to listen to music or even learn about it. But for Chris, to see someone perform—better yet, someone related to him—and rock crowds with his own words was proof that his passion wasn't a pipe dream. It was more like a family heirloom. Chris would tell his uncle Dave that when he became a famous musician, he'd be part of his crew.

"We was bound together. And from the first time Biggie heard me start to sing, that was it," Dave Wallace said in *I Got a Story to Tell*. "Many times we were out there, and he was rapping and I was singing."

For a natural-born storyteller, those excursions only provided more fodder once he'd return to Brooklyn.

"He'd tell me stories like his uncle was this ruthless dude in Jamaica," said Chico. "And that he'd have mad weed. His uncle was the man out there."

"Every summer, Chris would come back from Jamaica. Chris would bring back some Jamaican slang and music that we didn't listen to," Sam recalled. "Rock music, reggae, country. He said, 'You know, I can't sleep without country music on.' We were shocked."

For all the stories that came from those travels to Jamaica, exaggerated though they may have been, one part of his life that never came up was the part he had no real recollection of to begin with.

"I thought that his pops passed away or something. 'Cause he never mentioned his father too much. He really kept that too himself," Chico told me. "After a while, he'd say my pops bounced on my moms. He was like, 'I don't wanna talk about it, Chic . . . My pops ain't nothing, man.'"

"We didn't talk about his dad. That was a constant for a lot of us inner-city young boys that lived with our mothers," Sam said. "It was probably too painful or a mystery for him. In retrospect, it was wild that we never talked about that."

———

New York has always had a flair for the dramatic, especially in the underworld. Criminal figures were often celebrities, their influence coming not from TV ratings, record sales, or box office numbers but from money, power, and street respect, by any means necessary. Mobsters like Charles "Lucky" Luciano and Joseph "Crazy Joe" Gallo became household names. By the 1970s, Leroy "Nicky" Barnes and rival Frank Lucas battled for supremacy in the heroin trade. Their power was undeniable, but they went about it differently.

Lucas may have handed out frozen turkeys at Thanksgiving, but he mostly kept a low profile. In contrast, in 1977, Barnes posed on the cover of the *New York Times Magazine* emblazoned with the headline "Mr. Untouchable." And if that wasn't enough, what followed was one of the most ridiculous taunts in crime history, a subcaption that read, "The Police Say He May Be Harlem's Biggest Drug Dealer. But Can They Prove It?" Turns out, they could. President Jimmy Carter was so outraged that he ordered Barnes be prosecuted to the fullest extent of the law, and when he was convicted, Barnes was sentenced to life without parole. After seeing acquaintances, his wife, and girlfriends burn through his money, Mr. Untouchable agreed to testify against them, resulting in several convictions, including his ex-wife,

Thelma Grant, who'd serve ten years in prison. See? A masterclass in New York City drama.

In the 1980s, New York looked drastically different than it does today. Subways were tattooed with graffiti. It was a dirty, economically depressed, and dangerous place. Gentrification was nowhere close to remaking the city, and drugs had a vice grip on hundreds of thousands of residents. In 1986, New York State reported that there were 182,000 regular cocaine users in the city, and two years later, city officials estimated 600,000 users. At the start of the decade, New York City reported a record number of homicides, with 1,814 in 1980. Over the first six months of that year, the city saw its crime index jump 50 percent higher than that of the nation. In Brooklyn, there was a 15.5 percent increase in total crime. The Brooklyn Christopher Wallace was coming of age in was chaotic. And deadly. Some blocks had multiple abandoned buildings, and the rubble left over became makeshift playgrounds.

"Brooklyn was, and it is right now, one of the funnest places on Earth. Especially Brooklyn summers, there's nothing like it. It was very family oriented, and very Black. You knew everybody, everybody knew you," lifelong Brooklyn native Jessica Chong said. "But crack really was a major thing. There were crack vials everywhere. There was a lot of devastation as far as like family members being addicted. The dealers were on every corner, but they were a bunch of kids I knew. Brooklyn felt so good, but there were so many sad moments because of crack."

"The reality in the eighties . . . the drugs really came out hard back then . . . it was like a circus back in the eighties," said Chico Del Vec. "If you wasn't in the mix of what was going on, you either was in school or you had to have something else to do besides hanging out. It had to be something productive because it was really tough."

Paranoia ran the streets. Everyone was watching everyone. Money was exchanging hands at a blistering rate, and so were the bullets. Between 1980 and 1989, New York City averaged 2,042 homicides a year, peaking in 1990 with 2,605. What drugs did to New York was vicious. Street corners became makeshift offices for countless young Black men who saw money in the street as a better play than flipping burgers at McDonald's or working at a laundromat. Cocaine had a long history in America, and a reputation as a luxury drug, but crack was a game changer. It was cheaper. It was smokable, and when it hit a user's system, they almost instantly transformed into a zombie-like character. Crack wasn't just addictive, either; it was life-altering. It fractured homes and what once were tight-knit communities, dissolved legitimate jobs, and turned lives upside down quicker than it took to walk to the corner to purchase it. Some of the coverage surrounding the drug's lethalness was sensationalistic, but the carnage it inflicted on lower-income communities was generationally debilitating and stereotypically damning. Crack's high didn't last long, allowing fiends to cop multiple times a day. To do that, money had to be secured by any manner possible, including crimes like robberies, car break-ins, and muggings. The downsides to the life came in various forms—street rivals from another block, the New York Police Department, or even death. But for many, including Chris and Chico, the rewards made the risks seem worthwhile.

The era of Nicky Barnes and Frank Lucas had given way to a new one. Drug dealing in the 1970s came with organization and a certain sense of polish inherited from the Mafia, but in the eighties, it was anarchic, a free-for-all. The youth were out in droves in the streets. Whatever sophistication the game had had deteriorated. A new cast of street legends were holding court. Kenneth "Supreme" McGriff and Gerald "Prince" Miller of the Supreme Team, founded near Baisley Park Houses, ran Queens. Authorities said that at its height, the organization raked in $200,000 a day. Alberto "Alpo" Martinez, Azie "A.Z." Faison Jr., and Rich Porter were top dogs in Harlem—and would later inspire the cult classic film *Paid in Full*. And in Queens, Howard "Pappy" Mason and Lorenzo "Fat Cat" Nichols's names struck fear at the mere mention. And it wasn't just New York City. Kingpins existed all across the country. Crack was now as American as hot dogs on the Fourth of July.

Christopher Wallace, now in high school, wanted to take control of his life. He'd briefly spent time as a counselor at Park Slope's Congregation Beth Elohim alongside his mother at the Early Childhood Center. Like his mother, he was great with the kids. The adults there loved him, too. That was the thing about Chris: he could make anyone feel comfortable. But Chris wasn't comfortable, at least not financially, and he was tired of depending on his mom for money, especially when he saw so many people his age bringing in serious cash just by being outside in the mix.

"This nigga's coming through with the butter Fila velour suit, the big cables, four finger rings. I'm like, 'Yo, we the same age,'" Chris later recalled, sharing his impressions of Chico. "I'm sitting here fucked-up asking my moms to throw me down some money for ice cream. And this nigga is getting cash!"

By the time he was fifteen, Wallace was all in on hustling. Those close to him, like Hubert, were shocked when he chose the street life. But Hubert also understood. They were the same age, and he'd be lying if he didn't want many of the same things. He knew it wasn't a good road, but how was he realistically going to tell his lifelong friend not to walk down it? It was next to impossible, especially with Chris, who was already so headstrong, and the lure of easy riches was irresistible.

Money was king. It provided access to people, places, and opportunities, and the culture drilled into the country's psyche that wealth was good and poverty was evil. Coming from a community with few to no resources or avenues for upward advancement, drug dealing represented a way to acquire wealth in immediate fashion. By the time Hubert hit tenth grade, he noticed most of the dudes in his neighborhood disappearing. If you weren't a jock or your supervision at home wasn't stringent—hell, even if it was sometimes—for many young Black males at the time, graduation came in the form of a street corner instead of a cap and gown.

"It became about money. The eighties was just materialistic. Talk about the crack era and Reaganomics and all that," recalled Hubert Sam. "In Brooklyn, what we inherited was like the bastard child of the seventies in a way. Every summer would just get colder."

04

REAL CRACK, REAL MONEY

CHRIS AND CHICO HAD BECOME FAST FRIENDS, BUT IT WASN'T JUST CHICO WHO INTRODUCED HIM TO THE GAME. Suif "C-Gutta" Jackson was one of Chris's closest friends and lived nearby on Gates Avenue and Greene Avenue. Gutta had moved back to New York from Mississippi when Chris around twelve or thirteen. Returning to New York from the Deep South came with its own set of hurdles for Gutta, who already had a little-man complex and had to fight often after being teased for being perceived as "country." Gutta and Chris had a mutual friend in the neighborhood named Fat Eric. Chris and Eric were large in stature—and way more reserved in temperament. From there, one of Chris's lifelong bonds was established; he referred to Gutta as his "cousin" frequently. And it was Gutta who'd marvel at Chris's rhyming skills whenever he'd freestyle on the block.

Gutta and Chris moved through life together on Brooklyn's streets. So it makes sense that they entered the drug game together, too. Gutta recalled the first time he and Chris sold crack in the summer of 1988. They kept seeing Chico run around the corner. Gutta, whose primary source of income then was robbing people, and Chris hadn't yet fully immersed themselves in the world of street pharmaceutics.

Chico told them all he did was stand on the corner and the customers came to him. Chris and Gutta were flabbergasted. It couldn't be *that* easy to sell crack. As it turned out, it *was* that easy. The stressful part, as Chris would come to find out, came with committing fully to the lifestyle.

"I was getting a SSI check from my mom having cancer. Chic was like, 'Bro, you can get an ounce with that!' So we go cop an ounce," Gutta recalled in the 2021 Netflix documentary *I Got a Story to Tell*. "We go to Chic room. Chic bag it up. This was the first time me and Big ever sold crack. Now, at that time, we was bagging sixteen to seventeen hundred dollars in work off an ounce. And you don't even have the maturity enough to think it all the way through. Of course you gon' jump on that!"

Chris had grown to envy Chico's independence. But the two young Brooklyn boys just genuinely enjoyed each other's company. They both loved video games, and Chris would invite his friend up to his room to play. Chico was floored by how extensive his video game collection was.

"He'd go in the crib and play video games on his ColecoVision. He could be in the crib playing video games all day," Chico remembers.

Chris had *Donkey Kong*, *Jungle Hunt*, and more, and before long he was a neighborhood favorite for his entertainment system. A natural-born hustler, he even charged kids a quarter to play. Voletta didn't mind the new kids in the house as long as her son was home, too. Regardless of the games, though, he had his sights set outside. Chris was still in school at this point, and so long as his grades never failed, he could do whatever he wanted when his mom wasn't around. He'd smoke cigarettes and drink Calvin Coolers, sweet fruit-flavored wine coolers. He'd do everything he knew he wasn't supposed to do.

"It's funny because it'd only work in the daytime because at night he had to go in the crib," said Chico.

Initially, when her son would ask to go outside when she was there, Voletta would say no. He'd beg more. She'd say no again. And in his head, Chris thought about all the mischief he was missing. When she did let him go out, he had a strict curfew. As far as Voletta was concerned, no boys needed to be out on the street at night after 8:30 P.M. Especially not young Black boys. And *especially* not her Christopher.

"Nothing good happens after those hours," she'd later write.

"She just made me want to keep doing," he reflected as an adult. "Why does she not want me to play skelly, or 'run, catch, and kiss,' and do shit that little boys are supposed to do? Keeping me in the crib—that shit ain't doing nothing but stifling me, man. Let me loose a little, give me some air. I ain't got no brothers or sisters or nothing. You gone all the time. What? You just want me to be a lonely bastard?"

Voletta, of course, wasn't gone "all the time" for her own pleasure. She was trying to make a better life for her and her son. But he wanted a life of his own. As the years passed, Chris stayed in school, but he stayed on the streets, too. Where he had excelled in school before, now sitting in a class listening to a teacher talk just wasn't his idea of securing his future. It was a game he had to play. His mother, a terrific schoolteacher, knew the American educational system was far from perfect and that it was deeply flawed and systemically unjust in many ways. But she deeply believed in education as a way to improve one's lot in life. Chris didn't, at least not for himself. Voletta wrote in her 2005 memoir that one of her most painful memories with her son was "realizing that not only didn't he like school anymore, but he might actually drop out altogether."

By the time he reached high school, Chris had had enough. He was growing antsy from all the discipline. Plus, all those years of being teased for his uniform had run their course. He started at Sarah J. Hale High School in Boerum Hill and then transferred to George Westinghouse Career and Technical Education High School in Downtown Brooklyn, where future stars Shawn "Jay-Z" Carter, Earl "DMX" Simmons, and Trevor "Busta Rhymes" Smith were also enrolled. He did well at Westinghouse for a time; some teachers told Voletta that Chris was doing so well, he could receive a college scholarship as long as he maintained a B average.

"There's an alternate universe in my head where he's the world's funniest accountant," Cheo Hodari Coker, author of the 2003 biography *Unbelievable*, told me. "It's almost like that *Sopranos* episode where Tony, after he gets shot by Uncle June, has that dream about how he's a traveling salesman. He's a completely different Tony Soprano. There are alternate-reality Christophers that are completely different than what he ended up being."

It was never going to be. Chris started skipping school. As far as Voletta knew he was there, but he'd walk out the front door, then leave his stuff on the roof, and for the rest of the day, while she was at work, he'd be on the block hustling. She received a call from the police one night saying a neighbor reported seeing a prowler on the roof, and they found her son's school supplies up there. That caused a huge argument between mother and son.

And then when he did go to school, he'd often buck back at authority. Once, a teacher contacted Voletta to tell her Chris received a B on an exam. Normally, this would have been a good thing. But he had missed much of the instructional period leading up to it. When he was disrupting class one day, the teacher shot back that if he didn't get his act together, he'd amount to being a garbage collector. Chris was infuriated.

That same evening, Chris asked his mother how much a garbage collector made. For whatever reason, she had a magazine that listed professions and their salaries. And there it was. A teacher made roughly $22,000 a year, whereas a garbage collector made $29,000.

"You said some of us are gonna be garbage collectors," Chris shot back in class the next day. "But we're gonna be making more money than you. So that's cool."

School was far from Chris's main concern now. There was too much money to be made—even more than from garbage collecting—and learning about world history and whatever math they deemed was necessary for him to learn that semester didn't seem to matter. As long as he knew how much crack to bag up, how much to sell it for, and how much a re-up would cost, he knew as much math and science as he thought he needed to know. Crack was necessary. More important, the money he procured from selling crack was necessary. For a teenager making thousands of dollars just off hand-to-hand transactions, school was never going to be able to compete. His time in a classroom was nearing its end, not just because his interests waned on any sort of academic achievement, but also because there was no way his life in school and life in the streets would be able to coexist. It was either one or the other. And it didn't take a rocket scientist to figure out which option he'd choose.

While he was at Westinghouse, Chris got jumped by a group of teenagers called the Decepticons.

"They'd be going up to the schools back in the day. One time he got caught in a scuffle," said Chico, chuckling.

Chris came home bloodied up, with a cut on his wrist and a busted head that required stitches. By then, he already had his crew and this disrespect wasn't going to be accepted. Retaliation was swift.

"A week later, we went up there and we got the dudes that jumped him. We just wilded out!" an animated Chico said, almost as if he can still see the punches being thrown. "Me, him, and a couple of other dudes. It was crazy. After that, he definitely wasn't going back to school, after what we did."

Chris, now Big Chris or Fat Chris on the block, dropped out of high school in the tenth grade. Sure, he could make good grades, hopefully get into a good college, find a way to pay for it, earn a degree, and land a career in whatever field he decided on—like commercial art at the nearby Pratt Institute in Clinton Hill, within a mile from his apartment. Six years? Eight years? Maybe more before he got a job that was fulfilling in any meaningful way. Fulton Street provided instant gratification. "After I got introduced to crack—commercial art? Nigga please," he would reflect later in his life. "I can go out here for twenty minutes and get some real paper. That's your art, man. I didn't want no job. I couldn't see myself getting on no train for shit. I didn't want to work in no barbershop. I didn't want to do no restaurant. I wanted to sell drugs! I wanted to chop up keys, bag up work, and get paid. That's the only thing I ever thought I was gonna do."

Chris's decision to leave school wasn't uncommon. At his high school, less than half the students graduated in four years, and citywide, the dropout rate was around 20 percent. The streets were calling. As with anything else in life, hustling is a process. Chris didn't just jump off the stoop with his own corner or his own package. He'd move work for other people. Once he proved he could do that, the opportunities increased. The return was quick and fast.

In no time, Chris could have hundreds of dollars in his pockets. Real money. The juxtaposition between the two worlds—the one Voletta saw for her son and the one her son saw for himself—proved combative. The love they had for each other never wavered, but ideological differences absolutely left a strain on their relationship. Voletta would plead with him to return to school, but before long she understood that wish would never be granted. She wasn't totally oblivious. She saw the news and she understood what crack was doing to the city, but once the headstrong Christopher saw the benefits of selling crack, there was no convincing him he didn't make the right choice.

"We were sitting on six and seven grand a week, just living, you know what I'm saying?" he later said. "And we had all the chickenhead bitches on our dicks and shit. We were just doing our thing."

Chris and his crew did most of their thing on Fulton Street. The Ave. was in essence a graduation ceremony. No longer was Wallace confined to the stoop. On the Ave. came access to real money and real power. That's where the stores were. That's where all the foot traffic was. The routes going downtown to Albee Square Mall allowed him to see all the players and potential clients coming through. It was an entirely new world that was literally just outside his apartment window. But as exciting as this new life was for Chris, the pitfalls were potentially fatal.

"To live so close to Fulton, I never thought about that, but that could've changed his whole life if he lived on another back block," said Sam. "Not having access to Fulton as the strip could've changed the trajectory of his life."

"If you're gonna be out there on the Ave., you're gonna be out there for a reason," Sam added. "He came out to hustle."

The streets changed Christopher Wallace because they changed everyone. He was seventeen now, and his relationship with his mother was more strenuous than it had ever been. He wasn't a happy-go-lucky elementary school kid who'd bring home awards from school or honor roll report cards. That Chris was gone forever.

Hubert Sam and Christopher Wallace always remained friends. Sam never tried to talk Chris out of the path he was taking, but he would occasionally ask how deep down the rabbit hole he was actually trying to take this.

Sam was playing football at Thomas Jefferson High School in East New York. When he'd come to visit Chris, it would always be on the block. Not the stoop where they once saw the world whiz by them as young kids. Here he'd be with C-Gutta and a friend from the neighborhood named Roland. Known as "Olie" or "O" on the streets, he and Chris were in the trenches together selling crack on Fulton Street.

"O was the original hustler," said Damion "D-Roc" Butler, one of Chris's closest friends who hustled nearby on Bedford and Quincy. "O schooled everybody."

"O was always like a lone wolf in a big family," Sam remembered. "He had a lot of backing and he had a lot of hustle, so when he came around, he kinda elevated everyone's hustle. Him and Big got close, and Big would start to get game from O. They created a real bond."

Young grew up across the street from Sam and Chris's elementary school, St. Peter Claver. They didn't know O, but Sam does remember the junk the kids across the street would shout at them. They'd stand outside the rowhouses and just pelt them with insults. It wasn't until years later that they'd all put one and one together. O came from a very serious family in Brownsville, Brooklyn. He worked for his uncle, Carl Bazemore, aka I-God. And I-God wasn't someone to cross. Violence was a way of life, especially in his line of work. O brought the street knowledge he picked up in Brownsville over to Fulton Street, where Chris was, and spread game there.

"My man O. Like we used to be hustling. All of us dropped out of high school," Chris said. "We sitting on like six grand, seven grand a week. Just living."

So when Hubert came around the way that day, what he saw was more of the same. The same crew on the block and the same guys he'd grown up with. Chris was still the same Chris in some ways. The dude could still make him laugh at the drop of a hat. The streets hardened him because that was the nature of the beast, but it did nothing to sap him of his humanity. People naturally gravitated toward him, and he could hold court with anyone on the block, from fellow hustlers to fiends to even everyday folks from the neighborhood like store owners, young kids, and hardworking men and women going and coming from work. He was never an in-your-face type of cat, but he knew how to talk to people and how to make them feel at ease. And although it was different now, Chris had a clear vision of what it was he wanted out of life. He wanted money. And lots of it.

"You playing football?" an impressed Big Chris asked his childhood homie in a conversation that was replayed in the 2003 biography *Unbelievable*. "Man, you gonna break something."

Laughter erupted among the group of young Black males who, for a split second, weren't worried about the hazards around them. They were enjoying each other's company.

"I'm a'ight, yo," Sam rebutted while smiling. "I'm a'ight."

"You gettin' big though," Chris responded. Though they had taken different routes of teenage rites of passage—one of the football field and the other on the block—he was still proud of and happy for his friend.

Almost out of nowhere, Gutta decided to test his own tackling skills on Sam. Even in the midst of a war, the Black experience, no matter how fleeting, finds joy inside pain and hope inside of despair.

———

By the late 1980s, crack's impact on New York City was as vicious as it had ever been. A country that had favored punishment over rehabilitation, backed by a criminal justice system that came down hardest on those with pigment and without wealth or access to opportunity, was a powder keg waiting to explode. And now it had.

The city, much like others around the country with high concentrations of Black and brown people, couldn't control the drug's spread. Crack was just way too powerful, way too easy to produce, way too easy to distribute, and way too addictive.

The drug dismantled families with effortless precision. City officials blamed crack for an outrageous rise in cases of abused and neglected children, with 73 percent of deaths in those cases in 1987 compared with 11 percent in 1985. And, of course, the correctional system saw its own numbers rise, even declaring a "jail emergency" in 1988. Between July and December 1987, 13,601 misdemeanor and felony crack arrests had taken place in New York. From January 1988 to October 1988, that number ballooned to 31,223 arrests. By February 1989, per statistics kept at the time, the city's jail population was nearly 18,000 inmates—up from 9,815 in 1985.

If the numbers sounded astounding, which they were, being on the front line was even more harrowing. Big Chris dropped out of school and right into this world. No longer were pop quizzes the worry, but instead popups by the cops, and they were more than willing to haul young street-corner hustlers downtown. If they were beat up along the way, that was part of the game. The relationship between the NYPD and the city's Black and brown neighborhoods was historically tense.

And then, in the spring of 1989, five young teenage boys between the ages of fourteen and sixteen were arrested and later convicted of brutally assaulting twenty-eight-year-old white investment banker Trisha Meili, who was jogging through Central Park. Though the "Central Park Five" would be cleared of the crime in 2002 when the actual perpetrator confessed, in the moment, it became one of the tensest pre–Rodney King moments with Black bodies and police officers of its time. No DNA evidence from semen found at the scene connected any of the boys to the crime, but one certain New York City real estate mogul, who had been sued for housing discrimination dating back to Voletta Wallace's early days in New York in the seventies, thought otherwise. In four city newspapers, Donald Trump spent $85,000 on advertisements calling for the execution of the young boys.

"I want to hate these murderers and I always will," he wrote in the ad. "I am not looking to psychoanalyze or understand them, I am looking to punish them."

Then, in August 1989, the murder of Yusef Hawkins by a white mob in Brooklyn's Bensonhurst neighborhood poured gasoline on an already out-of-control racial firestorm. Hawkins and a group of friends were in the neighborhood, reportedly to purchase a used car. The mob gathered with the intention of attacking the group of Black people, reportedly operating off the rumor that one of the Black men was dating a white girl from the area. Whatever the reason, Hawkins's murder by a white mob bookended several of its kind, like Willie Turks in 1982 and Michael Griffith in 1986. Ironically, a month before the tragic incident, Spike Lee's *Do the Right Thing* hit theaters detailing the angst, bigotry, and violence Black Brooklynites experienced. Hawkins's murder ignited months of protest and civic uprisings. Being a young Black male in New York was enough to make someone like Big Chris a moving target based on appearance alone.

It was real in the field, and Chris knew it. He always had to keep his head on a swivel because now he was openly operating in a world where one misstep could crumble his entire operation. If he wasn't on the lookout for a rival crew, he had eyes up for the cops, who were all too eager to bust anyone's head if they even sensed the faintest hint of pushback. Big Chris could afford not to pay attention in the classroom if the material didn't interest him and still come out with an A or B on a test because he was smart.

He could tell you the distance between the planets in the solar system or memorize a jazz solo with ease. On the street, however, he didn't have that luxury. No matter how much of a lull some days were on the Ave., he had to pay attention if he wanted to get paid—and if he wanted to stay alive. These were the lessons older hustlers like Tony Rome and Cheese taught him, like veterans on a football team would do for a young rookie they take under their wing.

Big Chris never forgot a face. He couldn't afford to because the stakes were too high. Because of all this, too, he didn't trust too many people. There would be times when he didn't speak while he was on the block. He knew he could stand to learn a lot more just from observing and listening than he could talking.

"That's what I really liked about him, because he'd always be that dude to watch everything," said Chico. "To the point where he got a feel of it, because after a while he followed instructions."

Those closest to Chris knew he didn't have to hustle. Voletta sacrificed so much and worked so hard to make sure he didn't have to know that life. In fact, the only thing she was reluctant to give him was the one thing Chris wanted more than video games, clothes, or even food. He desperately yearned for his freedom and was fueled by capitalistic gain. Money was always the end goal. Though he'd later come to regret the damage he was inflicting on his own people, in the trenches he didn't have time for those thoughts.

As if there wasn't enough to watch for on the block for Big Chris and his counterparts, there was the one big truth they were always aware of: not every fiend was really a fiend. In 1988, the NYPD rolled out a new tactic in their war on drugs: TNTs, or Tactical Narcotics Teams. The first TNT was in response to the execution-style killing of a rookie police officer in Queens. The NYPD wanted to send a message, so it flooded the neighborhood with investigators and undercover officers. Buy-and-bust operations expanded to other neighborhoods and boroughs. This made dealers, Big Chris included, increasingly paranoid. Think season one of *The Wire* when Bubbles took Leandor Syndor, dressed as a dope fiend, with him to "the Pit" to see how Avon Barksdale and Stringer Bell ran their West Baltimore operation. Vans would park at the end of blocks while decoys would attempt to buy from some of the local dealers. Some, either too eager to make a dollar or unable to see a wolf in sheep's clothing, got jammed up.

Dealers would frequently require statements of recommendation when users brought potential new clientele around. There was no way to be too careful. TNTs were arresting so many suppliers and users that they were causing a backlog for the city's criminal justice system. Brooklyn district attorney Elizabeth Holtzman said her office was in "desperate shape—we are swamped with cases." The city, by 1989, had come under fire for its lack of proper drug treatment. Mayor Edward Koch's nearly $27 billion plan for the 1989–90 year envisioned converting one prison barge to a four-hundred-bed drug care center for inmates. This came after multiple harsh critiques from state drug officials after Koch failed to deliver on a promise to provide more space for treatment programs. There were ten buildings allotted for that exact purpose in 1988. Two caught on fire, two were condemned, and five had liens—leaving but one in working condition.

The "crack era" in New York City had an impact on every line of work from street corners to courtrooms, from newsrooms to dopehouses, and from precincts to state legislatures. For Big Chris, it was all about living to see the next sale. If people didn't know what to look for, Chris and all the hustlers just looked like guys standing around on the block. If one knew what to look for, however, Chris and the other guys were always moving around, making sure never to stay in one spot too long. But whatever tactics he used, the cops always knew who he was because he was the biggest kid on the block. Chris couldn't blend in if he tried. One time when Hubert Sam came to visit, they were trailed by cops when they both went inside a local bodega to get a turkey hero with cheese. Of course Chris was holding weight on him, but when the cops weren't looking, he popped the vials in his mouth. Then, when confronted, Chris put on the acting performance of a lifetime when he faked as if they were hurting him, screaming in pain so loudly that it caused a crowd.

"Yo, he could have won an Oscar. He was acting like they were killing him. And then he started crying," Sam recalled.

Big Chris got a kick out of the whole thing. That interaction with Sam wasn't the first, nor would it be the last police would ever make his acquaintance, and things didn't always go his way.

During another occasion, the block got a little too hot for Chris, said Chico: "Man, he swallowed a whole eightball. Police jumped out on him and he threw it in his mouth and swallowed." Chico laughed at the memory. "He was sitting there looking stupid all night!"

Chico and some friends went to get their comrade some magnesium citrate because Chris needed a laxative in the worst way possible.

The thing about hustling is that a person risks life and limb, all in the pursuit of a dream. Young men had visions of a Tony Montana rags-to-riches story, but in reality, dealing on the block was more like hoop dreams. No matter how much a kid dedicated his life to getting better at basketball, there are only so many selections in the NBA Draft each year. It wasn't as if Big Chris was expecting to be New York's biggest crack dealer overnight, but he did have dreams far beyond the Ave. On the block, he'd tell Chico about the visions he had for himself and his people.

"We gon' be like the mobsters," he'd say often.

But the road there was rough and oftentimes required putting the love of money ahead of morals. Around the way, there was a pregnant lady from New Jersey who used to visit every day looking for a fix. Somewhere along the range of ninety capsules a day. The crew had a rule—do not serve pregnant women. Big Chris decided to break that rule.

"I'm like, 'Fuck it. I mean, if I don't give it to her someone else will," he later reflected. "It ain't like she gonna go home and be like, 'Well, Biggie didn't give it to me, I'm going to sleep.' She's gonna get high. So I'm gonna handle my business. And niggas was like, 'Yo, you foul.'"

There was little room for sympathy on the streets. "I got into this game because I can't do nothing else. This is what's going to help me eat. So I can't pass up no mothafucka. That's bread and butter, you know what I'm saying? If I don't do that, I can't eat."

What he was doing in the neighborhood was no surprise. Selling drugs was the worst-kept secret in the hood. One of those people who took notice was Donald Harrison. He saw the young Black boys and men on the corner waiting for their next sale, and he was disappointed when he saw his promising mentee doing the same. Initially, he'd see Chris and tell him to go home. And Chris would, because of the respect he had for Harrison.

Despite those occasional moments when it was just the two of them, Harrison had come to accept that the Ave., the money, and the drugs were more alluring to Chris than his studio sessions. Those studio sessions, now a thing of the past, produced several tracks. Harrison compiled enough music between them to take demos to record companies.

"He was dealing with issues people of his generation were, and I guess they thought he was too young to be dealing with that," Harrison recalled of his attempts to get a then early-adolescent Chris a record deal. "It was more uplifting, but it was still the same kinda subject matter."

Once the companies found out his age, they balked. This disillusioned Chris, Harrison says. His pleas that Chris's time would come fell on deaf ears as the streets became his main source of inspiration. Chris had found his calling in another game.

"We were still friends. Sometimes he saw me and he would come walk with me and see what was going on. He'd turn into Christopher Wallace with me again," Harrison said. "I would just be like, I'm praying for you, brotha."

The guys on the block would look at Big Chris with exasperated looks, like *Who is this guy?* and *What the hell is his problem?* It got to a point where Voletta would call Harrison, begging him to do whatever he could. She'd seen what the young boys on the street corner were doing while she was headed to work. An entire generation was being driven into a world with no future, and she knew of the horror stories of mothers burying their sons. The last thing she needed was her Christopher adding his name to such a somber list. Maybe a male influence would shift the misfortunes of her son, she reasoned. But that wasn't enough, and after a while, Harrison stopped trying to interject.

As Chris dove deeper and deeper into the street life, there were still some who saw the innocence that he never completely lost. Lorna Pinckney, a renowned spoken word artist, posted on Facebook in 2016 about a friend she had once had in Brooklyn named Chris Wallace. The world knew him for his music, but she cherished the warm-hearted older kid who "made it his business to look out for me and my younger siblings." They'd swap comic books and video games. And he'd put her on to Boogie Down Productions, whizzing through lyrics from songs like "My Philosophy" and "Criminal Minded." According to Pinckney, he ended up becoming a big brother on the block to her. So much so that when he transitioned to life in the street a few years later, he kept the same commitment to her.

"I wasn't at the age of judging, but one day [I] asked him why he wasn't going to school anymore and his response was, 'I don't know Lorn . . . it might be too late for me,'" Pinckney wrote in her Facebook post. "I never forgot that. Then he made sure I got home . . . and would always make sure I got home in the house before those street lights came on."

The range of stories about Chris at this time capture the complicated, split sides of his life. He was a cold-blooded crack salesman on the street. To others, he was a protector. To others, he was the funniest guy on the planet. And to others, he was a musical prodigy who was wasting his gifts in a nihilistic world that had no future.

Whoever he was on the streets, when it was clock-out time, he always had to return home to Voletta and a relationship that had grown tense. Regardless of when she kicked him out for selling drugs and he eventually came back, and regardless of the time she left a Brooklyn courthouse in tears after filing a Person in Need of Supervision (PINS) warrant to keep him off the streets, Voletta and her son were still attached at the hip. She'd constantly threaten him that if whatever he was doing in the streets led to any harm for him—he'd always interrupt her with the same retort, saying, "I know, Ma, you're going to be a rich woman." Remember, her first love in America was her son—and the first example of love he'd ever known was his mother. The streets, and her frustration with her son's rebellious lifestyle, could never supersede that, though it'd be mighty difficult to tell at times. Voletta once said that for the first dozen years of his life he was an ideal child, one who never caused her any trouble and always did what he was told.

"He was a son that any mother would like," Voletta would say in the 1995 documentary *The Show*.

"Uh-huh," said her son, seated beside her. "Keep it real."

But they were always immensely protective of each other. Like that one time when Chris was sixteen and Voletta had come back home from a dentist's appointment to find her apartment had been robbed. Whoever the culprits were had gotten in through the fire escape. As if that wasn't petrifying enough, one afternoon while she slept on the couch, Voletta's apartment was robbed again. She didn't want to stay there alone and strongly considered moving.

Not long after the second break-in, Chris burst into her room. He had just come from the West Indian Day Parade, and he told her that the guy who had robbed her both times had been shot and killed after trying to pickpocket a man and steal his watch. For whatever reason, she believed him. She was relieved that she'd no longer have to live in fear in her own home.

A year later, she noted, she, Chris, and one of her friends were riding to AquaDuck Flea Market. Voletta was telling her friend about the break-ins and the death of the would-be burglar.

"Quack, quack, quack!" Chris said, laughing so hard he could hardly catch his breath.

"Christopher!" Voletta retorted. "What is the matter with you?"

"You were so afraid, Ma, I had to do something," Chris said. "You couldn't even go up the stairs by yourself. So I had to tell you that so you could forget about that nigga and stop being afraid to live in your own house."

"Even when I was wrong, I got my point across," he'd rhyme years later. That was his way of solving problems. It wasn't right, but the intention was so pure, it was hard to be mad at him. But that ruthless side was always there, too. He didn't really stop to think about the destruction selling crack was doing to the community. He was selling to men and women who, for the most part, looked just like him. The consequences of his decisions never took precedence over his own ambitions. He needed the money, not just for himself but because his supply wasn't free. If the connect didn't get his money, there'd be problems.

Like that one time while he was still at Westinghouse and a local plug gave him some crack to get off—and Chris never came back to school.

"I knew the guy. He was like, 'Yo, you know, what can you do? I mean, I'm gonna hurt him if I don't get my money,'" Chris's childhood friend Michael Bynum recalled in the documentary *Bigger Than Life*. "I was like, 'Just relax. Lemme talk to his moms.' So I was kind of the mediator. I stepped in and his mom and I, we arranged a meeting. His mother actually paid a drug dealer off for Big."

Nevertheless, Chris still attempted to hide that part of his life from his mother. By then, though, it wasn't like she was completely naive. She knew he was in the streets. "But it wasn't nothing she could do to stop a nigga," he said in 1995. "I'd tell her I'ma stop. I ain't gonna fuck around no more. I'd just come back in and tell her I ain't doing it—and still be doing it."

Chico Del Vec saw a lot of this happen in real time. It was Chico who introduced him and C-Gutta to the hustle, and in turn their bond developed far beyond street pharmaceuticals. It got to a point where Chico was as much a visitor to Chris's apartment as Chris was. But he'd also be the one who'd get in trouble for Chris' slipups. Voletta would constantly find drugs in his room.

"And I'd be like, it's Chico's," Chris explained the scenes years later.

"And I'm like, yo, what the hell?! Why you tell on me?" Chico responded.

"Well, it is yours."

One day on the street, Chris and Chico found themselves playing a quick game of Let's Make a Deal with a dope fiend. The fiend wanted to exchange a mysterious bag with a piece of treasure inside for some crack. Chico instantly rebuffed the offer. If it didn't involve money, he wasn't trying to hear anything about a deal. But it was Chris who was adamant on getting the bag. Like he had been his entire life—from watching *Ten Little Indians* to leaving the stoop—he was driven by curiosity. What could it be?

After a few minutes of bickering, Chico eventually lost out and they got the bag. Inside were a bunch of random items, the great majority of which neither Chico nor Chris wanted. Except for one item: a machete. It was like something Sylvester Stallone would've used in *Rambo*. For Chris, that was enough to make the transaction a success. For Chico, it was more like, *What the hell are we supposed to do with this?*

Jump forward to days later in Chris's room, when Chico fell asleep playing video games. And that's when all hell broke loose.

"What is this?!" Voletta yelled, busting through the door. "Where did you get this knife from? I don't want this knife in here!"

"Ma, what are you talking about?!" Christopher shot back.

Voletta, annoyed that her son was trying to play dumb, whipped out the machete.

"I jumped up scared as hell," Chico reminisced. "You know she Jamaican. I almost jumped out the window."

65

"Oh, nah, it's Chico's!" Chris protested.

But he never threw the knife away, and when Voletta found it again, it was the same routine. After a while, it became almost a twisted comedy show that all parties were involved in. If there was anything in Chris's room that didn't need to be there, it was always Chico's—even if it wasn't. The nice clothes he started wearing? Yep, Chico bought those for him.

Chris was notoriously messy, so it wasn't uncommon for his mother to come clean up behind him. Voletta needed everything in her house clean and in order. She'd always find plates of chicken bones in his room, so when she found a plate crusted with some white material on it, it didn't seem out of the ordinary, and she cleaned it up.

When Chris came back home and noticed the plate was gone, panic set in. He turned the room upside down in search of that singular plate that, on the street, was quite valuable.

"Ma, did you go in my room?" he asked.

"Yeah," she responded.

"Did you see a plate on my bed?"

"Yeah, the plate with mashed potatoes?" Chris recalled her saying, laughing at the moment in an interview years later. "Oh, they were so hard on the plate I had to flush it."

Chris felt his heart drop to his feet. If there was any hint of a saving grace, it's that some of it was thrown in the garbage. He ran outside to go through each bag of trash hoping to find anything. A morsel, a pinch. *Anything*. And, well, he did find some—but that crack had barbecued turkey wings all over it.

"Niggas is looking at me like, 'You fucked up,'" Chris recalled.

"I'm like, 'Boy, what are you doing?!' . . . But that's how hungry he was for money," Chico said. "His moms wasn't giving him a hundred dollars a day and all that. She was working. She paid bills. She was a schoolteacher."

In her own words, Voletta and Chris "grew up together." All Voletta wanted to do was protect her son. And Chris, despite the mischief he was now committing himself to, wanted to make his mother happy. If that meant keeping the truth about what he was really doing when she wasn't around away from her, then so be it. Chris knew that selling drugs wasn't how his mother had raised him—and he damn sure knew having drugs in his mother's apartment was a deep breach of trust. But Chris, ever the risk-taker, wasn't going to stop, either. But he also wasn't going to tell her until he was left with no other options. In a way, both mother and son needed to see the best in each other. Voletta knew her son was up to something treacherous. But the faux-safety in her denial was a lot more comforting than the truth.

"I thought crack bottles were perfume bottles," Voletta later admitted.

It wouldn't be until years later, after her son died, that Voletta eventually found out the truth of that story about the "potatoes."

"If he wasn't dead," she said in a 2017 A&E documentary, the ember in her eyes still ablaze, "I would've killed him."

05

LIFE IN THE GAME

THOUGH HE WAS NO LONGER AS CLOSE WITH DONALD HARRI-SON, MUSIC NEVER LEFT CHRIS'S LIFE. He still loved it, and he was in every aspect a student of rap. He could recite lyrics off the top of his head after hearing a song just a few times. He loved the classic albums of the late eighties like Public Enemy's *Yo! Bum Rush the Show* and *It Takes a Nation of Millions to Hold Us Back*, N.W.A's *Straight Outta Compton*, Eric B. & Rakim's *Paid in Full,* and EPMD's *Unfinished Business.*

"He had music, so we was always playing it," said Chico. "We had a room in his crib where he'd get on the floor and be break dancing. He's a funny dude, man."

Outside his close friends, few knew the musical side of Chris. Voletta knew because she'd always hear the music blaring from his room. Hubert Sam knew because he saw the musical evolution in his friend up close and personal from when they were in elementary school. He knew he had skills and the ability to tell a story with his wordplay that no one else in the neighborhood could even come close to mimicking.

But by the time they were in their teens, Chris had put music on the backburner. Hustling was his full-time career. Sam wasn't even using his turntables anymore. Music was almost like a past life.

"While he was on Fulton Street hustling, there was no balance of him as an artist and as a hustler. It was all hustle," said Sam. "He was already Big. Niggas was calling him Big already by then. But he wasn't known for rapping. Nobody really knew about his past."

Big was a fixture in the neighborhood. You couldn't miss him. Not just because of his physical stature, but because of his personality. Everyone came to know him, from elementary school kids to neighborhood elders. He was a hustler, and he was selling crack, but anyone who took the time to get to know him understood that he was just a jovial neighborhood conductor who just happened to move weight. He was the mayor of St. James. Big could even speak a little Arabic, which earned him a good reputation with many of the store owners in the area. He was Bed-Stuy's most famous hood politician.

On Fulton Street, Big experienced the entire repertoire of life in the drug game: stickups, shootouts, armed robberies, fights, and even death. How he moved around attracted young hustlers like Trice and Larceny and, in particular, James "Lil' Cease" Lloyd, who'd met Big when he was in elementary school.

"When we got older, like when I was twelve or thirteen, that's when I started hangin' out on the corner, cuttin' school and all that," Cease said. "That's when I started bonding with him. He wasn't serious about the rap thing yet. We was just hangin' on the Ave."

In early 1990, Big met a young Brooklyn woman named Jan Jackson. They grew up a block apart, but somehow fate had never brought them together. One day when she was getting off the subway, she stopped at a pay phone (the same pay phone that would be featured in the "Juicy" video) and Big, who had been hustling all day, stepped to her.

"I always see you getting off the train, [and] you always so serious. Why don't you smile?" he asked. Not exactly a pickup line women love to hear coming from a man, especially one they don't know. But to Jan, there was something endearing about this random guy who was now talking to her.

"Can you please leave? I don't know you!" Jan responded.

Each day when she got off the train, there was Chris walking her home. And over time, Chris—that's what she called him—won her over. What she really appreciated about him was his charisma. Chris had the gift of gab in surplus. He could make her smile and make her laugh all within the same conversation. She enjoyed his artistic side, too, but not in the way one would think. She had long heard his prowess on the mic from word on the street, but he never rapped in front of her. Instead, she revealed in an April 2004 *XXL* interview, Chris would "draw me pictures of things and make 'em into a ghetto style." Though he'd later become an international playboy, it was Jan who became the first woman in his life apart from Voletta to hold his heart. Things progressed quickly between the new couple. Months after their initial meeting, Jan moved out of her mother's house and in with Chris and Voletta. Though the young couple would experience their combative moments and even did that on-again, off-again thing that young couples tend to do, Jan was Chris's first serious girlfriend, and she adored Chris simply for being himself.

"That man had so much sex appeal," Jan said in *Unbelievable.* "It's not even funny. I couldn't think of five men that I've met since then that have the charisma of his one body. 'Cause when you'd meet him, he was just like . . . he was my friend. We would just talk and laugh, and you would feel so much at ease, and you wouldn't have a care in the world. It was nothing or no one else was there."

At eighteen years old, Chris's life was an emotional roller coaster. There was his love life with Jan. His tense but unbreakable bond with his mother. His friends like Chico, C-Gutta, Hubert Sam, and more, who all played separate but equally important roles in his life. And then there was his life in the streets. The blinding appeal of the money he started bringing in had lost some of its initial charm. He was still going to hustle because, at this point, he'd left himself no other viable option. Drug dealing was equal parts capitalistic and fatalistic, which made the money enticing, but at what cost? The murder rate in New York was out of control, with at least two thousand murders every year from 1987 to 1994. And cops patrolled the neighborhoods, in uniform and plain clothes, like their salaries depended on it. In 1989, Chris was arrested on St. James and charged with weapons possession. This earned him five years' probation. A year later, he was arrested again on violation of that probation. He could no longer keep his life of crime away from his mother.

The fairy tale of selling drugs, making millions, and smoking his weed off into the sunset had long since fizzled away. For Christopher Wallace, or "Big," as he was known on the block, his life was in clear and present danger.

And at this point, what else was he going to do except hustle?

—————

All across the country, the proof was in the pudding. Crack sold itself, and there was potential to make money anywhere, with the supply somehow never overtaking the demand. But at the turn of the last decade of the twentieth century, the risk of doing so wasn't just on every corner; the discussion around its exploits was oftentimes the discussion of some of the most powerful courts in the country.

A twenty-four-hour stretch in early September 1990 marks an important but largely unknown juncture in the history of America's complex history with drugs. On September 5, "Freeway" Ricky Ross pleaded guilty to a drug conspiracy count in a Cincinnati courtroom. The notorious crack kingpin had shifted his multi-million-dollar drug operation to the Midwest to stake claim on a higher profit margin. He was later sentenced to 121 months.

Exactly one day later and five hundred miles east, in Washington, D.C., Los Angeles Police Chief Daryl F. Gates sat in front of a Senate Judiciary Committee hearing on the state of drug use in America. The date coincided with the first anniversary of President George H. W. Bush's announcement of his administration's own war on drugs. It was there Gates would utter a statement that would come to define and symbolize how the country had always viewed drugs.

Drug users, Gates testified, "ought to be taken out and shot." He explained that this was more so directed at marijuana users than fiends who physically needed the drugs. That in and of itself was littered with racial undertones given the country's bigoted history with marijuana and race—dating back to the 1930s, when America's first drug czar, Harry Anslinger, argued that marijuana should be illegal because it made "darkies think they were as good as white men."

So whether or not Gates meant it with racial undertones, that's how many took it. Gates had a history with problematic statements toward policing and race, saying, in 1982, of the carotid chokehold, "We may be finding that in some Blacks when a [carotid restraint] is applied, the veins or arteries do not open as fast as they do on normal people." Given his history, Gates's comments about drug users needing to be shot caused a firestorm of commotion from civil liberties activists all the way to Capitol Hill.

A congressional panel's report discovered that 3.6 million criminal drug users over the previous year had been released without treatment, and that less than one in ten pregnant addicts were provided assistance. Despite whatever statistics politicians attempted to broadcast showing how great a job they were doing in the war on drugs, everyone on the street knew what the deal was. Crack was still moving, and until the communities hit the hardest by it were given opportunities and resources to sweepingly change their realities by legal means, the drug game was still king.

People like Gates took the war on drugs as an actual war because, in part, it was. And people like Gates also saw people like Christopher Wallace as the enemy. In Gates's eyes, there was no difference between someone like Christopher Wallace and Freeway Ricky. All he saw was a target—historically the American perception of young Black men. One who was personally responsible for the degradation of his country and had to be stopped at all costs—while ignoring his own role in the rotting of the moral fabric of society. But it's not like Chris gave a damn what someone like Gates thought of him. The police were the police, and as long as he could avoid them, life was much easier. If it wasn't about the money, not much mattered during those days other than the constant pursuit of paper.

And for Chris, doing that came with a change of scenery.

———

Hustling was no longer a local game. After weighing the pros and cons, Chris found himself heading to North Carolina to sell crack. Much like why Freeway Rick Ross expanded operations from a major metropolis like Los Angeles to a smaller city like Cincinnati, the money he was making in Brooklyn was cool, but he could double and triple his profits if he took his operation across state lines. What he was selling for $5 in Brooklyn could go for $20 out of state. It was a risky move, but all he saw were dollar signs.

Plus, Jan, who knew how deep he was in the streets, had family down there. The move, Chris felt, made too much sense.

"North Carolina was the transition point. It was an acknowledgment that, you know, I'm about to take my street shit to another level," said Cheo Hodari Coker. "I'm about to go out of town to make money."

Chris landed in Raleigh, North Carolina. It was there he linked up with an older hustler named Robert Cagle, who went by the nickname Zauqael. In an interview with Coker and *Unbelievable* editor Rob Kenner in the early 2000s from a Brockton, New York, penitentiary, Zauqael spoke of the kinship he formed with Chris in North Carolina.

"As I was getting to know him, he was very funny. He wasn't on no thug stuff," Zauqael said. "He was a good dude, man. All the way around, man. All the way."

Chris would make repeated trips back and forth down south for the better part of two years. The two bonded because of a common goal in making the most money possible, and they never stepped on the other's toes. When Chris arrived back in North Carolina one time, there was a young woman with him who was holding most of the work. According to Zauqael, he had told Chris he had to find someone else to help sell all his crack, which Chris did. The only problem was, the new guy took his work and ran off with it, leaving Chris stuck with no money and no drugs. In other words, the seventh level of hell for a drug dealer.

Zauqael felt bad because it had been his suggestion, and he helped Chris get back on his feet. How he did that is an outrageous tale in its own right. Chris needed money, and he needed it immediately. That's when he came up with the plan. He was going to rob the hotel he and Zauqael were staying in. After a few minutes of back-and-forth debate, they ultimately decided on Chris's original, outrageous plan.

"So I opened the back door of the hotel, put a garbage can down there. We went in there and . . . Yo, this is the funny part, right," Zauqael recalled, laughing. "He caught himself jumping over the counter—big as he is—and couldn't get over the counter. He didn't swing or hit the man, so the man was real cooperative. But he couldn't get over there. So he had to stop and go all the way around 'cause he couldn't jump over. But he attempted. So he gets back down, he goes around, and we do what we gotta do."

Their faces obscured by hoodies, the thieves got away. Minutes later, they came back downstairs, acting incredulous about what had just happened. The front desk man was talking to the police.

"Some guys just came in here and robbed me," he said. "Did y'all see anybody?"

"Damn," Chris responded with a deep note of fear in his voice. "Ain't no protection in here?"

Zauqael guessed that their time in North Carolina was roughly from late 1990 to 1992. The two, along with some other guys, lived in a one-story house at 2700 Alpha Drive in southwest Raleigh, about fifteen minutes from downtown. The house was the exact opposite of what Chris experienced in Brooklyn. Most nights it was quiet and very dark. With no streetlights, the stars shone brighter, and every rustle of a leaf or tree branch was its own individual concert. On cloudy nights, darkness was even darker. It was a desolate street, with no sidewalks out front and a seemingly infinite amount of trees. Chris never went to college, but the less-than-1,000-square-foot humble abode's one bathroom gave the house something of a dormitory feel. Such was the layout of was Christopher Wallace's trap house.

Raleigh lacked the hustle and bustle of New York. Sure, they were there to move weight, but they also had a ton of free time. From Zauqael's perspective, he got to know the young man and not just the hustler. They formed a brotherhood. He quickly learned Chris's appetite was insatiable. There are stories of Chris devouring endless Häagen-Dazs and eating Zauqael's ice cream without consulting him first—leading to everyone in the house having to write their names on their food in order to keep Chris at bay.

They'd regularly eat out, too, at places like Shoney's, Perkins, and the House of Pancake near North Carolina State University. A personal favorite, however, was a staple in affordable twenty-four-hour southern dining: Waffle House. It was there that Chris would order a meal that would later become a recognizable lyric—a carafe of grape juice, cheese eggs, and a T-bone steak.

And that's when Zauqael discovered Chris rapped. It was nothing Chris ever broadcast, but when the topic came up, he would never downplay his skills, either. He knew he was nice, and anybody who ever listened to him walked away with the same diagnosis.

"Back then it was different. The drug game was kinda big at the time. And at that time, everybody thought they was a rapper. I thought I was a little rapper. You know, I wrote a couple of rhymes back then," Zauqael said. "When I say it the first time, it sound good. But when you only got one rhyme and you keep saying it, then people start to realize you wack. So the rap game wasn't really that promising to me because I didn't have the talent for it."

At times in the car, Chris would freestyle to instrumentals and Zauqael would sit in astonishment. But even then, neither thought of making a career out of it.

"Son is nice," Zauqael reflected, "but we drug dealers right now."

And that's just how it was: he was a hustler who could spit.

"I just knew him by Fat Chris, and I knew he always had good product," a man by the name of Smoke told *The Fader* in 2011. "He was a respectable kind of dude, had a nice, clean, humble game. Everybody was making money . . . I had the west side of town locked down, and I guess he had the south side locked down."

The topic of rappers waxing poetic about taking trips out of town to sell drugs became a common theme. It's a question for some of them how true these stories actually were, but not for Fat Chris. In later years, he'd look back on the time not as a badge of honor but part of a cutthroat game he was lucky to have survived.

One night Zauqael and Chris were watching the 1975 film *Let's Do It Again* starring Bill Cosby, Sidney Poitier, Ossie Davis, John Amos, Calvin Lockhart, Jimmie Walker, and more. What happened next, per Zauqael's tale, was a monumental moment in Christopher Wallace's short adult life.

"One of the characters [Lockhart] was named Biggie Smalls. I said, 'Listen, ain't you say your rap name is Biggie?' I said, 'No, listen. That's a better name for you right there.' And he said, 'Yeah, I like that.' Because it was gangster, plus it was funny. But I told him if you're gonna be named that, I hope your MC game is nice."

━━━━━━━

Big made numerous trips back and forth between Brooklyn and Raleigh. He and Chico were still running heavy in the streets in New York, too. Their friendship was a connection, years earlier, that Chico had made that would further expand Big's worldview even if it was geographically only a matter of a few blocks. Chico introduced him to another one of his friends, Damion Butler, whom everyone in the neighborhood knew as D-Roc. He grew up on Gates Avenue between Bedford Avenue and Nostrand Avenue.

"My main street was his side block," D-Roc said in a 2018 *Rap Radar Podcast* interview.

They had long seen each other in passing, and one of Big's neighbors was a classmate of D-Roc's. It was Big's elementary and middle school uniforms that stood out to D-Roc—the ones that Big had hated because of the undesirable attention and bullying they'd elicit.

"I used to be amazed by the uniform Big used to wear to school. I used to think that was the ultimate shit because then you can't be judged," D-Roc said in *I Got a Story to Tell*. "There's no class. There's nobody better than nobody if we all wearing the same thing. Where I went to school, it wasn't that. I used to be telling him, 'Bro, I wish I didn't have to do the shit I was doing.'"

Big and D-Roc instantly clicked. For one, they were both bigger than damn near everyone. They were both laid-back, but still about their business when it came to getting money. Neither had their fathers around, and they both enjoyed a good meal. Voletta knew D-Roc truly cared for her son, too. Hustling connected the two Brooklyn teenagers. Despite the money it made, selling drugs on the corner wasn't D-Roc's idea of moving on up to that deluxe apartment in the sky *The Jeffersons* talked about. It was just a job that could put money in his pocket, perhaps the only viable one. It was the late eighties, and it wasn't like jobs were fruitful in their part of Brooklyn. However flawed the mindset may have been, in the moment, selling drugs felt like the realistic option. They'd always have conversations about Big getting into the drug game. D-Roc knew that hustling was something Big did because it was all around him, not necessarily because he had to. But D-Roc also knew there was no way to stop Big once he made his mind up.

"He used to be like, 'Man, I just wanna get out and about like what y'all be doing,'" D-Roc recalled. "I used to always try to talk to him like, 'I hear you, but I don't.'"

Early in their friendship, D-Roc quickly learned that Big was wickedly gifted on the microphone. Word of his rhyming skills was slowly beginning to make its way across Brooklyn. Fulton Street knew he could rip a beat because Chico had turntables and a tape recorder. He'd give Big the mic and the rest would be history. There was a common theme on each tape: he was going places, and he was going to be somebody one day, though at that time, he wasn't thinking it was going to be by rhyming. He'd devour local competition at open mics, but rapping wasn't anything to take seriously. Yet.

D-Roc soon came to understand what the Ave. already knew. His boy was *nice*. Not just like "neighborhood nice," either. Big had "it." Around this time, too, roughly circa 1990 when he was eighteen, D-Roc was bringing Big over to his neighborhood, to Bedford Avenue and Quincy Street. It was less than a mile from 226 St. James, but it was certainly more active in terms of its daily wheeling and dealings. It was here where Big's musical repertoire took on a new life. They still hustled on those blocks, but there were times when Big and his friends would get some weed, get some alcohol, and listen to music there for hours on end. These marathon listening sessions were usually spearheaded by Kevin Griffin, better known in the hood as DJ 50 Grand. 50 isn't only from there. He still lives there, in an area of Brooklyn that has been massively gentrified.

"Back then, we had a lot of abandoned buildings," 50 said. "A lot of vacant lots. A lot of stray cats, dogs, and rats. It was much wilder back then than it is now because certain places in Brooklyn, like Nostrand Avenue, you couldn't go down there if you didn't know anybody. A lot of drug activities. A lot of people getting shot, stabbed, or robbed. I was so young then. We never thought we'd see it look the way it looks now."

D-Roc and 50 hustled together, and it was D-Roc who introduced Big to 50 Grand. 50 Grand's crew was, and still is, dubbed the Old Gold Brothers, or "OGB" for short, the name inspired by the crew drinking Old Gold Beer like it was water.

By the time he met Big, the OGB were deep. They hustled together and they kicked it together, and when work was done, 50 would pull out his turntables and spin music for the block. Big was younger than nearly anyone in the crew, but they gravitated toward him, and he enjoyed the energy of the block all the same.

One day, not long after meeting Big, an innocent conversation turned into a life-altering moment. In his basement, 50 had two turntables, a mixer, and a microphone. D-Roc had already told him that Big rhymed, but he was only known as a hustler then. Now 50 was about to see for himself an entirely different side of the quiet, big dude from Fulton and St. James who just naturally fit in with the rest of his crew.

"I heard you know a lot of people," 50 recalls Big saying to him. "I want you to be my DJ."

Big, 50, D-Roc, and a few others piled into his basement for a studio session that would be nothing short of legendary.

The space was huge. A hot-water tank sat in the back, but other than that there was ample space for people to move around and be comfortable. 50 set up his Technics SL-1200 turntables and placed the needle on track four of *Ultimate Breaks and Beats, Vol. 24*. It was there that the Emotions's "Blind Alley" lived. That track was the foundation for "Ain't No Half Steppin'," the biggest record to date by the biggest rap star out of Brooklyn, Big's idol Big Daddy Kane. The tape deck started to record, Big started rapping, and all hell broke loose in the best way possible. He rhymed with the confidence of Kane, the fearlessness of Ice Cube, and the precision of Rakim. Whatever beats 50 threw on, Chris smashed all of them. His flow lived in the vein of every beat, almost as if they were tailor-made for him. 50 was in awe while D-Roc watched on like a proud brother.

That marijuana-smoke-clouded basement was the most important stage Big had been on up to that point. He had already chain-smoked so many blunts he'd lost count, but Big rhymed with the clear-cut aim of the Chicago Bulls sharpshooter Craig Hodges. The OGB crew had rhymers, but this was different. It wasn't the weed making their mind play tricks on them. Big was *that* good.

50 was sold.

"Let's make a tape," he said.

"Fuck it," Big responded. "Why not?"

And thus, a demo was born. A demo that would set in motion a chain reaction that would elevate rap to heights then unknown. And Big did it all in one take, too. A raw tenacity bled through the tape. He wasn't yet polished—there would be a long way to go before he'd get there. But his talent was undeniable. Big wasn't just nice for a drug dealer who dabbled in rap.

"Big came through last," said OGB member Money Twan. "He was like the last on the block. He came through when everything smoothed out, because it was a lot of killing and shooting on Bedford and Quincy. We ain't even know this nigga rapped. It wasn't about hip-hop. It was about us getting money."

But when crew members found out Big could rap, it was always a grand revelation. Twan's introduction to his microphone prowess coincided with a party that had gotten too far out of control. Back then, Twan says, OGB was known for causing a ruckus at parties. That was their rep. 50 Grand was DJing on St. James, and the entire crew was there.

"Thirty niggas and we was all fighters!" Twan yelled, with the excitement in his voice building. "We ain't need guns then! Well, we had one or two niggas holding, but most of the time we was just brawlers."

Twan was known to jump on the mic at parties and flow with whatever lyrics came to mind. Then Big stepped on the stage.

"Yo, who this nigga?!" Twan asked, damn near offended someone would try to follow him.

"Nah, that's my man right there," 50 responded. He knew what Twan was about to learn. If Big wanted the mic, give it to him and get the hell out of his way.

Needless to say, Big shut down the party—figuratively and literally. Everyone was amazed at how skilled he was, but around that time security was trying to get the mic back from being passed around. That's when the fight started and the party effectively ended.

"We ended up finding out that it was a church. We tore up a church! It was right across the street from Big," Twan said, the shock still in his voice. "But yeah, that's how we found out he could rap. We ended up tearing up his block, and the next day he came on our block talking about Fulton Street."

Hustling still took priority over rapping, but Big's musical acumen made others want to rhyme alongside him. This was the two turntables, a tape deck, and a microphone era—that was all that was needed to get a party jumping, and everyone wanted a turn. They'd write their rhymes in preparation, ready to challenge the neighborhood's best rapper. On the block's ranking, it was Big and then everybody vying for second place. Like a teenage LeBron James joining the Cleveland Cavaliers fresh out of high school, the precocious Big was instantly the best on his team and, on most nights, the best anywhere. He arrived a raw talent. The OGB crew and Bedford and Quincy didn't teach him how to rhyme, but the competition and camaraderie helped hone his skills, helped push him to get better, to prove himself. And in the process, an already-confident Big became even more so.

The more he rapped, the better he became. In essence, Twan became Big's first hypeman, too. If Big was going to jump on the mic, best believe Twan was going to be there to spice up the pot. There was something special about the way he could just spew this ghetto poetry at the drop of a hat. Their material took hours to write and Big's took minutes, and his rhymes were still far superior. There was something special in Big. And 50 Grand knew it.

"I'd cut, scratch, and niggas would just grab the mic and rap all day. Nonstop rhyming. Biggie would have his shit down in three verses. He knew what he wanted to use. He changed me," 50 said. "I cut my crew off for a while—in terms of cutting and scratching and playing music—and concentrated on Big."

For Big, rap went from being a minor hobby to one of those "Wait, there might be something here" realizations. He still didn't have both feet in the rap game, ready to push all the chips to the center of the table; but if there was a mic, a speaker, and crowd nearby, then why not show out? The neighborhood prestige that came with it was priceless.

"All we did was hustle and play music. One day, me and my boy just brought out the equipment," said 50 Grand. "I think Big and them had just come from outta town. We was just chilling and playing music. Big comes out, you know, just clowning around."

On May 27, 1991, less than a week after Big had turned nineteen—and eight weeks after he was given a suspended sentence for drug possession in Raleigh—they were hanging out in front of an old-school Brooklyn spot called the Pool Room. 50 Grand had set up his equipment, and nothing out of the ordinary was happening on the block. These makeshift block parties were regular occurrences in the summer. Big had recently returned from one of his North Carolina trips, and it felt good to be back home.

A local neighborhood guy named William Troy McClune (aka Supreme or 'Preme) got on the mic first. 'Preme wasn't Biggie, as he was already known by then, but he wasn't a slouch either. As the crowd drew bigger and bigger around the battle, 'Preme continued throwing lyrical darts at Big. The crowd was feeling him, but playing the cut was D-Roc, and his blood was starting to boil.

"Black-ass giant," 'Preme said before handing over the mic to his chubby competitor. "You scared? Don't be scared!"

The taunts about his appearance never bothered Big. His size, his lazy eye, his dark skin—he understood the calculus people would use to draw a reaction out of him, especially in battles like this. 'Preme ended his verbal barrage with the crowd behind him. Big, in his white pants and short-sleeved button-down asking for the mic, was ready to go. Now he had a crowd, D-Roc right beside him in an aqua-colored shirt and blue jeans, having the time of his life. But nobody realized, sans Big himself, what was about to happen. As far as anyone knew, it was just another battle.

"Warm it up, Chris!" the battle's hypeman chanted as 50 Grand spun that May afternoon in Brooklyn. "Warm it, warm it, warm it up, Chris! The B.I.G. wanna battle me!"

Something that 'Preme hadn't considered, or perhaps never knew, is that Big was so comfortable in battle settings not merely because he was a talented MC. These sorts of moments had been part of his bloodline. From watching his uncle Dave toasting and "chatting on the mic" in Jamaica, Big's cocky-yet-suave demeanor with a mic was all but a family heirloom.

Heads bobbed to the music, weed was passed around, drinks seemed endless, and jokes were cracked. Big was doing all four, just having a good time with his people. The Brooklyn heat didn't matter because the energy was electric. Then it happened. 'Preme finished rhyming, then gave Big the mic. What happened next is a moment that still lives in Brooklyn's storied cultural history.

"'Preme starts rhyming and then Big jumps up. They just started going at it, and you seen the outcome," 50 Grand said. As for 'Preme nowadays, "I don't know where he's at, but I see him off and on. I don't think he's rapping, though. But that's what he's known for! Battling Big!"

If Big's rhyming was known only among his closest friends on Fulton Street, that secret was out of the bag now. Big Chris the Hustler was now also Biggie, the best rapper on the block. His set wasn't long, less than three minutes. But what Big didn't provide for in time, he more than made up for in wordplay so wicked and storytelling so vivid, Bedford Avenue might as well have been Madison Square Garden that day. Jaws dropped, eyes nearly bulged out of heads, and everyone looked at themselves in disbelief. Meanwhile, D-Roc—the guy who had introduced Big to 50 Grand and the Bedford crew—sat back and watched with pride. This was the guy he brought around. The guy he was hyping up not just as a cool guy who could fit in with a block full of hustlers. This was a guy who could really rap, and now he was damn near hood royalty.

Big was a natural, and though he hardly moved when he was freestyling, everything about him was captivating. From the way he swayed back and forth to how he could pick metaphors and alliteration almost out of thin air without a moment's notice. The crowd hung on his every word, swaying back and forth and screaming whenever he dropped a line that blew everyone's minds. In 2007, 'Preme would sue Rugged Entertainment for $20 million for including footage from the battle in the documentary *Bigger Than Life*. He said the clip caused him "irreparable harm, mental distress, and disturbance of his peace of mind." That's how bad Big smoked him—sixteen years later and a video of the battle still caused him "mental distress."

06

THE TAPE AND THE COLUMN

50 GRAND KNEW HE HAD SOMETHING SPECIAL WITH BIG'S DEMO. The audio was rough, but it made Big's talent that much more palpable.

"When we did the demo, I felt something about it. I just couldn't put my hands on it," 50 said. "So I hunted down Mister Cee."

50 and Cee, born Calvin LeBrun, lived around the block from each other and had been friends for years. Cee heard 50 go on and on about this young Brooklyn kid named Biggie who was rhyming well beyond his years and he had to hear it for himself. Cee, who was Big Daddy Kane's DJ at the time, was accustomed to people coming up all the time saying either that they could rap or that their man was nice. Plus, he was about to go on the *Taste of Chocolate* tour with Big Daddy Kane, so it wasn't like he was truly interested in listening to the tape. But 50 kept pleading.

"Yo, you need to hear this kid Biggie Smalls right now," he said.

Cee promised that when he got back from the tour he would.

The truth is, Mister Cee always had a knack for being in the right part of Brooklyn at the right time. By luck, he attended Sarah J. Hale High School at the same time as Antonio Hardy, who the world would come to know as Big Daddy Kane. One day Cee was walking in the cafeteria and there was a rap battle taking place. One of the guys was named Austin. Cee was then DJing for a group from his Lafayette Gardens neighborhood called the Magnum Force Crew. Feeling froggy in the moment, Cee leaped in.

"I can battle you!" Cee told Austin, announcing it to the entire lunchroom. A crowd began to assemble as Cee dropped bars. The crowd went crazy because they didn't know he could rhyme. There was only one problem. Cee couldn't. He was rapping, but they weren't his rhymes. They were his crew's.

"A'ight, cool," Austin said, taking his loss on the chin. But not without a threat. "I'm gonna get my man MC Kane on you."

"Who the hell is MC Kane?" Cee thought to himself, leaving the lunchroom. He didn't give it much energy until later, when this guy walked up to him wearing a leather jacket cut off at the waist like Kurtis Blow. He reached inside his jacket, and for a moment Cee didn't know what the hell he was about to pull out. They did live in Brooklyn in the eighties, after all. But the guy pulled out a microphone.

"Yo, I heard you wanted to battle me," the guy said. "I'm MC Kane."

Cee wasn't a fool. "I thought the dude was nuts!" he recalled. "I started backing down! I was like I don't want no problems. In my mind, I was like, 'This dude is nuts carrying a microphone in school.'"

A few weeks later, Cee was back in the lunchroom. He wasn't going to battle anyone. He'd already learned his lesson. But there was another crowd gawking over someone else rhyming. Turns out it was MC Kane again, and Cee instantly saw the talent. And he was even happier he hadn't tried to battle Kane.

"I just remember this one line that he said: 'I got braids in my hair just like Stevie Wonder,'" Cee says. "You gotta remember a line like that back in 1982, when I first met Kane, was an ill line."

After lunch was over, Cee hit Kane with a business proposition. Join his group, the Magnum Force Crew. Kane initially refused.

"I don't rhyme with nobody," he said. "I rhyme solo."

Cee eventually convinced him to come to the Lafayette Gardens projects in Bedford-Stuyvesant to hear him DJ. If he still didn't like it, then he wouldn't ask him again. Not long after that conversation, Kane was there at Lafayette Gardens to see what was so special about Cee's skills on the wheels of steel. It didn't take long for Kane to realize how special Cee was as a DJ. He wasn't just great at scratching and cutting. He knew the right songs to play at the right time and had a brilliant read on the crowd's temperature. That's extremely important for an artist, because a DJ basically has to serve as the copilot during sets and shows. All of it came naturally to Cee. In the hood back then, the superstars were the drug dealers and the athletes. Cee grew up idolizing the New York Jets, Reggie Jackson, and, as one of the few Black kids in his neighborhood who loved hockey, Wayne Gretzky and the New York Islanders' Mike Bossy. He had two brothers who entered the drug game, but it was music that eventually won out for Cee.

House parties were extremely popular in Brooklyn. It wasn't uncommon for Cee to be DJing in somebody's bedroom with the speaker connected in the living room. Because he couldn't physically see what was going on, either he or a friend would have to run back and forth with status reports. Efficiency was the name of the game. A DJ had to know what the crowd wanted to hear, when they wanted to hear it, and, most importantly, how long they wanted to hear it. DJs played at house parties and in parks, where the challenge was sometimes finding cords long enough to plug into lampposts. Those days, DJs like Cee could play until midnight and oftentimes past that because the city wasn't so strict about permits.

"If it wasn't no fights or shootouts, we could play music really late," said Cee. "That was the vibe back in the eighties. That's what we came up on."

So when Kane came by to see Cee DJ, he was already watching a grizzled vet at work. He was sold.

"Yo, I'm down. Whatever you wanna do, I'll get down with the crew," said Kane.

Kane eventually got his original wish anyway. The Magnum Force Crew eventually disbanded. Some got jobs. Some started families and left music behind. Some went into the military. But Kane and Cee stuck with the music, eventually joining other posses. Kane was a member of the Queens and Brooklyn collective the Juice Crew, which featured a who's who of names like Roxanne Shante, Kool G Rap, MC Shan, Marley Marl, and Biz Markie, who helped them land a deal with Cold Chillin' Records.

Kane became one of rap's original superstars. He was a rhymeslayer who could carve any beat into a charcuterie board, but he also had the sex appeal that made him a crossover star. His first three albums, 1988's *Long*

Live the Kane, 1989's *It's a Big Daddy Thing*, and 1990's *Taste of Chocolate*, all entered the top ten on the U.S. R&B charts. Watching all this from afar was another young Brooklynite. Kane was a certified star while Biggie was still hustling. Now his demo tape was working its way into Kane's DJ's hands.

50 Grand's begging paid off. He had pleaded with Cee to listen to Biggie's tape, and when Cee got back from the tour on September 23, 1991, there was 50 Grand nearly beating down his door with that tape in hand. He couldn't put this off anymore, and 50's borderline obsession with him hearing the tape led him to believe there was something worth hearing on the other side of pressing play. Much like those who saw Big street battle with 'Preme, Cee was blown away almost immediately. Whoever this guy was on this tape, he had the total package. *The flow. The rawness. The lyrics. The storytelling.* It was all there.

And just when Mister Cee thought the tape couldn't get better, there was Big dismantling Kane's "Ain't No Half Steppin'" sample with his own flair, cadence, and charisma. It all screamed Brooklyn's next star. Cee had heard everything he needed to. There were big rappers from New York at the time who were releasing great music, like Brand Nubian, Pete Rock and C.L. Smooth, and Gang Starr, but at the time, the West Coast was on fire. To Mister Cee, this felt like the seeds of a resurgence.

"He said, 'Yo, you need to have this kid in front of my house,'" 50 Grand recalled. "When he came back from outta town, Big was sitting on his stoop waiting for him. From there, everything seemed like it happened overnight."

It didn't exactly happen that quickly, but Cee was hell-bent on helping Big. But first, he had to earn Big's trust.

Big showed up at Cee's apartment resembling nothing like the debonair playboy he would become in a few short years. Black jeans, a dirty white T-shirt, and boots. He had seen people pleading to DJs and people at labels to listen to their music. Big wanted to make music, but one thing he wasn't going to do was beg anyone.

"He wasn't one to pursue a rap career," Jan, Big's first girlfriend, told *XXL* in 2004. "If they wanted Chris, they would have to come to Chris. He was a very cocksure person."

This wasn't the first time he heard that someone liked his music and wanted to help him. His first words to Cee were simple. "Yo, you know, man, you know, don't be promising me nothing, Duke. You can't do nothin' for me, just tell me straight up, man. Don't try to gas me."

Cee wasn't trying to sell Big a dream. He legitimately wanted to help the husky hustler from Fulton Street land a record deal. But he was already thinking about his own next step. Cee saw people like Kid Capri, Pete Rock and C.L. Smooth, and Terminator X from Public Enemy releasing their own records at the time. That made him want to try it out on his own album. Cee compiled a demo, and on it was a track called "Biggie Got the Hype Shit." Cee, Big, Jesse West aka 3rd Eye, and 50 Grand recorded it in a studio in the Bronx (that has since burned down, destroying the original master reels).

"I started shopping that five-song demo to different record companies. Every record company I was going to was like, 'You know, Cee, the demo is cool, but who is this Biggie Smalls guy?'" Cee recalled via Zoom before playing the record. "Me shopping my demo turned into shopping Biggie because everybody loved 'Biggie Got the Hype Shit.' The two record companies in particular that were heavily interested at the time were Jive Records and Def Jam. The Mister Cee demo got thrown out the window because everybody was talking about how they wanted to sign Biggie."

Also in 1991, Biggie appeared on *The Stretch Armstrong and Bobbito Show*, broadcast from a Columbia University basement on WKCR 89.9 FM. The show often pitted demos from unsigned acts against one another to see which the audience liked better. Biggie ended up losing out to a group called Bronx Zoo. Similar to how Michael Jordan never forgot about how he got cut from his varsity basketball team, Biggie never forgot the loss.

"Biggie was pissed off that they beat him, so that's why he came up and he was like, 'I want to set the record straight.' He actually wanted to battle them live in the studio. That's why he came up there," Bobbito Garcia said in 2017. "[Artists] knew that the world was going to hear them, and for some of them who were unsigned, that was everything to them. They didn't know that they would get signed so they really took it seriously."

From the Bedford battle, his demo making its way to Mister Cee, labels asking Cee about him, and Stretch and Bobbito's show, Big's name was slowly but surely starting to ring bells around the city. What made it better was that it was for a positive reason and not just what he did on corners in Brooklyn and trap houses down south.

Big's demo was special, and Mister Cee knew it was a hood version of Willy Wonka's Golden Ticket as long as he got it into the right hands. All it needed was a little bit of polishing and that flair only Mister Cee could sprinkle on the tape. Big didn't push back when Cee told him the plan to rerecord the demo. There was a growing trust between the two, and as long as Cee didn't give him a reason to think otherwise, he was going to follow Cee's lead and see where it took him.

Chico went with Big when they rerecorded the demo. Cee lived on the top floor of a four-story Brooklyn brownstone on Gates between Bedford and Franklin. Not exactly the most conducive setting for a guy like Big, especially with no elevator. The walk from Chris's apartment didn't take long, but getting Cee to come to the door proved an exercise in patience.

"We'd be out there for like an hour! He'd never come out," Chico said. "Then after a while he'd come to the window and Big would be like, 'Nigga, I been out here calling you for an hour! Cee would be like, come upstairs, but it would be like a hundred steps."

Out of breath, impatient, and hot, Big might've been annoyed, but when it was time to record, he locked in. Cee, as promised, was going to put together something nice for Big to do his thing over. By the time Cee got the music set up and ready for Big to step in front of the microphone, the process didn't take long from there. Big, like he did with 50 Grand, knocked out the demo in essentially one take. From there, the ball was back in Cee's court.

Cee mapped out his grand vision for Big. Step one, rerecording the demo, was complete. Next was getting the tape to *The Source* for their Unsigned Hype column—the most important dose of publicity a new artist could pray for at the time. But it was up to Big if he felt comfortable moving forward. His response was short, but to the point.

"Whatever. Whatever you wanna do, Cee."

All Big knew about being a rapper up to that point was what he saw on TV and music videos and what he read in the magazines. He was as impressionable as any teenage kid across the country. It was rappers' access to wealth and a better life that made Big want to rap. He didn't even know how much being a rapper actually paid.

"All I knew is Doug E. Fresh had a nice link and a nice lil' piece. Slick Rick was mad heavy, you know what I'm saying," he reasoned. "Heav[y D] had a Montero . . . That's all it was, though. That's all it was, was a dream. It was never nothing I thought was really gon' take place."

Big still needed convincing, but that was fine. The wheels were in motion. Meanwhile, he still had a day job, the only thing paying him at the moment. It was dangerous work, but until Big saw any real money from the music game—if that was even possible—his two-week notice to the streets would have to wait.

———

Tennis drew Greg Dent to Raleigh, North Carolina. Growing up in Detroit, Dent's mom introduced him to the game when he was in elementary school, and it was always just part of his life from there. The historically Black college Saint Augustine's University was recruiting some of Dent's friends who had played in high school. They were all telling the coach, "Look, our boy Greg Dent can play. He just . . ."

In Dent's own words, he had the skills. He just couldn't play in high school "because I was a knucklehead." A deal was worked out. Dent took the GED and passed, and before he knew it, he was making the eleven-hour drive south to Raleigh. This wasn't the beginning of a rags-to-riches tennis career. Quite the opposite, in fact. His journey with tennis didn't last long at Saint Augustine's, but it did help lead to a new outlet for Dent's energy: party promotion.

Dent had been promoting house music—not hip-hop—parties since he was fourteen at locations from the local YMCA to people's backyards. When tennis was no longer a realistic option, Dent knew he was good at reaching out to large swaths of people and bringing them together for a good time.

"When I got to North Carolina, I started to meet people from New York," Dent said. "I met some cats that grew up in Roosevelt, Long Island, and that's where Public Enemy is from. They linked me up with Public Enemy before they blew up. I'd have them come to the gym at Saint Augustine's and do events. I looked like I was large as fuck back then!"

Dent was promoting all around the city at spots like Fevers and Tremors. But what really made him one of the area's most trusted curators of a good time was a spot called Cat's Cradle. It first opened its doors in 1969, near Chapel Hill, and in 2016, it was ranked number twelve on a list of the top one hundred music venues in America by the website Consequence of Sound. Dent helped bring Public Enemy to Cat's Cradle. From there, Dent says, the hip-hop world opened up for him, and he met people like Big Daddy Kane and Mister Cee and Maseo from De La Soul.

"It was easy to do an after-party and get a DJ instead of the whole group. First of all, it's a lot cheaper, and you still get the same influence. And you get a good party because it's the actual DJ of the group rocking the records. So Terminator X would look out. Red Alert and Mister Cee, too. So through Cee's relationship, he did my twenty-third birthday party at the Zoo. That put me on the map."

The Zoo was a venue Dent helped open up. A frequent visitor to the club was this young guy, bigger than everyone both in height and in weight, but he was cool. He never bothered anyone, and he was always playing the cut. Leaning against the wall and vibing to the music, it wasn't long until Dent and the patron, a young Christopher Wallace, got to know each other. Dent knew Big was hustling at the time, which honestly didn't shock him because he knew several guys from out of town in Raleigh on the same wavelength. But their conversations at the club often centered around Big jumping on the mic. His sales pitch was nothing if not quintessentially and hilariously on-brand. Even his lies would make Dent laugh.

"I'm Chubb Rock's little brother," Big would claim. "Let me get on the mic." Rock was four years older and also of Jamaican descent and called Brooklyn home, so it could have been plausible. His approach was to throw the claim up against the Zoo's wall and see if it stuck.

"He was slick! And he would spit," Dent said, laughing. "But I'd always get him off the mic because I would be like, 'Man, you're ruining the party. Nobody wants to hear that shit! Girls wanna dance!' I thought I was a little player. I just wanted people to party. I had no clue who he'd become!"

The Zoo turned out to be a sort of escape, a refuge for Big down in Raleigh. What he was in town to do made him quite a bit of cash. Down south, he could net tens of thousands of dollars if he played the game the right way. And Big was damn good at his job, too.

"He was a good hustler. People liked him. He knew how to talk, and he knew how to sell it," D-Roc said. "He wasn't one of the ones that was out there knocking folks over for it. Just basically came to him. If he wasn't there, they'll come back."

But with the money came stress. And with each passing day, Big began to wonder just how long he could realistically stay in the drug game. It's not that it came with a 401(k) or a pension plan, and any job where he could be considered a veteran even before the age of twenty-one didn't bode well for any sort of longevity. Dent says he'd constantly tell Big to fall back, and that selling crack, no matter how lucrative it was in the short term, was an unforgiving game. That reality came to a head on February 1, 1991, when Chris was arrested in Raleigh for possession of cocaine and marijuana with intent to sell. He pleaded guilty to the charges and received probation plus a ten-year suspended sentence on April 8, 1991.

"I was just like, goddamn! A lot of niggas was getting popped down there. A lot of New Yorkers in that time were coming down to Raleigh to hustle," said Dent. "It wasn't nothing that was super shocking, to be honest with you."

It may not have been startling to Dent, but Big's out-of-town trips—and out-of-town incarcerations, however brief—were still jarring. Per files from the North Carolina Department of Public Safety, Big seemed to serve, at most, two months for his possession charge. Still, the arrest shook Big. He operated in a game that had three possible outcomes. In one, he could stand to make a lot of money. But two others, possibilities that were only a single mistake away, were decades in prison and death.

For Chico Del Vec, Big's out-of-town trips were anxiety-inducing. He said he didn't initially know Big was even planning to head down to North Carolina.

"I was scared. Like, what did this dude do?!" Chico recalled. "His mom must have got him out, but he came back and told me some weird stories. He was down there doing something with somebody . . . It's funny because he wanted to do music because he didn't wanna hustle no more. It was more, 'Man, this ain't working out for me.' Sitting in jail was not a good feeling for him. He didn't like that at all. He didn't wanna hustle at all after that. He was like, 'I'm not doing this, man. I'm chillin'.'"

If only it were that easy. Big was a high school dropout and was hell-bent on never having a 9-to-5, so he didn't have much to fall back on. But he had Mister Cee working on his behalf. The respected Brooklyn DJ understood Big's talent, and he knew all it might take was getting the tape in front of the right set of ears.

Matteo Capoluongo was an editor at *The Source*. The magazine, founded by two white Jewish kids from Harvard, David Mays and Jonathan Shecter, initially launched in August 1988—the same month N.W.A's *Straight Outta Compton* dropped—as a two-page newsletter. It was an instant hit, and by 1991, the magazine was not only a full-length, nearly seventy-page magazine with advertisements and feature-length articles about rap, but it was seen as the genre's monthly bible, a professional publication dedicated to hip-hop culture and the politics and perspectives around it. So it made sense that Capoluongo—more commonly known as "Matty C"—fit in seamlessly at the growing rap publication. Born in Washington Heights, he grew up in the Bronx until his family moved to Washington, D.C. He always held onto hip-hop culture. In the early eighties, Matty lived and breathed hip-hop. He loved break dancing, but there wasn't a long-term career plan in break-ing. He wasn't a DJ or a rapper, either, so if he wanted to remain firmly planted in the culture, something else had to shake out. In 1988, when Matty returned to New York to attend NYU, a friend contacted him asking him if he remembered Mays.

"You wanna write some reviews?" Capoluongo remembered Mays ask-ing him.

The concept of writing rap reviews was still so new and so fresh, and provided so much real estate for the newfound journalist to make all his own.

"It wasn't even like my aim in life or my major in school," he said. "I didn't know what the fuck I was gonna do. [Mays] just knew that I knew the music and asked me if I wanted to help out. I was like, 'Cool.'"

The perks were sweet, exclusivity being the biggest. Capoluongo received all the new music before it came out. By the time it hit the streets, he knew the backstories, the lyrics, and the vibe of the record while every-one else was just getting their first listen. From there, the opportunities began to snowball. Contrary to popular belief, Capoluongo didn't start *The*

Source's now legendary Unsigned Hype column. It was something he was asked to take on, and from there, he made it his own.

Many of the demos he received came from people in the industry. At the time, the column wasn't the popular vessel it would soon become. What helped ignite its momentum was the deal Mays made with Alan Grunblatt at Relativity Records to put together an Unsigned Hype compilation in the early nineties. Grunblatt helped the label get its foot in the door bringing in artists like the Beatnuts, Fat Joe, and Common.

"I think everybody at *The Source* had dreams of being in the music business—not just being music journalists. The idea of being a music journalist happened as we were doing what we were doing," Capoluongo said. "I think Dave kinda had that goal too, so he was like, 'Yo, c'mon. Let's make some records and put some of these out. He took out an ad above the column."

That's how Mister Cee became aware of what was going on. Cee passed Matty C Big's demo tape, and like Cee before him, he couldn't believe what he heard. All he really needed to hear was the first ten seconds. The sounds, the stories, and the voice were unlike anything moving in hip-hop at the moment. Big felt like Big Daddy Kane 2.0, but different in his own way. Matty C couldn't stop playing the tape—for himself and anyone who would walk by at *The Source*'s office. Rap's next superstar was on that tape. All Matty had to do was press play and sit back. It didn't take long for the magic to spread like wildfire. Everyone at *The Source* had to hear the tape of this new guy from Bed-Stuy.

"I clearly remember feeling like something was happening. Like this cat was really incredible," said Kierna Mayo, then a reporter at *The Source* who often sat in with Matty C on listening sessions. "When Matty was cosigning or leading in this case, it was all ears. Biggie was a star, and his talent was really crisp and clear from the very first moment."

Life, too, was working in Matty's favor. He'd just recently moved to a house off Grand Avenue, a stone's throw away from where Big lived on St. James. The two would become lifelong friends, but how they met—at least according to Chico Del Vec—comes with quite the memory.

As fate would have it, Matty was on his first trip to the subway from his new house when he bumped into Big. Thing is, Matty knew who he was, but Big had no clue who Matty was. Biggie, Chico, and his crew were on the block hustling when the journalist came up to him saying he had heard his demo and he wanted to feature him in *The Source.*

"We were all like, 'Yo, nigga! What the . . . man, if you don't get up outta here!" Chico said, laughing. "Like, c'mon, man. How somebody gonna walk up on us after we been hustling all day talking about, 'Yo, I wanna do an interview on you. I work for a magazine.' Not to be funny, but you gotta be careful."

Like the police had done to them countless times before, Big, Chico, and the crew interrogated Matty with dozens of questions. In order to prove he wasn't an undercover cop, they made him smoke a blunt. The crew didn't know it at the time, but that was basically a peace offering, as Matty smoked like a chimney, too.

"We gave him some weed," Chico remembered, still unable to control his laughter. "He rolled up and started drinking, we was like, 'Yo, he ain't no cop, Big.'"

According to Chico, Big still wasn't convinced, but when Matty returned with his credentials from the magazine, everything opened up. Big didn't exactly know where being in *The Source* could take him, but he knew it was a step in the right direction. Mister Cee had come through on his promise.

"A'ight. What you wanna talk about?" he asked.

Matty conducted the interview, which already had those close to Big buzzing. Somebody they knew was going to be featured in *The Source.* Someone in the crew was making a positive turn away from all the negativity that surrounded them on a daily basis. What really sent the crew over the top was the photo shoot. Mister Cee hired the same photographer who did Big Daddy Kane's album covers to shoot photos of Big, 50 Grand, and his crew. Pride ran rampant throughout the neighborhood.

"Big was like, 'Yo, son, look.' Because, you know, we pulled out some things on the block. We getting the crew up together," said Chico. "Everybody was really hype. We took the pictures on the block. First at St. James. Then we went to Bedford and Quincy."

It landed in the March 1992 edition of *The Source.* Matty wrote, "His DJ, Hitman 50 Grand, threw a couple classic breaks and instrumentals and let B-I-G do what he had to do: he ripped shit. Straight outta Brooklyn, New

York, the heavy-set brother B-I-G has mad skills. His rhymes are fatter than he is." The placement in the magazine wasn't grand in word count, but being in the magazine and being dubbed "unsigned hype" was all the cosign that was needed at the time.

"It was a big deal . . . Everybody had [the issue]," D-Roc recalled. "It's like, 'Yo, you see Big in Unsigned Hype?! Yo, this is my man! Oh my God!' That shit got crazy."

But Cee wanted not just to get Big in the magazine, he wanted placement on the magazine's compilation album as well.

"That's what was so wild. They rerecorded the demo, and in between the songs, Biggie talks about wanting to be on the album in a very humble way," Capoluongo says. "He's like, 'Thank you for giving a brother an opportunity to be on this record. Right now, I don't have any songs, but my man 50 Grand got two turntables and got these beats.' It's just cool to know they were thinking about being on that record."

Big never ended up making it on the record, though. The money paid to each artist was small, roughly five grand a piece. Matty sat down with Relativity with then unknown artists like Biggie, DMX, Poetical Prophets (who'd later be renamed Mobb Deep), a girl group called Back to Back, Common Sense, and Freestyle Fellowship from Los Angeles. The label ended up going with Common because his No I.D. production gave the tape the best sound quality. Not that it mattered that much for Big. His name and face were already in a magazine that was being circulated all around the country. That meant it wasn't just people in Brooklyn or a select few clubgoers or his roommates in Raleigh who knew he had skills. Thousands of people in Seattle, Los Angeles, Chicago, Houston, Miami, Atlanta, and more knew who the Notorious B.I.G. was. And it wasn't for selling crack.

"Matt put that in the magazine, and when it came out it was like, 'Yo! That's wassup!' Chico said. "'What's next?'"

07

HARLEM, THE MECCA, AND A GUY NAMED PUFFY

BIG WASN'T IGNORANT. Every day he stepped on the block he knew he was a target. Selling drugs was part of that. But *how* he looked was an entry point into one of America's most consistent themes: the criminalization of the Black body and how it's been used to invoke fear.

In the months leading up to the 1988 election, George H. W. Bush's campaign unleashed a racially charged attack against its Democratic opponent, Massachusetts governor Michael Dukakis. The ad centered on a Massachusetts Black man by the name of Willie Horton. Horton was a convicted murderer who, while on a prison furlough, raped a white Maryland woman while tying up and stabbing her boyfriend. The incident became yet another brutally ugly entry point into the larger conversation around criminal punishment in America.

There were missteps all around, including by Dukakis. Massachusetts should never have furloughed a convicted murderer sentenced to life without parole. But it wasn't like Massachusetts was the only one furloughing inmates, even those convicted of murder. The Bush campaign blew a racist dog whistle and preyed on fear, with consequences beyond the 1988 election.

"The reason why the Willie Horton ad is so important in the political landscape—it wasn't just about a racist ad that misrepresented the furlough process," said Marcia Chatelain, a Georgetown University professor of

African American history, in 2018. "But it also taught the Democrats that in order to win elections, they have to mirror some of the racially inflected language of tough on crime."

Bush ran away with the 1988 presidential election, winning forty of fifty states, and tallying a whooping 426 electoral college votes. His victory marked the first time since 1836 that the sitting vice president received the country's most prestigious job promotion. But America was changing. This would be the last time the majority of the northeast and California chose a Republican presidential candidate, and the last time the party of Reagan would garner more votes from women than its Democratic challenger.

Public Enemy's landmark single "Fight the Power," with its state-of-the-union-like address, would be released in the summer of 1989. Months earlier, that same energy and unwillingness to stay silent lived on the historic campus of Howard University. It wasn't like the bulk of the students at Howard were fans of the forty-first president either. Multiple anti-Bush protests had been held on campus leading up to the election. And days before Election Day, the Reverend Jesse Jackson delivered an impassioned speech at Howard's Rankin Chapel blasting Bush's campaign and urging young Black voters to show up in massive numbers.

"Don't cry about what you don't have, but use what you've got. The hands that used to pick cotton can now pick governors, congressmen and presidents," Jackson pleaded to the nearly four hundred people in attendance.

Howard, founded less than two years after the Civil War, had grown to become one of the most important campuses in America. In the 1950s, *Time* and the *Saturday Evening Post* billed Howard as "America's Leading Negro University" and "America's Center of Negro Learning." The list of notable alumni seems never-ending: Thurgood Marshall, Toni Morrison, Kamala Harris, Phylicia Rashad, Stokely Carmichael (aka Kwame Ture), Elijah Cummings, Debbie Allen, Amiri Baraka, Andrew Young, L. Douglas Wilder, Donny Hathaway, Ossie Davis, Zora Neale Hurston, and, in later years, Chadwick Boseman, Taraji P. Henson, Anthony Anderson, Gus Johnson, Ta-Nehisi Coates, Wendy Raquel Robinson, and many more.

But by the early spring of 1989, the revolutionary spirit that lived on the northwest D.C. campus was put to the test. Geographically speaking, Howard and the White House are only separated by two miles. Culturally, however, they were worlds apart. Which is why the campus erupted in fury when Lee Atwater—Bush's campaign strategist—was named to its board of trustees. "If I can make Willie Horton a household name, we'll win the election," Atwater had said. Howard students erupted in fury over the decision, leading hundreds of them to occupy the Mordecai Wyatt Johnson administration building (or as it was known on campus, the "A building") threatening not to report to classes until Atwater was removed.

The protests, which began in early March, and which weren't only about Atwater, put the university in an interesting position. On one hand, supporting its students and hearing their demands was paramount. On the other hand, the school received federal funding each year—and Atwater's presence could potentially put Howard in a position to secure access to considerable amounts of money from conservative sources. Financially speaking, the school had done well under both political parties, but Howard's top brass, in particular the university president James Cheek, was particularly chummy with Republican presidents. The students and Howard's decision makers were on two different wavelengths. HOW FAR WILL HOWARD GO FOR A $? one sign read at the protests.

Local restaurants supplied food to students who were protesting. When famed civil rights activists like the Reverend Ralph Abernathy and the Reverend Jesse Jackson, and local D.C. political luminaries like the mayor Marion Berry and the delegate Walter Fauntroy, showed up to stand in solidarity with the student body, the media attention only increased. This wasn't just a protest for the sake of being heard and being loud. The students came with a list of seven demands they wanted swift action on: a more Afrocentric curriculum, a university-wide program that would grant academic credit for community service, a more efficient financial aid process, eliminating a 15 percent tuition increase, better living facilities for students, better campus security with higher-paid officers, and, of course, "the immediate removal of Lee Atwater from the board of trustees."

Howard students met with two Black Atwater aides, and then with Atwater himself. He wanted to state his case—that he wasn't some demon who wanted to impose on their freedoms as young Black men and women, and that their view of him was all wrong. Atwater, in the meeting, even told the students that he was a big fan of rhythm and blues. He also said that the

Horton ad was a "political stunt," and that he originally didn't know Horton was Black.

The pressure the students applied on both Atwater and the school was heralded in the media. And on March 8, 1989, Lee Atwater officially resigned from Howard's board of trustees. The victory proved symbolic.

"If the Republican Party—aware of Howard's importance in the Black community—had counted on Atwater's presence on the board as part of its outreach efforts to Blacks," wrote David Nicholson for the *Washington Post* on March 12, "it sorely underestimated Black opposition to the party's past policies. It's too early to tell, of course, but the protest at Howard just might be Black America's awakening from the long slumber of the Reagan years."

Black America's battle was still as uphill as ever, and heartbreaking losses lay ahead. But Howard students had fought the power and won. Their voices had been heard. Not every student participated in the protests. Some were on the front line, some decided to watch from a distance and see how it played out, and at least one, a freshman from New York named Sean Combs, figured out a way to promote the unrest.

With the campus protests, students wanted their voices to be heard. Combs, an enterprising young freshman from New York City, never had that issue. What he wanted, though, was his presence to be felt. Combs understood the value of a strong reputation and how that would only amplify his voice. He also understood the value of cultural currency and what that meant on a college campus—in particular, one that was historically Black. Combs arrived at Howard in the fall of 1987, roughly a few months before Christopher Wallace transitioned out of school and dove headfirst into the crack game. Combs wasn't a drug dealer, but he was a hustler. He wanted to bring people together, but he also wanted people to know he was the one doing so—a calling card that rings true to the present day.

For Combs, the student protests in the spring of '89 presented an opportunity to unite the student body—and put some money in his pockets at the same time. Combs took images from the protests—photos of students and police clashing, and students being whisked away—and printed up some posters.

"He made hundreds of them, and sold them for ten and fifteen dollars a piece," recalled his former Howard classmate and future coworker Deric

"D-Dot" Angelettie in the 2003 biography *Unbelievable*. "That's the type of nigga I saw. All this protest shit is well and good, but who's getting paid off of it? He was ready."

Combs was born on November 4, 1969, in Harlem, New York, to Melvin and Janice Combs. Anyone wondering where Combs got his flash, style, and charisma would have to look no further than his parents. "Pretty Melvin," as he was called, and his wife, Janice, stayed fly because that's all they knew. Legally, Melvin drove a cab, but he made other money that he couldn't exactly report on his taxes. In late 1971, Melvin was arrested for possession of heroin and $45,000 in cash. He had deep ties to the drug game, most notably with former kingpin Frank Lucas, who called Melvin a "good friend" in a 2010 VladTV interview.

That friendship, and what could've been for a father and his son, ended on January 26, 1972. Melvin Combs was murdered in a drug deal gone awry in Central Park. A year later, seven men and three women were convicted of being part of a conspiracy ring that sold wholesale price heroin in Harlem, the Bronx, and Westchester County. The case's lead prosecutor, W. Cullen MacDonald, told the court after the verdict that detectives believed Melvin's murder thirteen months earlier might "ultimately" be traced back to fellow members of the conspiracy ring. There were rumors that "Pretty Melvin" was a police informant, but Lucas, in his 2010 autobiography *Original Gangster*, came to his old friend's defense, saying that snitching "wasn't Melvin's style. And anyone who says different is lying."

"They say you can't miss something you never had, but that's only a little ways right," Combs would reflect later in life. "There's definitely been times as I've gotten older that I've missed my father . . . his presence—not being there."

It's impossible to say how much that murder altered the course of the Combs family legacy. Janice Combs made the decision to refrain from telling her son how her husband and his father was actually killed. For years, she told her two kids, Sean and Keisha, that their father had died in a car accident. Much like Voletta Wallace, Janice poured all her love, attention, and energy into making sure her kids never wanted for anything. And, most certainly, she wanted to make sure they stayed away from the world that made her a widow.

Janice moved the family to Mount Vernon, a suburb just north of the Bronx in Westchester County. It was a little less than fifteen miles from Harlem, but in New York City, when neighborhood cultures can shift by the block, this was an opportunity to reset. There, Janice lovingly spoiled her kids, once even getting a pool that was larger than the one their white neighbors had because Sean was never invited over to swim. Combs got what he wanted, and when he didn't, that's how he got his nickname—well, one of them.

"Whenever I got mad as a kid, I used to always huff and puff," Combs told *JET* magazine in 1998. "I had a temper. That's why my friend started calling me Puffy."

Even in Mount Vernon, though, that Harlem hustler mentality was impossible to shed. It was something he was born into. "My mother was always working," Combs said. "So I guess I was always trained that I should have multiple jobs, multiple aspirations."

It seemed like Combs came out of the womb knowing how to make money—and knowing how to activate others to help him. It wasn't like he wanted to be the biggest drug dealer or the biggest gangster in New York. That was never his mission. Combs wanted to make money his own way. And lots of it. Unlike Wallace, though, Combs didn't mind working anywhere as long as it came with a paycheck: amusement parks, restaurants, and even formulating his own newspaper delivery service, even though he was technically too young at the time. Combs was never satisfied with making one dollar when he knew two were possible.

Mount Vernon was the family's new home, but their heart never truly left Harlem. They had way too much history there, and family. They'd often go back to visit, and Combs would inevitably link up and tap in with old friends from the block like Paul "Big Paul" Offord and Anthony "Wolf" Jones. As Combs grew older, so did his knowledge of street politics. He'd heard through word on the street that his father was a hustler and that back in the day his family was the only one on the block to have a Mercedes-Benz. It became enticing to the young man affectionately known as Puffy. He wanted that same type of love and respect.

Combs was also coming of age during an era when the streets and hip-hop operated in tandem. Among Black youth, rap music was all the rage.

The dances, the house parties, and the energy rap brought was pure and authentic. Rhythm is the soul's more carefree form of expression. And there was real power that came with giving people a space to find it. Combs loved the music, the women, and even the money that came with that world, but what he really loved was the power and respect that came with being, in street lingo, "that nigga."

"Parties at the Rooftop—that shit was like one of the most incredible experiences ever," Combs told *VIBE* magazine in late 1997 of the legendary New York skating rink that turned into an after-hours spot for hip-hop. DJs like Brucie B and Lovebug Starski would DJ there, and those flush with street riches came in droves. "This was when crack first came out. Niggas was fourteen, fifteen riding around in Jeeps with the tops off. If you wasn't hustling, you wasn't on the list. I wasn't hustling . . . But I had to make sure my gear was up to par."

But behind nearly every successful rap artist of the early to mid-eighties was the truth that the hood wasn't too far away, either. Creatively, financially, and philosophically, hip-hop's entire existence was tied directly to the streets that served as its greatest muse. It wasn't uncommon for street impresarios like Queens's infamous Supreme Team leader Kenneth "Supreme" McGriff to throw parties where rap superstars like Kurtis Blow would be in attendance and even perform. Or James "Bimmy" Antney, also of the Supreme Team and who later became a respected music executive, and known for his close proximity to fellow Queens natives Run-DMC. Rap was loved by the community who created it, but outside of a select few, record labels weren't exactly drooling at the prospect of investing in the genre. And many rappers trusted the guys from their neighborhood more than the suits who still treated hip-hop like a novelty act rather than the genre on the pulse of young America. Directly or indirectly, street guys—most of whom lived the life many rappers painted on wax—propelled these careers.

Not even old enough to drink legally, Combs understood that the secret sauce was making music that appealed to the street while giving it crossover appeal. He'd seen both worlds, from private school to the streets of Harlem and Mount Vernon. With a vision in his mind as bright as Times Square on New Year's Eve, Combs headed to the nation's capital and the campus of Howard University in the fall of 1987.

He had an important task to handle first.

"As soon as I got to Howard, I went to the library and did some research. I used the microfilm at Founders [Library] and searched all the newspapers," Combs said in a commencement address at Howard in 2014. "When I typed in my father's name and the day he died, I read in the *Amsterdam News* that he had been murdered in a drug deal gone bad. Right there in that library, I realized there's nothing greater than a mother's love and desire to protect her child. I also decided to live my life in a way that would make her proud."

Finding out a truth of that magnitude can profoundly affect a person. Combs embraced the truth and understood that the best way to pay homage to the father he hardly knew was by forging his own path. He was a business major, but most of his education at Howard came from outside of the classroom. From nearly day one, he was one of the most recognizable people on campus. Freshmen normally have to pay their dues, but Combs bucked at that tradition. He was a party fixture and loved mixing and mingling with people on the Yard. Calling Combs a social butterfly would've been an understatement. He was a social lion, and love him or hate him, be you endeared to his personality or annoyed by it, Combs's swagger almost immediately had become synonymous with Howard's culture.

"I could get anything I wanted on campus. If I needed an English paper, I knew where to go," Combs reflected. "If I needed an exam or some weed, I knew where to get it."

On campus, Public Enemy's *Yo! Bum Rush the Show*, Boogie Down Productions' *Criminal Minded*, LL Cool J's *Bigger and Deffer*, Eric B. & Rakim's *Paid in Full*, Too $hort's *Born to Mack*, Salt-N-Pepa's "Push It," and Ice-T's "6 in the Morning" could be heard coming out of dorm rooms and across the Yard. Ever observant, Combs studied what crowds liked and what they wore. He knew what the best sound system was and the ideal aesthetics for the right ambiance. And most importantly—what the women liked the most, because if women felt comfortable partying and they were having a great time, then the party would ultimately be deemed a success. The math was simple. Guys love what girls like.

It was all part of his master plan to curate the ultimate entertainment experience. At Howard, Combs would meet the aforementioned Angelettie, the aspiring producer Ron "Amen-Ra" Lawrence, Mark Pitts, Nashiem Myrick, Robert "Don Pooh" Cummins, and Chucky Thompson—all of whom he'd eventually help make large sums of money in just a few short years. His future business partner, Harve Pierre, was also at Howard around this time.

Angelettie, a year older than Combs—who was already known around campus as Puffy—had spent much of his freshman year enjoying college life a little too much. The girls, the parties, the weed, the alcohol—all of that had taken precedence over the actual classroom. But it did allow him to create more social capital, and he started DJing at fraternity and sorority parties, where Combs was often in the mix.

"Puffy's in the middle of the dance floor getting all the young big-booty chicks on his dick because he's dancing and doing flips," Angelettie recalled in *Unbelievable.*

Combs and Angelettie joined forces and formed A Black Man and a Puerto Rican Productions.

"Their parties were really good. I do remember that," said the Howard alum and Brooklyn native Stacy Carmichael, who was the same year at Howard as Combs.

Puffy wasn't just the hottest promoter on campus. He was the biggest promoter in the city, usurping former nightlife kingpins like Maynard Clark and Todd Johnson. He relied on more than just the usual flyers posted around campus, cultivating word of mouth. Nothing topped the sizzle of having his party be on the lips of his peers. And he brought out stars. Fan favorites like Slick Rick, Heavy D, Guy, and more all popped up at Howard at one time or another, and Combs's after-parties were liable to be better than the actual concert. And their homecoming party became the stuff of legend as nearly 8,000 people attempted to pile into a church basement they dubbed "the Asylum." Charging basically whatever they wanted because the demand to be in that party was so high, Puffy and Angelettie stood to make a lot of money, but the fire marshal shut it down. The night would prove to be an ominous foreshadow to two of the worst nights of Puffy's life.

In that moment, though, what mattered is that Combs had found he could make things happen. He knew how to draw crowds and get them to move. But promoting parties wasn't the end game. Combs, like a young Christopher Wallace, wanted in to the music industry.

━━━━━━

Bernie Harrell worked at the Hunts Point produce market in the Bronx. His message to his son Andre, from an early age, was simple. At some point Andre was going to be an adult with responsibilities and a family of his own, so to handle both, he might as well do something he loved for a living. Andre, who grew up in the Bronxdale Housing Projects (renamed in 2010 after former resident Supreme Court justice Sonia Sotomayor), took the message to heart.

Andre Harrell loved music, even taking a shot at being a rapper as one half of the mid-eighties duo Dr. Jeckyll & Mr. Hyde alongside his childhood friend Alonzo Brown. In 1981, they landed a local club hit with the single "Genius Rap." They even released an album, *The Champagne of Rap*, in 1985. But Harrell quickly understood the stone-cold truth—he was never going to be a star. But that didn't mean he couldn't be part of the music world in other ways. He'd been working in radio and ad sales, but Harrell—who died in 2020 at the age of fifty-nine—acknowledged that his true expertise in the music industry came from being on the ground, in the mix, and among the people in New York City at hot spots like Bentley's.

Harrell met and quickly befriended Russell Simmons, who, along with Rick Rubin, launched Def Jam Records in 1985. Rap was still largely viewed as a trend, and Def Jam was the first rap label to secure national distribution. Harrell worked at Def Jam, helping to launch the careers of superstars like LL Cool J, but when he attempted to bring another young rapper named Dwight Myers—whose stage name was Heavy D—to the label, Simmons refused to sign him. Instead of sulking, Harrell switched up his hustle. He launched his own label and called it Uptown Records.

Simmons's Def Jam was more rugged, more reflective of the Queens he hailed from. Meanwhile, Uptown represented the energy of Harlem. It was still rugged, but flashy and more inclusive to a variety of sounds from hip-hop and R&B.

"I wanted hit records that make you feel a certain sexy way," Harrell said in 1995. "Records that would get a pretty girl to dance with you at two A.M. even if you weren't great looking. Girl-meets-boy, boy-meets-girl records."

It sounds implausible now, but at the time, hip-hop and R&B lived in two completely different universes. Harrell may not have been the one to originally merge the two worlds, but Uptown is most commonly credited with blending them. The label found massive success through names like Heavy D & the Boyz, Guy, Al B. Sure!, Teddy Riley, Father MC, and more.

"I used to see artists a little differently from Russell," Harrell said in 2003's *Unbelievable*. "He thought the sound that Teddy Riley was making was the commercial side of hip-hop—or not the authentic hip-hop. I thought it was a Harlem glamorous slick side. It was hip-hop that could also be R&B."

As the eighties became the nineties, Harrell was already considered a wizard executive whose music dominated senior proms, college fraternity and sorority parties, late-night after-hours spots, wedding receptions, and, if the mood called for it, the bedroom. Uptown, which cultural critic Naima Cochrane would later dub a "lifestyle label," could fit into nearly any pocket. He also had another star in the making on his label. Except this one wasn't an artist, it was an intern.

Harrell originally met a young Sean Combs in 1990 through Heavy D, a Mount Vernon native, and gave him a job at Uptown. As an intern, there was seemingly nothing that Harrell could ask of Combs that was too much. On his first day, Harrell asked Combs to get a tape from the studio. He came back with the tape in five minutes. The studio was ten blocks away. No one's hunger matched Combs's. He'd leave Howard and catch the train from Union Station at 5:00 A.M. to be at his unpaid internship by 10:00 A.M.

"I did everything. I drove Andre's car. If they needed something delivered, I would take a cab instead of a subway and pay for it out of my own pocket," Combs recalled. "I knew it was the place to be."

Much the way he had at Howard, Combs studied everything at Uptown: every meeting he sat in on; every task he was given, no matter how menial; every mannerism in the office. He may have been an intern, but the moment he was given a chance to exhibit his creativity and near peerless drive to be better than everyone, even the boss, Harrell himself, he would do it and never look back. That's just the way he was wired. He was a maniacal competitor fueled only by an obsession with success.

It didn't take long before Combs realized where his bread was buttered. He dropped out of Howard and moved into Harrell's New Jersey estate. Then the opportunity Combs had been waiting for all but fell in his lap. The late Heavy D must have had a third eye for musical talent. Not only did he introduce Harrell to Combs and crooner Al B. Sure!, but one day when he was walking through Uptown's lobby, he overheard two sets of brothers singing. They didn't even have an appointment. It had taken them over five hours to get to Uptown's Midtown Manhattan offices from their Queens hotel because they got lost along the way. Heavy D was convinced by what he heard, though. Harrell needed to hear them ASAP. Moments later, after the four brothers—Joel "JoJo" and Cedric "K-Ci" Hailey and Donald "Devante" and "Mr. Dalvin" DeGrate, otherwise known as Jodeci—performed, Harrell signed them on the spot. They were naturally talented, but they needed a curator. Following the resignation of Uptown's A&R director Kurt Woodley, Combs saw his opportunity. He asked Harrell for Woodley's position with the simple selling point: he was Harrell's target demographic.

"I was bugging that they were my age and able to sing like that," Combs recalled. "K-Ci was smaller than he is now. I couldn't believe all that came out of him."

Combs didn't just hit the ground running, he was a marathoner running at an all-out sprint. And it was through Father MC that Combs's grand vision began to take shape. A hustler-turned-rapper, Father MC was part of that first generation of rappers to successfully make music that both sexes gravitated toward. A large part of that had to do with Combs's influence. "Treat 'Em Like They Wanna Be Treated," Father's first single, featured Jodeci on the hook. And "I'll Do 4 U" featured a young up-and-coming singer from the Bronx named Mary J. Blige.

Over the next several months, Combs shifted his attention to Jodeci. Even if others at Uptown didn't see the appeal of the group—or perhaps it was jealousy of Combs's rapid ascension, or a combination of both—Combs knew what he had on his hands. He just had to chisel out the ideal R&B group. He wanted to keep their soulful, southern melodies intact, but he wanted to style them with hip-hop flavor—the sunglasses, the baggy clothes, the backward hats, the skullcaps. The group's debut album, *Forever My Lady*, dropped on May 28, 1991. Their first single, "Gotta Love," didn't garner much attention, but with its second single, the album's title track, "Forever My Lady," the group's sound was solidified. Hood, but sultry. Rugged, but smooth enough to take your girl at the same time.

Jodeci, guided and shaped by Combs as R&B roughnecks, the antithesis of Boyz II Men, became a runaway success with a string of hit singles. Puffy had managed to take the quartet's gospel foundation and make them into guys who never quite made it to Sunday school thanks to Saturday night's hedonism.

Combs was on, and everyone knew it. The "Puff Daddy" image was born. Partying with Puff Daddy was quickly becoming a status symbol. Every week there was a party at "Daddy's House," the nickname for the Manhattan club Red Zone. Each week, people from all over the city and out of town would crowd into the club, and in numbers that seemed to balloon by the week, rivaling bashes at the Rooftop in Harlem in the eighties.

Puffy wasn't a studio producer in the traditional sense, but his vision was tried and true. Triple platinum is triple platinum, and where Mary J. Blige was once an artist languishing on the shelf, he was already in the lab figuring out how to make her the next great Black female vocalist. Recording for what eventually became Blige's transcendent debut, *What's the 411?*, began in 1991 as Jodeci arrived on the scene as the industry's most talked-about new act. Combs's idea was to put two production teams in healthy competition with each other. In New Jersey were the Untouchables, and in New York were two of the album's main producers in Dave "Jam" Hall and Cory Rooney.

"So it ended up being a friendly rivalry. Puffy was right in the middle of it. It was kind of genius what he was doing, though," Rooney told *Ebony*. "He would use the records from one camp to amp up the other camp. I remember the day he played 'Reminisce' for us and we all said, 'Damnit!' We thought we had them and then he played us that record."

Maybe it was manipulation, or maybe it was Combs's way of bringing the best out of people. But there he was dancing all around the studio, gassing the record up, waiting to see what Rooney's and Hall's reactions would be. "Then," Rooney said, "we did the record 'Changes I've Been Going Through.' So we were trying to fire back. It was all love, though. It was a fun project to do. Puffy was really pushing us."

Puffy, in fact, pushed a lot of people. Not everybody liked his methods. Andre Harrell initially let it all slide. A father-son-like bond had formed between the two. But as Combs's name grew, so did his ego.

"He's not intimidated by youth, you know what I'm saying," a bald-headed Combs said in an early nineties interview with Harrell standing beside him.

"The whole company hated me," Combs later admitted. "People were like, 'Dre created a monster.' I was aggressive. I would trash the office. I'd call Andre a wimp and a house nigga."

As the hits kept increasing, the target became bigger and bigger on the man named Puff Daddy's back. Though, being a Black man in America, that was anything out of the ordinary.

———

The representation of Black men in American media proved pivotal in 1991. On March 3 of that year, Los Angeles Police Department officers tried to pull over Rodney King. He had been drinking, and worried that a DUI arrest would violate his parole for a previous robbery conviction, so he tried to get away. After a high-speed chase, King was eventually pulled over at an apartment complex in the San Fernando Valley. Four police officers savagely kicked and beat King, all captured on grainy video by a nearby resident. The incident would incite international outrage, and it became a landmark moment in the generations-long fraught relationship between the police and Black communities.

Later that summer, *Boyz n the Hood* hit theaters. Written and directed by the twenty-three-year-old John Singleton, the film was a cultural touchstone, an instant classic that provided an unfiltered view of the lives of young Black men and women living in South Central Los Angeles. It wasn't the biggest box office hit that year—that honor went to *Terminator 2: Judgment Day*—but it made $10 million its opening weekend, against a budget of $6.5 million, and went on to gross $57 million in theaters and earn two Oscar nominations. Singleton was nominated for the Academy Award for Best Director and Best Original Screenplay (losing to Jonathan Demme for *Silence of the Lambs* and Callie Khouri for *Thelma & Louise*). Because of how the film depicted the complexities, pressures, and emotional shockwaves of living in America's underbelly, what it's done to advance conversations around police brutality, gang violence, and socioeconomic disparities has proved immeasurable.

And then, on November 7, 1991, perhaps the most shocking news of the year broke when the famed Los Angeles Laker Magic Johnson announced he had tested HIV positive and immediately retired from the NBA. America was still struggling with understanding the AIDS epidemic, and Magic's diagnosis and openness helped increase awareness and shift the conversation—but it also left millions in fear of what the quality of Johnson's life would look like moving forward.

Nearly two months later, on December 28, 1991, Sean "Puff Daddy" Combs found himself in legal crosshairs. His incident didn't receive nearly as many national headlines, but he would be linked to the tragedy forever. It started innocently, and honorably, enough. Combs had organized a concert headlined by Heavy D at the City College gymnasium to follow an AIDS charity basketball game. Uptown artists would perform at the game as well. News of the event spread like wildfire. Combs was no stranger to the insanity of the party lifestyle, so having massive amounts of people arrive at his events wasn't anything new. In November 1991, another of Combs's Howard homecoming parties, this time at the Washington Convention Center, had to be shut down by police for overcrowding.

"I'm not very tall. I'm only five four, and I remember feeling like I couldn't breathe," Stacy Carmichael, Combs's classmate at Howard, said about that homecoming party. "I remember standing on my toes with my head up because I couldn't get air. So when the whole City College incident happened, I wasn't surprised. I felt it was going to happen eventually just from going to a couple of parties where that's how I felt waiting to get into."

Shortly after 7:00 P.M. at Jeremiah T. Mahoney Hall, the crowd began to take matters into its own hands. There had already been several fights from people cutting the line. But now thousands of people made their way into the gymnasium. The problem was that it was already full. The momentum led down a stairway and into a single door for ticket holders. A line stretched down the block on 138th Street. As many as five thousand people attempted to get into the gym that sat only 2,700. That's when the stampede began. In the chaos of that night, nine people were crushed to death, and twenty-nine more were injured.

"There were three people under me and two on top," said Keenan Gray of Queens, who was twenty at the time. "I was stuck for twenty minutes."

"A girl was sitting up on my chest," said Lynette Delane of Paterson, New Jersey. "She wasn't even conscious. I just thank God I'm still alive. No one even cared. They wouldn't stop pushing."

A day later, New York mayor David Dinkins refused to place blame on anyone until an investigation was complete. The finger-pointing, however, had already begun. Some blamed the college itself for approving the event and not staffing the adequate amount of security. Reports showed that the police had sixty-six officers on site, City College provided thirty private officers, and the promoters brought on an additional twenty. Others questioned whether the police department moved with enough urgency to limit the severity of the disaster. Others wondered out loud if the promoters, in particular Combs and Heavy D, had even taken the time to fully plan out their own event.

The two Mount Vernon residents spent the weekend trying to gather information on what had gone so grossly wrong so quickly. Phones were all but attached to their ears as they weaved in and out of conversations and cried with lawyers, friends, and, most importantly, those who lost loved ones. Combs's girlfriend at the time, Misa Hylton, had a close friend die at the event. As mayhem swirled all around him and Combs could only see bodies on the floor, he recalled to journalist dream hampton that as he fearfully sprinted between victims, he tried to resuscitate them. "I breathed in death," Combs said, pacing Heavy D's apartment. "I felt it happen."

Months later, in the March 1992 edition of *The Source*—the same issue in which Biggie was featured in Unsigned Hype—Heavy D penned an opinion piece shifting blame toward all the entities who prayed for hip-hop's downfall.

"I want you to keep in mind that all we have is each other. We can't depend on the police because they lie. We can't depend on the government because they lie. And we can't depend on the media because they lie," he wrote. "Remember the police, the government and the media have always tried to attack us and keep us down. There are exceptions to this fact, but very few. There were police, but no police assistance. I saw a lot of Black people helping Black people. All we had was each other."

The *New York Post* pinned the tragedy on a "Fool Named Puff Daddy." Perhaps Combs had gotten too comfortable and started to believe the hype around him. That his parties were petri dishes for insanity, and that that was good for business because, up until City College, he had no real reason to think otherwise. With the backdrop of charity, it wasn't like the Heavy D concert was strictly for public service, either. There was personal gain involved, too. Combs never denied that he mishandled some of the planning, but the moment shook him—the last thing Combs wanted was to be associated with such a tragedy. Criminal charges were never filed against Combs or the event's other organizers. Still, death threats came in droves, from people claiming to be loved ones of the deceased. Suicide, or at least the faint thought of it, crept into his mind.

"I started to lose it. I felt like I didn't wanna even live no more. I was so fuckin' sad," Combs said. His attorney, William Kunstler, advised him to keep his head down. "But I wanted to go to the wakes and funerals and try to provide some comfort, even though I knew my presence probably wouldn't have given comfort. But what I was going through with the blame and stuff was nothing compared to what the families were going through."

In a profile for the *New York Times* a few years later, Combs again addressed the incident, hammering on his innocence. He was guilty of too much delegation, he said. Not monitoring the situation with the precision he should've, too. But, he said, "I didn't do anything criminal, or else I wouldn't be here. I'd be in jail."

In 1992, lawyers for Combs and other promoters fired back at police and city officials who blamed them for the deadly tragedy. Seven years later, in 1999, a New York judge found City College partly liable for the deaths of the nine people. In between were the mounds of lawsuits piling up, including eight wrongful death claims and over twenty personal injury cases.

In May 2000, Combs paid an undisclosed amount to settle a final lawsuit. The *New York Post* called it the "last chapter [of the] tragedy." The moment set an example to Combs. No matter how many songs he placed on the charts, no man is bigger than life itself, and it could all be stripped without a moment's notice.

Back in 1991 into early 1992, rather than take a leave of absence as Andre Harrell suggested, Combs just worked harder. He was the youngest executive in rap, and he had more money than he'd ever had before. But his rep had been severely damaged by the catastrophe. Combs needed something to go his way. Then, seemingly out of nowhere, it happened for him in the form of a demo tape from this young rapper from Brooklyn.

08

THE DECISION: STREETS OR RAP?

ALL BIG ASKED OF MISTER CEE WAS THAT HE STAY TRUE TO HIS WORD. If he could do something, give it a shot. If he couldn't, just be upfront with him. Cee stayed true to his word when he got his demo tape to Matty C and got him in *The Source*. In early 1992, circulation of the magazine was at roughly fifty thousand copies a month. So, though Big didn't have a record or record deal, people from all over the country knew the name the Notorious B.I.G. He wasn't just rhyming on Fulton Street or battling 'Preme on Bedford and Quincy anymore. He had eyes and ears on him.

Around early 1992, the Uptown Records executive Sean Combs contacted Matty C asking if he knew of any artists on the rise he should be aware of. The truth is, he'd been wanting to make real street music for a while. Combs knew he could command the clubs, but he desperately yearned for that street credibility that came with an artist of Big's character. Matty's ear was like gold. He knew talent when he heard it, and those within the industry respected his judgment. Plus, Puffy had already missed out on another act called Poetical Prophets that Matty sang the praises of. Matty ended up throwing the alley-oop to his friend Bonz Malone, who had recently taken an A&R job at Island Records. Malone helped rename the group Mobb Deep.

Rap was still very much an insular game. The movers knew the shakers. The executives knew the journalists, often on a first name basis (for better and for worse). Matty C, who would often go back home to the nation's capital, knew Combs from his Howard University party days. Combs hit Matty up one day, telling him to come to his Uptown Records office.

The man now known industry-wide as Puffy paid more attention to the sushi he was eating than warmly acknowledging Matty's presence when he walked in. Before long, Matty pressed played on the demo tape that Mister Cee had given him and let Big do his talking. The storytelling was there. As was the charisma and attention to detail in every syllable. He may have been trying to pull himself out of a personal hell following the City College melee, but in Puffy's eyes, this demo tape was a gift straight from the rap gods. Combs's poker face, however, never broke. Once the demo ended Combs's demeanor eased up, and he asked one question.

"What's he look like?"

Truthfully speaking, there wasn't anyone who looked like Big. He wasn't a chiseled sex symbol like LL Cool J or Big Daddy Kane, or a high-energy small guy like Eazy-E or Phife Dawg. He didn't even, at least initially, have the Big guy sex symbol vibes like Heavy D. Combs wanted to know how big Big actually was. But Matty told him it'd be best if he set up a meeting with Mister Cee to answer whatever questions he had. The bait had been cast, and the big fish, Combs in this instance, had already shown interest. It didn't matter if he had no clue what this young, grimy Brooklyn MC looked like, or even what his personality was like outside the few minutes he hear him rap. There was no way Puffy was letting the Notorious B.I.G. slip by him.

Cee eventually brought the news back to Big. This was his moment, their chance to turn a demo tape into a legitimate career in the music industry. When Cee got to Fulton Street, there was Big in the middle of an intense game of cee-lo. A blunt hung out of his mouth. D-Roc wasn't playing, but he was keeping an ever-watchful eye on the scene and making sure no one or nothing suspicious pulled on them. Cee told Big that Puffy loved the tape and he wanted to meet him.

"Puffy who?" Big asked.

Cee went through an entire spiel about who Puffy was and what he could potentially do for Big's career. Puffy was looking to take a more hard-core approach with his next act, and Big's demo tape had told him everything he needed to know. Still, he was skeptical.

"Uptown? Heavy D and the Boyz? Jodeci? Guy?" Big asked while taking a deep pull of the blunt. "They ain't gonna know what to do with a nigga like me."

Eventually, Big agreed to a meeting with Combs, on one condition.

"I ain't gonna be doing no talking in the meeting," he told Cee. "You gon' do all the talking. I don't really know Duke and I ain't talking to him. *You* talk. You make everything happen." Those who knew Big intimately understood the full range of his character. The intelligent, inquisitive, rebellious, and undeniably hilarious sides of him were on constant display if he felt comfortable in his environment. But he was skeptical of anyone and everything until proven otherwise. As far as he was concerned, Puffy was Mister Cee's connect, so he should handle the flow of the meeting. Plus, Puffy had to sell himself to Big—not the other way around.

Cee gathered Big and the two headed to Uptown's offices on a cold New York day in early 1992. On the cab ride there, the two didn't speak much. Cee wanted to give Big every opportunity to shine, though he had no clue what to expect from Combs once they walked in his office.

"Yo, man. He used to be a dancer," Cee told Big. "You remember the City College incident? When the people got trampled?"

"Yeah."

"That was Puff's celebrity basketball game where it happened."

Big nodded and continued looking out the window as the New York skyline whisked by.

When Cee and Big walked into Combs's office, Combs didn't waste any time and asked Big to freestyle. What he heard on the tape was so great it hadn't even seemed real, so he wanted to make sure he wasn't getting a fast one pulled on him. He quickly learned what Cee and everyone on Fulton Street and Bedford and Quincy already knew: there may have been a lot of talented young rappers in New York at the time, but none was hotter than Biggie Smalls. The demo tape was incredible, but Big wasn't one of those guys who needed certain requirements to rhyme. He could rhyme on the block, in a car, or in an office. He didn't need to cut his talent on because it was never off.

Below the surface, Combs was bursting at the seams with excitement, but the entire time Big was freestyling he sat there motionless and emotionless. When he finished, Combs broke his poker face and came with an offer. Everything Combs wanted in this idea of a new artist was there in Big. The look and marketing package was all Combs. He could do those things in his sleep. But Big had the flow, the storytelling, and a voice that made him this one-of-one anomaly that seemed almost unfair for one artist to have. From day one, minute one, Combs knew he had a superstar in the making sitting in his office. This wasn't just a dude rapping graphic street narratives and it sounded good. He was, for the most part, living what he rapped about—a reality that would come with its own set of headaches in the months moving forward. But as Big rhymed in his office, Combs knew the blessing he'd been praying for since the City College tragedy was looking him square in face.

Combs stood up and leaned over his desk asking Big one question. "I can have a record out on you by the summer," Combs said with the excitement in his voice rising. "Would you be cool with that?"

"You gotta talk to Cee, man," Big responded. "Whatever Cee say."

He put a lot of faith in Cee. Cee had shown himself to be a man of his word. Cee had wanted to rerecord his demo to make it a little cleaner—and he did. Cee had said he'd get the demo to Matty C at *The Source* to try and get him placement in the magazine—and he did. And now Cee had him on the brink of a record deal. Big was loyal to people who were loyal to him, and now he and Cee were bonded at the hip forever.

"Big was not the type of person that was decisive on what he wanted to do," Cee told me. "He really trusted me to make the best decision for him."

Cee's decision was obvious: sign with Puffy and Uptown and let him make Big a superstar. But the ultimate decision rested with Puffy's boss, Andre Harrell. Big may have looked like a thug straight out of Brooklyn's roughest street corners—in part because he was—but the man had an unrivaled talent to paint pictures with his words. He was poised to be a breakout star—with some grooming, of course. But that's what Combs was for.

Harrell, Combs, Cee, and Big linked up at Sylvia's soul food restaurant in Harlem a few weeks later. As short ribs and collard greens populated the table, Mister Cee once again gave his greatest sales pitch for Biggie Smalls as the future of rap music. Big was more like Michigan J. Frog, the fictional cartoon character who'd only perform in front of certain people and appear mute in front of others. Harrell hadn't seen anything that convinced him Big was the future of rap, but he'd give it one last shot. Something *had* to be there if Combs and Mister Cee were vouching so hard for him.

"Yo, Money, I want you to rhyme right now, in the car," Harrell said on the ride downtown from Sylvia's to the record label's offices in Midtown.

Mister Cee put on a beat from a cassette and Big took care of the rest.

He unleashed a string of rhymes that damn near made Harrell stop the car. Big wasn't the type of artist Harrell originally envisioned for Uptown—but talent was talent. He promised Puffy he would draw up the paperwork and from there it would be on. Just like that, Big had the promise of a record deal. And the idea of a better life.

———

Combs was Uptown's brightest, most envied and loathed rising star. But he was already thinking about the future. Uptown was great. It had given him the foot in the door he needed once he left Howard, and he wasn't necessarily thinking about leaving Uptown. But he did want his own imprint underneath the umbrella. This is how the idea of Bad Boy Records was born. Combs had worked his way up from unpaid intern to vice president, but he wanted more power. He envisioned a world where he not only signed artists, but saw them become bona fide superstars. And Combs would be there right alongside them. But that's what Bad Boy was for the most part in its early days—a dream. He had the vision. What was important for Combs—this was a reality that was hard for him to avoid at times—was making sure he didn't get in his own way.

For all the knocks against Combs, his attitude, or even his character, one thing that was undeniable was that he could always read the temperature of the culture. It wasn't that he was tired of helping to create classic R&B albums like Jodeci's *Forever My Lady* or Mary J. Blige's *What's the 411?* That would always be in his blood, but Combs wanted that hard-core street sound, too. In the early nineties, rap was experiencing a myriad of sounds from all parts of the country. Combs feverishly wanted in on that world. He saw an opening and an opportunity to make exorbitant amounts of money.

But, again, with Combs it was about the power. It's not that Combs didn't know anything about rap. That was anything but the truth. In the entertainment world, especially in nightlife, it was the soundtrack. But for all the acts he had been credited with developing, he was still missing that breakout rap star. An artist with that street edge and that credibility that came with telling honest truths about life in America's ghettos—sprinkled with a little Puff Daddy seasoning, of course. He wanted in on that action, and in Biggie Smalls, he found just that.

"I don't like no goody two-shoes shit. I like the sense of being in trouble," Combs said during the early days of the label's existence. "It's almost like a girl, you know what I'm saying. Girls don't like no good niggas. Girls like bad boys."

For Big, maybe this was it. He'd been writing in notebooks since he was in elementary school. He loved rap. He loved rapping, too. But for so long, the pathway to making it happen felt impossible. He didn't know where to begin. In the totality of his journey up to that point, it was never Big who sought to get his music in front of others. He opened his mouth to spit and everyone else did that for him.

Each served a purpose the other couldn't. Combs, not yet at least, wasn't interested in being an artist. And Big, not yet at least, wasn't interested in being an executive. Combs was boisterous, loud, and flashy while Big had no problem playing the cut until someone handed him a microphone. It was the start of a storied and an all too tragically brief partnership.

───

Voletta Wallace was awoken one morning by her son. He kneeled right by her bedside so they could be eye to eye. Christopher wasn't going to stop drug dealing unless given a reason to, and now he believed he had one. He knew she was disappointed in him for the choices he'd made and the lifestyle he was living. Christopher didn't like to upset Voletta, though he did it anyway. But he was serious about this. He wanted her to know the music dream he was chasing was legit. It made him happy. It made him feel worth a damn, and it made him feel like he didn't have to risk death or his freedom every day.

"You know, ma, this is your life," Christopher said to his mother. The weight of what he was about to say was an invisible blanket on both of them. "You know, you're a teacher. You went to school. You're teaching. You're happy. You want me to be happy? Ma, this is what I'm gonna do, and this is what's gonna make me happy."

"And who is going to help you, Christopher," Voletta recalled in the 2021 documentary *I Got a Story to Tell*.

"This guy named Puffy."

"He said goddamn Puffy," Voletta recalled, unable to hold back her laughter.

Voletta might have still needed convincing that music was a viable career option for her son. But one person who couldn't have been happier about Christopher's meeting with Puffy was Roland Young, otherwise known as Olie or O. They were still young, age-wise; Big had just turned twenty by the summer of 1992. Their time on the streets and the intensity of their line of work, though, aged them because of what they saw and, more importantly, what they survived. Big and O's bond had grown far beyond crack. Through music, O saw something special in his friend that would allow him to escape a world that felt like an inescapable hell at times. Now Big had a potential way out, and a way to take the hood with him. O wasn't going to let Big fumble that bag under any circumstances.

"O was actually Big's biggest cheerleader," said Hubert Sam. "I was more laid-back about it, but O was hype, and he was thinking about the fact that none of us would have to hustle anymore."

They were inseparable. If O was riding around in his Honda Accord, best believe Big was in the passenger seat. If O took Big over to Brownsville, then considered arguably the roughest part of Brooklyn, there was Big rhyming with O's people there—oftentimes with O gassing Big up the entire time. If they were on Fulton Street with some time to kill, it was almost expected that Big, O, and C-Gutta would engage in fierce hip-hop debates. Think of *First Take* long before *First Take* became a thing. They'd argue all day about the best MCs in rap. Gutta's favorite was KRS-One. O's was Rakim. And Big's, of course, was Big Daddy Kane. Even between sales, they'd break down rhymes, flows, and content of songs. Nobody ever really budged from their favorites, but it was something that helped pass the time.

Big was an only child, so he appreciated the fraternal bond that had formed with O. Rapping came naturally to him, but to see someone so excited for him made him want to make that much more of an effort to get this off the ground. Hustling was still a reality, but if they could make the same money, if not more, in a safer line of work, then they owed it to themselves to see it through. Following his meeting with Puffy, O was ecstatic. Their dream was turning closer and closer into a reality. Nearly a year after his legendary street battle on Bedford and Quincy, Big was already on his way, and nearly every place he went, there was O hyping him up along the way.

"Watch, I'm telling you when my man get on, it's gonna be some shit," Big would later recall O preaching on the song "Miss U." "We ain't gonna have to sell this shit no more! I'm telling you!"

Big wasn't just rapping to get out of the drug game or to make a lot of money on his own. Those were certainly motivations. But he wanted to change the reality of everyone he held close to him, from his mother to people like D-Roc, Chico, Hubert, O, 50 Grand, and Mister Cee. Even at a young age, he understood the power of creating a meaningful legacy. It wasn't all about him, because what fun would success be without the ones who held him up during his darkest times?

Big was, at this point in his life, double-dipping in the streets and the studio. But it was in the studio where O pleaded with Big to spend his time. O still had to get money. He found himself in Brownsville a lot more. In spite of the separation, the two remained close and excited for what the future held. Unfortunately, O's life came to a heartbreaking, screeching end nearly month after Big's twentieth birthday. On June 18, 1992, two people were killed inside a Brooklyn bodega after a man walked in with a 9-millimeter semiautomatic shotgun and opened fire. The man with the gun was thirty-three-year-old Carl Bazemore, aka I-God. The victim? His nephew, Roland "O" Young. O was shot in the stomach by his uncle, and then Bazemore was shot in the back by a store employee. Both died on the scene. Detectives said at the time the double homicide was believed to be the result of a drug-related beef.

"Some things is about principle, and some things is about loyalty. When you a man of principle, and a man that stands for a code, and somebody violate those things, shit happens," said street lieutenant Frank Nitti. "And O's death wasn't really about money. It had a lot to do with principle."

O had taken a liking to Hubert Sam really quick. They'd known each other for a while, but once they started making moves together, their friendship, much like O's with Big, tightened.

"If I had to paint a picture, his sense of humor was kinda like 50 Cent's. He had a real sinister side, but he had a warm heart at the same time," Sam said. "He liked me because I was real quick. We kinda hit it off, and I rode out with him to Brownsville a few times."

Sam and O made those trips for a few weeks straight, getting money. It wasn't until Sam's girlfriend at the time sarcastically asked him why didn't have his own drugs and why he was so dependent on O to get them that he stopped going. The spot they'd travel to was the bodega where O was killed. It was a few weeks after he stopped making the Brownsville runs with O that he was murdered.

"Big didn't even really know that me and O was doing things," Sam continued. "I never really got to talk to Big about that. I don't know what would've happened if I would've stayed with him, but that day I might have helped—or I might've gotten killed. I don't even know. It's like this weird space for me when it comes to talking about O . . . You talk about 'spread love the Brooklyn way,' Big was really on that. It wasn't just words, but the streets is not all love. The streets actually is perverted love. You gotta find pockets of the real love in the streets. Just cause they show love, that's already telling you it's not just love. To be down is to show love. Every handshake ain't genuine if your hug ain't real. Big was moving a certain way, and he had a lot of love for O. His death definitely left Big in limbo for a while because he knew he was gonna take O with him."

It's impossible to overstate the role Roland "O" Young had on Christopher Wallace's life. He was a friend, a brother, a hustler, and perhaps his biggest champion. The streets had long told Big that death was the most unfortunate part of doing business in their chosen line of work. He wasn't immune to it, but he'd seen people in the streets come and go—and the business never stopped. Fiends kept buying crack as long as the dealers had it on them. But O's death was different. And everyone around Big understood that part of Big, spiritually at least, had died along with O. As he sat outside on their stoop the day O died, Voletta was returning home from work. Christopher told her about O's death. The pain from a friendship torn from him far too early sat on his wide shoulders. It scared him deeply, even more than getting arrested in North Carolina had. This was a guy he'd been in the trenches with and a guy who he was supposed to share in the fruits of his future success. With the flash of his uncle's gun, O was gone.

But O's memory never left Big. The best way Big felt he could pay homage to his fallen street soldier was by becoming the star O told all of Brooklyn he would be.

But even the best-intentioned plans often go up in flames. He wanted to rap, but things weren't progressing nearly as quickly as he had envisioned. Combs had stayed true to his word and gotten him placements on major remixes like Super Cat's dancehall anthem "Dolly My Baby," Heavy D's "A Buncha Niggas" and the remix to Mary J. Blige's monster hit "Real Love." The official contract paperwork was still in progress, though.

"His whole thing was like, 'I want cash. I don't want no check. I want cash,'" Mister Cee said. "He'd go in the studio and get five grand from this person, seven grand from this record. He'd do his verses and be out. In between all that, he was still hustling. He was selling drugs, but he was also hustling by being on those verses. He wasn't telling Puff what he was doing."

The truth is, it wasn't just the wait for the Uptown contracts that had Big stressed out. It wasn't the easiest conversation with his mother, and she all but had to pry it out of him, but he was expecting a baby. The conversation with his mother went about as expected. She couldn't believe the words "Jan's pregnant" even after she heard them. Despite her son being known as a jokester, she knew this was serious.

Voletta was so worried about her son making an honest living, and she still wasn't convinced this music dream of his with this Puffy guy was actually going to work. She was traditional, and in her heart, she wanted her son to be. The type of person who worked a 9-to-5, earned a consistent paycheck, worked his way to the middle class like she did, paid his taxes, and came home to his family. But her son was never that guy. He was never going to be that guy.

Voletta wasn't the only person he had to convince that he was ready for a kid. Most importantly, he had to be on the same page with Jan. The first year of his relationship with Jan was riddled with drama.

"There was always some woman lurking around the corner, or some woman's phone number that I was finding. When you look back, I can't count how many girls I approached," Jan recalled. "He always had the women. It wasn't about the money. That man had charisma out the wazoo. I don't care what anybody says about his looks, his weight. There's something about his personality that makes him able to pull almost any woman he wants. That didn't start after the money, it was that way in the beginning."

Big felt it from both sides. Jan was constantly on him about the life they were bringing into the world, and deservedly so. And his mother was pressing him about how exactly he planned to support said child, deservedly so.

"Is it yours? And are you getting married?" she said, interrogating her son.

"Yes. And no," he responded.

"Can you afford a baby emotionally?"

He perked up, beaming with pride. "Of course I can." But in a moment of ill-timed emotional levity, he just had to have one more statement to really set his mom off. "If I can't take care of it emotionally, you can."

In Voletta's eyes, her twenty-year-old son was still a child. So how the hell was he legitimately supposed to raise one? She continued to press about how he was going to support his unborn child.

"I got a deal," he shot back, annoyed he had to defend himself this much.

"Where is this deal? For weeks, you've talked about this deal. It's not cemented yet. You have to do something."

In his heart, Big knew his mother was right. He had a verbal agreement, but he knew nothing was official until it was in writing. Combs was in his ear telling him to be patient. That it would all work out in due time. But patience was a luxury he couldn't afford. So Big decided to make money the best way he knew how. Jan had understood him making those moves hustling when he was a boyfriend, but now they both had something to lose.

"I don't have to tell you everything I'm doing," he reasoned with Jan. "Just trust in me to know that I'm making sure she's gonna be okay. I'm doing everything I'm supposed to do."

Big's mentality was: get money by any means necessary. So he returned to the world he already knew. He went back to North Carolina to hustle.

"I'm like, yo, okay, it's all good. But let me just do what I gotta do, you know what I'm saying? And when you ready, just let me know," he later said, explaining his reasoning for continuing to hustle even after Combs informed him his deal was imminent.

Big returned to North Carolina, a risky move considering his 1991 arrest. This time, though, it wasn't about him just trying to make the most money he could for sheer capitalistic gain. Sure, there was that purpose, but ultimately what drove Big was his daughter. It was no longer about the thrill of being out of state hustling or keeping his pockets fat to satisfy his own materialistic urges. It was about understanding that hustling wasn't just about the next brick, the next sale, or the next payday. It was about surviving for the life he was responsible for bringing into the world. That and keeping Combs out of his business. Hustling was partially about helping fiends chase a high that they'd never truly grasp. But now it had become all the more sobering. He knew that by selling crack for the most part to people who looked like him that he was helping cripple his own community. But now, after all those years of hustling, he still wasn't as financially secure as he thought he would be when he was sixteen. Neither world had a happy ending, Big understood. Still, though, during his down time, Big would talk about this guy named Puffy and the weight he held at Uptown Records.

"Listen, man, if that's the case, when we need to clean the money up, let's do it through Big," said one of Big's street-pharmaceutical colleagues.

"Nah," Big responded.

"He was actually seeing money. We doin' our thing. We go to the club [and] it's like we're celebrities. He had a celebrity status in a different way," said Zauqael, Big's original hustling partner down in Raleigh.

Big and Zauqael, according to *Unbelievable*, were grossing north of $30,000 every two weeks. He could only keep that under wraps for so long. Combs discovered his new artist's whereabouts, but more importantly *what* he was doing, and he was enraged. He understood why Big made the decision he had, but even still, he was pissed because he knew the risks didn't outweigh the ultimate reward.

"I know why you down there, nigga. You know that is gonna only lead to jail or death. But you don't need to be down there. I just got a call from your lawyer. Deal's closed, man," exclaimed Combs. "You can come by the office Tuesday morning. I got a check waiting for you, ready to cash, right here."

The $125,000 Wallace was to receive was a lot of money, but it wasn't like he was set for life. There was studio time, and then there was paying for necessities like finding the dopest producers. But it was the single biggest check that he'd seen at that time. Mister Cee's lawyer negotiated the deal through his production company. But Big warned Puffy that this better be legit, because the money he was making in North Carolina was incredibly hard to turn away from. In the back of his mind, though, rattled a lingering thought that maybe he should pack up and head back north. The longer he stayed with crack in his pocket, the closer and closer he came to losing his freedom, or perhaps even his life.

"This is so crazy, and a lot of people don't even know this, but the day Puffy called me and told me the contracts would be there . . . I was going to leave Tuesday, but something told me, yo, just leave Monday," Big said later. "Don't you know Monday night, police ran up in the house we were staying in and locked them niggas up."

That was the sign. He had been so close to his life effectively being over and any semblance of a rap dream dying in a North Carolina jail cell. Big knew that he had to focus on music full-time, because there was no going back after this. It's what O had been telling him, and as far as he knew, that was O that got him out of that trap house just in time.

"He was one hundred and fifty percent focused on rap," D-Roc noted.

Yet it wasn't like the rap game didn't come with its own set of stresses.

09

TWO BUBBLING SUPERPOWERS

GROOVEY LEW JONES, BY HIS OWN ADMISSION, IS THE KING OF HIS CITY. That city is Mount Vernon, New York. And Mount Vernon is the city that first introduced him to one of his lifelong friends, Sean Combs.

"And when you come in that city," Lew said, with a slight chuckle in his voice but not enough to hide the fact he was very much serious, "you gotta get with the king if you wanna be part of the culture of what's going on."

Lew and Combs originally met at one of the most sacred spaces where Black males of all ages congregate: the barbershop. Fourteen at the time, they instantly clicked, having many of the same interests in dancing, music, and fashion. It's fashion where Groovey Lew would eventually make a name for himself, styling some of rap and R&B's biggest names, including Lauryn Hill, Nipsey Hussle, and Combs himself.

In late 1992, Lew was in Mount Vernon working in a candy store—which also served as a dope spot—when an excited Combs pulled up on him.

"Yo! I got something you gotta hear!" Combs said, unable to contain his jubilation. "It's my new artist."

This wasn't uncommon. Combs would bring new music to him all the time. He respected Lew's opinion, but there was a different excitement about Combs this time. He was already an animated individual, but he was nearly bouncing off the wall now. He put the cassette tape in and pressed play. The first voice Lew heard was Mary J. Blige on a remix of her hit single "Real Love." Combs, like he had with Jodeci, had helped take Mary from a relative unknown to a superstar with a bona fide classic debut album in *What's the 411?* Mary was sensual, yet street. Vulnerable, yet ferocious. And the sharpness of her voice made every lyric she sang sound believable whether she'd written it or not. So, yes, Lew knew the first voice quite well. Then, out of nowhere, there was a voice he had never heard before:

"Look up in the sky! / It's a bird, it's a plane!" the nasally, unfamiliar lyricist exclaimed. "Nope, it's Mary Jane / Ain't a damn thing changed!"

"Homie is hard!" Lew yelled back—like Combs, unsuccessful in keeping his true excitement at bay. "Who the hell is that?!"

"This kid named Biggie Smalls," Combs said. "He's my new artist."

Lew was happy for Combs. He was happy for all the success he had achieved in such a short time at Uptown. And he was really pleased to see that Combs hadn't allowed the City College tragedy to derail him. Lew didn't want his friend staying at the candy shop too long, mainly because of the environment. Lew and his crew in Mount Vernon would always look out for Combs, making sure he didn't get caught up in any nonsense when he had so much going for him as Andre Harrell's understudy. But that voice stuck in Lew's head.

"I met the voice," he says, "before I met the physical."

———

Big damn sure didn't think Matteo "Matty C" Capoluongo was a cop anymore. He not only had gotten him in *The Source,* but he had played a vital role in getting his music in front of Combs, which led to the deal with Uptown Records. But it wasn't just because of what Matty C did for him that the two became close friends. There were two things, specifically, that Matty and Big loved—weed and music. And if they could listen to music while smoking weed, even better.

Matty would see Big every day on his walk to the train. Even still in '92, he was a fixture on the block. And everyone wanted to be around him. Fellow hustler or not, dope fiend or straitlaced neighbor, it didn't matter.

"Crackheads maintain a respectful distance till they catch some attention. They always acknowledge Big," wrote dream hampton. "Invariably one of the kids reaches into a brown paper bag stuffed in the crevice of the wall and blesses the addict with a white top."

Anyone who lived in Brooklyn in the early nineties—dream, Matty C, and more—saw it. Big was the mayor, the governor, the president of his block, and no one really challenged that rule. No one really wanted to because he was such a natural representative, despite whatever illicit dealings were part of his life. Christopher Wallace was a first-generation Brooklynite. Everything he came to know about his borough and America as a whole came through his own experiences. He taught himself what "being Brooklyn" was all about, and in return—especially in later years and after his death—he became an eternally symbolic figure of what Brooklyn represents.

"Biggie was always out on the block," said Matty C. "During this era, there was definitely still a very open-market crack track. A lot of hands were involved really quickly if a fiend showed up. It was just part of the landscape at the time. Who exactly was doing what was like a flash. To say that's what was always going on is wrong. To say that was never going on is also wrong. Even standing right there, like who's doing what, that's not really obvious. I'm not saying he was this kingpin and not touching anything. That's not the fact, either. It was just a lot of shit going, and he lived right there . . . But Big was pretty much friendly to everybody."

He'd be there on his porch listening to music, but before long, Big would occasionally bring those sessions to Matty's brownstone nearby, off Grand Avenue. Matty lived with several roommates at the time, one of them a Stanford graduate named Drew Dixon who had moved to New York in 1992 because she "wanted to make rap records." Another was a young lady named Betsy Jones who had just graduated from Howard University. The Brooklyn Dixon and Jones moved to is almost unrecognizable compared to the one Dixon currently lives in.

"You couldn't get cabs to take you to Brooklyn," Dixon said. "If you were on the subway going to Brooklyn, all the white folks got off before you left the city. Maybe some white folks would stay on for the first stop. But that was it."

At the time, Dixon was answering phones at Empire Artists Management. DJ Premier was signed as a producer there, as was Gang Starr as a group. Jeru the Damaja, Group Home, and a mix of dancehall artists, too. Dixon was bringing home $199 a week—"I was on struggle!" she laughed—but somehow it was enough to fund the kickbacks in the backyard that would feature music, alcohol, and copious amounts of weed. They'd hear gunshots from time to time, but that was Brooklyn in the early nineties. It never stopped the fun, mainly because they were too drunk or high to really care.

Jones remembers getting to know Big through so many of her friends, like Matty C and dream hampton. And, through that, forming a musical bond with Big, over one of their mutual favorites, Too $hort. Whereas Dixon doesn't remember how or when she met the guy everyone around the neighborhood knew as Big. To his mother, he was still Christopher. But by then, and after the Unsigned Hype feature, most people called him Big, Big Chris, Fat Chris, or Biggie. It all depended on how a person met him. Big, as Dixon met him, would occasionally show up at their backyard parties, a lot of times with Chico Del Vec, and, she remembers, he'd always have weed. *Lots of weed*. And, in a moment's notice, rhymes, too.

"We had our own little blunt crew going," Jones laughed. "I remember Lil' Kim would smoke with us sometimes. She was so sweet. All those people were just really nice. It was never anything but nice and well for me."

"What I remember about Biggie is that he was always smiling, in my experience at least," Dixon said. "He was just fun to be around. A really, really funny guy, man."

Dixon and Big, who became friends, couldn't have come from more different households. Dixon's mom, Sharon Pratt Dixon, was the mayor of Washington, D.C., and her dad had been chair of the Council of the District of Columbia. She grew up knocking on doors, shaking hands, and smiling at people while asking for votes. People, like Alamo from Brand Nubian, had told her to stop smiling and nodding at everyone and expecting others to be as friendly as she was in New York.

Big, who would often see Dixon walking home by herself at night, told her the same.

"From now on, what I need you to do is walk down St. James," he instructed her. "I'll tell my people you're my people."

"So, I did," Dixon told me. "And I always felt safe."

Jones experienced that same hood protection, too.

"Biggie really was the king of our neighborhood. He looked out for me. He took care of me like family," Jones said. "Him, Damion, Chico. I'd just pass them every day on Fulton, and Big would be like walking me to a certain point and be like, 'Go straight home.' He made sure nobody bothered me."

A lot of the time Big spent at Matty's brownstone was spent upstairs. He and Matty would smoke weed and listen to music and beats for hours. Those marathon marijuana cyphers would represent some of the greatest times of Matty's life. They were pure. They were innocent. And they were his chance to see Big at his most relaxed and most inquisitive. Without fail, many times their high debates would center around who was rap's best wordsmith.

"Over time, I realized that he was luring me into that more and more," Matty laughed. "He wanted me to say him!"

The truth was, with Big, Matty C was watching one of the greatest MCs he had ever heard evolve right in front of him in real time.

Getting music well before it hit shelves was part of Matty's everyday life. On rare occasions, like Big's demo, a project came along that made him stop everything he was doing and pick his jaw up off the floor. That's exactly what happened in September 1992 when the debut album from Dr. Dre, *The Chronic*—soon to be released on the newly minted Death Row Records—landed on his desk.

"Big, nah, come to the crib *now*!" Matty demanded. "Trust me!"

Big was floored by what he heard. The cinematic production, the attention to every minute detail exploded through the speakers. "Stranded on Death Row" hit Big square in his chest. "Let Me Ride" sounded like the perfect rap song to experience in a car with the windows down, a fat-ass blunt in his hand, and a pretty young thing by his side. Months before the rest of the country would hear the genre-altering album, there was Biggie Smalls sitting in a Brooklyn brownstone high as hell both in awe and inspired.

Big had heard enough.

"Nigga, fuck that!" he said. He cleared his schedule and went home. "Yo, Matt. I'm out!"

"That was it. That was when he went to write *Ready to Die*," Matty C says. "*The Chronic* is when New York changed all the way up."

———

The block had long been hot in Los Angeles. If it wasn't crack cocaine pillaging its largely Black and brown communities, then it was gang violence. Or it was the gang violence that came with competing factions over the crack cocaine trade. Or if it wasn't that, it was the growing racial divisions between many of the city's different communities. And on top of everything, there was the Los Angeles Police Department exerting its will over it all.

N.W.A's colossal 1988 battle cry "Fuck tha Police" resonated across communities nationwide, but at its epicenter in Los Angeles, the tension between the Black community and LAPD was already on the brink of revolt. All it would take was a lit match to burn the city down. In this case, literally.

Thanks to a grainy videotape, Rodney King's savage beating by four LAPD officers in 1991 laid bare the brutality inflicted upon Black bodies by police. For white audiences, the assault on King brought forth a moment they couldn't ignore or simply cast off as an issue that Black people needed to figure out on their own. Black people knew that violence by law enforcement on Black men, women, boys, and girls wasn't a myth—it was an American tradition.

And then, thirteen days after King's beating, fifteen-year-old Latasha Harlins was killed in South Los Angeles, shot in the back of the head by a Korean grocery store owner named Soon Ja Du. The two had been in an argument at Du's Empire Liquor Market over a bottle of orange juice that cost $1.79. The details of the final moments of her life are gut-wrenching. Harlins, witnesses said, stuck the bottle partly into her backpack but walked to the store counter, presumably to pay. Captured by the store's security footage, Du grabbed Harlins's sweater, prompting Harlins to punch Du multiple times. Harlins avoided a stool being thrown at her, placed the juice on the counter, and started to walk away. Du grabbed her pistol, and in the blink of an eye, Harlins's body collapsed to the ground. She died instantly.

The two incidents exposed two very ugly truths. One, that police brutality wasn't an allegory or some wild exaggeration but rather a terrifying reality for a large segment of the population, who understood it as a threat to their humanity. The second was that there was a very real disconnect between Black and Korean American communities. Fairly or unfairly, there was a belief that Koreans would place businesses in Black neighborhoods but never truly care about the clientele whose money they would willingly accept for things like alcohol or unhealthy food. The Black dollar was powerful, but the Black body was expendable—or so the logic went. This understanding was further cemented when, following a conviction for voluntary manslaughter, Soon Ja Du was sentenced on November 16, 1991.

Superior Court Judge Joyce A. Karlin said in her statement that "it is not a time for revenge," and that embarking on a path of healing was the proper course. That may have sounded great in a prepared statement, but for the Black community, it was never about revenge. It was about justice, and how could they feel there was justice when it was their blood on the pavement, their bodies being laid into the ground, with so few consequences? Judge Karlin, citing Du's lack of a criminal record, then handed down a sentence of time served, four hundred hours of community service, a $500 fine, five years of probation, and payment of Harlins's funeral expenses. That was the penalty for shooting a teenage Black girl in the back of the head.

"Thank you, God!" Du exclaimed while walking out of the courtroom, according to the *Los Angeles Times*.

She claimed she had killed Harlins out of fear and that her store had been terrorized by gangs. Her reasoning did little to quell the tension. If anything, it only exacerbated the situation. The courtroom was heavily guarded, but in the hallways, above the sobs of Harlins's family and friends, lived the shouts of "Murderer!" and the even more ominous "We'll take this to the streets!"

State senator Diane Watson, a Democrat from Los Angeles, had an even more ominous premonition: "This might be the bomb that explodes," Watson said.

It didn't go off, not right away. But then, a little over six months after the unacceptable sentencing of Soon Ja Du, on April 29, 1992, four LAPD officers were acquitted in the beating of Rodney King. Enough was enough. The sharp, familiar pain of the injustice over Latasha Harlins was still too raw for the Black community. Rodney King getting beat within an inch of his life by those sworn "to protect and to serve" and them getting away with it was all too much. Knowing that basic human rights afforded to white communities again and again would be denied to the Black community was too much. The bomb exploded, and what happened over the next six days tattooed itself in American history. It's easy to assume it was just because of the King verdict, but it was about so much more. That was just the match.

Anyone familiar with the arc of American history couldn't be surprised by what happened in Los Angeles over six days, from April 29 to May 4. More than a thousand buildings were attacked or completely destroyed, with estimates north of $1 billion in damages. Sixty-three people lost their lives, more than two thousand were injured, and nearly ten thousand state National Guard troops descended upon the city. The entire country watched in horror on television as L.A. quite literally burned because Black people had once again grown tired of America failing to live up to its most basic promises of freedom and justice for all. Everyone, especially in Black America, had an opinion about the riots. Including Michael Jordan's teammate Craig Hodges, who blasted his teammate for not having an opinion.

"When they came to Michael after the L.A. deal went down and asked him what he thought, his reply was that he wasn't really up on what was going on," Hodges said as the team was in the midst of the second consecutive title run. "I can understand that, but at the same time, that's a bailout situation because you are bailing out when some heat is coming on you. We can't bail anymore."

The world's greatest basketball player may not have been paying attention—or at least didn't want to speak up because of a fear of what it might cost him. But the world's most dangerous rap label was watching, and wasn't shy about letting their voices be heard.

———

Marion Hugh "Suge" Knight Jr. was born on April 19, 1966—after the assassination of Malcolm X and the Watts Riots, but before the formation of the Black Panthers, Muhammad Ali's boxing exile, and the assassination of Martin Luther King Jr. At his peak, Knight would represent the essence of Black independence in an industry that historically pillaged Black talent but never allowed it to assume true ownership.

Knight was the product of many things in Compton. Blessed as he was, he had two adoring parents. His direct home life may have been loving, but what wasn't loving were the rising tensions in the city brought on by an elixir of gang violence, crack cocaine, and police brutality. Knight grew up around all this drama, but his original terror dome was the defensive line. It's where he starred for four years at Lynwood High School, twenty minutes from Compton, California's much-loved Tam's Burgers. Football, and to a lesser extent track and field, was a buffer. That is, if being secure was ever the goal.

In 1981, Harvey Hyde became the head football coach at the University of Nevada, Las Vegas. At the time, the UNLV Rebels were new to Division 1 sports. The school had gained national prominence via basketball coach Jerry Tarkanian's "Runnin' Rebels," and now it was up to Hyde to make UNLV a two-sport school. Hyde met Knight—nicknamed "Sugar Bear" or "Suge"—on a recruiting trip to Los Angeles County's El Camino Junior College, where Knight starred. Hyde, impressed by Knight's prowess, brought him to the city in the desert, and as a junior, starting at nose guard and defensive tackle, he immediately became one of the Rebels' best defensive players. In 1985, Knight was voted the program's Rookie of the Year, named defensive captain, and won first-team all-conference honors. In a city full of sins, Knight was UNLV's biggest blessing.

"Suge played his butt off," Hyde told me for a story years ago on Knight's pigskin days. Hyde coached future NFL stars Ickey Woods, Randall Cunningham, and Terrell Davis, and said that "[Knight] was a 'yes sir, no sir' guy . . . the type of player any college football coach would love to have on his team." Knight, a part-time bouncer at Vegas's then-hot Cotton Club, didn't register on Hyde's disciplinary radar. "He never, ever gave me a problem in any way."

Knight may have been yes-sir-no-sir, but he had a side-hustle: selling books. Jon Wolfson, who in the early 2000s was a publicist for Death Row Records and is now the manager of Hall & Oates, recalled a conversation he had with Knight about his UNLV days. "He'd say something like, 'Then I'd play the dumb athlete role and say, 'Oh, Coach, I lost my books.'" The staff never second-guessed Knight, said Wolfson. "They'd give him brand-new books, and he'd sell them to make some extra cash."

Knight's demeanor became more ominous and reclusive during his senior campaign in 1986. Visitors from his hometown of Compton were frequently sighted. Knight moved into an apartment by himself and was seen in several late-model sedans. His reputation evolved from being a friendly jokester to the biggest drug dealer on campus.

According to teammates, Knight dropped out of UNLV prior to graduation. But before turning to hip-hop to plant the seeds of a future empire, Knight had one last gridiron itch to scratch: the National Football League.

NFL players went on strike in 1987 after Week 3, after the players' union and league failed to come to a new collective bargaining agreement. The players had a list of demands, including the right to free agency, the elimination of artificial turf, and better pension benefits as well as severance packages. Player movement in the 1980s wasn't like it is today, with hundreds of players changing teams annually. "This was before free agency," said veteran *Los Angeles Times* sports reporter Chris Dufresne. "[NFL players] really were indentured servants. They couldn't go anywhere!" Players were, for lack of a better phrase, property—bound to teams for life.

Teams *could* sign free agents, but the cost was steep. The Rozelle Rule, named after storied league head honcho Pete Rozelle, stated that the NFL commissioner could reward the player's original team with draft picks, often first-round selections, or players. NFL salaries did rise in the eighties, primarily because of the brief existence of the United States Football League and its willingness to lure NFL players with large contracts. But by 1985, the USFL was defunct, destroyed by New Jersey Generals owner Donald Trump.

In 1987, without its actual players to suit up, the NFL brought in replacement players, and one of the "scabs" was Suge Knight. His career didn't last long, but Knight did suit up in the NFL, playing in two games. His true calling would present itself soon.

In October, as the regular NFL players reported back to work, Knight's rap sheet ballooned, and his boogeyman persona began to take shape. Knight was charged with domestic violence in Los Angeles after grabbing his future ex-wife Sharitha Golden by the hair and chopping her ponytail off in the driveway of her mother's home. That Halloween, he was arrested in Vegas for shooting a man in the wrist and in the leg, and stealing his Nissan Maxima. With felony charges looming, Knight skated away from any serious penalty in part because of a contrite courtroom appearance and his history in the city as a famed football player. The felonies were reduced to misdemeanors: a $1,000 fine and three years' probation. "I shot him with his own gun," Knight would later say. Three years later, in Vegas once again, he pleaded guilty to felony assault with a deadly weapon after pistol-whipping a man with a loaded gun and breaking his jaw. Knight again evaded serious penalty.

Knight by then was immersing himself in the music industry, serving as a bodyguard for superstars such as Bobby Brown. He eventually maneuvered his way into the circles of rappers like Tracy Curry, aka the D.O.C., and Dr. Dre, formerly of the electro-rap group World Class Wreckin' Cru of the early eighties. The latter was the superproducer behind the country's most popular and most reviled rap group N.W.A, which featured members Dre, Ice Cube, MC Ren, DJ Yella (also formerly of Cru), and the charismatically gangsta Eazy-E. When Knight was back in L.A. by 1987, the biggest song on the streets was Eazy's seminal hit "Boyz-n-the-Hood." The gangsta rap bellwether was produced by Dre and established Eazy, a Compton Crip, as a bona fide star, and for all intents and purposes, put Compton as a force to be reckoned with on the hip-hop map. Whatever Eazy put his name on had instant credibility, and that fact rang true for N.W.A and the label he helped start alongside businessman Jerry Heller. Every facet about the group was countercultural, from its name—Niggaz Wit Attitudes—to its graphic "street knowledge," as Dre dubbed it on the landmark 1988 single "Straight Outta Compton." The album of the same title, which took only six weeks and $8,000 to make, became a call to action that opened the entire country's eyes to what Black life in the ghetto was like growing up in South L.A. Rap was undoubtedly birthed in New York under the belief that it was music both to party to and to address societal concerns through. But now music was coming out of Compton that was doing both—at the same time. *Straight Outta Compton*'s most profound generational heirloom was its articulation of police brutality in a way that made America clutch its own pearls. N.W.A's music was banned from MTV, and the FBI wrote a letter to the group demanding they stop performing "Fuck tha Police." N.W.A was labeled as the first gangsta rap group, a subgenre of hip-hop that focused heavily on violent lyrics and violent themes to get its point across. To them, though, it wasn't a pose. They weren't playing at being gangstas; they were peeling the curtains back to show the reality of Black communities.

"We ain't talking about all police, man, but there's bad police out there. A lot of people pretend that police brutality and stuff like that don't happen in their city," Ice Cube said in a 1989 interview. "They're saying that we're infesting their kids to believe that cops are bad. We just tell the truth, and it goes for, you know, damn near every city."

There was so much chaos in the group's formation and its content that it was not surprising the original N.W.A ended seemingly as quickly as it came together. Ice Cube left the group to go solo after realizing he had no publishing or royalties in his name. The D.O.C., who had appeared on "Parental Discretion Iz Advised," filled in for Cube. With D.O.C. on the scene more and more, and his hit single "It's Funky Enough" in constant rotation, his bodyguard worked into the fold and learned more about the music industry firsthand. Knight overheard conversations and saw how deals were finalized. And, for the most part, he didn't like what he saw. Through the D.O.C., Knight's bridge from bodyguard to businessman was taking shape. D.O.C. was a rising star, and his debut album, *No One Can Do It Better,* still stands as one of rap's most aptly titled projects. He had a world of potential in front of him with a combination of showmanship and lyricism that few artists can not just understand but implement. All of which made the horrific car crash that crushed D.O.C.'s larynx on August 20, 1989, all the more tragic. Even worse, his medical expenses were skyrocketing, and he didn't have the money to pay them. Knight was confused. Here was a member of one of the hottest rap groups in the country, and his debut solo album was going gold, so how could he not be financially secure? The former defensive lineman went on the offensive and got a copy of D.O.C.'s contract. What he found was brutal.

"If they fuckin' with mine," D.O.C. warned, "you know they fuckin' with Dre, too."

So Knight did. He knew Dre was growing more and more annoyed with his contract situation at Ruthless Records. Per D.O.C.'s suggestion, he read through Dre's paperwork. Then Knight saw an opportunity. Knight managed to get Dre out of his Ruthless contract, but it's *how* he allegedly did it that sent shockwaves throughout the industry. Knight and several cohorts either beat Eazy-E with metal pipes or threatened to do so, and the encounter between Knight and Eazy left three undeniable truths. One, Dre was finally a free man. (Eazy-E would later file a multimillion-dollar lawsuit against a litany of parties, Dre and Knight included, for multiple instances of money laundering, extortion, and racketeering.) Two, Dre's departure officially closed the door on N.W.A, which had the number one album in the country with 1991's *Efil4zaggin*, the group's dark, more sexually explicit, and less lyrical album sans Ice Cube. And three, Suge Knight's reputation as an enforcer was no longer a dark secret.

"Suge is cool. He's just temperamental," an unnamed friend of Knight's was quoted as saying in 2003's *Unbelievable*. "He's the type of brother who can't take no. He just feel like he gotta always have that last word. Don't get me wrong—Suge'll smack the shit out of you. I done seen niggas get the shit beat out of them. Believe me. I seen a hallway of niggas at the Palladium get cleared out by that nigga. I done see him make two niggas slap each other. He ain't no coward. I'll tell you that. That nigga'll demonstrate in a second."

Knight was always most loyal to himself, but if he saw his friends being taken advantage of—or people he could stand to be in lucrative business with—he had no problem going directly to the source. More times than not, too, he got something out of the deal. Case in point: another client he was managing, and another high-profile artist he paid a visit to. Mario "Chocolate" Johnson, also from Dallas, was a producer who had worked on some songs for a rapper named Robert Van Winkle, better known as Vanilla Ice, including 1990's "Ice, Ice, Baby," the first rap song to top the *Billboard* Hot 100.

"They paid me $1,500 for the two songs that I was supposed to do," Chocolate explained. "And when I got there I ended up doing five more songs. I did ["Ice, Ice, Baby"] for free . . . Next thing you know, a year later, the song blew up. That's when I called Suge and told him, 'Look, man, that's a song I did.'"

If Chocolate wasn't getting paid, that meant Knight wasn't getting paid. And Knight didn't take too kindly to not getting paid. So he did what he always did—he took matters into his own hands. One night, in a Beverly Hills hotel, Knight and six other men showed up uninvited at Van Winkle's room and took the white rapper out on to the balcony, fifteen stories off the ground, to have a little talk.

"I needed to wear a diaper on that day," Van Winkle later said. "I was very scared."

Van Winkle claimed that Chocolate didn't write the song, but he signed over points of the song to Chocolate and Knight anyway. Those points were worth anywhere between three and four million dollars. With Dre released from Ruthless and Knight with some money in his pocket, the world was their oyster. Both wanted their next move to remain loyal to their Compton soil. Equally as important, both had seen the ugly side of the music business in terms of ownership and being paid their actual worth. They wanted it all.

"First thing to do was to establish an organization, not just no record label," Knight told *VIBE* for a 1996 cover story. "I knew the difference between having a record label and having a production company and a logo. First goal was to own our masters. Without your master tapes you ain't got shit, period."

Dre and Knight had seen the ugliest sides of the business and how the talent, largely Black talent, was treated. That wasn't going to be the case with them, or at least, that was their original intent. If they were going to take over the music industry, it wasn't going to be with someone else calling the shots. They wanted the money, the power, and respect to all trace back to them.

———

There was already a groundswell of talent waiting in the wings. Dre's half brother was Warren G, and he was already rocking with two artists named Snoop Doggy Dogg and Nate Dogg out of Long Beach. And Dre was the mastermind, the conductor, and the quarterback. With Dre's musical vision and Knight's business savvy and muscle, they had all the makings for a ferocious Black powerhouse. The first offering came in the form of "Deep Cover," from the soundtrack of the 1992 crime drama of the same name starring Laurence Fishburne and Jeff Goldblum. This was Dre and Snoop's first collaboration, and as fate would have it, the L.A. Riots erupted just weeks after the single was officially released. Snoop's "'cause it's 1-8-7 on an undercover cop" hook suddenly carried more dark power, and the single had the streets on fire. All eyes were on Dre.

A quarter million dollars. That's what it would take for Dre to craft whatever first project would come of this partnership between him and Knight. They had money, but they also needed a third party to bring the idea in complete formation. Knight could've fronted the money himself with the funds he strong-armed from Vanilla Ice, but a lot of that money was tied up in the courts. Roughly around this time, the attorney David Kenner began showing up at Dre's recording sessions. He had an idea. There was a potential third party as long as Dre and Knight were willing to hear him out. Kenner represented accused high-level drug dealers, and one of them was a Bounty Hunter Blood with mutual associates with Knight named Michael "Harry O" Harris.

The meeting had to take place at the Metropolitan Detention Center in downtown Los Angeles because Harris was locked up. He had amassed much of his wealth in the eighties through the drug game. But at the time he and Knight met, Harris was in the early stages of a lengthy sentence for attempted murder and drug trafficking. Harris, however, was no stranger to the entertainment industry. In 1988, he coproduced a Broadway show called *Checkmates*, in which a then-unknown Denzel Washington made his debut. Whatever was said during the meeting met the satisfaction of both parties. Harris had money to invest, said to be $1.5 million, and he believed in Knight's vision and Dr. Dre's promise as a solo artist. Godfather Entertainment, which ultimately became known as Death Row Records, was born.

"We called it Death Row 'cause most everybody had been involved with the law," Knight later explained. He wasn't lying. His rap sheet record was already long, and Dre's was trending that way, too. Though Dre would have multiple run-ins with the law in the coming years, the worst up to that point was the horrific assault on journalist Dee Barnes in 1991. Barnes, who hosted the show *Pump It Up!*, which aired on Fox, conducted an interview with Ice Cube following his split from N.W.A in the fall of 1990. It was Barnes's intention to try to get Cube and his former groupmates on the show at the same time to iron out their differences. That never happened, and Dre, Eazy-E, and the rest of N.W.A felt Barnes and the show were trying to instigate the situation. When Dre and Barnes found themselves at the same industry party in January 1991, tensions boiled over quickly. The incident remains one of music's most infamous examples of domestic violence, with Dre telling *Rolling Stone* he just "threw her through a door." Yet it didn't do much, if anything, to derail Dre's career in real time. He pleaded no contest in August 1991 to misdemeanor battery charges and later settled out of court. Decades later, a deeply remorseful Dre would call the assault a lifetime scar on who he was as a man. But in the moment, the thugged-out image Death Row would come to represent was all part of its business model.

Death Row was a risky investment by nearly every metric. They lived what they rapped, which gave them instant credibility in the world of hip-hop but also presented multiple red flags from corporations wary of doing business with such an unpredictable startup. Dre graced the November 1991 cover of *The Source* in poetic-yet-graphic fashion. There he was, in a white Death Row hat, boldly letting the world know the days of Ruthless were long in the rearview. He also held a revolver to his head, with the caption reading, "N.W.A's Notorious Producer Puts His Head Out." No one knew what the future held for Death Row Records, but one thing was for damn sure. They weren't going to operate by anyone's rules but their own.

Jimmy Iovine and Interscope Records agreed to a $10 million label deal that gave Knight and Dre exactly what they wanted: complete control. Over the artists signed, their masters, *everything*. That's because Iovine had, like a young Christopher Wallace some three thousand miles east in Brooklyn, heard what the entire country would soon hear in Dr. Dre's debut album, *The Chronic*.

Everything proved true. The almost-instant return on investment with the massive success of the album after its December 1992 release. And the drama. A whole lot of drama.

10

FUN TIMES AND BIG PROBLEMS

THE WORK SEAN "PUFFY" COMBS HAD PUT INTO JODECI DIDN'T
GO UNNOTICED. Not only were they one of the hottest acts in music, but
the group was one of the big winners at the 1992 *Billboard* Music Awards,
taking home four awards, including Best R&B Album for *Forever My Lady*.
It was a landmark moment for Combs and Uptown, but what happened a
week later put every person in the industry on high alert: Dr. Dre and Death
Row Records released *The Chronic*.

Influenced by a myriad of Black cultural flashpoints, like Parliament-
Funkadelic, Blaxploitation, and the gangsta rap Dre helped launch, *The
Chronic* had no sonic comparison. Records like the hypnotic single with
Snoop Dogg "Nuthin' But a 'G' Thang" were instantaneous hip-hop clas-
sics. "Let Me Ride" would eventually earn Dre his first Grammy. "Bitches
Ain't Shit" was misogynistic to the core, but it was known to get any party
jumping off its infectious first ten seconds alone. Songs like "Lil' Ghetto
Boy" and "The Day the Niggaz Took Over" were direct responses to the
L.A. riots. And as a result of the album, Snoop Dogg's upcoming solo debut
almost instantly became the most anticipated project since, well, *The
Chronic*. Death Row Records didn't just hit the ground running. They were
in an all-out sprint.

Nearly three thousand miles east in Brooklyn, Big was paying attention to Death Row's movement. He loved the energy, and to be honest, he loved the style of West Coast music as a whole. He loved Too $hort's *Freaky Tales* for its X-rated musings. And there was another guy who lived in California named Tupac Shakur whose music was so violent, so political, and yet so transparently soulful that it drew him in almost immediately. Big loved that graphic music, whether it be sexual or depictions of life in the street.

By the start of 1993, the focus of hip-hop was no longer in New York. It was still the mecca, and that year saw the release of Wu-Tang Clan's *Enter the Wu-Tang (36 Chambers)* and A Tribe Called Quest's *Midnight Marauders*, but it was clear now that great rap could come from any multitude of locations. Rap grew from the Black experience, and the Black experience took place all across the country.

Big was inspired. By the spring of 1993, he'd been on a remix with Mary J. Blige that had become a hood staple from house parties to summertime cookouts and even on records like "A Buncha Niggas" with Heavy D & The Boyz. The overweight tandem of D and Big again hooked up on "Jam Session" alongside the rapper Troo-Rula on *NBA Jam Session* VHS. His appearance on the remix to Super Cat's dancehall anthem "Dolly My Baby" was the standout and a hit on the New York rap scene, where the Caribbean influence on music dated back decades. So, yes, the Notorious B.I.G. was on the scene. He wasn't as hot as Snoop Dogg at the top of 1993, but his name was bubbling. Big was in the process of recording his debut on Uptown, a distinct departure from what had traditionally been the label's sound. Harrell was all about the feel-good, sexy vibes that had become the soundtrack for young Black America. In his own way, Big was attempting to do the same. Just the young Black America he knew, the one that revolved around selling crack across state lines, surviving beatdowns from the cops, and what it looked like to be an unwilling soldier in the country's war on drugs—while also having an obscene amount of sex and smoking an even more obscene amount of weed. Big's songs sounded as if they were recorded on a Brooklyn street corner or in a Raleigh trap house, in part because that's where they were born.

The record that put Big on the map, and effectively changed his life, was a solo cut titled "Party and Bullshit" produced by Brooklyn maestro Easy Mo Bee circa 1993. Mo Bee lived on Clinton Avenue between Gates and Greene

Avenues, not too far from Big's homebase of Fulton and St. James. His manager wanted him to meet with Andre Harrell and Combs for a new artist they were working with named Biggie Smalls. Mo Bee came to learn what many already knew about Big. He was very accessible in Brooklyn. On any given day, he could be standing outside with his crew hustling. Mo Bee pulled up on him one day, saying he wanted him to listen to a beat he had for him.

On their 1970 cut "When the Revolution Comes," the Last Poets, one of the original architects of hip-hop, had said that until the revolution comes, "niggas will party and bullshit." Mo Bee sampled the line and Big instantly loved it. But his vision wasn't exactly the same as the Poets. He was talking about fighting at parties, carrying guns, and casual sex on a whim.

"When we rapped, it was all about raising consciousness and using language to challenge people," one of the group's founders, Abiodun "Dun" Oyewole, would say years later. "When I wrote [about] 'party and bullshit,' it was to make people get off their ass. But now 'party and bullshit' was used by Biggie, used by Busta Rhymes, but in a nonconscious way. That's difficult for us to deal with." (Oyewole later sued Biggie's estate for copyright infringement; after several years, a New York federal judge ruled that the use of the words did not constitute infringement.)

Big wasn't trying to start the revolution, but "Party and Bullshit" would revolutionize his career. And though Big didn't preach like the Poets did, he was about the betterment of his people, specifically a core group. Toward the end of the song, Combs strategically introduced two new terms to the public lexicon: Bad Boy and Junior M.A.F.I.A. The former, of course, was the label he was hoping to form. The latter being the crew Big always had around him. They hustled together, but Big felt a sense of kinship and responsibility to take care of them, too. There were so many members of the crew that it made it impossible to shout everyone out on every song. Big was committed to making this rap mission shake, but he was just as committed to bringing his crew along with him.

Junior M.A.F.I.A. (short for "Masters at Finding Intelligent Attitudes") was more like family than friends. Some lived around the corner from Big, others up the street, and they saw each other everyday. Chico Del Vec, a member of the M.A.F.I.A., was around the same age as Big, whereas others, like Lil' Cease, Lil' Kim, Nino Brown, and more, were a few years younger.

"We grew up watching *Scarface*, watching *Hell Up in Harlem*, watching the mobster movies with Al Capone, Al Pacino. So we was more trying to paint that type of picture and put a character to every member: Bugsy, Capone, Nino, Klepto, Lil' Cease, Lil' Kim, and La Bella Mafia," Chico explained. "He wanted to paint that picture of that clique—young, but still family orientated like the mob. It was the mafia, but a lot of them was young so it was Junior Mafia."

"Party and Bullshit" was the standout track from the 1993 Ed Lover and Dr. Dre–led film *Who's the Man*. Neither the movie nor its accompanying soundtrack was a huge success—though the movie did receive a favorable review from Roger Ebert—but it was Big's song that garnered the most juice. It sounded new, fresh, and vibrant. Brooklyn was buzzing. This was one of their own with a bona fide neighborhood smash.

"We would be sitting on the corner and watch cars drive by playing 'Party and Bullshit' and I remember saying, 'Something ain't right. We done seen about four different cars come through playing the music and we still on this corner,'" said D-Roc. "We was blowing up and learning at the same time."

The single maintained the momentum that had started with 50 Grand's original demo tape. Big was invigorated to be in a position that just a few years earlier didn't seem feasible. He was a rapper. He was making legal money. And he was living out a dream.

"We all lost our minds when we heard 'Party and Bullshit.' He was just very happy to be in the game. We were all excited to be in the middle of this thing," said Drew Dixon. "Just happy to be in the game."

Normally, when he was taking trips out of town to go down south it was to sell crack. Now he was taking trips out of town to get paid to rap. Even as the notoriety around his name began to rise and people in other cities began to recognize the name the Notorious B.I.G. or Biggie Smalls, Christopher Wallace was still Christopher Wallace. Like that one time in 1993 when he, DJ Premier, and Jeru the Damaja had a show in Virginia.

"We were real hungry, and Big was sitting in his hotel with no clothes and a bucket of chicken, clipping his toenails," said Premier. "Jeru said, 'You need to stop eating that.'"

"My name is Biggie," he responded. "*Not* Rakim."

"Party and Bullshit" was, by every metric, a success for Big. Now Combs wanted the Uptown/Bad Boy crew to go out to the West Coast, do some promotion, and rock a few shows. In just a year's time, he'd gone from selling crack to selling actual records. The West Coast was on fire in 1993, so the logic was to soak up that energy and try to create a fan base out west.

Prior to making the trip, Los Angeles might as well have been a fantasy land to Big. It was the home of the chronic and *The Chronic*, two major influences in his life. It was the city that birthed one of his favorite rap songs in Spice 1's "Trigga Gots No Heart." But now he was here. The Fat Burger and Roscoe's Chicken and Waffles hit the spot. The Mustang 5.0 convertibles they were afforded for the trip gave them the proper rides they needed to stunt all through a town that was known for stunting. Almost immediately, he fell in love with the women, the weed, and the weather. Los Angeles's speed appeared to mesh well with the laid-back Biggie (though legally he couldn't call himself that, since there was a white rapper from California who went by Biggy Smallz).

Combs was happy with his success with Jodeci and Mary J. Blige. And the City College tragedy appeared to be in the rearview, at least in terms of headlines. With Big, he had just the ghetto wordsmith he needed to launch Uptown's next star. They were in town promoting a show at Prince's Glam Slam West, a new club the artist had opened in January 1993. It was there that Suge Knight allegedly beat a security guard so badly that he needed multiple surgeries to fix his spleen. For Big, though, the Glam Slam was his chance to win over fans nearly three thousand miles from Brooklyn.

"I just think that everybody out here think that all East Coast rappers is like Tim Dog, and we all about dissing. It ain't about all that," Big said, referencing the Bronx-born rapper who released the 1991 diss record "Fuck Compton," aimed at N.W.A. "We got flavor just like they got flavor," he said. "We need to get together."

The show at Glam Slam was also a first for Lil' Cease. Just as they were about to go onstage, Big had a request.

"Here, take this mic," Big ordered.

"What's up?" Cease responded, genuinely surprised.

"Just hold me down." Big didn't want him to say the whole verse, but just to feel the crowd and rock out.

"I was scared, but they was loving Big so much that they lovin' me too," Cease said. "That's how Biggie made me feel."

———

Outside Big's inner circle and the borough of Brooklyn, there wasn't a person in America who loved "Party and Bullshit" more than Tupac Shakur. The legendary filmmaker John Singleton once recalled Shakur playing the song on a loop for hours while they sat in a limo.

"You heard this shit yet?" Shakur asked Singleton. They were working on the director's new film *Poetic Justice*, starring Shakur and pop superstar Janet Jackson.

By the spring of 1993, Shakur was a growing star nationally, but already beloved in hoods across America. His music represented his background. The son of the Black revolutionary in Afeni Shakur, Tupac Shakur was born raging against the system from the moment he entered the world. Born in New York, raised in Baltimore, and spending his early adult years in the Bay Area, Tupac's crash course to being Black in America was spent on the front lines, and his music represented such. Topics like drug abuse, police brutality, and the rage of Black violence in Black communities were constant themes.

Singleton heard all the critiques about Shakur prior to bringing him on board—that he was a live wire, was unpredictable, and courted drama on the regular. That his role of the sadistic Bishop in the 1992 film *Juice* wasn't Tupac acting but playing himself. But for Singleton, sure, they had their lively debates on what should happen on-screen, but the two became close. It was during the filming of *Justice* that Shakur found some down time to get THUG LIFE tattooed across his abdomen. And one of the greatest memories Singleton gained from working with the controversial rapper came when they traveled to the Black college spring break congregation in Atlanta known as Freaknik. They partied all weekend, chasing women, spreading the gospel of the film, and enjoying the fruits of their success. In their rented limo, Shakur made sure the soundtrack for the debauchery was but one record: "Party and Bullshit."

148

Big had long been a fan of Shakur. He had movies and music. The ladies loved him, and the "thug niggas" Shakur coveted embraced his graphic and explicit manner of street poetry, too. 'Pac kept his ear to the streets, so he always knew of talented artists on the rise. Especially ones who paid attention to life in the ghetto like himself. When 'Pac heard that Big, the architect behind his current favorite song, was in town, he headed directly to the Sheraton Hotel in Studio City. By the time Big, Groovey Lew, and company pulled back up at the hotel, there was Tupac sitting in his green Jeep Cherokee smiling from ear to ear.

It was almost as if from the moment they saw each other in person that first time, the two Gemini twins, 'Pac born in June 1971 and Big eleven months later, became instant friends. As the two chatted, Greg Nice from Nice & Smooth came downstairs.

"Yo, what else you gotta do today?" Shakur asked Big.

The truth was that they had more to do in terms of promotional runs and marketing obligations, but if an artist like Shakur asked a question like this, he was doing so with a purpose. It wasn't every day an opportunity came knocking.

"Big looks at me, and I knew at that point, cancel anything else we had scheduled," the Uptown intern Dan Smalls told *The Fader* in 2011. "It was gonna be a wrap."

Tupac had come to scoop Big and show him around town, but Big was fiercely loyal. Smalls and Lew were his people, and they were all enjoying the same sights at the same time.

"Yo, B.I., can I roll?" asked Lew, who was now working as Big's personal stylist.

"C'mon." Big gestured.

'Pac was driving while Big sat in the passenger seat passing blunts back and forth.

"Yo, we in L.A. for the first time and 'Pac is our tour guide," Lew reflected nearly thirty years later. "That was the best shit ever."

Not too long after arriving at Shakur's house in the Valley did the rapper/actor/son of a Black Panther come out with a massive freezer bag full of weed. Big could barely contain his excitement. An assembly line of blunt rollers immediately went into action. 'Pac was rolling blunt after blunt, as were Big, Groovey Lew, and Greg Nice. Lew was so high that he asked Tupac if he could make some peanut butter and jelly sandwiches, to which Shakur, equally as high, agreed. Then, seemingly out of nowhere in an act preordained by the rap gods, 'Pac and Big broke out into a cypher.

"Big was new, so 'Pac was getting the best out of him. 'Pac is rhyming, rhyming, and rhyming. And he's telling Big show me what you got," Lew recalled.

"C'mon, nigga!" 'Pac said, putting a battery in his new friend's back even more. "Spit that shit!"

"'Pac would spit for fifteen minutes. Then Big would spit for fifteen minutes," Lew said. "'Pac would spit ten. Big would spit ten. Rhyme for rhyme. Verse for verse. Song for song. The most incredible day in my music- and fashion-industry life."

None of this marathon freestyle session was ever recorded. But following the cypher, 'Pac once again retreated out of sight, only to return moments later with a gigantic green army bag, the contents of which he proceeded to dump on the floor. It was a show-and-tell type of moment. More than twenty-five guns hit the floor, ranging from handguns to TEC-9s.

"So now, here we are, in this backyard running around with guns, just playing," Smalls said. "Luckily, they were all unloaded."

It was a moment of pure innocence even if actual arms were involved. Big and 'Pac ran around the backyard all but playing cops and robbers like grown little kids. From the moment they first met, there was an intense brotherly love between 'Pac and Big that lit up a room. They laughed, they cracked jokes, and they enjoyed each other's company. In this very moment, the possibilities of their friendship were limitless. 'Pac left the organized chaos a tad early because he was on to his next task: cooking. Much in the same vein of Big, Shakur loved making sure everyone around him was in good spirits.

"We were drinking and smoking, and all of a sudden 'Pac was like, 'Yo! Come get it!'" Smalls said. "We go into the kitchen and he had steaks, and French fries, and bread, and Kool-Aid. We just sitting there eating and drinking and laughing."

"'Pac and Biggie," Lew sighed to me as we spoke on the phone, "were like brothers."

For Big, life felt like it was finally coming together.

Christopher was making a lot of decisions that tested Voletta's patience, but it was her love, her approval, and her smile that drove him. He couldn't imagine a world without her until he learned of news no child wants to hear about a parent.

In 1993, doctors found a malignant tumor in Voletta's breast. She had known two women who had been diagnosed with breast cancer, and both of them had since passed away. The way Voletta figured it, she only had five years to live. She left the doctor's office in a fog, but she knew what her next move was. She had to tell Christopher.

It was an impossible conversation, and her son was angry. Not with her, but with the situation. He'd survived so much in the streets, and now he felt as if he was that much closer to taking care of her the way she deserved. But cancer was threatening to take the person who loved him unconditionally. Whenever Voletta would try to bring the topic up to him, he'd walk away and cry uncontrollably.

"Ma, you're going to live," her son said as tears streamed down his face. "Now, come on. I don't want to talk about this."

The stress found residency in his music, too. Big grieved largely on his own. Jan knew, but not even many of his closest friends knew of his mother's diagnosis. Part of it was young Black men being unable to process multiple forms of trauma all at once. And part of it stemmed from him not even knowing how to speak about his feelings outside the recording booth. So when many people heard the early recordings of a song like "Things Done Changed," where he said, "Shit, my mom's got cancer in her breast / Don't ask me why I'm mothafuckin' stressed," it was a shock.

"I'ma keep it a hundred with you. Nobody knew. He didn't tell nobody that," Chico told me. "I didn't know until I heard the song. Being with him all the time, certain things he kept to himself. It was more like a 'I ain't gonna tell nobody that' because it might really break him down feeling like, 'Yo, my moms gon' die.'"

Chico continued, "When he started recording and he'd say certain things, I was like, 'Yo, is that true?' He'd be like, 'Yeah, Chic.' I'd be like wow. I ain't know that. But we brushed it off like that. Let's drink, let's smoke.

When he put that in the music, that's how I knew. Everything he said was real because he couldn't talk about nothing phony. He had a lot on his mind at that point. Through a mix of trying to do music and hustling and people trying to get at you for this and that, you know, it gets to a point where he was really ready to die. I was like, 'Duke, are you crazy?!'"

Voletta underwent surgery ten days after her diagnosis. The operation was a success, but Voletta had a long, hard road of rehabilitation ahead. Normal arm movements came with an ungodly amount of pain. As Voletta sat in the hospital, initially Christopher never came to see her, though she was never upset by his absence. She knew it wasn't out of cruelty. And she knew that while so many people around Christopher saw this giant of man, what she saw was, in her own words, "a scared little boy." Eventually, though, he did show up. He wasn't used to being in a hospital, and he damn sure wasn't used to seeing his mother in a hospital. He apologized for his absence.

"I was afraid to see you because I didn't know what you would look like," he reasoned. "I didn't know what I was going to see."

That day he finally came to see her, Christopher never left his mother's side. He was always nervous. That feeling never left him. But if he needed to take a phone call, he'd do so at her bedside. And when Voletta returned home, he was the most caring drill sergeant she could ever ask for, checking on her every day, ensuring she took her medicine and was doing her rehab exercises. He'd cry in front of Jan over seeing his mother in such a vulnerable physical state, even if she was well on the road to recovery. But in front of her, he'd be her rock—or as best he could.

"That's mom dukes. What I'm 'posed to be like when she had cancer and shit? 'Fuck you! Get your own tea!' Nah, that's mom dukes, you know what I'm saying?" he later explained. "I got to take care of my moms. I'm the only nigga she got. Ain't nobody else in this motherfucker."

Trouble always seemed to follow Big. He and D-Roc were walking down Gates Avenue one night after leaving D-Roc's grandmother's place. The two were excited, talking about what life could be like once Big's rap career really got off the ground. Then the cops pulled up. They took off running down the block, with Big ditching the gun he was holding along the way. The cops eventually caught up to both. And they found the gun, too.

"There's two of you, but only one gun," the cop said. "Take some time and figure it out."

Big and D-Roc sat in that 79th Precinct interrogation room looking at each other and wondering what their next move would be. They weighed their options. The gun was Big's, but he had priors, including a weapons case and drug case. If he took the rap for this, he wouldn't see the outside world for a long time, and that rap career he was trying to get off the ground would be derailed. The choice was easy for D-Roc. After convincing his friend it was the right move, D-Roc took the gun charge. He was later sentenced to four years. They'd always been close, but now it was a brotherhood that could never be separated. Big never forgot the loyalty D-Roc showed him in that moment, and he vowed to make sure whenever he came home, he'd be looked out for. His mother's breast cancer, albeit on the road to recovery, had shaken Big to his core. And now one of the most loyal people he had ever met was taking up to a four-year bid for *his* gun so he could he continue to live *his* dream. There was really no turning back now.

As if that weight wasn't enough, in July 1993, Combs's tenure at Uptown met an abrupt end. He was Harrell's star pupil, and one the boss had fought to keep on board following the intense pressure to fire Combs after the City College tragedy. But Harrell was also the only person who could control the rapidly rising star whose ego had grown out of control. Long gone was the intern who'd make the five-hour trek from Howard to New York to get coffee, cars, and whatever else his boss could begin to think of. In early 1992, while Puffy took some time off, Mark Siegel, a white guy, had been hired to be the general manager of Uptown. The two almost immediately clashed over many of the things Puffy was used to having his way on, like studio time and overall production budgets. Combs didn't like being told what to do by a white man when he felt he was working for a Black company. Siegel, on the other hand, labeled Combs as "out of control" and declared that he "had no sense of how to function in a corporation" and that he "treated Andre like shit."

"Puffy never appreciated what Andre did for him," Al B. Sure! told *New York* magazine in October 1995, alluding to the City College incident. "I mean, he had a bottle of pills by his head, ready to kill himself, and Andre saved his life."

But there was only room for one of them, and in a glass-half-full sort of way, Harrell saw letting go of Combs, who had the drive to be one of the game's most successful businessmen, as a gift.

"I started to branch into movies, into television," Harrell explained to the *Wall Street Journal*. "So then Puff wouldn't really listen to anybody but me. My full-time job became managing Puff, and I was doing other things. I knew it was time for him to grow and the only way he could grow was if he was gonna have the same kind of corporate compensations that I was subjected to."

"He asked me to leave the same day. It was like leaving home," Combs said. "I ended up on the stoop of his brownstone that night, crying my eyes out. I wish I never left."

Despite how bitterly it all ended, there was still love there—Combs saw Harrell as a father figure, and Harrell saw Combs in a son-like light—though Combs wanted desperately to prove he could make it on his own. Weeks after the firing, both Harrell and Combs attended a private party following the annual T.J. Martell Foundation dinner, then considered one of the industry's most prestigious events. For the great majority of the night, Combs and Harrell hung out in a corner of the room just talking. Jessica Rosenblum, one of hip-hop's most influential people connectors, described it at the time: "I've known these guys forever. It's so sick. It's like a never-ending drama."

Harrell agreed to extend the payroll of Combs's staff for a limited time. That was a gracious offer, and it helped Combs keep his head above water for a certain period. But Big was well into the recording process for his debut album, as was another artist Combs had invested a lot into named Craig Mack. With Big in particular, word around MCA, Uptown's parent company, wasn't good. His music was too graphic, too violent, and too vulgar. One record that specifically upset higher-ups at the label was "Just Playing (Dreams)"—short for "Dreams of Fuckin' an R&B Bitch"—in which he went through a string of women singers and openly gloated about wanting, or *not* wanting, to have sex with them. Quite a few of the singers he mentioned were on the same label, like Patti LaBelle, who was none too pleased at Big's lyrics referencing her. The story goes that the legendary singer demanded he be dropped from the label, but she also got in touch with Big himself, who promptly apologized.

While the industry wondered what Combs's next move was going to be, those close to Big were concerned. He had a lucrative enterprise down in North Carolina, and he had walked away from it because he had believed in Combs. And now Combs was technically unemployed, so where did that leave him?

"When Puff got fired, I remember everybody feeling like, 'What we gonna do?' . . . My concern was really, 'What's Biggie gonna do?'" said Mark Pitts in the 2021 Netflix documentary *I Got a Story to Tell*. Pitts had started off as Combs's personal assistant and become Wallace's manager. The two grew closer while Voletta battled breast cancer. Pitts's own mother had passed from the same illness when he was fifteen, so he understood Big's fear. He promised Voletta that he would always look out for her son. She believed him. So when Combs was attempting to make his next play after leaving Uptown, Pitts knew he had to keep Big focused.

"Even though it wasn't a huge explosion yet, I seen just enough for me to know that he got a shot, and he's about to fuck it up," said Pitts.

A mother battling breast cancer, a best friend doing time for willingly taking a charge that wasn't his, and suddenly his music career in jeopardy. As if all that weren't enough stress for Big, on August 8, 1993, he and Jan's baby girl, T'yanna Dream Wallace, was born. His mother still wasn't pleased that her son and Jan had allowed a child to be born into a world her parents were still trying to figure out for themselves, but Christopher begged, pleaded, and softly demanded his mother meet her. She put up a good fight but eventually caved. Voletta hadn't even thought of the baby as her granddaughter because she was so angry at the entirety of the situation. That was until she saw her for the first time.

"That moment," she reflected, "felt like the first time I laid eyes on Christopher. I didn't think it was possible to duplicate that overwhelming feeling of love that I had had for Christopher, but I was wrong."

The tears started flowing—and her son delivered the comedic relief he was so known for.

"Oh my God! You're not crying, are you?" he asked. "She's not *that* ugly!"

Big loved T'yanna, and through her a different fire ignited in him. She was here now. The conversations around predicting what life would be like once she was born were no more. It was game time. Ever the hustler, he would pay people to clean his room so he could have his daughter's bassinet beside his bed. It wasn't that long ago that he had dropped out of high school to pursue the streets full-time. Like any legit hustler understands, the streets are not a long-term career. It's just not feasible. So even if he wanted to go back, it's not like it would ever be the same as it was in Raleigh. Too much had changed, and the block was still hot. Plus, he wanted to be part of his daughter's life, and the streets just came with way too many risks.

Combs knew he had to convince Big that his dream was still achievable. Circa November or December 1993, Combs made the rare trek to Brooklyn. In a way, he felt he owed it to Big to make him feel at ease. Combs met Big and his close friend, journalist dream hampton (T'yanna's middle name was in honor of her), at Junior's.

Combs, while eating strawberry cheesecake, did whatever he could to make Big see the light. This next situation he was working on would be the one to put him on and, more importantly, *keep* Big. He was so close to achieving this dream.

"I'm a visionary," Combs said. "You have to trust me."

━━━━━━

Rob Stone can paint a picture of his first meeting with Combs like he just walked out of the room five minutes ago. By late 1993 and early 1994, Stone had been working in the music industry for a few years, primarily in hip-hop, the music he grew up on coming up in New York. At the time, the twenty-four-year-old Stone, who is white, was doing some A&R work at SBK Records. SBK had artists like Vanilla Ice and Wilson Phillips and was merging with EMI, who had acts like Gang Starr. It was well known throughout the industry that Combs was looking for a home for his Bad Boy Records since he had been relieved of his duties at Uptown a few months earlier.

Because Stone had a deep understanding of hip-hop, his bosses, Daniel Glass and Fred Davis (the son of Clive), invited him to the meeting with Combs. Stone was quite familiar with the man known in the industry as Puffy from his Daddy's House parties and all the work he'd done with Jodeci and Mary J. Blige. The meeting took place in the ostentatious lobby of the Mark Hotel on the Upper East Side. Glass and Davis wore suits, while Stone kept it casual with jeans, sneakers, and a polo shirt. Shortly thereafter, Combs walked in, already intense. Glass and Davis wanted to bring Combs in as their vice president of Black music at EMI and give him an imprint for Bad Boy. Combs was with it.

"Well, what do you want to do?" Glass and Davis asked.

"Look, I'll be VP," Stone recalled Combs saying, with the confidence in his voice seemingly rising with every syllable. "If you need me to be a VP for EMI, I'll make your shit hot . . . But I need Bad Boy, and I need my label, and I need to be able to decide who I want to sign, and put out music for who I want to sign."

Combs was just getting started.

"I have the textbook on how to do this, and I could show it to any-body . . . because nobody can do it like Puff," Combs said. "The reason I talk on my records is so when people hear my voice, they know the artist is hot. They don't even have to hear him. They know by the time they get to him or her, the shit is already hot. That it's certified in the streets."

Stone was confident, but he had never seen anyone like Combs. The meeting progressed and drinks were had—though not by Stone, because his dad had taught him never to drink during business meetings. Davis and Glass loosened up as time went on, but not Combs. He never lost his game face.

"You felt like you were dealing with somebody who was in a rush to get something happening," said Stone. If only he knew at the time how much was on the line, he would know that this statement came with an almost dizzying amount of truth.

"What would you do to help us with Vanilla Ice?" Glass asked. Ice was already at the tail end of his fame and was basically a lost cause by then.

Combs was shocked, damn near offended that he was asked the question.

"Vanilla Ice? I can't fuck with that guy. Rob knows I can't fuck with that guy!" he yelled. "Rob knows I can't go on the street with that guy. That guy's the devil. I can't do anything with him."

What happened next, Stone recalls, was the greatest two-minute offense he's ever seen. With the possibility of Combs resurrecting the pretty much comatose career of Vanilla Ice out of the window, the question was posed to Combs of what he wanted to do next.

"Next step?" Combs asked rhetorically. "When you guys go back to EMI, and you get in a room with all them suits, and you decide what you're going to pay Puff—just when you get to a number that you think is going to make Puff happy, *double it*."

He wasn't done. "And just after you double it, don't stop there. I want you to put whipped cream and a cherry on top because I don't want money to be an issue . . . Don't be coming at me with no nigga money."

Rob Stone, who was quiet for pretty much the entire meeting, sat in stunned silence and amazement. He had never seen anything like that. A few minutes later, Combs shook everyone's hands and left.

"That meeting happened, and I ended up getting recruited probably a month or two later to go work at Arista to handle all the crossover stuff," says Stone.

Even at Arista Records, the temperature on hip-hop was still pretty much the same. The people in power at most labels weren't rap fans. They were pop fans who had to learn the value of hip-hop, and that's if they even chose to do that. Stone grew up idolizing Rakim, Run-DMC, and LL Cool J. Hip-hop for him wasn't just some new edgy musical genre. It was his lifestyle. About two or three months after that meeting with Combs at the Mark Hotel, Stone's boss at Arista, Rick Bisceglia, called him to tell him to rush to his office quick because "Puffy's coming."

Combs walked in with Paul "Big Paul" Offord, his head of security, and one or two other people in his entourage. Bisceglia was really savvy at getting records played and strategizing, but he needed Stone there for credibility.

"Puff, you know Rob Stone?" Bisceglia asked.

Combs looked at Stone for a few seconds and walked toward him.

"They taking care of you?"

"What do you mean?" Stone responded.

"I mean, they paying you, right?" Combs asked.

"Yeah, yeah," Stone responded.

"A'ight, because if you're working my records," Combs said, making sure Bisceglia heard him, "they better be paying you right."

The deal with EMI never materialized, but it only opened the door for Puffy's next move. In early 1994, Combs and Arista agreed to a 50/50 joint venture deal. Bad Boy Records finally had a home. The play was inspired, in part, by Andre Harrell. The day after Combs was fired, he called his former boss asking for advice. Call Clive Davis, Harrell had said. Davis, a longtime power player in the music industry, had formed Arista Records in 1974 after (like Combs) being fired from his original company at Columbia Records for (also like Combs) blowing budgets wide open. Arista would help launch the careers of Whitney Houston, Kenny G, Sarah McLachlan, Monica, Dido, and Barry Manilow, and would attract A-list talent like Aretha Franklin, the Grateful Dead, Dionne Warwick, Daryl Hall and John Oates, Carly Simon, and more. And in 1989, he entered into an agreement with L.A. Reid and Kenneth "Babyface" Edmonds to launch LaFace Records. That roster, by 1994, included superstar acts like TLC and Toni Braxton, a child prodigy Combs would help develop named Usher, and a still-unknown-but-not-for-long duo out of Atlanta named OutKast.

"I guess Clive realized he needed his young promotion guy to interact, and understand hip-hop. They didn't have that on the pop side," said Stone. "Especially back then, the music industry was like your pop staff, or your white executives, and your white staff. Urban music, or Black music, as it's really called, was Black employees, and they worked different stations."

Like Combs, too, Clive Davis had a legendary ego. There was an inside joke in the music industry that the famed executive thought so highly of himself he believed the CD was named in honor of him.

"Puffy was probably thinking, 'I'll show [Clive] how to do street records, but he's going to teach me how to do Michael Jackson, Whitney Houston–type records. I'm going to go big-time with this guy," Stone said. "[Clive] had such a respect for the creative process, and I'm sure whatever Puff's first check was was probably significant. I don't know if EMI would've come to him the same way."

Agree with his tactics or not—even like the guy or not—it was undeniable that Combs had come through on his promise to himself, and to Big. They were officially back in the game. Now all that was left was making the music that would satisfy a proper return on investment. Quiet as he kept, Biggie Smalls was working on just that.

11

MATTERS OF THE HEART

BIG'S MIND WAS BLOWN BY DR. DRE'S *THE CHRONIC* FROM THE
MOMENT MATTY C LET HIM HEAR THE PROJECT MONTHS IN
ADVANCE OF ITS RELEASE. It was one of those albums that made Big,
as confident in his own skills as perhaps any MC before or after him, realize
he had to step his shit up. *The Chronic* was a sonic boom, and if you weren't
putting out a project at least in the same zip code, then you shouldn't even
waste your time.

If *The Chronic* wasn't enough, Death Row followed it with Snoop
Doggy Dogg's *Doggystyle* a year later. That one-two punch in terms of
debut albums for a label is perhaps the greatest in rap history. Snoop's
project was a slightly different speed, but it encapsulated the same attention to musical detail that drew Big into its predecessor. Big loved the
tag team of albums, and honestly loved pretty much everything he was
hearing from the west and the south with artists like Scarface and UGK.
New York hip-hop had become complacent. For years, New York had
been the alpha and omega of hip-hop. The city was coming out with good
music, but a lot of it was on the conscious wave, like Brand Nubian, A
Tribe Called Quest, De La Soul, and more, whereas a prolific lyricist
and storyteller like Kool G Rap was never going to truly break out of the
niche lane of gritty, noncommerical rap he had carved for himself. Simply put,

there was a vacant throne for whoever wanted to reclaim New York's top spot in terms of gritty street narratives combined with commercial appeal.

In late 1993, the Wu-Tang Clan planted their flag in the ground with *Enter the Wu (36 Chambers)*, a chaotic, pristinely produced group album with a motley crew of legendary MCs. And in the spring of 1994, a gifted young wordsmith from Queensbridge named Nas released *Illmatic*. The project was *The Source*'s original five-mic album, and in its review, the magazine claimed, "If you can't at least appreciate the value of Nas' poetical realism, then you best get yourself up out of hip-hop."

With Bad Boy firmly in place under Arista, Big had the comfort of stability—but there was also intense pressure to deliver. He wanted to create the hardest street album New York had ever heard, and he wanted the world to embrace it. He didn't need to imagine fictional tales. His life, all twenty-two years of it, provided more than enough material. Big wanted to bring listeners with him into the violent, dark, and often depressing world he knew. One of the most notorious crime figures in New York at the time was mob boss John Gotti, and Big wanted to call the album *The Teflon Don*, the nickname Gotti had earned after evading convictions during several high-profile trials during the eighties.

"We can't do that," Combs reasoned, saying the title was too New York–specific. "We gonna hit 'em hard, but we gonna do it in a way where we're gonna represent for the masses."

Big ultimately agreed, but in terms of the content, he knew what he wanted. To be in the studio with Big around this time of his life was to expect any and everything. Easy Mo Bee played Big countless instrumentals. If he didn't like it, he didn't waste any time passing on it. But when he did find one that tickled his fancy, that's when the real magic began. The process was pretty much the same throughout his career. While the beat blasted in the studio on loop, Big would sit in the room chain-smoking blunts and just nodding his head. Oftentimes, many people didn't know if he was paying attention or not, but he'd be in a zone that would last for hours listening to the same beat. Studio time wasn't cheap, so spending marathon sessions in there would create feelings of anxiousness or impatience. All that would fly out the window when Big would stand up, go into the booth, put headphones on, and knock an entire song with ease.

Watching Big record was both sublime and, if you weren't prepared for just how vulgar he could be, cringeworthy. Take Big in the booth recording the song "Ready to Die"—the very first song they laid on wax for the forthcoming album at the Soundtrack recording studio circa 1993. The process was what it always came to be for Mo Bee. The beat was on loop, and Big went through his usual routine of mumbling, smoking weed, zoning out, and looking like he was under hypnosis of some kind. And when he was ready, he hopped in the booth and spit the verses off the top of his head. Oftentimes in one take, too.

The harsh lyrics were no surprise to Mo Bee. This was hip-hop, after all. But even he had a limit. In the booth, Wallace delivered a lyrical dismount that, to this day, still hits with the force of a Mike Tyson right hook: "Fuck the world, my moms and my girl / My life is played out like a Jheri curl / I'm ready to die."

Mo Bee was stupefied. He couldn't believe what he just heard.

"Big, you know what you just said?" a visibly perturbed Mo Bee asked.

Big just took his headphones off and shrugged. It wasn't anything shocking for him.

"Yo, I'm not ready to die. That's just like an extension of how I feel. It's serious for me right now," he explained. "A nigga just be like, 'Yo. Fuck! If I was dead, I wouldn't have to worry about nothing. I could just lay up. Either I'd be in heaven or hell. I'd be laying the fuck up, chilling. I wouldn't have to worry about no problems.'"

It was quite the unique perspective to have about mortality. But for Big, given everything going on in his life and what he'd experienced, it was, in its own way, logical. Mo Bee would have more moments like this. On "Gimme the Loot," a standout on the album, Big had the idea of rhyming in two different voices representing two different characters with two different outlooks on how to operate in the streets. In his normal voice was Big himself, a more reasonable, if not hardened, dealer who had seen everything possible hustling. In a higher-pitched voice was his alter ego, a deranged, maniacal, and bloodthirsty young Brooklyn firecracker who would do any and everything for a dollar.

"Slick Rick played different characters, but the characters sounded the same. And with 'Redman Meets Reggie Noble,' he played two different people, but both characters sounded the same," he reasoned. "I wanted to make them two completely different dudes, to the point where someone could wonder, who was that rapper with Big on 'Gimme the Loot'?"

It wasn't like he was the first to ever put the concept on wax, but "Gimme the Loot" was a brilliant display of everything that made him the no-brainer signing that Combs saw. Not only was he lyrical, but if you closed your eyes, the images he was creating played more like the gangsta flicks and hood classics. A rapper and an actor all at once. He was sharp, witty, and hilarious, and, just when Mo Bee thought he knew what to expect, Big was there with a verbal uppercut that'd stop him in his tracks. Big rhymed about robbing both men and women for their jewelry and that "I wouldn't give a fuck if you're pregnant / Gimme the baby rings and the number one mom pendant." It was quintessential Big—outrageous, darkly humorous, inventive all at once. (On the album, "pregnant" would be blurred out.)

Like Voletta Wallace, Mo Bee was a devout Christian, and a line on the song like "If I Should Die Before I Wake" that featured Big boasting about having sex with Mary and leaving her body in a sewer was just too much. But it wasn't like he could stop Big, either. He was going to say whatever he wanted, whenever he wanted, and however he wanted. Everyone in the studio, including Combs, Lil' Cease, and Big, was rocking out. But Mo Bee asked Combs if he was comfortable releasing that song with that reference. Combs didn't understand the issue. Mo Bee tried to explain the flak they could get for the line from women's rights groups and the church. For him, the reward wasn't greater than the risk. The entire studio erupted in laughter. None more than Cease, who told Mo Bee he was being too sensitive, with Mo Bee insisting he wasn't.

"Big ain't stress it. Big was like, it's just a rhyme," Cease would later explain. "I guess he was testing his waters, like, let me go write some outlandish shit. 'Cause when you got that type of mind where you intelligent like that and you really got that pen sharp? You can talk about anything. He was just experimenting."

One of the biggest misconceptions surrounding the album was that it was strictly a New York-inspired project. Big's experiences on those corners by the Ave. or Bedford and Quincy, those trips down south to North

Carolina, or even those annual vacations to Jamaica were undoubtedly critical sources of inspiration—the last being prominent in Diana King's patois opening on "Respect." But he listened to wide swaths of music. One, because he was a fan of rap, but two, and most importantly, he wanted to hear what others were creating at the time. One album that Wallace held close to his heart was OutKast's *Southernplayalisticadillacmuzik*.

"A lot of people felt like he got that Southern twang on the 'Pac side, but he didn't. He got it from OutKast," said Jacob York on Bossip's *Don't Be Scared* podcast, in 2015. York, along with Lance "Un" Rivera, would later help Big get into the managerial side of the business through Undeas Entertainment. "A lot of people don't know Diddy directed OutKast's 'Player's Ball' video. And so Big knew a lot about that. He listened to 'Git Up, Git Out.'"

That diverse catalog of music Big listened to now had to play out on his own album. For the most part, Puffy let Big cook on his own, recording the hard-core raps he could spit in his sleep. But Puffy knew that to really meet people where they were, especially with a new artist like Big, they had to give them something they could vibe out to. He needed a radio hit, something that could spin in the clubs and the women would want to dance along with. Big might not have seen the vision off the rip, but if Puffy knew one thing in the music industry, it was how to make money. And if Big wanted to make money, he best figure out how to make one of those records Puffy was imploring him to make.

"You can give me my little limitations, but when I get a track, I ask him, 'What do you want from this, you let me know,'" Big said later, reflecting on the chemistry between him and Combs. "And he might be like, 'You need to be partying on this joint. You don't need to be killing nobody's mother on this one. Take it easy.'"

They'd bump heads from time to time, but that's largely how Big came to understand the importance of making a radio record—something like "Big Poppa"—without fully sacrificing his integrity as an artist. Being in the studio with Big, you never knew what you'd see or hear—and you'd never know how quickly he'd put his real life into his music. DJ Premier—aka Preemo—found that out firsthand. Ever the rap historian, Big was already well aware of Premier's background as one of the hardest producers in the game. He knew his work with Guru in their group Gang Starr, but also with artists like Jeru the Damaja, Heavy D & The Boyz, and more. And he heard the heat the Houston, Texas, producer had given Nas for *Illmatic* with songs like "N.Y. State of Mind," "Memory Lane (Sittin' in da Park)" and "Represent." Big wanted that same type of energy.

The album was almost done, but it still needed that street slapper for Big. That one track where he didn't have to worry about anything except rapping. That one track where he could flex his skills and by the end of the record there would be no denying not just who the hardest rapper in New York was, but the hardest rapper in the game, period. Big, in his own, words, needed "that gutter shit." He told Preemo to loop the Honeydrippers' "Impeach the President."

"Flip that and just do some shit to it," Big said.

So Preemo did, and two days later at Preemo's favorite workspace, the B room at D&D Studios on West Thirty-Seventh Street in the Garment District, which he would later purchase. He was toying around with the beat until Big showed up with his crew several hours later. Preemo played the beat for Big, who bobbed his head and gave his seal of approval, telling Preemo that he had laced him with a smash. All it needed was a slight tinker with a counter rhythm and it was perfect. Big now had the gem, the knockout blow he needed to lay his game down quite flat and come out the gates swinging.

So Big went into his normal routine of sitting in the corner mumbling to himself, smoking blunt after blunt, and living in his own universe. This happened for quite some time, then he got up and left. Preemo didn't think too much of it and continued to toy around with the beat until Dave Lotwin, one of the two co-owners of the studio, approached him asking if he knew what Big was doing. Preemo, not too fazed by the question or whatever it is he was doing, asked what.

"Go check it out," Lotwin whispered.

On an impromptu scavenger hunt, Preemo walked down a short hallway to get to the vocal booth, which had a lounge a little farther off to the right. He opened the door to find Big sitting on the couch, pants open, with two attractive women, their heads in his lap, performing oral sex.

"Yo, Preme," Big asked, unfazed that the producer had walked in the room, "You want some of this?"

Preemo declined, closing the door and laughing on his way back to the B room. A short time later, Big returned fully refreshed. Preemo and Mo Bee didn't share notes on Big's studio etiquette, but now Preemo was getting nervous about the long hours in the studio with nothing to show. Then, like clockwork, Big said the two words that let everyone know it was about to go down.

"I'm ready."

He went in the booth, closed his eyes, and let the beat ride for a few seconds before launching into one of his most lauded verses and songs. The first lyrics out of his mouth were a homage to Bed-Stuy and the corners that raised him, and most of the rest of song found Big asserting his dominance in ways that were, unlike the song's sampled loop, unimpeachable. He even managed to get a reference in about what Preemo had just walked in on in the back room.

Preemo couldn't believe what he had just witnessed. Big had hovered around the studio—and back room—all night with nothing to show for it. Then, out of nowhere, a mammoth of a song was on wax. They came up with the title "Unbelievable" after Big said it repeatedly in his verses and scratched the hook from R. Kelly's "Your Body's Calling" as the final piece of the puzzle.

Every studio session with Big was memorable. There was the skit with him and the first lady of Junior M.A.F.I.A., Lil' Kim, that depicted the two engaged in a heated and passionate sexual liaison. The relationship between Big and Kim would become clearer and more combustible as the years went along. But even the songs that were obscenely morbid were indelible. The album's closing track, "Suicidal Thoughts," was its graphic vortex, with Big claiming that he wanted to go to hell when he died because he was a "piece of shit," before committing suicide. All the wrong and unlawful things he did in his life would finally catch up to him in the afterlife. The Lord Finesse–produced record was conceived through copious amounts of weed, liquor, and about six or seven pizzas. Chico Del Vec was growing impatient with Big and was ready to leave.

"Chill, Chic!" he pleaded. "Just chill, son!"

"Man, we been here for four hours!" Chico shot back.

The smoking and drinking continued, and Chico was growing more and more impatient by the minute. Big, per custom, was sitting in the corner vibing out and mumbling to himself, not writing anything down. Some time later, Big, per tradition, said he was ready and went in the booth and knocked out the track, but not before a special surprise. At the end of the verse, he left with this bar: "Call my nigga Chic / Tell 'em that my will is weak." Chico couldn't believe what he had just heard. He had known Big—or Chris, as he calls him—could rap for years, and he was even in Mister Cee's sweltering apartment when they rerecorded the demo. But he'd never been shouted out in a verse before. Chico was on cloud nine.

"Yo! Is you serious right now?!" Chico exclaimed.

"Don't worry 'bout it, Chic!" Big responded, unable to hold back his smile. "I told you I got you, nigga."

Chico said they listened to the song all day, and that all throughout the neighborhood, it was like a parade for the song. His mind started racing about all the marketing and promotion they could do to market the song. In Chico's mind, the song was an undeniable hit. That was, until Big had to bring him back down to earth. It wasn't that Big didn't love the song. He did, and it was the perfect swan song for the album. But there was only so much marketing they could put behind this song outside of putting it on the album.

"Yo, you should do a video for this song," Chico said. His suggestion was dead serious.

"Chic, is you crazy, son?" Big responded, genuinely shocked at the idea. "How the hell we gonna shoot a video for this? What's wrong with you, man?!"

Chico was blinded by his own mention.

"Nah, this gonna be a dope joint! You called me out on it!"

"Nigga, you didn't hear what the song's talking about?!" Big said.

It was quite the opposite. Chico had heard the song so much he probably could've recited it better than Big himself. That's when clarity hit him.

"Ohhhhhhh, you killed yourself on there," Chico said. "Nah, I don't wanna do a video for that. I'm stupid."

"Yeah," Big said, laughing. "You stupid."

What wasn't stupid was the vision Puffy had for the album, titled *Ready to Die*. With such a morbid title, Puffy knew the album needed some polishing. He wasn't trying to block Big's creative vision on coming up with the hardest bars imaginable. He wanted him to do that. That was part of the reason he signed him in the first place. He wanted him to paint that graphic picture of being a young Black man coming from the hood who survived the streets and Reaganomics alike and what kind of animal that made along the way. That's something Puffy couldn't teach, nor did he want to.

Puffy wanted to allow the casual fan to find out who and what Biggie Smalls was all about. And to do that, he had to again come with singles for the radio. Big wanted to make you *feel* something in his music. Puffy wanted you to dance while you were feeling it. Puffy wasn't a producer in the sense of Easy Mo Bee or DJ Premier, a beat maker, a track mixer. He was more like a high-end travel agent, someone who could come in and create the vibe a song needed not just to become a hit—but to become an anthem that would become the soundtrack to a generation's life. Case in point: the day when he brought an idea to the table for a song sampling James Mtume's 1983 smash single "Juicy Fruit." Mtume had a meeting with Andre Harrell at Uptown one day. He'd already known Puffy, so the conversation was natural between him and the upstart soon-to-be mogul and musical legend. Puffy was interested in sampling the song for his new artist named the Notorious B.I.G.

When Puffy originally brought the idea to Big, he was none too receptive. He had no interest in chasing a radio single. For Big, whatever he did had to come naturally.

"I'm not getting on anything like that," Big told Puff. "It's too soft."

"I just kept telling Big to trust the process. I had to explain to him that Puff is letting you do what you do, but you gotta sprinkle some other type of joints too so you can have that balance," said Mister Cee. "I'm not gonna try and toot my own horn and say me having that conversation made Big at ease doing those type of records. But I feel like at that time I was probably in Big's ear the most outside of Puff that could influence him."

It was with "Juicy" that Big truly learned the formula.

"[Puff] wanna make hits. That's what he thrives on," he said. "So whatever he tell me to do, you know what I'm saying? If it ain't too outlandish, I'll roll . . . I'm down."

It had already been simmering in the pot, but now one of the greatest combinations in music history—Biggie Smalls's artistic value and Puff Daddy's vision—was about to erupt. Now it was time to take this show on the road.

12

WORD ON ROAD

IN JUNE 1994, PUFFY CALLED ROB STONE AND TOLD THE ARISTA EXECUTIVE THAT HE HAD SOMETHING HE WANTED HIM TO HEAR. So Stone made the trek from Fifty-Seventh Street to Bad Boy's offices on Nineteenth Street. There was a quote on a wall in the lobby at the office from Puffy: "Don't be afraid to close your eyes and dream, and open them and see." And all around, the label's street teams were hard at work. It was like everyone had a thousand different tasks they had to complete at once.

"The energy there was insane," remembered Stone. "It felt like Times Square during New Year's. It felt like mayhem. It felt like organized chaos in an office, which was amazing."

Stone sat in the lobby for nearly an hour before being brought back to Combs' office by Norma Augenblick, one of Combs's most trusted employees. Walking into Combs's office felt like a scene in a mobster flick—there he was sitting behind his desk with a look so serious it could make Denzel Washington break character.

"Hold my calls," Combs demanded. "Don't let anybody interrupt me."

"It just made me feel like, wow, this is important," Stone told me. "His intensity was crazy."

Combs played Big's entire album, titled *Ready to Die*. He didn't speak much outside of asking Stone what he thought of certain songs and mouthing lyrics every so often. Bad Boy's head honcho and the man tasked with getting the songs on the radio spent more than ninety minutes dissecting Biggie's debut. Stone knew the project was good enough to get airplay, and as a body of work, he knew it was going to shake up the industry in much the way Dr. Dre's *The Chronic* and Snoop's *Doggystyle* had done in years prior. Combs even let him keep the cassette—different from the version that hit shelves months later—which he still has to this day.

"I remember leaving Puff's office, and I called Mike Kyser, who was doing at Def Jam what I was doing at Arista," Stone said. Kyser is currently the president of Black music at Atlantic Records.

"I just heard one of the five best albums of all time," Stone told Kyser.

"Hip-hop albums?" Kyser asked.

"No, albums. This is one of the greatest albums I've ever heard."

Stone knew what lay on the horizon, but Big wasn't Bad Boy's first star artist. That honor went to Craig Mack. Like Big, Mack was brought over to Bad Boy with the Arista deal, and Mack had a single that was heating up all the clubs. "Flava in Ya Ear" dominated radio stations and helped introduce Bad Boy as a force to be reckoned with. A month before that impromptu listening session in Combs's office, the Welcome to Bad Boy/Arista Party was held at the Trump Plaza on Fifth Avenue. In essence, it was a way to announce that Combs's new label would operate under the umbrella of Clive Davis, and that a new day of hit records was on the horizon.

On the way to the party, Big rode with Stone, who was playing Smif-N-Wessun's album demos. That caught his attention.

"Yo, where you'd get this?" Big asked with his hat pulled down over his lazy eye.

"I'm friends with Dru-Ha, who works with them over at Nervous Records," said Stone.

"Those are my boys," Big responded, referencing a mutual respect stemming from Brooklyn.

Big was impressed Stone had the juice to get those demos. There wasn't much conversation in the car at that time. In the back sat Lil' Cease and Big's tour manager, Hawk Burns. Stone struck up a conversation with Big, telling him he had been at one of his first shows in New York at a club in the Lower West Side called the Muse. Other hip-hop luminaries were in the building that night, too, like Buckshot, Black Moon, and Redman, the third of whom was weaving through the crowd in a hoodie with an aluminum baseball bat. Big performed less than five minutes that night. The only song he got to perform was "Whatchu Want," in fact. That's because mid-song, a fight broke out and cleared the club. But Big left an impression on Stone.

"That was my first show," he said.

"First show in New York?" Stone asked.

"Nah," Big responded. "My first show."

And thus a friendship was born.

Ever the marketing savant, Combs understood exactly what he had in Big and Mack. Hence the B.I.G. Mack tour of 1994. The idea was birthed within Bad Boy and Arista's creative teams and enlisted famed hip-hop photographer Chi Modu to execute the vision. The now famous picture of Mack, Puffy, and Big behind the counter of a fast food restaurant was a brilliant concept.

"I think in some ways that campaign was a little bit of a leading edge because it wasn't really about a particular album release or a song. It was a campaign for a kick-off for a label, which we really hadn't seen prior to that," said Modu, who passed in 2021. "It was kind of the start of the label owner being part of the brand, because prior to that, those guys tended to stay out of the picture. You knew Berry Gordy, but you didn't really see him in ads, right? It was always artist-first."

The tour itself was a humbling experience for Big, who found out what it was like to play Robin to Mack's Batman. It was impossible to deny how big a record "Flava in Ya Ear" was becoming, ultimately peaking as a top 20 song in the country. Every club in the country was playing the record, and at that very moment, it was hard to doubt anyone who thought Mack would be Bad Boy's star of the present and future. Big wasn't envious of the love Mack was getting. He just knew he was worthy of the adulation as well.

Big was opening for Mack. And on that West Coast road swing, Stone and others would often pay club DJs a few hundred dollars just to let Puff's artists get some time on the mic. Oftentimes, they could do a whole show.

"Big would get annoyed because people wouldn't even be listening to him because they didn't know his music yet. I just remember this one show in San Jose," said Stone. "By the second song, Big was spinning the mic around on the cord, not even doing the lyrics. He was whistling into the mic at one point. It was probably the third or fourth show of the day and nobody was listening to him."

Big and Mack just had different energies. It wasn't that they didn't like each other, but they weren't exactly the best of friends, either. There was one time the group had a dinner with staff and executives of KMEL in San Francisco.

"Craig would be all loud and screaming shit out. That wasn't Big's style at all. Big was respectful, and nice to waiters and waitresses," Stone recalled. "Craig would be like, 'Hey, waiter. Where's my drink?' He had that voice you could hear from a mile away anyways . . . Big rolled like they was serious."

Stone continued, "They started to get annoyed by each other. Radio guys thought, and some DJs thought, Craig Mack was the shit, and was the bigger artist. Big had to play the back sometimes, and it would bother him."

If Mack was loud and boisterous to get his point across, Big would do the same, but in a subtler manner. One night in San Francisco, three or four guys from the Bay Area walked in Big's dressing room unannounced. Big's crew, including Harve Pierre, Hawk Burns, and Lil' Cease, let them know their presence wasn't welcomed. They weren't pleased about being told that in their own city. Pierre was growing more visibly angry by the moment. Cease was preparing to hit somebody with anything within arm's reach.

"I came in and tried to defuse it, and I guess I did a bit," Stone said. "But Biggie's crew was not looking to defuse it. I felt like they were going to handle it quicker than Craig's crew would've handled it."

Ahead of a visit to Los Angeles's Power 106, Big rocked a particular T-shirt that stunned Stone. Not because he was offended by it—he wasn't—but rather he didn't want this to be the reason Big was blackballed from radio on his very first radio walk-through. He rocked a black tee of a Ku Klux Klan member holding a baby in Klan attire with bold type that read FUTURE POLICE OFFICER. To some it might've come off as offensive, but for Big, as for many Black folks across the country, it was a reality he knew all too well from his time in the streets.

All Stone wanted to do was come through and do the job that Clive Davis and Puffy had sent him out west to do. All he could see was radio executives getting mad and him being out of a job.

"Big, you know we're heading to radio stations to get your songs played," Stone said.

He nodded in agreement.

"Well, these are white-owned radio stations. The shirt might offend them and get in the way of us getting your record played."

Big had no clue what the hell Stone was talking about until he looked down. There was a lot of truth in that shirt as far as Big was concerned. He couldn't help but laugh.

"We're good, Rob Stone," Big said. "We're good."

He never changed the shirt. And his songs still got spins on the radio. Stone learned a valuable lesson. Big was always going to march to the beat of his own drum, and he would always speak from his own experiences. He and Stone's bond only deepened during the West Coast road swing in 1994. Perhaps it was not as deep a bond as those Big had with 50 Grand, Chico del Vec, D-Roc, Mister Cee, or Matty C, but Big did appreciate how seriously Stone took his career and how he looked out for him. He wasn't yet a superstar, but that would soon change. The vow he made to take rap seriously—one he seriously considered reneging on at times—was finally starting to take shape. That wouldn't be the only vow he'd take on, either.

———

It wasn't like Faith Evans was looking for a husband, but that's the thing about love. It often comes to find you. Just like drama. And little did Evans know that both were on her horizon.

Combs had a photo shoot for Bad Boy's new artists in June 1994—Craig Mack, Biggie, and Evans, an R&B singer whom Combs had first noticed while she was singing background. Evans had gone on to write on and sing background on Mary J. Blige's *My Life* and Usher's first album, and her own album would be released a year later.

At the shoot, from the moment he first laid eyes on her, Big was awe-struck by Evans. He was there to do a job, but instead he was focused on getting to know Evans. But first he had to find out who she exactly was. He'd seen Evans in and around different studio sessions before, but he figured she was a session singer. She was far more than just that.

Evans was born in Lakeland, Florida, but moved to Newark, New Jersey (aka Brick City), before she was a year old. Her mother, Helene, was barely out of high school when Faith was born. She never met her father. All she knew was that his name was Richard Swain, and that he may have been Italian, but he was definitely white. When she got older, Evans would hear her aunts speaking about her, thinking she couldn't hear.

"You see how light she is? It's 'cause her daddy's a white man," they'd say.

"Poor girl. Can't dance for nothing. Guess that's 'cause of that white daddy she got. Gave her that flat butt, too."

Yet still, Evans never felt the reality of being raised as biracial. She saw herself only one way.

"I was raised 100 percent Black and have always considered myself a Black woman," she wrote in her 2008 memoir, *Keep the Faith*.

Raised by her grandparents, Evans was a regular fixture in the church, where the soul, vulnerability, and power in her voice was cultivated. She won all sorts of talent shows and pageants and sang at funerals and weddings alike. She'd created a name for herself in her community as a voice to know and behold. Combs came to know this same voice years later through a couple degrees of separation. Evans had dropped out of Fordham University and decided to pursue music. Her boyfriend, Kiyamma Griffin, was working with Christopher Williams, an Uptown artist. Griffin introduced Evans to Puffy, and she soon found herself in a studio session for Usher's album singing background.

Puffy believed in Evans something terrible. He knew she could be a star because she had the coveted combination of a lethal pen and lethal voice. And she had a serious work ethic. Even with a young daughter, Chyna (whom she had with Griffin), to care for, Evans cowrote three songs on Blige's album in addition to singing background. She didn't turn much work down.

During some downtime at the shoot, Big peeped Evans looking at some pictures she had just gotten developed of her daughter's birthday party. That was his in. He walked over and started the conversation. They were both artists on this new, well-funded label. They both understood the intricacies of working with a guy like Puffy, and they both knew how frustrating the music industry could be already. And they both had young daughters. Evans saw Big's gift of gab and ability to make her feel completely at ease almost instantaneously. Evans also didn't mind cooking—and Big sure as hell didn't mind eating.

"I was attracted to, first of all, his sense of humor," Evans said in a 2014 interview. "That was the first thing that caught my attention about him, aside from his confidence, because I didn't know this guy."

Big was intrigued by the fact that Evans knew her way around Brooklyn, too. She was dropping her homegirl Gloria, aka the rapper Hurricane G, off there after the shoot, so Big asked if she could give him, Cease, Nino, and a few other Junior M.A.F.I.A. members a lift there, since she was already going to be in the area. The entire trip back to Brooklyn, Big held court, cracking jokes, smoking blunts, and having the entire car nearly in tears with his impeccable sense of comedic timing. When she dropped off Big and the M.A.F.I.A., he made her a promise.

"I'ma call you tomorrow," he said.

"Yeah," she said, smirking. "Okay. Whatever."

Evans was flattered by the gesture, but she was confused. She never gave him her number, so how exactly was she going to call? He had copied it down earlier from the envelope of Chyna's birthday pictures.

"He called me later that day, and I thought it was cute. And attractive," she said. "We just started talking, and I started going to Brooklyn. Every day it would be, 'What we gon' eat today?' That's pretty much how our thing started."

The two fell for each other quickly and hard. Everyone around them saw it happening, too.

"She was coming around and hanging out all the time. You know, that was his girl. He was in love," Lil' Cease said. "There was something about her that was making him feel good about himself, made him feel love. He wanted to be around her. He embraced her. I think he wanted somebody that was on the same level as him as far as chasing the same dream he was chasing, successful like him. I think that's what really made them gel."

He and Jan parted ways for good when T'yanna was eight months old. Meeting Evans at the time he did, only months before his debut album was to hit shelves, just added one life-altering moment on top of another.

In the summer of 1994, Faith and Big were falling more and more in love by the day. They'd met in June, but by late July, while sitting in Faith's car on the way to pick up some Chinese food from a spot near Big's apartment on St. James, he popped the question. Well, more so, posed the statement.

"Let's get married," he said.

"Wait. You serious?" Faith asked.

"I'm dead-ass," Big promised.

On August 4, 1994, Faith and Biggie drove to Rockland County in Upstate New York. They were married by the justice of peace at the local courthouse. Neither had regrets.

"I'm not mad I did," Evans said years later. "He's certainly the first true love of my life."

As for Big, his perspective on what Evans brought to his life was, if nothing else, brutally honest.

"When you start hustling, you get introduced to shit real fast. You be getting pussy real quick, because you be fuckin' the users sometimes. I done had every kind of bitch. Young bitch, old bitch, users, mothers, grand-mothers, dumb bitches, every kind of bitch I done fucked, and I *never* met no girl like my wife," he reasoned. "I ain't never met no girl like this, never in my life. She talks to me like nobody ever talked to me before. Not only do I enjoy her company, just being with me, but just the conversations just be striking. The honey got me. I knew I wasn't going to find nobody like her."

He was in love. But the news of his marriage caught a lot of people by surprise.

"A lot of the girls in the hood—I'm not gonna name names or any-thing like that," said Betsy Jones, who lived in the Brooklyn brownstone with Matty C, Drew Dixon, and others, "thought they were in a relation-ship with Big."

Puffy thought Evans and Big were joking when he first heard about their decision to tie the knot. His reaction paled in comparison to the two leading women in Big's life. Jan, his daughter's mother, was shocked.

"Up until that point, I still had hope alive. He was still coming to see me. We were still interacting with each other. I really thought I was going along for the ride," she said. "We were such kindred spirits. I had this impression nothing would come between us, but I guess rap came between us."

In the moment, Jan had one question for the man she shared a child with. If he had a chance to let her go, why didn't he? Why did he make her believe that something could still happen between the two of them? Big knew he wasn't in the right by leading her on, but he told her he was afraid he'd lose T'yanna. Jan wasn't that type of woman. No matter how saddened she was over the official closure of their romantic relationship, she'd never withhold her child from her father. The happier he was, the happier he could make their daughter, and that's all either side wanted. But at least Jan had closure and could carry on with the rest of her life.

The same cordial separation could not be said of Big and Junior M.A.F.I.A. member Lil' Kim. That's mainly because there was never truly a complete separation.

Kim had met Big when she was seventeen and he was nineteen, but even then she had already lived a long and complicated life. From a broken home shattered by domestic violence and, at times, homelessness, Kim never shied away from talking about what she'd overcome, from pushing drugs for former boyfriends, to working in retail, to having sex with men who gave her shelter. Big had met Kim through a mutual friend, on whose voicemail Kim would leave raps. The friend told Big that Kim could rap, too. She also lived not too far from Big in Bed-Stuy.

"Yeah, right," he told the friend. "She too pretty to rap."

That was a common misconception with Kim. That her petite size and pretty face somehow made her too dainty to get busy on the mic. Truthfully speaking, Kim knew the streets damn near as well as any of the dudes who called those corners their offices.

"Kim used to be around the thugs and gangstas back then," Chico Del Vec says. "Kim and Big's relationship was—how can I say this—funny buddies."

Years later, on an episode of BET's *106 & Park*, Kim rehashed the story of their first conversation. Kim was working at Bloomingdale's in the early nineties. One evening, after she got back to Brooklyn, there was Big was sitting on a trash can near his St. James apartment engaging in one of his favorite nonmusical activities: shooting dice. That's when he challenged her to spit something.

"I ain't really doing it for nobody like that," Kim told him.

"See, I told you she couldn't rap!" he responded.

"He was good at manipulating you to get you to do what he wanted you to do," Kim said. That's all she needed to spit a verse. Big was taken aback. Not only could she rap, but she had a swagger about her that he'd never seen in a woman on the microphone before. He went from originally being stunned by Kim's beauty and ferocious personality to also seeing something artistically in her that, under the right circumstances, could make her a star.

"It was a funny relationship, because Kim rhymed and Kim was *hard* with it," said Chico. "Big used to take note on her like, 'Yo, she's dope! She could be a nice MC.'"

From there, their artistic, frequently romantic, and oftentimes combative union was formed. Kim would still see him on the block shooting dice everyday with his friends. "And if he only won five dollars that day," she later said, "and I was like, 'Big, I'm hungry,' he would give me two-fifty of his five dollars."

"When you don't have any money, you can think of more romantic things to do. One Valentine's Day, I went over to his house and he said he was gonna buy a bunch of roses and put them on the bed, but he didn't have enough money. So he wanted to put a bunch of pennies on the bed instead, in the shape of a heart, but he thought I'd be mad."

There's no clear date when Big and Kim's emotional roller coaster of a journey began, though it was sometime in the early nineties. When Big married Evans, it didn't sit well with Kim. This would be far from the last time the three would ever butt heads.

But he wasn't worried about Kim's reaction to the news; the person Big was the most scared to tell about his impromptu marriage was, by far, his mother. Voletta came home one day from work to find her son sitting on the stoop in front of their apartment building. He couldn't hide the strange look on his face.

"Christopher, what's wrong with you?" she recalled in her memoir.

"I did it."

"Did what?"

"I just got married."

Christopher had put Voletta through a lot over the last couple of years, from dropping out of school, to slinging drugs, getting arrested, and spending time in jail, and to having a baby far before she felt he was ready. And now, out of the blue, he was telling her he was married? Voletta just couldn't understand how. He had different women calling her house every week, and *now* she was supposed to believe that he had found the one woman he wanted to spend the rest of his life with? Christopher followed her into the apartment, pleading with her that what he was saying was real. This wasn't a practical joke.

"No one believes I got married," a frustrated Christopher told his mother.

Voletta's denial would last only a short time, though. Her sister called and told Voletta she'd heard him on the radio sending a shout-out to his wife, Faith. Voletta confirmed it with Mark Pitts, her son's manager. Christopher was still living at home at the time, so when he came home later that day, Voletta decided to do some inquiring. She asked to see a picture of Evans.

"Is she white?" a perplexed Voletta asked.

Hardly able to speak through the laughter, Christopher said, "No, Ma! She's Black. She's pretty. That's what I told you."

If Voletta was annoyed that her son had gotten married on a whim, what happened next infuriated her. Evans called the house a few days later, and Voletta recognized the voice who had called her home several times before, but Voletta had never stopped to ask who it was. Now she had confirmation and proceeded to let her newfound daughter-in-law know how upset she was that she had never introduced herself. Evans was eager to get the heat off herself and was nearly in tears when she spilled the beans.

"I know, Miss Wallace. You are absolutely right," Evans said. "But it's not my fault. Christopher told me to stay away from you."

At that point, all Voletta saw was red. She wanted to wrangle her grown, giant of a son by the neck—and her grown, giant of a son wanted no smoke with his mother. She demanded to know why on Earth he would present her in such an unflattering light. He was like a puppy with its tail between its legs. But leave it to Christopher Wallace to come up with, given the circumstances, a logical explanation.

"First of all, you weren't supportive of this marriage and you know that," he said, looking his mother square in the eye. "Ma, I love you. But I love my wife and I did not want her to come around here and for you to insult her or disrespect her, because I did not want to have to choose between my mother and my wife."

Voletta was still mad as fire, but she understood the reasoning. A day after she spoke with Evans on the phone, husband and wife came by the apartment for Voletta and Evans's first meeting. Mother-in-law and daughter-in-law instantly hit it off.

"This should've happened a long time ago," Evans told Voletta with her husband right beside her. "That's Christopher's fault that it didn't."

All he could do was smile and walk away. His mom and wife liked each other. If they wanted to blame everything else on him, then so be it. It was far better than living with the alternative. Evans and Big would soon get a duplex of their own in nearby Fort Greene. He was officially in the honeymoon phase of the marriage, though that didn't last long at all. Evans estimated that within two weeks their lives were in a whirlwind of promotional tours, album rollouts, and studio sessions that would inevitably play a role in the strain on their relationship.

For now, though, everything felt on the upswing. Big loved Faith. Faith loved Big. And their careers were trending upward.

13

FRIEND OF MINE

BY THE FALL OF 1994, PRESIDENT BILL CLINTON HAD BEEN IN OFFICE FOR NEARLY TWO YEARS. He inherited the office with a stigma surrounding Democrats that they were too lenient on crime, a belief that had taken shape during the Reagan years and was hammered home by the Willie Horton ad and during George H. W. Bush's lone term. Throughout all of the 1980s and into the '90s, Republican leadership in the White House argued that if the voters were foolish enough to give power to Democrats, they'd also be giving away their own safety.

The Democrats took that framing to heart and acted. Or overreacted. On September 13, Clinton signed into law the Violent Crime Control and Law Enforcement Act. Or, as history would come to know it as, simply the "Crime Bill." On its surface, the legislation was enacted to curb years of high crime rates and place more power in law enforcement's hands in dealing with would-be criminals.

Not every provision in the Act was viewed negatively, either, like the Violence Against Women Act, which allocated $1.6 billion to prevent rape and domestic violence and punish offenders. Likewise, the Federal Assault Weapons Ban banned the manufacture of some semiautomatic weapons and magazines. There was also funding for "drug courts," which directed nonviolent drug offenders to probation, treatment, and services rather than incarceration.

Violent crimes had been increasing for decades dating back to the 1960s, and the crack cocaine epidemic in the '80s and '90s only helped increase the hysteria around violence in America. With Clinton in office, this was a chance for Democrats—like then-senator Joe Biden, who helped spearhead the legislation—to prove the shots taken at them by Republicans were wrong. They weren't scared to crack down on crime, and this bill was proof. The bill even expanded the federal death penalty. As a result of Clinton's signature, the Crime Bill envisioned that states would fall in line with the implementation of severe sentences at the federal level. There was money in building prisons, and the law did just that, along with funding a hundred thousand more cops and supported grant programs that incentivized cops to perform more drug-related arrests.

The Crime Bill has historically received a lot of heat for the epidemic of mass incarceration in the years that followed, and it shouldn't escape blame, but it was more reflective of a change already underway than the cause of it. The country had seen a terrifying rise in crime, fueled by racism and disinvestment, and looked to punishment as the solution. Then-First Lady Hillary Clinton said in 1996, "We need to take these people on, they are often connected to big drug cartels, they are not just gangs of kids anymore. They are often the kinds of kids that are called 'superpredators.' No conscience. No empathy. We can talk about why they ended up that way, but first we have to bring them to heel."

Poignantly, on the exact same day that President Clinton signed the Crime Bill, the dream Christopher Wallace had been chasing for so long finally came to fruition. His debut album, *Ready to Die*, hit shelves. Fueled by its infectious, rags-to-riches lead single "Juicy," the Notorious B.I.G.'s voice was on the radio across the country more times a day than he could count, and his face was on MTV every hour on the hour. His hesitations about doing the song went completely out the window now. In the history of rap, it's hard to think of many songs—if any exist—that serve as a more powerful introduction to an artist than "Juicy." In less than five minutes, Big managed to paint his life story in a way that, a quarter century later, the BBC would dub rap's "quintessential Cinderella tale."

Just like that—just like his fallen comrade Roland "O" Young had envisioned—he wasn't the dude performing to crowds in faraway cities who didn't know his lyrics, which had been the case only months earlier. And he wasn't that dude who had to sell crack to spoil his daughter. If he wanted to, he could start the first few words and let the crowd finish the verse for him. And that was on damn near any record throughout the album. The Notorious B.I.G., Biggie Smalls, Big—whatever one called him, the truth was evident. A star was born. *Ready to Die* would sell 57,000 copies in its first week—and would sell a half million copies before Thanksgiving.

At its core, *Ready to Die* was a product of crack-era New York City and the policies that helped involuntarily morph Black kids into criminals because of their skin tone and the environment they were raised in. If the 1994 Crime Bill was a way to combat crime, an honest listen to Big's album was a way to understand why the crimes were happening in the first place.

"I want them stressed-out niggas to be like, 'Yo, this nigga be hitting it right on the nose, man,'" he said. "That's what I'm trying to do . . . I got a lot off my chest with that album."

"I think my music is being so well received because it's some real shit. It ain't no gimmicks behind this shit. I'm just a nigga that live in Brooklyn that get busy. The shit I be talking about don't be no bullshit," Big said. "I'm not trying to be no role model for nobody. I'm not trying to tell nobody what's right and what's wrong because I lived my life doing wrong. All I can say is, if you listen to my shit, and you say, 'Damn, that nigga been through some hard shit.' And if you think about getting involved, think twice. I'm just a warning."

He continued, "I'm not trying to commit suicide when I say that. I'm just saying a nigga come out here every day hustling and risking his life. Risking his life from the police, the stickup man. Anything can happen to a nigga in the streets. So when I say a nigga 'ready to die,' a nigga ready to go all out for his. Ready to die for that money. Ready to die for his respect. Whatever a nigga gotta do."

It wasn't just Big gassing up his album, either. Critically, it was moving the needle, too. The *New York Times* dubbed the album "perhaps the most balanced and honest portrait of the dealer's life of any in hip-hop."

Wu-Tang with *36 Chambers* and Nas with *Illmatic* had announced the resurgence in East Coast rap before *Ready to Die*. But Big managed to achieve the rare combination of both commercial and critical stamps of approval. He seemed to check off every box an album could. Hard-core rap? "Warning," "Machine Gun

Funk," and "Gimme the Loot" handled that. Introspective numbers? That's what "Everyday Struggle," "Suicidal Thoughts," and "Things Done Changed" covered. Lyrical exercises? Look no further than "Unbelievable," "The What" with the album's lone guest Method Man, and "Respect." Pop-friendly singles? "Juicy" and "Big Poppa," which hit number one on the *Billboard* rap charts and number six on the Hot 100 (climbing higher than Craig Mack). There was no limit to where *Ready to Die* was set to take Big. Through it all, he remained the jokester, even at the expense of his friends sometimes.

A plethora of guns were on the set of Big's "Warning" video, albeit guns with blanks in them. He loved the firearms on set nonetheless. And there he was pointing a gun at everybody, much to the chagrin of Chico Del Vec.

"He was acting stupid with them guns," Chico said, laughing at the memory. "I got a scar on my back where I was sitting down and he ran up on me and I'm like, 'Stop playing! Stop playing!'"

Chico jumped up but, in the process, hit his back on a speaker. He fell to the floor in excruciating pain, holding his back. Big thought he had accidentally shot one of his closest friends. Everyone ran over to him to check on his condition.

"Y'all better check these guns!" Big yelled, looking at the gun, unsure of what exactly just happened.

"I'm like, 'Nah, son. I hit my back on the speaker. My back is bleeding because you scared me, duke! Don't do that!"

Two weeks after the release of *Ready to Die*, journalist Cheo Hodari Coker caught up with Big in front of his apartment near Fulton Street to see how Biggie Smalls was really living. He'd long been "hood famous," but now the Mayor of Bed-Stuy was famous enough, as he said, to be up close and personal with Robin Leach.

"I run this, dog. I mean, I've been doing this for the longest. Everybody know Biggie," he told Coker. "There ain't a nigga out here that don't know me. From down in that area they call Park Slope to all the way up in East New York, you know what I'm saying? And they all go through me. If they don't know me, they know of me. And they give me respect—a lot."

Big was right. He might not have had a 100 percent approval rating in Brooklyn, but it was pretty damn high. Just being outside caused a commotion. Some were brave enough to speak to him. Others just wanted to hear him talk about whatever topic under the sun. Coker told a fascinating story of two younger dudes who rolled up on Big smoking blunts during the interview. Trife and Larceny were M.A.F.I.A. members, but they also were part of a neighborhood crew of youngsters called the Snakes. They were looking for a gun to rob a guy for his VCR. Big played incredulous as to where a gun actually was the entire time.

Once they walked away, he admitted something to Coker.

"I know exactly where the gun is," Big said, "but I'm not gonna be a part of that shit there. Fuck that!"

He was now a household name, but he still had an ear to, and partially a foot in, the streets. Not because he was still hustling, but rather because he still felt an obligation to those there. Success from his music was always the goal. It was never the end goal. Ever since he was a kid and he and Hubert Sam first met in elementary school, he always thrived on the company he kept around him. The plan was always for Big to get on, become a star, and bring his friends from the neighborhood with him.

"Even if niggas don't go to school, you're going to be something," he demanded. "You ain't just going to be sitting there disappointing your parents. You're going to get some kind of paper. Try to play some ball. You're going to do *something*, man. You can't just sit there, because that's what really hurts parents the most, to just watch their son give up and not do nothing to fix it."

That was Christopher Wallace talking, not Biggie Smalls. In a way, he was speaking from experience and the grief he had caused his mother over the past several years, and what the drugs he sold did to his community. But it was also him wanting to be a provider for young people from his neighborhood; hence the formation of Junior M.A.F.I.A.

"Oh, nah, man! We ain't care about none of that," said 50 Grand when asked if the OGB felt slighted that Junior M.A.F.I.A. became Big's project and not them. "I was following his steps, but OGB, we ain't think like that. They was a bunch of young kids doing what they do . . . The ones who could rap made the album. The ones who couldn't rap just hung around. They were on the same block anyway."

"He never said, 'Take this bag and go hustle it.' He never said, 'Go around the corner and shoot this nigga,'" Lil' Cease reflected. "Instead, it was always, 'Get in this room, write these rhymes, get that pen and paper. I'm gonna make moves, and when I come back you better have a rhyme.' That's what Big did."

Around the same time, Lance "Un" Rivera came into the picture. Truthfully, Rivera had always been around the neighborhood. Un, like Big, hustled and came across some money as a result. His brother, Justice, had put him on to Big's music. He was impressed, but initially his interest didn't expand past that. In the past he loaned Big money when he needed it and was always a street figure Big trusted. Big liked having him around, but Un didn't exactly know how he wanted to be involved in the music industry—which was originally his brother's dream. Big brought Un to a Jodeci video shoot and could tell immediately Puffy didn't necessarily enjoy his presence.

"Puff pulled up across the street and he called Big over," Un recalled in *Unbelievable*. "I seen him talkin'. Then I seen Big put his head down. Something told me they was over there talkin' about me. So when Big came back across the street, he just looked at me, and he ain't want to say nothin'. I was like, 'You ain't got to explain.'"

From that moment on, Un vowed to get back at Puffy. Not in a street way, but in a way that would benefit him and have no legal ramifications.

"I knew the nigga Big was dope," Un said. "And I knew the nigga Puff needed Big. So I would get in the middle of they shit, not to really be disruptive, but to manipulate certain situations."

Big's life was changing seemingly by the minute, and he was thinking about what it would look like moving forward—as well as who he wanted to keep close to him. This was a natural progression of fame. He was only twenty-two, but despite the money, the fame, and the women, he did wonder what happiness would resemble as he grew older. One rainy night, shortly after *Ready to Die*'s release, Big and Rob Stone rode to Providence, Rhode Island, to do a radio station appearance. It was just the two of them in the car, which was rare, because Big would always have someone like Lil' Cease or Hawk with him. They spoke about many things on the ride there: women, growing up in Brooklyn, the industry. Big's love for his mother and Puffy's undeniable influence on *Ready to Die*.

"I remember him saying shit was starting to get hectic and people were coming at him. He was already starting to talk about the next album," said Stone. "And that he just wanted to get away, that he didn't think he could record it in Brooklyn and make it the best it could be. He just wanted to go to an island somewhere, like Jamaica . . . and just bury himself in the studio with Puff."

But if Big was adapting to the newfound success and the occasionally suffocating weight of celebrity, Sean "Puffy" Combs was seeing the celebrity around his name increase tenfold. Two days after his twenty-fifth birthday, the *New York Times* published a big feature on Combs and the success (and drama) that seemed to follow the man predicted to be the next great Black music mogul.

"He's one of the best young executives who is rolling with the big guys," said Havelock Nelson, a rap columnist at *Billboard* at the time. "Right now Puffy has his finger on the pulse of the music industry. Older executives could learn a lot from him."

With the success of *Ready to Die* and Craig Mack's "Flava in Ya Ear"—on top of his sweeping success with Jodeci, Heavy D, and Mary J. Blige at Uptown—this was the acclaim that Puffy had so feverishly coveted. A year earlier, he had been fired from Uptown and unsure of what exactly his next move was going to be. Now he was sitting on top of the world with established veterans like Andre Harrell and Russell Simmons at Def Jam racing to catch up with him. Yet as Puffy's star power was rising, it wasn't as if his former boss, Harrell, was jealous. He had other issues to worry about.

———

"[People] like Suge Knight are just takers. They make no legitimate contribution to the music business," Jerry Heller said in the fall of 1994. "They just extort people out of the fruits of their labor."

Three years after Knight successfully managed to get Dr. Dre out of his Ruthless Records contract, he shifted his attention to Uptown Records. Knight got his hands on the contracts of Uptown's most prized artists in Jodeci, Mary J. Blige, and producer-artist DeVante Swing. All three ended up signing West Coast management deals with Knight. The coup happened so quickly that many in the industry believed Knight had physically intimidated Harrell into signing his prized acts over to a man who was growing more and more fearsome within the industry.

Knight denied all allegations, instead heaping praise on himself, saying that his artists knew he would do everything in his power to "represent them to the fullest." Whatever tactics Knight used, he did manage to overhaul what the artists felt were one-sided contracts with Uptown. According to Swing, Knight helped Jodeci land greater creative control, get a massive retroactive back payment, and double its royalty rate from 9 percent to 18 percent.

"I have had so many people take advantage of me that it's nice to finally have someone on my side," said Blige then. "Suge's like that guy in the movies who goes around getting the bad people—like Charles Bronson, right?"

"It's true that I try to do everything in my power to protect the people I love and to make sure everybody in the Death Row family prospers," Knight said in 1994. "I know there are still individuals in this society who can't stand the thought of a young Black person with a gang of money in the bank."

All parties involved denied any threats or physical altercations, but the Fruit of Islam were hired by Harrell shortly after the transfer of power took place. It was rumored that Knight even showed up at a recording session for Big to see Puffy. The two may not have been the best of friends, but they were cordial, and there was a sense of respect from young Black music executives achieving success.

It wasn't as if Puffy was in competition with Suge, though. At least not yet. He was too busy flying high on his own triumphs. The City College tragedy was still very much on his mind, but he'd proven that nothing could keep him down. Which is why his twenty-fifth birthday at the Roseland Ballroom in New York City on November 4, 1994, was such a pivotal moment. Dressed in a three-piece suit, top hat, and bow tie, Puffy was the man of the hour and newfound King of New York. Big, the author behind the hottest album on the streets, rocked the mic in a striped suit. Also in attendance that night was Big's close friend Tupac Shakur.

Biggie and Tupac's friendship was as genuine as any in rap. Born less than a year apart, they had completely different personalities. 'Pac was the more vocal, not just in rap, but in everything he did, and Big respected the fact that 'Pac came from a lineage that tied him directly to the streets and the struggle painted in his music. He'd speak about injustices toward Black women in the same vein he'd talk about shootouts in public with rivals and the same way he'd hold America accountable for systemic injustices toward his people. And he was charismatic enough to record songs taunting the police while starring in movies alongside pop dynamos like Janet Jackson. Big was by far the reserved of the two, though 'Pac deeply respected his ability to paint truly graphic expressions of the Black experience through his lyrics. Both oozed an elixir of charisma, wisdom, and at times recklessness. Their future was bright, and neither was twenty-five yet. They had years and years to create magic together, though, and their star power was only going to shine brighter. Or at least they figured it would.

In the year and change since they had first met, so much in their lives had changed. Big was no longer just some up-and-coming raw talent from New York. And Tupac was fighting for his freedom in the aftermath of a crime he vehemently denied, stemming from a rape accusation a year earlier. Shakur's life had always been lived at a hundred miles per hour, but now it felt as if he was going even faster, and without brake pads. Shakur's name was ringing heavily on the streets of New York at that time, too, as he was calling out real-life street dudes, saying that he was being set up. Some of those same guys were at Puffy's party that night, including a man respected and feared in the streets known as Haitian Jack.

That party and the blunts, bottles, and beauties it would bring would be the last time Biggie and Tupac would enjoy each other's company. The next time they'd come face-to-face, Big would hardly recognize the man he had once considered one of his closest friends.

Little did anyone know at the time that a chain reaction that would ultimately lead to two of the darkest days in rap history had already begun. They were both living on borrowed time.

Much of Tupac Shakur's early life was spent bouncing from city to city, coast to coast, all the while battling the constructs of intense poverty and a mother who had become addicted to crack cocaine. He slept on mattresses with springs coming out of them and often wore the same clothes to school because his family could barely afford to keep food on the table. The lights were hardly on. Despite the odds stacked against him, Tupac's brilliance was blinding. His intelligence, bolstered by the fact that he was constantly reading books and newspapers, gave him a more defined worldview than most people his age. He attended the Baltimore School for the Arts, where his creative and artistic capabilities made him stand out among a school full of talented peers. It was there that he established a lifelong friendship with a classmate named Jada Pinkett, who would evolve into an accomplished thespian herself. It was there, too, where so many people saw Shakur's immaculate potential as an actor—and more important, they say, the deep love he had for his community and the obsession he had with creating art that mattered. And art that represented his people—Black people.

"I could have seen him as a Denzel Washington," Richard Pilcher, the Baltimore School for the Arts principal acting teacher who helped Shakur hone his fondness for Shakespeare, told the *Baltimore Sun* in 2017. "I think he would've become one of our finest film actors."

"You know, if you look at the career that Will Smith has," Cheo Hodari Coker told me, "Tupac was as good, if not better. If Tupac started making the right decisions, he could've been a ten-, fifteen-, twenty-million-dollar actor. He was poised to do that."

Shakur wasn't a "street dude" in the sense that he was out there putting in work and selling drugs. But he more than understood that world because he had no choice but to live in the communities where a lot of these things happened. Shakur was the bastard child of government interference with the Black liberation movement. He came up in the hell that public policy and counterintelligence created, at the same time hip-hop was coming of age in Black communities across the country.

Hip-hop provided Shakur the avenue of self-expression he needed. Much like Big, the rap moniker the world would come to know him by wasn't his first. Shakur started off as MC New York, an homage to his birthplace, but by the time he hooked up with Shock G and Digital Underground out of Oakland, he kept it simple: 2Pac. Shakur was originally a roadie with the outrageous, platinum-selling group. Even then, though, everyone around him knew 'Pac definitely had more to say and offer. That opportunity came on the 1991 single "Same Song," where 'Pac highlighted his potential as solo artist. Not long after, Shakur branched out on his own.

His debut album, 1991's *2Pacalypse Now*, didn't hit the top of the *Billboard* charts, but it was an explicit societal critique from a young man who had seen so much in the first twenty years of his life. Songs like "Trapped" encapsulated the angst of growing up Black in a country that historically loathed Black skin. And "Brenda's Got a Baby" told the real-life story of a young, pregnant Black girl abandoned by the system and, feeling no other options were available, entering a life of prostitution and eventually taking her own life.

"A woman had thrown her baby in the trash, and he was just so rattled by that," recalled the actor Omar Epps, years later, who acted alongside Shakur in the 1992 street classic *Juice*. Ironically, Shakur's character of "Bishop," a maniacal, coldhearted teen who lives with a chip on his shoulder and a bullet in the chamber of a gun, was the polar opposite of the young man who couldn't stop talking about the story of the discarded baby. While it's not clear which story in particular Epps was referring to, there were multiple accounts in the *New York Times* of young girls giving birth and leaving their babies in the trash in 1991, when *Juice* would've been in production in Harlem. "The whole day, he kept bringing it up. At lunchtime, he was like, 'Yo, O, come into the trailer. He starts rapping this song to me. Months later his album comes out and I see the video . . . I thought that was incredible. That was real-life art."

2Pacalypse Now also landed on the desk of one of the most powerful people in America, Vice President Dan Quayle. On April 11, 1992, a drug dealer named Ronald Ray Howard shot and killed a Texas state trooper named Bill Davidson. Howard, who was driving a stolen car, said he was listening to Shakur's "Souljah's Story," and according to the Associated Press, his attorney "said his client would not have done it 'without the music riling him up.'" Davidson's daughter filed a lawsuit against Tupac and his label, and in September, Quayle demanded that the album be removed from shelves. He called the release of the album "an irresponsible corporate act." Asked later if he was upset that Howard used his name, Shakur chose the side of the Black man, saying he understood Howard had to do whatever he needed to help his case. But asked if he felt remorse for a string of cop killings, Shakur was far more blunt.

"No. I mean, I would if I could, but I can't," Shakur said. "It wasn't no remorse for Latasha [Harlins]. It wasn't no remorse for Yusef Hawkins. And it wasn't no remorse when them mothafuckas kicked my ass," he said, referring to the 1991 beating he took at the hands of two Oakland police officers who attempted to arrest him for jaywalking. He sued the department for $10 million, and the police later settled. "So they can all mothafuckin' die until they respect me as a muthafuckin' man—and every Black man out there. They can all mothafuckin' die, and that's real. Until they do, more mothafuckas gon' die. As long as they got bullets, it's gon' be some justice around this mothafucka."

Like a moth to a flame, controversy always seemed to find Tupac Shakur. Truthfully, sometimes he would go searching for it himself. He was always in the news for something. An August 1992 altercation at a Marin City, California, park between Shakur and his camp with a rival crew ended in six-year-old Qa'id Walker-Teal being accidentally shot and killed. The bullet was fired from a gun registered to Tupac. The incident deeply bothered Shakur, who cared immensely for young kids. It would be far from his last run-in with the law.

By 1993, Shakur's status as rap's most beloved and notorious rebel had only grown tenfold. He was critically praised for his role in *Juice* and was preparing for the release of his second feature film, *Poetic Justice*, starring alongside Janet Jackson. In June, he appeared in an episode of *A Different World* with his childhood friend Jada Pinkett. And his sophomore album, *Strictly 4 My N.I.G.G.A.Z. . .* , released that February, became a smash hit, fueled by diverse singles like the rebellious "Holler If Ya Hear Me," the sexually promiscuous "I Get Around," and the women's empowerment anthem "Keep Ya Head Up." All three singles represent different sides to Shakur, and for anyone paying attention, it was evident that Tupac Shakur was far more than just a rapper. There was this Malcolm X–like spirit to him that endeared him to Black folks regardless of where he was from, because he understood "the struggle" was not confined to one region. It was universal to the Black experience in America. Speaking at the Indiana Black Expo in the summer of 1993, Shakur delivered perhaps his fiercest speech about the value of Black life as he saw it.

"My mother put mothafuckin' work in! Do you hear me?" Shakur fired off. "And this why I'm telling y'all, if we gon' struggle, the struggle gotta come from our heart. It can't come from because we looking for a key back in. It's gotta come because I'm looking at you and you look goddamn good to me and you my sister. And I ain't gonna let none of these crackers take you down!"

Even when he was self-destructive, Shakur was still reflective of all the issues and rages that burned deeply within the souls of Black folks. At his best, Tupac was part of the lineage of great Black orators and activists, many of whom caught bullets to silence them. Like those same leaders, Shakur often found himself on the wrong side of the law. He sued the Oakland Police Department and was awarded $43,000 after the jaywalking incident led to the assault by the two officers. He was charged with physically assaulting movie directors Albert and Allen Hughes after being removed from *Menace II Society*—a fight he infamously admitted to partaking in on an episode of *Yo! MTV Raps* that would later result in jail time. In April 1993, he was charged with felonious assault after attempting to hit another rapper with a baseball bat at a Michigan State University concert.

By the time Shakur and Big met, they found something else in the other they both cherished. Big loved the fact that Shakur's story was as real as it got. While his mother showered him with video games, fresh clothes, and annual trips back to Jamaica during his formative years, it was Shakur who experienced the abject poverty that so much of *Ready to Die* would come to represent. And Shakur deeply cherished Big's penchant for storytelling, and his street prowess. Plus, they both loved weed, Hennessy, and cracking jokes. Big was smitten with Shakur that first meeting in L.A. Now, whenever they'd link up again, it was all love. And whenever they were around each other, they were always the center of attention. Like that one time 'Pac and Big held club goers captivated in New York's beloved and equally infamous nightclub the Tunnel. All they were doing was talking, but their presence was so magnetic in the club that it became its own event. That was, at least, until Big and his crew got into a brawl with bouncers for reasons no one really remembers. For a point in time, too, Shakur was a regular fixture on the corner of Fulton and St. James.

"Tupac used to call my house often asking for Christopher," Voletta said.

"'Pac pulled up on Fulton Street one time with a garbage bag [of weed]," Lil' Kim reflected. "Nas just happened to come through, too. Everybody was just talking like, 'Shoot, Nas, Tupac, and Big is out there.' Cease was running back and forth to the store getting mad blunts 'cause they couldn't keep up with the garbage bag of weed! They was out there in front of a little chicken spot and the liquor store was right there."

"Tupac would be done with the movie shoot and they'd come through Fulton Street. They'd smoke, drink, and hang out," said 50 Grand. "Now Big is signed and everybody would come on the Ave. to see him. Nas would come through. Treach, too, because he hung out with 'Pac a lot. Fulton Street was really shining at the time."

Shakur would take Big, Cease, and the crew to shows with him and watched with pride as they ripped the same stages together. Like at Bowie State University's homecoming concert in 1993 when 'Pac turned his show over to the Live Squad and Big, who performed "Party and Bullshit" to a raucous crowd. Or at the Budweiser Superfest on October 24 at Madison Square Garden that held their now legendary onstage freestyle, and Big repeatedly asking the crowd "Where Brooklyn at?!"

Big slept on Tupac's couch in L.A., and when Tupac was in New York, Big always made sure Tupac had protection. Like when he took Chico Del Vec to meet Tupac for the first time. An encounter that came with the oddest grocery list Chico had ever heard.

"Yo, Chic, let's go meet this nigga Tupac," Big said. "We gonna go uptown. He in this hotel. I gotta link up with him to do this song. Go get the thing and come back."

"What the hell am I getting a gun for this nigga Tupac for?" Chico wondered. He went and got the gun, and by the time he returned, Big had an even odder request.

"Yo," Big said, "let's get a bouquet of flowers and let's get on the train."

Flowers? Chico was confused. He had a gun on him and some flowers. To go meet Tupac. The math, for Chico, wasn't adding up. Chico was quiet the rest of the way to Manhattan until they got to Shakur's Times Square hotel. Shakur opened the door with energy that was recognizable from the moment the doorknob turned. It was the happiest Chico had ever seen anyone while wearing a bulletproof vest on. Chico didn't know if he was walking into a gunfight or not. But at the same time, too, he was excited.

"Wassup, Bishop!" Chico blindly said. He looks back on the memory with laughter. "I'm over here calling this man Bishop."

Shakur appreciated the reference. "I like this nigga already!" he said. "Big, who's this?"

Chico sat in amazement. Damn, he thought, it's really Tupac live and in the flesh. The crazy dude from the movies who said "I don't give a fuck" and made Chico feel it in his chest. 'Pac was his usual bouncing-off-the-walls self, chain-smoking cigarette after cigarette when he noticed the flowers. He was flattered.

"Yo, Big, you brought me flowers, man?"

"Yeah, man, I brought the flowers for you, man."

Now Chico was even more confused. He was saying every curse word imaginable in his head, alternating between a mixture of awe at Shakur and sheer confusion as to what was really taking place. Big then told Chico to give 'Pac the gun, which Chico did but not before taking the clip out.

"Oh, nigga, this for me?!" Shakur asked.

"Yeah, something to hold you down, playboy."

If Chico was confused about what was going on, what happened next caused him to pick his jaw off the floor. There was a knock at the door. It was Madonna. Chico was so starstruck that he couldn't even say her name.

"That's the girl from 'Like a Virgin!' 'Like a Virgin!'" he blurted out. "Big's telling me to chill. But she's just smiling and she gives 'Pac a kiss on the cheek and he gives her flowers. I was like, 'Ohhhh snap!' She left out the room and 'Pac sat back down. I'm just sitting there in shock."

For the next several hours, it wasn't 2Pac and Biggie talking. It was Tupac and Christopher. America loves a rebel, as long as they aren't Black. And in their own separate ways, 'Pac and Big were rebels. They bonded over their talents and where they could take them, but at the root of everything was a mutual respect. A genuine love, too. Chico took the gun back and dusted the prints off it before they left, but whenever Tupac needed anything in New York, it was Big and crew who made sure he had it.

"Them niggas was together every day. He had to prove something to Big, and Big had something to prove to him," Cease said. "'Pac was that thug nigga in the industry. And Big was the next thing to come from the hood that was gonna fuck niggas' heads up. And they were building together. That shit was looking strong. They was really looking out for each other, and they did records together."

Big introduced Shakur to Easy Mo Bee, who would later produce records on Shakur's aptly titled *Me Against the World* album—and who would produce "Runnin,'" their first-ever collaboration, originally meant for Shakur's *Thug Life* album. In turn, Shakur introduced Big to his close friend Stretch of the Live Squad. So it was no surprise when Big and Stretch became good friends.

Yet as their friendship was blossoming, it wasn't like Big was his only friend in New York. For much of the latter part of 1993, Shakur was in New York frequently, filming his third feature film in as many years. Shakur's character Birdie in the 1994 coming-of-age hoops film *Above the Rim* was its charismatic yet terrifying street figure. Those in the know had long known that 'Pac had been running with Jacques Agnant—or, as he was known in the streets, "Haitian Jack."

Jack's reputation in New York was storied. His family emigrated from Haiti to East Flatbush, Brooklyn, which by the seventies and definitely the eighties had established itself as a hotbed of crime. By the time crack had its cobra clutch on the hood, Jack was already deeply immersed in the street life. He was known, in his own words, to "clean corners" and shoot entire blocks up to send messages to his enemies. Walking into clubs with his gun on him was normal. Drug dealers were often the most respected and feared guys—and Jack was the one robbing them. Not because it made him a ghetto Robin Hood. He did it because it made him a lot of money. *A lot.* His reputation in the streets earned him respect in the music industry that, with its dog-eat-dog ethos, was not all that different from the underworld that turned Jacques Agnant into Haitian Jack.

By the early nineties, Jack was known around New York not only for his weight in the streets, but as an epic figure on the nightlife scene. Party promoters respected him, DJs saluted him, and everyone from athletes to entertainers knew of Jack. So it wasn't too surprising when a chance meeting in an Atlanta studio connected him with Madonna. The two instantly hit it off. He was alluring, and his ties to the streets gave him the bad boy image that Madonna gravitated toward in the nineties.

"[Jack] got [Madonna] chillin', eating jerk chicken, nigga. I saw that flex," the rapper and fellow Flatbush native Spliff Star said in the 2021 FX docu-series *Hip Hop Uncovered*. "It was the swag. It was the persona. She felt it. I couldn't understand. I was like, 'Does this bitch know who she hanging with?' This a real street nigga."

Because rappers and people of power in the streets frequently ran in the same circles, and energy finds energy, Haitian Jack met Tupac Shakur. Drug dealers, pimps, and prostitutes had been unintended role models in his childhood, but hanging around Jack offered a masterclass in how to operate within the ghetto political infrastructure, or so Shakur figured. "They made me mature," Tupac later said. "They introduced me to all these gangsters in Brooklyn."

"One day ['Pac] said to me, 'I'm glad I met you when I did because it really helped with that character I was working on,'" Jack recalled. "Then I said, 'You got something from me?' He was like, 'Yeah, man. Just your swagger, the way you handle yourself, how everybody's always around you. That was important for me to see that that happens. That people gravitate to a gangster.'"

14
THE CHAIN REACTION

ON NOVEMBER 2, 1993, TUPAC WAS CHARGED WITH SHOOTING TWO OFF-DUTY ATLANTA POLICE OFFICERS. He claimed the cops were harassing a Black motorist and pulled guns out first as he intervened. The case was serious, but the charges were eventually dropped. Plus, one of the cops ended up being charged with lying and for firing the first shot. But the charge that lay on the horizon just days away would prove to be the moment that changed the course of Shakur's entire life. A few weeks later, shortly before Thanksgiving, Shakur went with Jack and company to the popular Manhattan nightclub Nell's. Shakur was enjoying his time there, meeting Ronnie Lott of the New York Jets and Derrick Coleman of the New Jersey Nets, who showed him love, and appreciating the many beautiful women in attendance. He was introduced to a young woman named Ayanna Jackson, who took an instant liking to the star. Though Jackson would deny this claim, Shakur said they went to a dark and empty portion of the dance floor where she performed oral sex on him.

"That shit turned me on. I wasn't thinking, like, 'This is going to be a rape case.' I'm thinking, 'This is going to be a good night,'" Shakur said. "We drive back to the hotel. We go upstairs and have sex, real quick. As soon as I came, that was it. I was tired. I was drunk. And I knew I had to get up early in the morning, so I was like, 'What are you going to do? You can spend the night or you can leave.' She left me her number, and everything was cool."

Everything changed for Shakur after that night. And later, for Big, too. A few nights later, on November 18, Jackson returned to 'Pac's thirty-eighth-floor Parker Meridien hotel room before he headed out to New Jersey to perform at Club 88 at Jack's request. Shakur said that he was getting a massage from Jackson when Jack and Shakur's tour manager entered the room. Up until that point, the stories were in alignment. Jackson would accuse Shakur and company of raping her. Shakur said that he left the room once the other men entered and awoke a short while later to Jackson yelling at him that this wouldn't be the last he heard from her.

Shakur and two others were charged with forcible sodomy and unlawful imprisonment. The charge came as 'Pac's pro-women anthem "Keep Ya Head Up" sat at number sixteen on the *Billboard* Hot 100. Over the course of the next year, Shakur's star power came under the microscope like never before. *Above the Rim*, before assuming the cult status it has now, initially received lukewarm reviews. But if there was one thing that received universal praise, it was Shakur's performance. "As the strong-arm hustler, Tupac Shakur proves, once again, that he may be the most dynamic young actor since Sean Penn," said *Entertainment Weekly*.

Throughout it all, 'Pac and Big remained close. On April 4, 1994, journalist dream hampton captured one such occasion on camera. They chain-smoked blunt after blunt and drank Hennessy in Shakur's Midtown Manhattan hotel room. Shakur was joking, but there was an element of sincerity in his voice.

"I'm staying right here in this little-ass room," Shakur told Big. "Nigga got to stay out of trouble . . . From now on, bitch wanna fuck with me, I'm getting it all on tape. Whatchusay? You wanna give me some pussy? Repeat that. What's that? You want to engage in consensual sex in my hotel room?"

Shakur and Jack's relationship, however, deteriorated over the course of 1994. Agnant's case was eventually separated from Shakur's, which raised an immediate red flag for the rapper. Several people in the star's orbit attempted to warn him about the gangster. From prison, Mike Tyson told him he was "out of his league" running with Jack.

"I would often have conversations with him about some elements around him, but I wasn't abreast of it all because I wasn't there every time he was getting in trouble," Tupac's *Above the Rim* costar Marlon Wayans told me in 2019. "I'd just say, 'Yo, you have the power to make different decisions, watch out for this, watch out for that. You have to dodge traps. You can't run into them.' 'Pac's greatest attribute is that he was super courageous, but sometimes that can also become your Achilles' heel. Sometimes the thing that's your superpower is also your flaw."

'Pac's paranoia slowly began to seep its way into his bond with Big, too. He was hurt he wasn't mentioned in *Ready to Die*'s liner notes. But Shakur understood the inner workings of the industry. He didn't allow that to come in between their friendship. Big had always shown him nothing but love. It was at Puffy's party at Roseland that Shakur was annoyed even more. Jack was at the party, politicking with the people he thought were his friends.

"I was hurt," a heated Shakur later said. "I was like, I'm going to trial, I'm probably going to get convicted, and this nigga's showing up at a party with champagne, hanging with Biggie. I was like, 'Damn, he's just bouncing from rapper to rapper.'"

Big, as he always had, greeted Shakur with open arms, even introducing him to his wife, Faith Evans, that night. But when they were by themselves, Big asked him if he was still kicking it with Jack. Shakur said no.

"Don't," Big demanded. "Be careful."

Shakur committed a major breach street etiquette at the party that night, too. He saw Jack there, but he didn't acknowledge him. He didn't even look in Jack's direction. But Shakur was done with Jack, and the bad blood would only grow more public in the coming weeks. Through the press, he called Jack a "hanger-on," and on November 29, he delivered one of his most emotionally charged interviews when he pleaded his innocence once more and expressed resentment that his rape case was being tried separately.

"My whole life has been turned around. I lost every job. I lost everything. I lost every opportunity. I can't buy cars. I can't get rent," he said, coming out of court. "But I'm still a survivor. I'm still coming to court. Still signing autographs. But soon, I'ma go crazy. And it's up to the world. America eats its babies. No matter what y'all think about me, I'm still your child."

As his trial trudged on, Shakur became more and more strapped for cash. All the money he'd made from his movies and the overwhelming success from *Strictly 4 My N.I.G.G.A.Z.* . . . had been used to pay his attorneys. This is how songs like "Dear Mama," "If I Die Tonight," and more from his next album, *Me Against the World*, came to fruition. It was that stress, that drama, and that fear of the unknown that inspired arguably his greatest body of work.

Shakur would go to court during the day and prepare for marathon studio sessions at night. If he slept, very few people seemed to see it. Hours before the ruling in his sexual assault case, Shakur set off on a whirlwind of errands.

———

Tupac knew his freedom was no longer in his hands. His fate rested in a jury he felt saw him as a menace to society. But he still needed money. Acting was complicated by schedules and the stigma of his case, but he knew he could always get money in the recording studio. As long as a producer or manager had cash on hand, he'd be there to deliver a verse. On November 29, after a meeting with the cast of *New York Undercover* about the possibility of appearing on a future episode, Shakur, Stretch, and a few of his homeboys headed to lay some verses for Ron G, one of rap's most impactful mixtape DJs. Shakur had heard of Ron G through Big, who also saluted Ron on "Juicy." Because of their friendship, and because 'Pac knew a feature on a Ron G mixtape would keep his name on the streets should he have to do a bid, he didn't charge Ron. The verse eventually landed on the song "Representin' 4 Ron G," which also featured Stretch and Keith Murray.

"I think niggas is trying to kill me," Shakur rapped that night. "Picturin' pistols, spittin' hollow points till they drill me."

Not even 'Pac realized how immediately ominous this would become.

Little Shawn was signed to Uptown, and his manager wanted Shakur to come record a verse. Shakur agreed, but this time he wanted his money—$7,000, to be exact. He wasn't in a rush and made sure to stop by a local weed spot when he noticed his pager was blowing up again. He knew Shawn's manager, Jimmy Henchman, through some street dudes and saw himself as doing Henchman a favor by helping him try to go legit. Word got back to Shakur that the money was off the table, and Shakur told him that if there was no money involved, he wouldn't waste his time heading to Quad Studios. Moments later Henchman called back saying he'd give him the money out of his pocket, but to just come to the studio. Shakur agreed and made his way to Quad Studios in the early morning hours of November 30.

Drew Dixon, Big's friend from Brooklyn, was working at Def Jam at the time. Earlier that day, she said, Big called her and told her to come to Quad that night, as he was working on the Junior M.A.F.I.A. project and he wanted her to hear what they were cooking up. *Ready to Die* was tearing up the streets, and he was already thinking about how he could get his young protégés on. Dixon and her friends had made weed brownies that night and fell asleep. Shakur, though, pulled up to Quad that night on edge. Something felt off about the entire situation, but then again, that could be the pressure of his case weighing on him, too. Lil' Cease, Nino Brown, and Matty C were all on the balcony smoking weed. They had already smoked out the actual studio.

"The engineer was like, 'I gotta mix this song down,'" Chico said. "My God, we was just blowing it down!"

Cease, Nino, and Matty could tell by the bop it was Shakur. His walk and bald head with the bandana tied around it was a dead giveaway. No one in Big's immediate circle knew Shakur, Stretch, and company were pulling up to the studio, so they were all ecstatic to see him.

"Yo, Big! 'Pac's downstairs! He was just walking right down Forty-Seventh Street!" Cease and Nino relayed.

Big and company were in the studio working on the record that would become "Player's Anthem."

"Word?!" he responded excitedly. "Tell him to come upstairs!"

Cease and Nino rushed downstairs to get Shakur. All throughout Quad that night were significant studio sessions from SWV, Deborah Cox, Mobb Deep, and, of course, the M.A.F.I.A. On another floor, Puffy and Mark Pitts were talking to Harrell. Puffy had just finished shooting his parts to Big's "Warning" video and was intending to go upstairs and check on Big. By then, word around the studio was that 'Pac was pulling up and everyone was happy to see him. As for Shakur himself, the trepidation that had left him once he saw Cease on the balcony calling out for him had immediately returned. Something seemed off. He saw guys in fatigues near the lobby but figured they were Big's security. It tripped him out, though, because even Big's most loyal street soldiers had always shown him love.

By then, the jig was up. Those same unidentifiable guys he saw in the lobby pulled guns on him by the time he got to the elevator.

"Don't nobody move! Everybody on the floor! You know what time it is. Run your shit! Run your shit!" the gunmen yelled.

"All of my homeboys dropped to the floor," Shakur recounted. "But I wanted going to get on the floor. I'm thinking Stretch is going to fight because Stretch is so big he was towering over those niggas. And from what I know about the criminal element, if niggas come to rob you and they see the big nigga, they always hit the big nigga first. But they didn't touch Stretch. They came straight to me."

"I'm the nigga that goes for mines, always forever," Stretch said later. "But I ain't no dumb nigga. Niggas run up on me with guns, and I ain't got no gun? What the fuck am I supposed to do. I ain't fighting no niggas with no guns. I can be towering over niggas, but I'm not towering over no slugs."

Shakur's stubbornness to comply with their orders only agitated the gunmen. 'Pac moved to draw his gun, but the gunmen pulled their triggers first. All in all, Shakur was shot five times—twice in the groin, twice in the head, and once in the hand.

The elevator door opened with an enthusiastic Cease and Nino. Those jubilant emotions they had felt coming down immediately evaporated as they saw a bloodied 'Pac and company on the ground, with masked gunmen demanding they get back into the elevator. Following the armed robbery, the gunmen ran back into Times Square and disappeared into the night. Within minutes of the shooting, Haitian Jack—who says he told his soldiers in the streets to refrain from touching Shakur—received a phone call saying what went down.

"The person, at the time, we were real cool. And he felt like Tupac had no right to say what he did about me, especially in New York City. They wanted to discipline him," Jack would say in a later interview. "I got the call within thirty seconds after it happened. He said, 'Listen, man. I got it, homie. And it went all bad.' I said wrong number and hung up."

Shakur, Stretch, and company limped outside, asking a stripper who worked next door what she'd seen. Shakur was screaming for the police.

"We asked this bitch, 'What did you see? Did you see something? Where'd the niggas go?'" said Stretch. "And this bitch was like, 'I don't know nothing. I didn't see nothing.'"

Bloodied, confused, and admittedly scared, Shakur and his crew went back into the studio and stumbled upon the elevator. Meanwhile, back up in the session where Big was, an exasperated Cease and Nino stumbled out of the elevator to relay the news. Shakur had just been robbed, and he was shot. The mood immediately shifted.

"The fuck? You fucking lying," Big said. "Y'all niggas don't move!"

Big and a gang of people waited minutes for the elevator to come. Those minutes felt like hours. They knew something serious was going down in the lobby, and they all wanted to get there to protect Shakur.

"Thank God Big ain't grab no piece or he would've been going to jail," said Matty C of that fateful night at Quad. "Because by the time we got to the lobby, it wasn't nothing but cops searching us."

Meanwhile, the elevator carrying Shakur, Stretch, and company got off on the floor with Little Shawn—the artist he was originally supposed to be recording with at Quad. Everyone looked as if they were seeing a ghost when a groggy Shakur struggled to get off the elevator. An already paranoid Shakur, due to his trial and falling out with Jack, became even more so. Now he really didn't know who to trust.

"You were the only one who knew I was coming," a bloodied 'Pac said.

Everyone in the studio was shocked to see Shakur in such a vulnerable state. But they also knew what was on the way: the police. And they knew the cops would be more than eager to search every young Black male on the property. Especially if they knew it was a rapper-involved shooting. Shakur was so in shock and so traumatized that all he could do was roll up a blunt. He'd later say that the first cop on the scene was the same who testified against him in his rape trial. Nothing was adding up for Shakur.

In the lobby, Big and company were being questioned by police. They'd come down to protect their friend, and now they were being treated as suspects. Big smelled the gunpowder in the lobby, and there was blood by a bandana on the floor. He couldn't believe it. One of his closest friends was in trouble, and Big felt helpless.

"They had multiple people come off the elevator, and they was throwing them against the wall like us. It was a bunch of us against the wall," said Chico. "Police was asking everyone for ID, what floor they were on. They were saying it's a crime scene. Then the elevator opens up and 'Pac was on a stretcher coming out. Big turned around and looked at 'Pac, and he had his middle finger up like, 'Fuck these niggas.'"

Big, Chico, Matty, and more were all questioned by police and ultimately let go. But the damage had been done. Tupac had been shot and no one quite understood why, especially Tupac. As he was rushed to Bellevue Hospital, the bullets still lodged in his body, Shakur began to think about who did this to him and why.

"I just kept thinking, 'They really did shoot me.' I really did believe at one point, up until I got shot, that no Black person would ever shoot me," Shakur said in a 1995 interview. "I was their representative. I didn't have to fear my own community. I represent them. I'm their ambassador to the world. They would never harm me. They would never rob me. They would never do me wrong. But as proven by this false rape charge, as proven by these gun shots, as proven by a lot of the comments you read in the news and the media, that's not true. I'm just one man. I just thought about how I would change. What would I do? How could I make them sorry they ever did this to me?"

He was the only one ambushed, attacked, and shot, and he already had his suspicions. He originally thought it was hired guns by Ayanna Jackson. Then he remembered that the men who robbed him looked like "the type of niggas" Jack was introducing him to.

Inside Bellevue Hospital, Tupac simply tried to remain calm. He needed emergency surgery to repair a damaged blood vessel in his leg. Less than three hours after coming out of the operating room, overly suspicious that whoever had tried to kill him would try to finish the job at the hospital, he checked himself out against doctor's orders.

"I knew what type of niggas I was dealing with," Shakur said.

So the story goes, 'Pac's gun that night was hidden in a piano at the studio when the police arrived. Big went to retrieve the piece and return it to Shakur at the hospital the next day. Tupac, however, had already left. Nobody knows what could've happened had Big had a chance to speak to Shakur that night after the attempt on his life.

Big was in a daze of emotions. He was confused about why 'Pac was holding his middle finger up in his direction as he was being wheeled to the ambulance. He was worried about the safety of his friend, because he knew the sort of company he was keeping and alienating. And he also had no clue what would come of the trial.

Not only could Big not get to 'Pac in the hospital, but less than twenty-four hours after the shooting, he learned of 'Pac's legal fate. The media called him dramatic for showing up to his verdict hearing in a wheelchair, bandages, and a New York Yankees beanie. And the jury was sequestered, so when they saw Shakur in the condition he was in, they were equally flabbergasted. In his heart, Big knew 'Pac wasn't going to miss that moment. All year long, to anyone who would listen, from BET's Ed Gordon to Arsenio Hall and reporters waiting for him outside the courtroom, that he was innocent. It didn't matter, though. Shakur was convicted of felony sexual abuse—finding that he groped and touched Jackson without her consent—and weapons charges from the November 1993 incident. He was acquitted of the most serious crime of forcing Jackson to perform oral sex on him and his friends. Though he would check himself back into the hospital under the name Bob Day, and no one was supposed to know he was there, Shakur still received ominous calls to his room asking why he wasn't dead yet.

The next several weeks in New York and in hip-hop in general were tense. Big's career was ascending thanks to *Ready to Die*'s success, 'Pac's shooting had everyone shook, and his conviction opened the door for a litany of questions, ranging from how Shakur's conviction would change the conversation around sexual assault to what Shakur's career would look like moving forward.

"I hope the verdict in this case causes men and women in the music industry, and fans, to think more carefully about male-female relationships in the music business and the culture of celebrity and the too-often-held belief that a consent to sex is a consent to whatever the more powerful partner wants," said the author Tricia Rose shortly after the verdict. "There's a culture of sexual abuse of women in the music business, a presumption that women are objects to be consumed on and off the set in music video production, not just rap music. So what I'm hoping is that the threat and the fear of some kind of legal implication, the specter of it, will give the men who act this way pause in presuming that women are consumable goods."

Everything in Tupac's life was spinning seemingly on its head. As he prepared for sentencing, he was recuperating from his gunshot wounds at the house of Jasmine Guy, whom he had become friends with on the set of *A Different World*. His biological father, Billy Garland, reentered his life at this time, too. The journalist Touré penned a scathing piece in the *Village Voice* essentially calling Tupac a marvelous actor who treated the world as his stage, and that his theatrics outweighed any creative work he'd ever done up to that point. The piece, in Shakur's own words, gutted him and made him cry "like a bitch."

Rumors are like uncontrollable wildfires, especially in the music industry. And *especially* in hip-hop. There was talk throughout industry circles about what happened to Tupac that night at Quad Studios, who may have been behind it, and what the long-term ramifications would be. Everyone was talking about Tupac except Tupac. That was, at least, until he granted the journalist Kevin Powell an exclusive interview from Rikers in January 1995. All of hip-hop wanted to hear what Tupac had to say about his case, his life, and the rumors of who he thought had him shot. And now Big's and Puffy's names were circulating in the mix.

"If I hadn't eaten those weed brownies and fallen asleep," said Drew Dixon, "I might've been in the fucking lobby at Quad at approximately the same time Tupac was shot. There was no fucking way Biggie would've told me to come to Quad that night if he had ordered a hit on 'Pac. No fucking way."

There was no one more shocked or hurt by the allegations than Big. He considered Shakur a friend. A brother, really. Not just an industry friend, but someone he could actually trust. There was so much they still had to accomplish together, Big thought. He didn't know where Shakur was coming from with these allegations, but he knew they weren't true. His part in them, at least. The Kevin Powell–Tupac jailhouse interview was making its way around the industry before it hit shelves in the April 1995 issue. Puffy read it during a break from a studio session.

His advice to Big was simple. Say nothing.

"Niggas come up to you, start asking questions, reporters start asking you shit . . . nothing. Complete silence," Puffy instructed, recounted in *Unbelievable*.

Big was cool with remaining quiet on the entire situation. Puffy was heated, but he knew not to fan the flames or else they could get out of control. Shortly after Tupac's interview with Powell ran, Puffy, Big, and more all spoke with Fab 5 Freddy in an attempt to clear their names. They had nothing to do with Shakur being shot, they said. Shakur, in later interviews, would become more and more venomous with his accusations that it was Big who set him up that fateful night at Quad.

"I used to share my experiences in the game and my lessons, and my rules and my knowledge on the game with him," Shakur said. "[Biggie] owed me more than to turn his head and act like he didn't know niggas was about to blow my fuckin' head off. He knew."

As Big's career continued to climb, the responsibilities he carried on his shoulders began to pile up. There was his widely successful album *Ready to Die*, his daughter, his marriage and what was to become of that, and Junior M.A.F.I.A. and their careers, and now he had to worry about one of his closest friends insinuating that he, of all people, put a hit out on him. It was a lot to carry for a twenty-two-year-old.

All the while, Big never spoke ill of 'Pac. At least, not in public. He wanted to understand why he felt the way he did. He still very much cared for Shakur despite his allegations. He wanted an apology, but he reasoned that getting shot and then having to serve time for a crime he vehemently denied had done a number on Shakur's mental state.

"I always said that he was the realest nigga in the game," said Big. "He knows that I was at the hospital with his mother when he got shot in that studio. He knows me and Stretch was there. He knows after he left the hospital and went to his girl house uptown, me and Stretch went up in some weed spots to get this nigga a half ounce of weed, and bring him some weed to his girl crib. He knows this."

All 'Pac needed was time, Big figured. This would clear itself up eventually. They were too close of friends to fall out over something that could easily be squashed with a conversation—and some weed and some Hennessy. They'd get that moment at some point, he thought. And when they could have a real face-to-face conversation, they'd look back on everything and laugh.

15

HOW YA LIVIN', BIGGIE SMALLS?

BIG COULDN'T SHAKE WHAT WAS GOING ON WITH TUPAC, BUT IT WASN'T LIKE HE DIDN'T HAVE HIS OWN CAREER TO TEND TO. "Juicy" was an anthem of socioeconomic advancement. That rags-to-riches story—or "ashy to classy," as he framed it—endeared him to nearly every walk of hip-hop. There was an everyman, everywoman type of appeal to that song that was palpable far beyond Bed-Stuy. But now it was time to hit people with the follow-up. To show the world that Biggie Smalls was a lot of things, but a one-hit wonder wasn't one of them. He could make a hit in his sleep if wanted to.

By the start of 1995, Big had two singles heating up the charts. The first was "Warning," a dizzying display of lyrical paranoia that featured him addressing rumors of enemies coming to take his life. It was "Big Poppa," though, that would elevate his career to another stratosphere. Perhaps it was the Isley Brothers' "Between the Sheets" sample. Or maybe it was the fact that Big revealed a side of himself those closest had known for years, but now the world was finding out: Big was a playboy, and he had the gift of gab by the surplus.

The video was filmed in Nell's, the same nightclub where Shakur initially met Jackson. "Big Poppa" became an instant hit. He was blowing up just like he said he would. The ladies loved him, and the fellas wanted to be just like him—just like his teenage rap idol Big Daddy Kane was. He could be a sex symbol, and at the same time, he could drop the hardest verses known to man. Big coveted that diversity in his music because it kept Puffy happy and it kept money in his pockets. The success also allowed him to look out for his people.

Mister Cee's career had slowed down by the mid-nineties, and his radio career at Hot 97 was still in the early stages. His money hadn't dried up, but it wasn't pouring in at the rate it once did. It got to a point where he owed his landlord, who just happened to be his uncle, six months of rent.

"Nephew or no nephew, if you don't gimme this rent, I'ma evict you," Cee's uncle said.

Big was on the road at the time, so Cee got in touch with DJ Enuff, Big's tour DJ. He told Enuff it was an emergency, and a day or two later, Enuff called back with Big on the line. By this point, Cee was in tears.

"The fuck are you crying for? The fuck?!" a bewildered Big asked. "What's wrong with you?"

Cee told him the story, but he tired of hearing this grown man cry.

"Man, stop that fucking crying. Stop crying!" Big yelled. "Yo, man. I want you to go see my accountant. He's gonna have something for you."

Cee, as instructed, went to the accountant's office the next day. A check for $10,000 was waiting for him.

"You wanna talk about generosity?" Cee reflects. "I never told Big how much I needed."

Big was truly enjoying the spoils of his success. But he never truly forgot about the days hustling on the corner or taking trips down south to sell crack. Had one thing gone wrong, had he been late one time, none of it would have been possible, not the videos on MTV or the singles on radio stations across the country.

"[Being in the streets] had its ups and its downs. I can't be the one to say it was all bad because it wasn't really all bad," he said in a 1995 *Rap City* interview in Toronto. "But I guess just living an illegal life makes it all bad. I lost a lot of friends and I made a lot of money. It had its ups and its downs, but it's nothing that I would want to be involved with again."

Big deeply respected how the West Coast was releasing so much great music and changing the game in the process. But he knew he was, too. Big didn't resurrect East Coast hip-hop, but he did bring it back to the mainstream with an album that was flying off the shelves quicker than it could be stocked. "Big Poppa" peaked as high as the number-six song in the country, and Big was on every rap radio station in every city. Within six months of its release, *Ready to Die* was already platinum, and by the end of 1995, the album would sell over two million copies. Biggie Smalls was a superstar, and it felt as if the reign was just getting started.

"First Brooklyn nigga to go platinum, you know. It's all good," Big bragged. "Got my gold [plaque] from 'Juicy.' Straight out the hood, a hood nigga."

So now it was all about what was next. In the nineties, an album had a much longer shelf life than it does today. Instead of every track hitting streaming services instantly on release date, labels carefully doled out singles over many months, boosting album sales and keeping an artist in the spotlight. But that meant that the decisions about which tracks were singles was crucial. "Juicy" was an undeniable success out the gate and served as a pristine introduction for Big. "Big Poppa," with "Warning" as the B side, showed that just as easily as Big could take your girl, he could eliminate haters trying to stick him for his paper.

But by the summer of 1995, Bad Boy Records was in full swing, and it was Big leading the charge. Big had more than enough product on the streets. His "Flava in Ya Ear (Remix)" verse was blazing the clubs. And his feature on Total's smash hit "Can't You See" made the opening lines, "Gimme all the chicken heads from Pasadena to Medina," as infectious as anything to come out that year. Big wasn't just in-demand in rap circles, either. He was in the studio with pop icons like Michael Jackson for the record "This Time Around." But Puffy was also looking for Biggie's next single. Rob Stone was in a marketing meeting at Arista when he heard the news. The next single was going to be "Machine Gun Funk." Stone loved the Easy Mo Bee–produced heatrock, which was one of the hardest on the entire album. But as a single? In particular a summer single? That didn't sit well with him. His boss asked him what it should be if not "Machine Gun Funk."

"I'm not sure," Stone said. "I think it should be 'One More Chance.'"

There was a problem, though. "One More Chance" was far too explicit—with Big talking about "licking clits" and how big his dick was in Karl Kani jeans—for it to have a chance of ever getting played on the radio. An hour after mentioning his suggestion to his boss, Stone was told he needed to report back to his boss's office immediately. Stone didn't know what was going on, but he didn't have to wait long to find out.

Puffy was on the phone, and without saying a word, Stone already knew what Puffy he was getting.

"Hey, Puff," Stone said, preparing himself for what was to come.

"Sup," the young mogul responded, his voice in a monotone.

Stone's boss had told Puffy that he didn't think "Machine Gun Funk" was the best choice for Big's next single. Stone had a very respectable working relationship with Puffy, but it's not like they hung out or anything, so he had to keep this strictly business related and get to his point quickly. If not, he ran the risk of Puffy going berserk.

"I think you're making a mistake with 'Machine Gun Funk,'" Stone said. Not exactly the greatest way to start a conversation with the budding executive. Before he could even get his next thought in, the reins to the conversation had already shifted.

"All you motherfuckers think you know what the fuck I should be doing!" Puffy screamed. "What the fuck you should be doing is getting my shit played on the radio! And I'll worry about what the fuck Puff needs and does."

Stone lost count of how many "motherfuckers" Puffy yelled over the course of the call. He felt sick. He thought he had just botched one of the most important relationships he had in the music industry. But there was something he noticed. Puffy was still cursing, but he hadn't hung up yet. Stone's boss was looking at him. He put the phone on mute and demanded, "Fucking tell him! Fucking tell him!"

Stone had the idea in his head, but he'd never rehearsed it. It was now or never, and Stone went for it.

"Yo, Puff, you gonna scream at me or you want to hear my idea?" Stone remembers asking. "Look, Puff, you came with 'Juicy.' Anyone could understand that struggle. It was very relatable. Then you have Big becoming 'Big Poppa.' He's now got that style and pizzazz, and he's in the clubs and the girls are loving him. And then you come in with 'I live for the funk, I'll die for the funk.' It's a really cool record. I just don't think it's telling the story like you should be."

Silence. That's what the next several seconds consisted of. Silence. Stone was still petrified, but there was no turning back. Puffy still hadn't hung up, and he wasn't cursing anymore. At worst, he was tuning Stone out. At best, he was at least listening.

"I think it should be 'One More Chance.' You go from 'Juicy' to 'Big Poppa' to now women begging him for one more chance," Stone said.

"But that's nothing but curses. I can't make that," Puffy replied. "That's not a radio record."

"Puff, you made the 'Flava in Ya Ear' remix," Stone said. "Do the same thing with this. Go make a remix to this record and put Janet Jackson, Madonna, Aaliyah, Total, Faith, Mary J. Put every big-name woman in the industry, begging this guy for one more chance."

Silence again. Stone was nauseated. Puffy didn't say anything for what felt like an eternity. Then he said it.

"Oh shit," Puffy said, the idea now racing through his head. "*I got that good love girl, you didn't know.* I'll call y'all right back."

Stone and his boss looked at each other, completely lost. What the hell just happened on that phone call? Stone knew that Puffy had it from there. He just didn't know how the record would turn out. If anyone could make a fire remix, it was Puffy—the man who would later claim to have invented the remix. Two weeks later, the "One More Chance" remix was delivered. Sampling DeBarge's 1983 hit "Stay with Me," the Rashad "Ringo" Smith–produced remix completely overpowered its pornographic original. Everything about the remix was magnetic, from Big's syrupy-smooth, Billy Dee Williams–like delivery to the video, with what appeared like the world's greatest house party with guests like Luther "Uncle Luke" Campbell, D-Nice, Heavy D, Da Brat, Queen Latifah, Tyson Beckford, and more, and a who's-who of R&B starlets like Mary J. Blige, Aaliyah, Zhané, Miss Jones, Patra, a group called Changing Faces, and more all requesting one more chance. While everyone on set was having fun, one person in particular who wasn't was Faith Evans. Evans was nervous around all the other women in the video. Puffy took notice and pulled her to the side.

"You see all these chicks up in here? But this is yo' nigga!" Evans recalled of Puff's pep talk in her 2008 memoir, *Keep the Faith.* "You can't let these chicks be hotter than you on *your* shit."

Unbeknownst to Evans, her work on set wasn't done. There was a scene set up to show Big sitting on the corner of the bed and a model dressed in hardly anything to play the scene's lead. That's when Big called an audible. He called an impromptu meeting with Puffy and the video's director, Hype Williams.

"I want Faye in this scene," he told them.

"I was shocked that Big would want me in the video for that scene. I figured he'd want some video chick to be next to him. I knew it was Hollywood and not real life," she said. "But Big wanted his real-life woman next to him in that scene. And of course, I loved that he was making it clear who the main woman was in his life as well as in the video."

The shoot might have been an emotional roller coaster for Evans, but the end result was the single dreams are made of, winning both critical praise and commercial acclaim. The remix that began with a tense phone call between Puffy and Rob Stone would ultimately peak at the number-two spot on the *Billboard* Hot 100 by July 1995.

"If I had to mark a moment when Biggie-mania was about to become a real thing, I would say when the 'One More Chance' remix dropped," said the cultural critic Naima Cochrane. "That's when we all said, 'Okay, there's really something here.' It's the perfect microcosm of the best part of Bad Boy's hip-hop at that moment. And a perfect microcosm of how much rap could be outside in these streets at that moment."

"I had nothing to do with that. That was all Puffy," said Stone. "He didn't tell me to just shut up and do my job. Well, he did, but he was appreciative enough to listen. When 'One More Chance' hit and it was huge, Puff was now a force in the industry. You'd see Puff in the clubs, and you'd see him in VIP buying all the champagne."

One night Stone and a friend were walking on the West Side by the Hit Factory on West Fifty-Fourth Street. Puff was a regular there, and on that night in particular, he was outside with about twenty-five people surrounding him. Cars were lined up down the block. That's when he saw Stone walking by.

"Yo! Rob! Rob Stone!" he yelled. "Come here!"

Stone was pretty much the opposite of Combs, who loved crowds and being the center of attention.

"Hey, wassup, Puff."

Combs's face turned serious. "Yo, I told you 'One More Chance' was a hit."

Stone was confused. "Huh? You told me? I told you!"

Combs was unable to contain himself. He burst out in laughter and dapped Stone up. The truth is, Big had a lot to smile and laugh about. *Ready to Die* was still a force in the streets and the charts. Big's singles were on fire. Even the tracks not pushed as radio friendly tunes, like "Unbelievable" or "Me & My Bitch," were hood staples. But he was cool with lending out a helping hand, too. The self-proclaimed Black Frank White—a name he adopted from Christopher Walken's character from the 1990 film *King of New York*—might've been rap's MVP, but he tapped back into his hard-core essence on the freestyles he'd record for Mister Cee. He was even living up to a promise he made to himself and his neighborhood with the release of Junior M.A.F.I.A.'s debut album *Conspiracy* on August 29, 1995.

It wasn't anywhere near the classic that *Ready to Die* was, but the album, largely off his association, did well. The album was released through Big Beat and Atlantic Records and debuted at number eight on the *Billboard* charts, going gold before the end of the year. Its two biggest singles were "Get Money" and "Player's Anthem"—the latter being the song Big and company were working on at Quad Studios when Tupac was ambushed and shot. Big once again delivered standout verses, but now Lil' Kim and Lil' Cease were becoming the group's most recognizable faces not named Biggie. Getting that album out was an accomplishment for Big, and a labor of love.

"They just all kids from the neighborhood, man. People I grew up with, hustled with. Just be with everyday," Big said. "I told them once I got on, and things work out the way we want them to, they all gon' live and we all gon' eat. It ain't no need to [keep them in line]. They ain't stupid. They see how I do my thing and how I leave the street stuff in the streets."

Biggie had been trying to get Junior M.A.F.I.A. signed even before his first album. One person in particular who'd seen this firsthand was Drew Dixon. By 1995, Dixon was in A&R at Def Jam. She was the brainchild behind the classic rap documentary *The Show*, and her musical acumen was respected across the industry. Dixon and Biggie had been cool since he was still hustling on Fulton Street and, by Dixon's account, they were equally proud of each other's success. But that came with commitments, and made it so they didn't talk every week, or every month for that matter.

Dixon had already tried to get Junior M.A.F.I.A. a publishing deal at her previous job at Zomba Music Publishing. Now she was at Def Jam, and the first call Dixon received during her first week was from none other than Big.

"Drew, what?!? I see you, ma!" he said. Big came to her office, which she says was the size of two bathroom stalls, along with Lance "Un" Rivera and the Brooklyn-based producer Daddy-O, who had been working with the M.A.F.I.A. and Lil' Kim. Dixon called Russell Simmons on speakerphone, but didn't get a chance to tell him he was on speakerphone before he immediately began talking.

"Drew, Drew, Drew. Lemme just cut you off right there. Biggie Smalls is not gonna sell ten thousand records outside of Brooklyn," Simmons said, according to Dixon. "That dark-skin, fat, ugly motherfucker is never gonna be a pop star. The only people that give a fuck about him are hardheads in Brooklyn and you. I don't get why you and Puffy and everybody is so obsessed with this guy. He's not gonna cross over. And I definitely don't wanna sign a band based on some female artist. Female rappers don't sell. I tried it with Boss. It doesn't work!"

Big was shocked when Dixon bucked back at Simmons, telling him was tripping for not even giving Junior M.A.F.I.A. a chance. Dixon believed in Big, and if he believed in something, she did, too. The entire time Dixon was yelling back at Simmons, Big was trying to give her the kill sign. Dixon eventually told Simmons he was on speakerphone.

"I don't give a fuck!" Simmons said. "Yo, Big, it's Russ. You know how I feel, man. I told Puffy this. I love you, and you're dope and shit. But, yo, it's a business. I'ma keep it real. And Drew, don't ever put me on speakerphone without telling me, but yo, I fucking stand by what I said."

"Nah, man. It's cool," he said. "I get it."

Dixon, fuming, hung up the phone.

"Yo, sis. Yo. When I met you, you was answering phones. This is your dream job. You ain't gotta go that hard for us. I don't want you to lose your job over this. You tried at Zomba. You tried at Def Jam. We're good. How about this—no matter where we go, no matter what we do, you're going to be our honorary A&R." Months later, and true to his word, Dixon was thanked in the liner notes on *Conspiracy*.

Big's superstar ascension also coincided with the rise of the newly minted twenty-four-hour hip-hop station in New York, Hot 97. It didn't always live in that format, though. Because of the stigmas that came with Black music being niche, the concept of an all-hip-hop, all-the-time radio station, for many managers and executives in the radio world, could never generate revenue. Hot 97 wasn't doing well in its current format at the time, either. They were largely a dance-format station with hip-hop sprinkled in between. The station decided to shake things up in 1993 when they brought in Steve Smith, a programming director who took the risk and went all in on rap.

"It didn't take me that long in my first few days there to realize that hip-hop was what was going on in the street," said Smith, who originally planned on being a lawyer before going into radio. "I never took the typical approach to radio that other people took because I never wanted to be in radio. I found it by accident."

Smith discovered Big's music through a meeting Rob Stone set up with Puffy. Initially hesitant, Smith did an about-face once he began hearing the music Combs and Bad Boy were preparing to unleash on the world. Craig Mack's "Flava in Ya Ear" won him over, but it was Big's voice on "Juicy" that stopped him in his tracks. He'd never heard a voice like that, with an effortless penchant for storytelling. He initially felt weird about two songs from the same label in rotation at the same time, but good music was good music. And this was undeniable.

The working relationship between Hot 97 and Bad Boy grew from there. Bad Boy made music the people of New York wanted to hear, and Hot 97 had a platform to make sure that happened. Instead of bringing DJs from outside the city to come spin on air, too, Smith decided it was best to give that time to the artists. That's who the people wanted to hear anyway, he surmised.

"The whole radio world hated me. But I was like, are you fucking kidding me?" Smith said. "Everybody wants to hear Treach from Naughty by Nature on the air. They want to hear Queen Latifah on the air. They want to hear Biggie on the air!"

Big had an open invitation to the station. The word on Big, at this time, was that he was extremely affable. People genuinely loved being around him. He may have looked hard and intimidating, but he was funny, and he could talk about any topic, from the best weed spots in Brooklyn to whatever was on the front page of the *New York Times* that day. Whatever people thought about Biggie, it was Christopher Wallace they eventually fell for.

"He was always willing to do anything for us. He loved us. And we loved him so much. It was such a love affair," said Smith. "It was amazing radio, but it was real, and many times Biggie filled in with Puffy. I loved when they came in. Biggie would sit in the control room, and he got very fidgety. He'd go into his bag and pull out some weed and start rolling joints right there on the console. I'd have to walk into the control room and say, 'Biggie, you gotta stop doing this, man.' And he'd just go, 'My fault, man.' He was such a humble, very nice man. I really loved him. He was such a good-hearted guy, and that's the part you never see any of. You see how hard he was, but you don't realize that side of him because he was so comfortable to be around."

Everyone knew Big. It was a complete 180 from when he was performing in California when no one was paying attention and he was left spinning the mic. He was living better now. The grungy white tees had been replaced by leather coats and Coogi sweaters. The Timberland boots remained constant, but he had an entire different energy and bop to him now. Combs's girlfriend at the time, legendary stylist Misa Hylton, was the one who originally convinced him that Big's look wasn't a hindrance but rather a gift. And Voletta Wallace was in her son's ear about always making sure he looked presentable whenever he was on camera. In his own way, he did. No one looked, talked, and dressed like Biggie Smalls, and that was by design. And damn sure no one rapped like him. Everything about him was singular and signature. So when Big and company showed up to Howard University's homecoming in the fall of 1995, he was unmistakable from the size to the gear and the overall energy. Christopher Wallace was the sun in his own solar system. Everyone and everything else revolved around him.

Big, Groovey Lew, and more were posted up in the apparel store Up Against the Wall on Georgia Avenue right across the street from the McDonald's by campus. Lew knew the owner and organized a private shopping session before the general public was let in.

"They was letting us in the stock room and everything. We was taking people layaway stuff. We was wilding!" Lew said, laughing at the memory. "Big had the big yellow bubblegoose on, and he took a pair of Timbs. He put one under one arm the other under the other, right? Then he told me to walk behind him."

It was all good until it wasn't. Lew continues, "When we get outside, a girl outta nowhere—like just around the homecoming scene—seen Big take the boots out and she's like, 'Oooo, Biggie! You stole a pair of Timbs!' We was laughing so hard, man!"

At that point in time, it felt like Big's career was impenetrable. Musically, he could do no wrong. But music was only one part of his life. And while he seemed to be batting 1.000 from an artistic perspective, peeling back the layers revealed a different story.

So much had changed in Big's life in such a short amount of time. Less than three years earlier, he was selling crack in North Carolina, wondering what a legit exit strategy from the drug game looked like. Or if it even existed, for that matter. Now people all over the country of all races and backgrounds were rapping his words and idolizing his every move. The music game wasn't all that different from the drug game.

"I look at y'all as my customers," he said. "I gotta sell my product. They both exactly the same to me."

Voletta Wallace was happy her son was doing what made him happy and she didn't have to worry about him. But she wanted to make sure he was being careful with the money he was making. Satisfaction in the present meant nothing if it came with headaches in the future. She had read about this rapper named MC Hammer who amassed such a massive fortune and lost it all. She didn't want that for her son.

"Ma, I'll never be poor again," her son said. "Trust me, Ma. If I have a question about my money at five o'clock in the morning, I'm calling my accountant like, 'How much money I got?'"

His life was a whirlwind at the moment, but he always remembered that it was Voletta who loved him first. Now that he was making money (and money that couldn't be tied back to selling crack), he wanted to make her life better. He wanted his mother to move to Florida, because it was the closest he could get her to Jamaica. Voletta wasn't necessarily interested in that. She had her own life in America, and she wanted to stay close to Brooklyn. Per the *New York Times* in 1994, he decided to move his mother into a house in Park Slope, Brooklyn. She'd ultimately move to Pennsylvania. It was close enough to New York, but far enough away that life could be different.

How he understood his place in Brooklyn was changing, too. He'd always love Brooklyn, and he'd rep the borough until his last breath. That was never in question. He once spoke of never seeing himself leaving his hood because he wondered how it would impact his music. He couldn't keep it real in the suburbs. But that was before the money started piling in, his face was on TV every day, and his voice saturated radio stations from Brooklyn to Long Beach and everywhere in between. He was too well known, too successful, and too hot. He had to get off the block.

"One thing I learned about the game is when you get a lot of money, niggas don't like you. I'm getting more money now," Big said, months after *Ready to Die* dropped. He still kept a pair of 9-millimeter Rugers under the mattress in his bedroom. "I'm not paranoid to the point where . . ." he said, catching his thoughts. "Yes, I am. I'm scared to death. Scared of getting my brains blown out."

This was a part of success Big never saw coming.

"I'll keep it one hundred with you. When he realized that we not around the hood anymore and he was living with a whole 'nother place with a big house, his whole mindset was a whole different character," says Chico Del Vec. "He couldn't be around certain people like he used to because certain people would try to take advantage of him because he's a cool dude. That was more scary to him because the majority of the people he didn't even know. They see you on TV and then you outside the next day? It was a lot going on.

"Can you imagine coming outside and you got ten cars doubled parked on your block and you don't know who's in the car? And you're just going to the store," Chico said. "He used to tell us, 'Yo, I feel like somebody's going to kill me one day.' I'd tell him, you're talking crazy. What the fuck is wrong with you? One time I came in the room and he was asleep and I scared him. He jumped up and started swinging on me. I'm like, yo, it's me! He's like, 'Yo, Chic, what the fuck?! Don't do that!' Life went somewhere else after a minute. It was a different life."

For as much as Big enjoyed the success he found in 1995, it came with its own wave of stresses, too. "Who Shot Ya," the Nashiem Myrick–produced banger was recorded in 1994 and was featured as a Keith Murray interlude on Mary J. Blige's *My Life* album. Big's verse didn't make the final cut. He had also been hearing from DJ Clark Kent that another Brooklyn rapper he was working with at the time, who went by the name of Jay-Z, was just as talented as him. In an effort to prove that no one in Brooklyn, or anyone for that matter, could rhyme harder than him, Big went back in to record the second verse later that year. That, in essence, is the backstory behind the B-side single for "Big Poppa."

Beyond its lyrical potency was its timing. It was released in February 1995, the same month Tupac was sentenced to up to four and a half years in his sexual abuse trial, and the talk around the industry of course centered on a narrative of its being a subliminal shot at the incarcerated superstar. Tupac was still hanging with Big around the time "Who Shot Ya" was recorded, but he took it as disrespect that the song would be released so soon after his own shooting and while stowed away in a maximum-security correctional facility in upstate New York. It was in that same facility, too, that 'Pac's anger began to stew more and more. On the outside, it was Big was who becoming rap's top star. Meanwhile, 'Pac claimed to hear little from the man he once saw as a brother.

"My homeboy Stretch is going to Biggie's concerts. Niggas is abandoning me. But then on the air and like on TV they like, 'Yeah, 'Pac . . . keep the struggle on," Shakur said in a later interview. "Niggas is just gonna act like I'ma just be in jail and they gonna give me shout-outs. They trying to take my position. And if you watch, that's what Biggie did."

Shakur continued, "While I'm in jail, strangers is telling, 'Yo, you don't know? Biggie's homeboy shot you.' 'Cause they bragging. They telling they niggas in jail. 'Yo, we just got 'Pac. Whoo, whoo, whoo."

The miscommunication of the song's intent was far from the only headache in Big's life. He was so famous now that everyone who saw him expected him to be Big. To be the gangster playboy. He wasn't acting, but it's hard being that person twenty-four hours a day. He was constantly on tour, constantly doing media in a different city. And that came with a different set of requests from a different set of fans, groupies, radio DJs, and venues. Big's headlining performance at San Francisco's 1995 KMEL Summer Jam was cut short because of extreme heat warping DJ Big Kap's records. Big was always cool, calm, and collected for the most part. But this sent him over the edge. There was a rule that each mistake during a live performance cost $100. The rule applied to everyone, including Big. Kap's records were cooking like bacon under the extreme heat, but Big didn't care. He threw a water bottle at Kap and walked offstage. Kap, who had to take a cab back to the hotel that evening, was embarrassed. He knocked on Big's door, only to find him laughing with a bunch of girls in his room.

All Kap wanted to do was apologize. Even though it wasn't his fault, he felt bad. People didn't like letting Big down.

"Man, I knew! I saw those records," he said. "I knew it was the sun. But I couldn't let them think it was me out there messing up!"

Not everything was resolved so easily. In May 1995, Big was set to perform at Club Xscape in Camden, New Jersey. The show was canceled, but Big still wanted the back half of his $20,000. The show's promoter, Brook Herdell, was missing in action, which left Big annoyed. Nathaniel Banks Jr., an associate of Herdell's, bore the brunt of what came next. Big warned that if he didn't get his money that he was "going to start punching mothafuckas." And so his crew did. Banks had a bracelet, necklace, watch, cell phone, and $300 in cash taken from him that night. Big and his crew denied that he ever took part in the fight. "Who knows who beat the shit outta duke?" he said in a later interview. "That whole block was lined up with cars."

"People tell me he's really not that type of person," Banks reasoned to *SPIN* a few years after the incident, and after a $41,000 settlement. "Maybe he had to do what he did because he might look like a punk if he didn't. Maybe he had to act out what he says on his records."

A month and a half after the Jersey incident, Big was arrested after performing at a club in Concord Township, Pennsylvania, roughly an hour outside Philly. Big was drunk, holding a bottle of Dom Pérignon in his lap, and initially he thought it was a police escort, but that thought quickly turned when police were pointing guns at the car. Then he was on the ground, with rocks and bugs near his mouth while a cop held a shotgun and flashlight near his head. In the precinct, the police seemed to bask in their headlined-inducing arrest—all the while asking him for autographs.

"They were like, 'My daughter Meghan loves you,'" Big was quoted as saying in *Unbelievable*. "So I'm talking to Meghan on the phone, and she telling me she want to go to my concert. I'm like, 'Yo, Meghan, talk to your pops.'"

Big was held without bail, since he was technically on the run stemming from robbery and aggravated assault charges in the Camden altercation. He was released three days later, but much like the experience of being locked up in North Carolina during his hustling days, the time in the can shook him. That's what he was rapping for—to avoid that. And it hurt that his mother was deeply disappointed in him. So much so that she didn't speak to him for a while.

"I'd rather be dead than in jail," Big said.

A show in Raleigh came with its own harrowing experience and would later have Big questioning the price of fame as a result. He and the M.A.F.I.A. had a show at a local spot called the Taj Mahal—in what would ultimately be the venue's last-ever performance. For Big, it was a homecoming of sorts. He'd made a lot of money in that city, and now he was coming back to make some more in the limelight.

During a performance of "The What," he surprised the crowd by bringing out Method Man. Things went left almost immediately. Their collaboration was already a hardbody record, with both MCs going bar for bar with some of the rawest lyrics in rap at the moment. That same energy bled into the crowd. Some concertgoers in the front row were talking shit to Big. They were testing his gangsta, demanding a battle.

"Big was cool about his shit, but while Big is talking to the nigga, [Big's] man slides him the piece," Method Man recounted later.

Big entertained the fan, but he wasn't just going to battle some random dude to give him that satisfaction. He told him that he'd battle him, but if he—when he—won, that fan would have to strip. If he was going to mess up the flow of Big's show, then Big was going to emasculate him in front of his entire city. While the fan was trying to jump onstage, a member of Big's entourage snatched the gun from Big and pistol-whipped the fan. Earlier in the day, Big was telling people he hoped the club had security. Turns out Big's premonition held weight. A melee erupted.

"Everybody was scrapping in that motherfucker. Like four niggas got shot that night," Meth said. "But what was so deep about it, it was just me and [my boy], but when that shit went down, like four niggas I ain't never seen before were like, 'You a'ight? We got you.' That was Big, nigga."

Being in Raleigh also gave Big an opportunity to connect with an old friend in Greg Dent. The transformation was incredible to witness for Dent. He'd known Big when he was just the out-of-town kid selling crack and who'd jump on the microphone at Dent's parties to rap whenever Dent turned his back.

"I was so happy to see him," Dent said, the pride in his voice still very much present more than a quarter century later. "I saw him when he wasn't famous to, like, an icon. And through it all, he was still the same cat. Still silly as hell."

Dent was excited because he'd been hanging with Big, Cease, and the crew all day. He even took Big to the local hip-hop station 97.5 to promote the show. Dent was at the show when the shootout went down, too. The after-party was supposed to be at Dent's club the Vibe, but the Raleigh Police Department put a stop to that following the brawl.

"I actually called my attorney," Dent says. "My attorney was like, 'They can't stop you from opening. That happened somewhere else, so fuck them!'"

Dent opened the Vibe anyway, but the police blocked the entire radius off. No one showed up. Dent was upset. Not just because he missed out on some serious cash, but also because he didn't think Big would show up. Dent barely got out of the Taj Mahal himself, so he understood if his old friend wanted to lay low.

"I'm thinking, *Damn, man. Big ain't gonna come to this shit after that crazy shootout and fights*," Dent recalled to me. "I barely got outta there myself to get back to the club to open it up."

People who worked at the Vibe were starting to doubt that Dent even knew the Notorious B.I.G.

"Like one in the morning, this motherfucker pulls up with some shit in an old beat-up-ass fucking SUV," Dent says. "My security guard comes in like, 'Yo, Big's outside looking for you!' They couldn't believe it. They were like, 'Yeah, we know you know some people, but you don't know Big!'"

Dent walked outside. It was a ghost town. Nobody in sight except two people standing outside of, as Dent recalls, a "beat-up-ass fucking SUV." There was Big, and a lady friend, standing outside with a huge smile on his face.

"I told you I was gon' make it," he chuckled.

The two friends walked inside and sat at the bar throwing back Heinekens for nearly two hours. They laughed about the good times. About how Big would damn near cry when he couldn't go eat. And Dent still doing his thing on the party scene. Big opened up about his newfound life, and Dent was surprised at his old friend's vulnerability.

"He was telling me, 'G, this shit ain't what you think it is.' He was actually kinda not happy," Dent told me.

"Yo, this fame shit ain't what I thought it was. It's cool and all that, but I'm just tryna do me," Big admitted. "Shit is kinda fucked up out here."

Dent remembers Big repeating that over and over. *This fame shit ain't what I thought it would be. Shit is kinda fucked up out here.* Fame was bringing him a lot of money, but the price tag of it all was weighing on him. He was married—more so by law than by actual emotional attachment, as his union with Faith Evans was constantly being tested because of Big's infidelity. And the rumors of him setting Shakur up were still permeating around the industry.

Shortly before three in the morning, Big and Dent exchanged their goodbyes with pounds and hugs. Dent gave Big an entire case of Heineken. Big gave Dent some weed. It would be the last time Dent would see his friend.

16

GROWING PAINS

COMPETITION IS A NATURAL ELEMENT OF MUSIC, ESPECIALLY
IN RAP. So by August 3, 1995, it was obvious that heading into the Source
Awards, all eyes would be on the two record labels that had hip-hop in a
chokehold: Bad Boy and Death Row.

Combs was no longer in the shadow of Russell Simmons or his mentor
Andre Harrell. He was the one calling the shots, and in 1995, nearly every
shot he called felt like money. If anyone was Combs's "competition," it was
Knight, but he didn't seem to harp on that.

"I really had thought we were cool—cool acquaintances, just being
respectful as people coming into other cities," Combs would later say on a
2016 *Drink Champs* episode.

Suge Knight came to Madison Square Garden's Paramount Theater to
make a statement. For many in attendance that night, it was their first time
actually seeing Knight up close and personal. Rap's most feared boogeyman
was in the building, and he was going to belittle Combs every chance got.
Death Row got it cracking from the very beginning. Dr. Dre, Snoop Dogg,
Tha Dogg Pound, DJ Quik, Lady of Rage, and Sam Sneed showcased the
label's deep catalog with a medley of hits. Onstage was a cardboard cutout of
Tupac Shakur, a subtle hint of a future game-changing free-agency decision.
Very few people in the industry knew that Death Row was working behind

the scenes to bail Shakur out of prison, but for anyone paying attention that night, the writing was quite literally onstage. But it wasn't until Death Row won the Motion Picture Soundtrack of the Year category for *Above the Rim* that things went from friendly competition to something far more personal. Knight grabbed the mic and launched and chose proverbial violence.

"Any artist out there that want to be an artist, and want to stay a star and don't want to worry about the executive producer all up in the videos, all on the records—dancing, come to Death Row!" Knight declared.

There was no denying Combs had the secret sauce when it came to not only making hits, but making superstars. But this was far from the first time Combs was criticized for his attention-seeking ways. Many even silently agreed with the critique, too. But doing that in Combs's hometown, though, was considered the ultimate sign of disrespect. Everyone knew exactly who he was talking about and to.

"When Suge got up there and threw that wild pitch, we felt that heat from the audience," Quik revealed on Questlove's *Questlove Supreme* podcast, in 2019. "Me and Nate Dogg was sitting next to each other. We stood up and just stood back-to-back. Nate Dogg said, 'Quik, if you don't let nobody hit me in the back of my head, I won't let nobody hit you in the back of your head.' I'm like, 'Bro, you ain't gotta say nothin' else.' We knew it was bad."

"We loved Puffy. We loved Biggie," Kurupt of Tha Dogg Pound said. "Suge pushed the line. Now what are we supposed to do? Only thing to do is smash."

It felt like the entire building had something to prove, and that any moment anything could pop off. André 3000 of OutKast put on for rap below the Mason-Dixon line with his iconic quote that "the South got something to say." But when Dr. Dre captured the Producer of the Year award, the night's next landmark moment took place. The late John Singleton, who presented the award with then-Houston Rockets guard Sam Cassell, said before announcing the winner, "Uh-oh, we gon' have some trouble here."

Snoop Dogg accompanied Dre onstage and, like Suge before him, grabbed the mic, asking if the East Coast had love for Death Row. There were always tensions between east and west in rap, mainly stemming from New York's rap scene being so insular. Other regions wanted New York's respect because it was viewed as the genre's mecca, but New York was incredibly stingy when distributing that respect, too. In a way, Snoop was trying to mend whatever divisions Knight had sowed earlier. But in another, the tensions were already so thick that night that nearly anything could be taken as disrespect. Combs attempted to squash any feelings, saying that he had love for Death Row and the West Coast and that he wanted everyone to win.

Years later, Combs would admit the night took him by surprise. "I was like, 'I could blow this thing up right now.' I just decided . . . I felt it was really dangerous. 'Cause the crowd was really, really, really with me and with Bad Boy. They were just looking for the word, like, 'throw something up.' It's just crazy."

One person who wasn't paying attention to the drama was Big, who was the night's MVP in a crowd full of all-star talent. But that's not to say he wasn't pissed off that night, either. Two days before the Source Awards, Raekwon's *Only Built 4 Cuban Linx . . .* had hit the streets. On the soon-to-be classic album was the "Shark Niggas" skit with Rae and his Wu-Tang brother Ghostface Killah. Without naming names, they blasted MCs who they say copied styles from other rappers—like rappers biting Nas's *Illmatic* album cover that featured him as a child. Big's *Ready to Die* featured a baby on his.

"We're mastering the album. Ghost was like, I wanna do a skit . . . and I'm like, 'Ahhh, man. You had to do it,'" said Matty C, who was working on the album at the time. "Then I had to go through all types of shit with Biggie and him thinking I was purposely trying to do something to him. He took it a whole kinda way. He *loved* Rae and Ghost's shit, and then they clowned him on their album. That shit hurt him bad. He was tight. He wasn't fucking with me for a second."

At the Source Awards, Matty C was stressed out because now Big and Rae and Ghost were all in the same building. But whatever anger Big had, it didn't show. He took home several of the night's major awards, including Best New Artist, Solo, Best Live Performer, Best Lyricist, and the most coveted of them all, Album of the Year. For the last award, Big was accompanied onstage by what felt like all of Fulton Street. Faith was there, the entire Junior M.A.F.I.A. was too, and even D-Roc, who had come home from serving time from the gun charge he took for Big a few years earlier. He shouted out his daughter, T'yanna, his mother, his wife, and his manager, "Gucci," aka Mark Pitts. It was a celebratory moment for Big, then the undisputed heavyweight champion in rap.

"We did it, Brooklyn!" he exclaimed. "We did it!"

"Half of Brooklyn was in there. If Big would've been like, 'Fuck you dudes,' it would've been ruckus in there!" said Chico. "But it was more of a respect thing, and at the end of the day, we felt no way about insults or nobody. We just felt like we made it."

Similar to Death Row at the beginning of the show, Bad Boy performed their own string of hits, with Big as the main attraction—though Lil' Kim's fierce "Player's Anthem" performance was a crowd favorite and one of the most electric moments of the night. Combs, who in a way backed up what Knight said about him earlier by starting the performance with an intro of his own, stating that he "lived in the east and I'm gon' die in the east." But he did end the performance once again by shouting out the West Coast. The night was over, but the drama was just beginning. Later that night, Death Row had a kickback at Le Parker Meridien hotel in Manhattan. And the amount of people there who had direct connections to Puffy wasn't lost on anyone.

"We were there, and Suge had Misa come over," Quik said, referring to the famed stylist Misa Hylton, the mother of Combs's oldest son, Justin. "I'm goin', 'Suge, what are you doing?' Like what the fuck? Like, that's Diddy's baby mama! She was just like hanging out . . . Mary J. Blige popped up. I didn't get it. It just got weird to me."

Combs would say years later that he and Knight ran into each other at the Tunnel that night and Knight supposedly said his comments were directed toward Jermaine Dupri and So So Def. Dupri would deny that claim. A day after the Source Awards was a New Music Seminar convention. DJ Premier, Big, and the rapper Buckwild were in attendance when Knight approached the producer. Knight told him he wasn't a fan of some beats he had given Lady of Rage, but he still wanted to work with him for Dogg Pound's project. There was no tension or threat of hostility. Premier and Knight even hugged at the end of the conversation. Knight's emotions quickly turned cold, though, when Big spoke to him. Big clearly wasn't that affected by the previous night's events. He wasn't thinking about going to war. In fact, he was thinking about a Bad Boy–Death Row collaboration.

"Big walks up to Suge and says, 'Ayo, I want to get in touch with Dre to do a couple of songs on my new album," Premier recalled in a 2010 interview. "Suge just looks at him and goes, 'Yeah, a'ight.' And walks off."

It was a wasted opportunity to hear arguably rap's greatest producer and arguably its greatest wordsmith join forces. The Source Awards would become a watershed moment in rap. It could've been far worse than what it ultimately was—one CEO being mad at another CEO and using a public platform to vent his frustrations. Things, though, would turn far more dire and dark quicker than anyone could have imagined.

———

Big was doing exactly what he said he was going to do. He got on and he put his people on. And he also spoke of bringing his own company into existence with Undeas Entertainment, which he formed alongside Lance "Un" Rivera. The idea for the label was actually birthed in 1993 at a Clinton Hill chicken stand. Like Big, Un was a product of the crack era and had even spent two years in prison for an armed robbery conviction. And like Big, he wanted out of that life and into the music industry in hopes of making money without having to look over his shoulders every day. But now Undeas was the label that released Junior M.A.F.I.A.'s debut album and was working on Lil' Kim's solo debut. Big was expanding his portfolio with other ventures. One of them was acting.

Toward the end of the summer, Big flew to L.A. to film an episode of the hit sitcom *Martin*. He and Martin Lawrence were huge fans of each other. Lawrence often listened to Big while driving to work. Before and after filming the episode, Big went over to Lawrence's house, where the two got high, laughed, and chopped it up about life. Even for a comedian who'd seen it all, having Big on set with him was special.

"We never really saw Martin excited about anybody that came to the set other than Biggie," actress Tichina Arnold, who played the character of Pam on the show, told HipHopWired, in 2012. "When Biggie was on the set, we just made sure all of us were on good behavior."

They were as in awe of him as he was of them, and that mutual admiration played out in the episode—one of the funniest in a sitcom that had no shortage of hilarious moments in its run during the nineties. During the reading of the episode, Big didn't say much. His lack of talking wasn't to be confused with a lack of interest. He observed how each actor treated the process, and similar to how he treated recording music, he'd much rather be with his own thoughts until it was show time. Plus, as anyone who knew Big could tell you, it wasn't like he was ever going to quit rap and pursue a career in Hollywood.

"If you thought he was acting, Big cannot act at all!" Chico said, hardly able to control his laughter. "But you know what's funny with that episode? He basically freestyled it. For one thing, he don't eat seafood. He allergic to seafood. But he was on *Martin* talking about them shrimps was banging! We all started laughing. It's funny because he had that Sergio Tacchini sweatsuit [he had on in the episode] on for a whole week after that!"

The episode, entitled "Blow, Baby, Blow," aired on September 23, 1995. That same night, some three thousand miles away, outside an after-party for Jermaine Dupri's birthday at the Platinum House in Atlanta, a murder would occur that would set the course for the next eighteen months and beyond. Dupri had invited parties from both Bad Boy and Death Row, including Big, to his city with the intention of popping bottles and having a good time. He wasn't even thinking that what had happened a month earlier at the Source Awards was that deep. Just a few weeks earlier, Quincy Jones had held a summit aimed at ceasing the rising tensions in hip-hop. Combs and Big attended, as had Knight and Dr. Dre. Whatever progress was made there, if any, was about to be railroaded. Both sides reportedly barked at each other all night. Bad Boy hadn't forgotten what Knight had said, and Knight wasn't the type to backtrack. After both sides were asked to leave, emotions boiled over in the parking lot outside the club. This left Knight and Combs face-to-face.

"[Suge and Puffy] were, like, in the middle of the street. It's not a calm conversation. It's a very hostile conversation," Dupri reflected. "Suge got one dude with him. Puff got a crew."

By the end of the fracas, shots were fired and Jai-Hassan Jamal, aka Jake Robles or "Big Jake," was left bleeding on the pavement. Robles was with Knight that night and would lose his life weeks later due to a gunshot wound.

"After Jake," said Mob James, former muscle for Death Row, "it just went crazy . . . It's just sad that all those guys is gone because of stupid shit."

Cops suspected one of Combs's bodyguards, Anthony "Wolf" Jones, to be the trigger man. In a *VIBE* interview months later, Combs claimed he was waiting for his limo when he tried to help Knight, who had gotten into it with some guys in the club. He said his back was turned when Robles was shot, and that Knight's blaming him for the murder was a sign of his "insecurity."

None of that mattered. There was blood on the street. It was war now.

October 1995 was one for the books as it related to celebrity Black men and the criminal justice system. On October 3, the NFL Hall of Famer and former Heisman Trophy winner O. J. Simpson was found not guilty in the double murders of his ex-wife, Nicole Brown Simpson, and the waiter Ron Goldman. One person who wasn't surprised? Suge Knight.

"I thought O. J.'d get off," Knight said the night of the verdict from his all-red office at the Can-Am studios in Tarzana. "He's O. J. jumping over shit, O. J. run for a touchdown. What the fuck Juice done for us? I don't want to see anybody behind bars, but I've never seen O. J. in the ghetto."

Nine days later, another Black man who commanded his own fair share of headlines scored his own legal victory. On October 12, Tupac Shakur would walk out of Clinton Correctional Facility free on bail pending an appeal of his conviction. Originally, Shakur's bail was $3 million, but in May 1995, a New York judge reduced the price to $1.4 million. For weeks, Knight and his team at Death Row worked on securing the money, and now it was official.

It was reported that those close to Shakur—like his manager and former Black Panther Watani Tyehimba and lawyers Stewart Levy and Charles Ogletree—pleaded with him not to sign with Death Row. Tyehimba later told the *New Yorker* that during his last meeting with Shakur in prison, the rapper hugged him and cried and reportedly said, "I know I'm selling my soul to the devil." Nevertheless, in September 1995, roughly a week before Big Jake was murdered in Atlanta, Shakur signed a handwritten, three-page memo drafted by Death Row lawyer David Kenner. The terms of the deal said that Shakur would record three albums for $3.5 million. Approximately $1 million of that was to be used for his advance and other miscellaneous expenses. Also in the agreement was a massive conflict of interest—Knight was now Shakur's manager, and Kenner was his lawyer.

"It wasn't a legal contract . . . It was absurd that anyone with an opportunity to reflect would agree to those terms," said Ogletree, who represented Shakur in many cases. "It was only because he was in prison that he signed it. Tupac was saying, 'My freedom is everything. If you can get me my freedom, you can have access to my artistic product.'"

Knight had done what he'd always done.

"I don't know that it felt shocking," former *VIBE* editor in chief Alan Light told me of the signing. "It felt like, 'Yeah, okay. Once again, [Suge] had an opportunity and he took it."

Shakur left prison and went straight to a private jet. And on that private jet was a briefcase full of money, courtesy of Knight. The jet landed in L.A., and another limo brought him to the studio where Knight was waiting. Immediately, Shakur got to work chain-smoking blunts and drinking Cristal. The first song he recorded eventually became "Ambitionz Az a Ridah." For months, Shakur stewed in prison—sometimes in solitary confinement—for a crime he vehemently denied. Prison guards made his life hell, performing unwarranted cavity searches, according to Shakur's lawyers who visited him. All the while, his former friend and a man he was accusing of trying to have him killed, Biggie, became rap's top star. Shakur, too, was never able to properly promote his third solo effort, *Me Against the World*, the only album to debut at number one from an incarcerated artist. All of his anger came roaring out of him in the studio.

"He was like, 'Shit, what you think?'" Knight recalled. "That shit was bomb! But I said it was just a'ight because my pops used to tell me that in football and it'd make me work harder. He started rapping again, and I told the engineer whatever you do, don't erase it. Just save it and go to another verse."

The crowd in the studio that evening could hardly contain themselves. Shakur took his shirt off in the booth and asked for a Newport cigarette. He took two long pulls and launched into another lyrical onslaught. By this point, Knight could no longer contain his excitement. They knocked out several songs that night until Shakur literally passed out. He was too high and too drunk, and just twenty-four hours earlier, he'd been in a prison cell. And had it not been for his now-ex-wife, Keisha Morris, Knight said, the moment might have never happened. Knight sent him home in style, too. Morris, who met Shakur at a nightclub in 1994, married him in prison on April 29, 1995, and the marriage was annulled shortly after his release.

"I put him in a limo. I got him the biggest suite at the Peninsula, and I had seven of the baddest bitches in California," Knight claimed. "I told them, 'Don't try to steal none of his money, don't try to steal none of his jewelry. Give him a bath, massage him. Do everything for him. All y'all bitches get naked for him. Take care of him all night until the morning.' That mothafucka called me in the morning like, 'Hey! I thought I was dreaming! They already got me a blunt rolled up . . . I ain't never felt so good in my life!"

———

Big could talk his way out of damn near any pickle. Like that one time in Sacramento when he and his road crew were the recipients of an elaborate setup by the rapper E-40. Months earlier, he was extremely high—even higher than normal for a chimney like Big—while giving an interview, when he was asked to rate other artists. When it came to E-40, his response was harsh, saying, "No rating! Zero! I don't fuck with that dude at all!"

Big was in town to perform months later, and when he got to the club, he noticed it was hardly full. This was odd, because he was one of the most in-demand rappers in the game, and here he was potentially about to perform to no more than fifteen people. When he did get around to performing, people began to throw coins at him. Needless to say, the show didn't last long. Something was definitely off; Big and company just didn't know what. When they left the venue and went back to the limo, there was no driver. What they heard next was the sound of trunks popping open.

"I turn around and I'm like, 'Oh, shit!'" Larry "Hawk" Burns, Big's road manager, remembered. "It's a gang of dudes with guns."

"What up, Big?" one of the gun-yielding men said. "You in Sacramento now."

They were irate about his comments and were willing to go any length to prove their loyalty to E-40. During this entire showdown, though, Big never broke his Brooklyn cool. He knew how the streets operated, and it wasn't like it was the first time he'd ever had a gun pointed at him.

Hawk knew the situation could be smoothed over if Big and 40 could just speak man-to-man. Moments later, Big was handed a phone with 40 on the other line. After a few minutes, Big handed the phone back. And just like that, it was a wrap. Everything was fine. The same guy who spoke to Big while pointing a gun at him even asked for an autograph once he was told by E-40 to stand down. In fact, 40 even made sure to offer Big and his crew added protection until they got out of town the next day.

"For the way he got us there, because he booked the show himself, to make sure he knew where we were gonna be . . . for the way he got us, I respect him," Burns said of E-40. "And for the way he took care of us after we resolved the situation, I respect him even more."

Life on the road for Big wasn't always so death-defying. Way more often than not, life treated him well. From even before *Ready to Die* dropped, it felt as if Big was always on the road. There was always some show, some radio interview in some city. Some video shoot. Some concert. There were the marathon bus rides that sometimes featured broken air-conditioning systems. His diet ebbed and flowed depending the city he was in, and he could shop in a different city damn near every other day. And business got hectic every now and then with all the side projects he was working on, to the chagrin of Combs and Clive Davis. But it wasn't like Big was slacking on his responsibilities at Bad Boy. He was the label's franchise player. Following an October 1995 performance at BET's Phattest Concert in the '95 in Chicago, the *Daily Egyptian* said of Big's performance that his "vocal delivery made it unmistakably clear" why he was the year's biggest star, and that he could "execute rhymes unlike any other rap artist." Plus, his crew was living, and Big couldn't have been more proud.

"We wild, we young, and we tight like how a Mafia would be trained. These niggas is actually get ten thousand [dollars] a show right now," he said, beaming with elation. "They're getting paid. They're like fucking sex symbols. They're in magazines. Yo, this is great, man. I love it."

Many may have looked at Big as just a supremely gifted rapper, but those in the know, like 2 Live Crew's legendary frontman Luther Campbell, saw how much he was operating behind the scenes.

"A lot of other people take a lot of credit for the business aspect of that whole crew," Campbell said in *Unbelievable*. "It may have been Un running the label, but Biggie was the brains behind it all. Puffy takes credit for a lot of things with Faith and Kim, but a lot of that was Biggie. This cat did it without receiving the glory."

While Big saw the field of play in rap better than almost anyone, he wasn't also selfish in making sure the wealth—and the wild times—were equally distributed.

"You know how Big was depicted in that video for 'One More Chance'? Well, when girls were around Biggie, that's how it was," said the stylist Sybil Pennix. "They were rubbing his back or his neck, whatever. He was really Big Poppa like that."

Life on the road came with women. *Lots of women.* Tupac Shakur wasn't the only one who got around. Big told ladies across the country he was never a heartthrob and was "Black and ugly as ever," and in turn he morphed into one of the marquee sex symbols of his generation. At any given show, in any given city, there were women rubbing their breasts to the "Player's Anthem" hook and begging him to take pictures. It didn't matter what they looked like. He liked for women to be comfortable around him, and if it meant gassing up the least-attractive woman in a crew of friends to impress her homegirl, then he'd do that, too. Big Poppa was always accessible.

"He would get introduced to people, and when he said 'pleased to meet you' to a girl, it rang a different way," Combs said. "I guess they was caught off guard by how much of a gentleman he was, how smooth he was, and also how he didn't try to continue on the conversation. That made her feel comfortable. They'd lay in the cut, something else would happen, and then they'd start laughing. They'd see the humor and it was a wrap."

"I know I ain't no pretty nigga," Big said. "But I got a little, a little style to me. I don't know what it is. I just think that I'm cool to be with."

Being the self-proclaimed Player President meant he had to meet with his constituents, and it wouldn't take long for him to convince them of his platform. One time, the producer Stevie J invited two young ladies up from Philadelphia, and after picking them up and stopping at the studio, J told Big he was going to make a run to pick up some liquor and some weed.

"I got 'em. Don't worry about it," Big pledged. "They'll be in good hands."

When Stevie J returned some time later, he found exactly what DJ Premier walked in on when they were recording "Unbelievable."

"My man in the booth doing an interview getting topped off," Stevie J said on a 2017 appearance on *Desus & Mero*. "Right there! I was like, 'That's my man.'"

That's just how life was when you rolled with Biggie Smalls. You could end up seeing a classic show. Or you could end up in an orgy at the end of the night, because women would flock to him like bees to honey. And, in a lot of cases, both happened.

"The power of Big Poppa was like, 'Ain't no questions.' It's just, 'What you want?' 'I want some head right now.' 'Just go upstairs and take care of that,'" said Lil' Cease. "It's like, Big got three upstairs. I got one over there. Roc got one over there . . . in the car, the dressing room, backstage, you know. They was happy to have fun. This when the M.A.F.I.A. was out. And we wasn't no ugly niggas, either. No, we were sharp. We were flashing. We was with the hottest nigga running the game right now. Every bitch wanted a piece of that shit. Every bitch. We was getting paid so everybody had the jewelry, the suits, we had the cars. Extra rooms, suites. And mad bitches."

Big was getting it in at an extremely high clip, but there was one problem, and a pretty massive problem at that: he was still very much married to Faith Evans. In reality, the couple who married some two months after they met never truly had a chance to be newlyweds. Big basically lived on the road, and she was promoting her debut album, *Faith*. Big was featured in the video for Evans's lead single, "You Used to Love Me," and was said to be the inspiration behind her Chucky Thompson–produced single "You Don't Understand."

It wasn't like Big was trying to be a jerk. But he wasn't about to stop what he was doing, either. He was twenty-three years old, with a career that seemed unstoppable. Everything he put his voice on became a hit, and his debut album was at two million copies sold and counting. Even with all the life experiences he had in just a short amount of time, he was still in that part of life where he was trying to figure things out. None of that excused the misogyny in his life, yet it's not as if Big was betraying years of commitment, either. But not only did he make the decision to say "I do," it was his idea to do so in the first place. And his actions didn't affect just anyone. This was his wife. Big reasoned his infidelity wasn't that bad when looking at it in context.

"Temptation is a mothafucka. You're in the industry. Girls sucking your dick for nothing. Suck your man's dick just to get to suck your dick. That's the way it goes. It's crazy, but it's real," Big said.

"Now you got me. I'm going from state to state. It's possible for me to fuck ten bitches a day if I wanted to. It's crazy, but it's true," he reasoned. "Now, if you're in a relationship for how long? Let's just say two or three years. And in that time I fuck four bitches, you gonna flip over that? I mean, shit, I could've fucked four thousand bitches. And you gonna scream on me like, 'You cheating mothafucka!' You in Louisville, Kentucky, somewhere, and the shit come over you. Everybody make mistakes. Shit happens, you know what I'm saying? As long as it ain't no keeping-in-contact-type shit, like the girl from Louisville is trying to move to New York and be part of your life and shit. Just take a fuck for what it is. A fuck.

"You're my only girl. You're the one that I love, the one that I'm with,'" he said, mimicking the conversation he would have with his wife. "'If I happen to fuck up and make a mistake, I apologize, man. Just don't lose it. 'Cause it could've been a lot worse. Give me an E for effort, at least. Goddamn. I couldn't get an A, so I got a B+. Don't be mad at me. My feelings for you ain't changed.'"

That grading scale might've made sense in Big's eyes, but his wife wasn't trying to hear that arithmetic. Evans's professional career was blowing up, too. Her first single, "You Used to Love Me," was certified gold. But her personal life was in shambles. She was lonely and wondering how feasible it would be to continue a marriage when she hardly saw her husband. And even when they did see each other, there was always work to complete. Like their October 1995 *VIBE* cover story that positioned them as rap's definitive power couple. Or even the time Faith and Big had gotten into a heated argument and Big saw her later that day talking to one of her longtime friends on Washington Street while holding her daughter, Chyna. Though Chyna,

Faith's daughter from a previous relationship, was not biologically Big's, she still called him "Daddy," and he accepted her as his own. Big, D-Roc, and their friend Buck pulled up on them, and after Big asked Faith's friend to give Chyna to him, D-Roc and Buck jumped him. Big knew she wasn't seeing this guy, but Faith was pissed that her husband would react as if she was. Especially when he would flaunt other women in front of her. It didn't matter if he had the hottest album out or his singles were on the soundtrack to people's lives. They had made a commitment to each other, and her husband wasn't honoring his vows.

Big was pretty consistent about calling his wife and checking in with her whenever he got to a new city to do a show. But when he called this time after a show in Virginia Beach, something seemed off. Big said he was letting someone else use his suite that night because they had a girl with them. Faith didn't believe it for one second. It was a struggle to figure out what to be more insulted by: the fact that her husband was cheating or the fact that he thought such a poorly constructed lie would work on her. She found someone to watch Chyna, and before Evans knew it, she was on a 6:00 A.M. flight to Virginia Beach. She knew she had plenty of time to get down there after a quick flight, because it wasn't like they were going to check out of the hotel early. She snuck past Hawk Burns in the lobby and went straight to Big's room and began knocking on the door.

"Who is it?" a woman's voice asked from behind the door.

"Housekeeping," Evans said.

As soon as the door slightly cracked open, Evans went to town. Big, in a future *VIBE* interview, said he guessed his wife punched the woman in the face "like, thirty times." Evans said she didn't know how badly she beat the woman up because she was looking at her husband the entire time, as if to say, *You know this is all your fault, right?* Big and the woman were fully clothed, but Evans didn't give a damn. She didn't need to be in a married man's hotel room anyway.

"I ain't fuck her!" Big pleaded. "I ain't fuck her!"

Evans's reply was as witty as anything her husband ever put on wax. "You should've!"

"By the time I was done hitting her, all the guys had come—you know he done called everybody from their room—Cease, [Money] L, whoever else was out of town with him—all just standing there looking at me," Evans recalled, laughing. "I was just standing there putting my coat on to leave by then. I was like, 'Bye, y'all. I'm done.'"

Evans was back in Brooklyn by noon, and Big wasn't far behind. He actually wasn't mad—not that he had much of a leg to stand on. But he respected his wife's tenacity. He was a nervous wreck the whole flight back and eventually caught up with Evans as he attempted to work his way out of the doghouse. He wasn't there long. Big always knew what to say and when to say it, especially to his wife.

"I was definitely weak," Evans said, smiling at the memory. "Weak for him. Definitely so."

It wasn't the first or only time Evans had to get physical to defend her marriage.

"I definitely did some things where I'm like, 'What was I thinking?!'" she said years later. "Some near-death situations . . . I was just a little too bold when it came to that man and my heart. But you live and you learn."

Evans didn't think too much of it when her husband began asking her to hang out with Lil' Kim. Big believed in Kim's talent, and despite her small stature, the Brooklyn mami could hold her own in a room full of men, whether shooting cee-lo or penning verses for Junior M.A.F.I.A.'s debut album. He knew that Kim, perhaps more than any member of the clique, had a chance to be a superstar in her own right, despite whatever ignorant stereotypes around women MCs existed.

Nevertheless, Faith and Kim did hang out on occasion, going shopping and to the gym together a few times. One time Big found out Kim was over at his and Faith's apartment with Faith and was none too pleased—and Faith couldn't understand why. She wasn't looking for anything because, in her mind, there wasn't anything to look for. Things got weird when Faith heard Kim on the radio speaking to Wendy Williams about her and Big's marriage. Kim told Williams that their marriage was over and that Faith had moved out. The truth was that Evans *had* moved out. She had gotten word through two of her good friends, Doobie and Creamy, whom she'd met through Big, that word around Brooklyn was that some guys from Fort Greene had been talking about robbing her and her husband. That led to Faith's moving out of their Fort Greene apartment immediately. She was beginning to put the pieces together, and she eventually caught Kim and Big in bed together. She was embarrassed, and angry at herself for being played by both. Suddenly, the "Fuck Me (Interlude)" on *Ready to Die*, which featured Big and Kim engaging in raunchy sex, wasn't just a funny skit anymore. It was art imitating life.

"It was a shock, but it wasn't the first person I found he was messing around with. But it was her, and I thought it was just the artist thing," Evans said. "But by that time, we were going through it because of a bunch of other women and a lot of other situations."

In a September 2000 *Washington Post* feature about Kim, Voletta Wallace said that her son and Kim "were like peanut butter and jelly" and "had the same voice." There was a lot of truth in that. Big and Kim's on-wax chemistry was impeccable. She was the firecracker to his laid-back, Brooklyn-chill demeanor. And neither minded painting the most graphic and explicit pictures imaginable through their lyrics. Yet their real-life chemistry was perhaps best described as passionately volatile. Even to this day, Kim speaks of Big in an almost religious manner—calling him the best lover she's ever had in 2018 interview with Power 106 in Los Angeles. They experienced many highs together, and many of their songs are still in constant rotation a quarter century later. They'd been romantically involved but also verbally combative. They were arguing on the way to the 1995 Source Awards. And there was once a time when Evans remembered walking in on him screaming at Kim for something music-related. He was threatening to replace her with Foxy Brown.

"You ain't special!" he yelled. "I'll replace your ass with the quickness. Don't forget that shit!"

It was Big, though, and Lance "Un" Rivera who cultivated her image focused heavily on tough street talk and lascivious lyrics that left no room for doubt. By the fall of 1995, Kim's star power was rising, in part because of her close association with Big, but also because anyone who ever saw Kim live understood that her star power carried its own weight. But the personal affair between the two came with its own share of harrowing moments, like when Big reportedly dragged her by her coat after finding her talking to members of Jodeci in a hotel lobby and later prohibited her from recording a song with them. Or like when Big pulled a gun on her in the studio after she refused to record a verse he had written for her for the Usher song "Just Like Me." Jermaine Dupri recounted the story on a *Drink Champs* podcast episode, which had already been told on an episode of VH1's *Undriven*. Dupri said Kim was upset because this was around the time Big had reportedly had sex with a close friend of Kim's—an entanglement Big hinted at on "Friend of Mine" on *Ready to Die*.

"We did have a very violent relationship," Kim confirmed during a 2017 interview on *Ebro in the Morning*. "I hate that, for a while, that was all I attracted . . . It is what it is. He was *everything*."

Big and Kim's relationship, however toxic at times, and however undeniably creative at others, is something those close to them saw play out in real time. Including when Kim, reportedly, made the agonizing decision to get an abortion while recording her solo debut, *Hard Core*, and Junior M.A.F.I.A.'s *Conspiracy*.

In many ways, Big knew what he was doing by helping to dictate the direction of Kim's career, from how she said things on record to the image of a sexually liberated Black woman who could spit as raunchy as he could, and keeping her in his life as his mistress.

"My strategy was [consistent] when it comes to Kim: she wasn't the wife. She was the high-end side chick to drug dealers," Rivera said in Clover Hope's *The Motherlode: 100+ Women Who Made Hip-Hop*. "We placed her in a world that we were living in, and it was: you wear all of the finest things because the number one drug dealer, you're his side chick, and he buys you everything. It's all driven by the male hormones, the male ego, the fantasy. It's not about love. It's about being nasty."

In the nineties, the conversation around topics like domestic abuse wasn't just different; it hardly existed. For years, rumors have circulated about the long-term effects from Kim's time with Big. Had Big lived to see fifty years old, there's no telling how he would have spoken on this part of his life. Award-winning playwright Pearl Cleage published *Mad at Miles: A Blackwoman's Guide to Truth* in 1990, and in it she famously took jazz icon Miles Davis to task for his history of violence against women, including Cicely Tyson. When asked by *Atlanta* magazine years later if people should feel guilty about listening to his music, she responded no, and that if Miles's spirit were ever to return, that hopefully it would be as beautiful as his music—and that she never stopped listening to his *Kind of Blue* album, either. Those who knew Big personally, like Cheo Hodari Coker, said the man he knew would've been upfront about the misgivings in his life and knew that certainly wasn't the way his mother raised him to be.

"Miles lived to be in his sixties, and he talked about it and hopefully had evolved past that," said Coker. "Not excusing any of what Big did or what happened, but I think you have to reconcile the fact that when you're that young, one would hope one would have the opportunity to apologize. It's an imperfection that needs to be talked about and needs to be dealt with. I think you need that for the full three-hundred-sixty-degree person. And Big never shied away from being that person."

"When I hear people who were close to them and still are talk about that, there is still a separation of Big as a person. And maybe had he still been alive that'd be different, but there's still a separation there," said cultural critic Naima Cochrane. "We also have to put in context this nigga was twenty-four years old. He was a kid. How much had Big really learned about himself? About how to cope? Because it's not like men in this game were sitting around talking about self-care and talking to each other and airing it out. That level of self-awareness wasn't a thing yet. I think there is also some grace in thinking about it. I don't know a person in this business, that's me included, in the nineties in their twenties who wasn't problematic, because the culture was problematic. The priorities in the culture were problematic. I'm not excusing Big, [but] that might be part of why now there's this ability to separate his behavior and disrespect from his memory."

Yet those close to Big knew how hectic these falling-outs with Kim could get because they'd be the ones left to pick up the pieces.

"The only thing I said to Big is, 'You really shouldn't have never messed with your artist,'" said Mister Cee. "And Big was like, 'Well, it's done now, Cee.' I felt like as much as Big felt like he had it under control, he didn't have it under control. Big was really in love with two women at the same time."

"It wouldn't take more than five minutes for Big to fall in love. And he meant it. I had to cover and patch shit up for him a few times," Rivera told *VIBE*. "Once he made Kim so mad that she wouldn't come to the studio. He called me and was like, 'I fucked up and Kim's mad.' I'd call her and say,

'C'mon, you know he love you,' and she'd be like, 'So why he treat me like that?' I'd have to smooth shit over."

If Big wasn't already flying close to the sun with the high-profile, intimate relationships in his life, he further tempted fate by trying to feature them all when it came time to shoot the video for Junior M.A.F.I.A.'s hit single "Get Money." Rivera called Faith, asking her to be in the video. Husband and wife, at this point just by title only, weren't speaking at the time, so she declined.

"Tell him to ask his girlfriend," she said.

When Big recorded the verse, he and Faith were still on good terms, so the hypothetical woman Big rapped about being disloyal to in song couldn't have applied to her—outside of the tattoo on her breast that said "B.I.G." That part was true. But she wasn't playing video games with Cease and Nino and answering the phone.

"Now," Evans said in a 2014 interview, "maybe that was about Tiffany. I don't know."

The "girlfriend" and "Tiffany" that Evans was referring to was Big's new love interest, Tiffany Lane Jarmon, better known as rapper Charli Baltimore. The two had met at one of Big's concerts in Philadelphia. They took pictures together after the show and instantly hit it off. How Big learned Baltimore could rhyme, at least according to Baltimore herself, was learning firsthand you were never the *only* woman in Big's life. Baltimore once got the code to his answering machine, which housed hundreds of voicemails from women leaving outrageous and sexually explicit messages. As a Christmas present, Baltimore wrote a rap with all the girls' names from the voicemails. As she rapped the verses to Big, he just sat in silence.

"When I was done, he got real quiet. He was like, 'You got my passcode or something?'" Baltimore laughed. Big nodded, almost as if to concede guilt. "I said, 'Yeah.' And he said, 'So you can spit?' And that was it."

By the time of the "Get Money" video, Big knew there were too many moving parts to have a peaceful shoot, and so did everyone else. Evans had already told Rivera that there was no way she was participating, but now Big was going to have his current girlfriend wearing a platinum-blonde wig playing the role he originally intended for his wife in the video that many suspected was directed at her. Not only that, but Lil' Kim was featured on the song, too. Rivera warned Big that it wasn't a good idea to do something this messy. Big moved forward anyway.

Shortly after Kim's appearance on Wendy Williams, Faith—in a move she'd later regret—returned the volley and aired her grievances with Wendy as well. She directed her anger at Kim and Charli, telling both it was on whenever she saw them. After the radio appearance, Faith went to go see Big at a Manhattan hotel he was staying in at the time.

"Wassup with you and Kim?" she recalled asking in *Keep the Faith*.

"Yeah, we get down like that," Big responded without hesitation.

"All this time?" she asked. "You been fucking this girl all this time?"

"Yeah . . ."

Husband and wife slept together again that day. But in Faith's eyes, it was far more about emotional detachment than the passion they once had. She was done. "If Big wanted to fuck the entire world, that was on him," she wrote. Big had put his own personal life on wax. But this was far from the last time that would ever be the case. And not by him, either.

———

While Big was on the set of the "Get Money" video shoot, he received some news that would rock his world. He was busy all night on November 30, 1995, and when he finally checked his messages, the first was from Randy "Stretch" Walker. Big met Stretch through Shakur when the two were on speaking terms. Stretch was also with Shakur when he was shot multiple times at Quad Studios. Stretch and Big's friendship continued to evolve, a reality that left Shakur none too pleased.

"Yo," Stretch said, "how do I get to the shoot, dog?"

The last message hit Big like a punch in the gut. It was Stretch's wife, bawling in tears delivering the news that Stretch had been murdered shortly after midnight. Reports said Stretch was chased by two Black men in a black Acura. He flipped his SUV over at the corner of 112th Avenue and 209th Street in Queens Village. The assailants unloaded more shots into his car before fleeing. Stretch was shot four times.

The news was tragic and stunned a hip-hop community that was still reeling from Eazy-E's passing from AIDS earlier in the year. But the timing was nothing short of an eerie coincidence. Exactly a year earlier, Stretch and Shakur had been ambushed in the lobby of Quad Studios. That one event set off a chain reaction that was still being felt.

"The shootings were one year and about five minutes apart," Lieutenant Vito R. Spano told the *New York Times*. "It's weird."

Stretch took offense to Shakur's critique of him not attacking the shooters in Quad and complying with their demands. He implied that Shakur had accidentally shot himself trying to grab his gun and openly asked why the man so many still saw as "Bishop" would take such street issues to the media.

"Tupac made disparaging remarks about him in *VIBE* magazine, and it really hurt his feelings a lot," said Ed Lover. The famed TV and radio personality had introduced Stretch to the music industry. "I think—just my opinion—after Tupac got shot, I just think Tupac kind of turned against everybody."

Tupac spoke of a self-metamorphosis when he spoke to the journalist Kevin Powell at Rikers Island for their *VIBE* interview. He wanted to make a change in not just how people saw him, but how he saw himself. "The addict in Tupac is dead. The excuse-maker in Tupac is dead. The vengeful Tupac is dead," he said. God let him live for him to do something extremely extraordinary, he saw of his life's purpose. But now he was out of prison with months of abuse, confinement, and countless remarks from people in prison about who set him up.

His feelings toward a lot of people had changed. Those close to Shakur, like the former Tommy Boy publicist Laura Hines, who had known him since his Digital Underground days, said that he suffered from a "profound sense of victimhood," and that he took slights against him to the point of obsession. Yet when asked about Stretch's passing, Tupac's response was particularly cold. "I felt for his mother and his wife. I didn't feel anything for him. Honestly."

"He didn't do what your dog is supposed to do when you get shot up," Shakur told *The Source*. "When I was in jail, nigga never wrote me, never got at me. And he started hanging around Biggie right after this. I'm in jail, shot up, his main dog, and he hanging out, going to shows with Biggie. Both these niggas never came to see me. Ain't no words. The rules of the game are so self-explanatory."

Across the country, Shakur was hard at work on his post-prison album. Without saying Stretch's name, the first verse on the song "Holla At Me" carried those same accusations of disloyalty, clearly directed at Stretch, claiming that he had "lost respect for" him and that they "could never be friends." Ever since he had gotten out of prison in mid-October 1995, Shakur's focus remained on releasing an album as quickly as possible. He wanted the rap world to know that not only was he back, but there would be no prisoners taken on his climb toward rap's Mount Olympus. And, perhaps, for a far more subtle reason, it would help him fulfill the terms of the agreement he made with Death Row to secure his release.

Whatever the case, it was all hands on deck at Death Row, and under Suge's orders, everyone was to help Tupac. Originally intended to be a Dr. Dre solo, "California Love" was gifted to Shakur as sort of a welcome-home present. To Shakur's credit, he didn't waste anyone's time. Written with so many emotions flowing through him, the songs flowed directly from his heart to the pen. And by February, just four months after being released from prison, Shakur was ready to release the new album. If *Me Against the World* felt aptly titled, then *All Eyez on Me* would double the fold. Tupac's work ethic had long been one of his most Herculean qualities, as well as being able to record under intense emotional stress. But now he recorded a double disc full of songs within three months after getting out of prison.

Throughout the entire process, Big, Puffy, and Bad Boy were never far from Tupac's mind. During the filming of the "California Love" video, Shakur taunted MTV cameras with an insinuation that made a personal conflict even more so.

"Faith my homegirl," Shakur said sarcastically with a smile while flashing a handful of cash.

The truth is, the two had met a few weeks earlier at the Hollywood Athletic Club in Los Angeles. Evans was in town to pursue some musical opportunities of her own, and, more important, to clear her head. Her marriage was in disarray, and she felt as if the relationship with Big was overtaking her own successful album, which had already surpassed gold status and was charging toward platinum. Shakur and Evans were introduced by their mutual friend, Treach of Naughty by Nature, whom the R&B star shared New Jersey ties with. They took a few pictures together and afterward, Shakur said he was a fan and wanted to work with her on his new album, and according to Evans, that's all that happened. Evans even called Big, despite them not being on the best of terms at the moment, to let her know she had run into Shakur. She'd heard of 'Pac being angry at Big for his shooting a year earlier, but Big told her not to trip about it, and that 'Pac knew in his heart that that wasn't the truth. So when Big found out from Faith that she was planning on recording a song with him for his upcoming album, all he asked was whether she going to do it. To Evans, there was no animosity in Big's response at all. No one knew at that moment just how far Shakur would take things.

The two ran into each other again at a *Waiting to Exhale* soundtrack release party. Or, the way she put it in her memoir, Shakur attached himself to Evans and her friend Nicci Gilbert of the group Brownstone. Evans understood how the optics looked. Her heart sank when she saw Whitney Houston at the party that night looking at her and Shakur in such close proximity. Despite all the tension in her head, Evans agreed to hop on the song with Tupac for $25,000. Yet it wasn't until she arrived at the studio with Tupac, who had originally promised to send a driver but instead picked her up in his drop-top Mercedes-Benz, that she felt the energy completely shift. According to Evans, she had heard about Tupac getting out of prison, but she was completely oblivious to his signing with Death Row. She was well aware of the escalating bad blood between Suge Knight and Puffy, and now she was in the middle of even more drama. They knocked out what eventually became the song "Wonder Why They Call U Bitch," and Shakur said he'd hit the Bad Boy offices up to potentially clear the song. When she asked for her check, Shakur, per Evans's memoir, began to reveal his true intentions. He told her that Big and company had set him up, and then he asked if she was going to give him oral sex. He cursed and yelled about her husband and Bad Boy Records and about how they would feel his wrath.

Evans has always held the same stance: she didn't know the beef between Shakur and her husband was that serious. Only time would reveal just how consequential the chain of events since they met in the club would become, but the ferocity between Death Row and Bad Boy only intensified. Following Robles's murder in Atlanta, according to the *New York Times Magazine*, Combs sent Mustapha Farrakhan, son of Louis Farrakhan, to speak with Knight, but Knight wouldn't speak with him. "He's going to settle the beef his way," a friend of Knight's was quoted as saying. "On the street."

When the How Can I Be Down rap conference took place in Miami weeks later, the tension was undeniable. By its billing, the summit was intended to provide insight on how to navigate the music business. Rumors circulated that Knight was bringing an army with him while *VIBE* reported that Combs would be bringing his own army of "drug lords and thugs." Ultimately, Combs chose not to attend, with *Billboard* reporting at the time that the reason was because of threats from Death Row.

On December 15, 1995—three years to the day since *The Chronic* dropped—Death Row made another statement. This time, reportedly, violent. According to reports, Suge Knight, Tupac, and several other Death Row affiliates cornered Mark Anthony Bell, a record promoter Combs had known since high school, at a Christmas party. They demanded he hand over the addresses of Combs and his mother and what he knew about Big Jake's killing in Atlanta. The story goes that it was either give that information over or get beaten up and forced to drink urine.

"He mighta got a few punches and he probably drunk about twenty shots of piss, you know what I mean?" Knight would later say. "Literally."

Bell's attorney said he would sue Knight and Death Row, but he accepted an estimated $600,000 settlement and moved out of the country. Bell's assault was never front-page news, but it spoke volumes to those in the know. There was a real beef, and as Dr. Dre somberly said, it was going to be hard for either coast to visit the other and not be wary of mayhem.

A day later, on December 16, 1995, a Dogg Pound music video trailer was shot up on the set of their "New York, New York" video shoot in Red Hook, Brooklyn. Big was the one who announced it on Hot 97. Death Row was enraged, believing Big had encouraged the shooting.

"Aye—Biggie and them caused that," Snoop Dogg said while speaking on the incident years later in 2018 *Rap Radar Podcast* interview. Big and Snoop would speak months later and squash any bad blood between them following a tragedy that had an impact on both camps. "And that's all in the art of war. And because we didn't try to fuck him up—because we had so much love for him. Me and my team, we loved Biggie. So we took it on the chin, like, 'Fuck' . . . But the homies were hot. Death Row was hot."

A tense situation grew even more tense when Death Row's *New York Times Magazine* feature landed. On the cover of the January 14, 1996, edition, Knight was dressed in all red and flanked by Snoop and Tupac, and the feature itself proved to be a masterclass in access and reporting. It was a king's ransom of details and tidbits, but one exchange stood out above the rest.

"The wife of a top rapper bought this for him," Suge said, purposely trying to draw a reaction.

"Who's that?" Tupac smiled.

"Notorious B.I.G.'s wife, Faith Evans . . . She bought him this and a suit and some other stuff . . . And how did you thank her, Tupac?" Knight trolled.

"I did enough," Shakur said.

Rumors were also swirling that Knight was involved with Misa Hylton and that Death Row had printed a magazine ad with Hylton and Knight holding Combs's toddler son with a caption that read "The East Coast can't even take care of their own." Hot 97's Wendy Williams discussed this on the radio, but the ad never ran anywhere, and Death Row said no such thing ever existed.

The news of Shakur boasting about an alleged affair with his wife reached Big, and he was furious. Evans had moved out of their Fort Greene apartment and into a Midtown Manhattan hotel. Big was nearly beating her door down. She contemplated calling the cops, but ultimately decided against it. She let Big into the room, and he was the maddest he'd ever been. Cursing, screaming, grabbing her by her arms. That anger eventually gave way to tears, and as Evans stayed in the bathroom, Big left the room. Moments later, it was D-Roc who was knocking on her door. D-Roc knew his best friend was wilding, but he'd come to check on Evans, whom he cared about deeply, too. If the allegations weren't easy for Big, it couldn't have been easy on her.

"You know that shit ain't true," she said.

"I know," Roc said. "Chris don't believe that . . . The nigga just mad, you know? He mad."

Despite all their drama, the husband still very much cared for his wife. Ask anyone on the tour bus with him. Whenever the two would go through their spats, Big would wallow in his wife's album for hours on end. He always preferred to be left alone. His sole attention would be dedicated to *Faith*. He played it so much the rest of the bus would beg him to put something else on. To which he'd say over and over again that Evans was "my baby" and that he loved her.

"Faith did something to him that no other woman did to him," said DJ Enuff, his tour DJ. "I don't know what it is, but he really did love his Faith."

For Evans, the internal and external chaos was all becoming too much. She and Big had their own issues revolving around how little time they could spend together and his very public infidelity. Then she had Lil' Kim speaking about her marriage across the New York airwaves and his new girlfriend Charli Baltimore in his music videos. Now the whole Tupac, Suge, and Death Row beef had intensified, and in her eyes, she'd been used as a pawn in a situation that had nothing to do with her. But she did go to see Big one last time. It was Valentine's Day weekend in 1996, and Big and Junior M.A.F.I.A. had a show down in New Orleans. She went, and if nothing else, it would give her an opportunity to keep an eye on Kim at the same time. But love is the hardest drug to kick. The pain of its absence can never replace the high of its presence. Even if it is fleeting. Big used that charming gift of gab, and the rest took its course.

A few weeks after that Big Easy one-night rekindling, Evans found out she was pregnant.

17

ALL EYEZ ON MAYHEM

BIG HAD MORE THAN ENOUGH DRAMA IN HIS OWN PERSONAL
LIFE. The last thing he needed was to entertain someone else's issues. By
the time Big, Faith, Puffy, and the Bad Boy crew landed in Los Angeles for
the Soul Train Music Awards in late March 1996, it wasn't lost on anyone
just how much they had to pay attention to their moves in what was increasingly becoming known as enemy territory. But for Death Row, while they
were on their own turf, the label was in the midst of a major transition. On
the surface, Death Row had everything a label could possibly want—a major
feature in *VIBE*'s February 1996 issue titled LIVE FROM DEATH ROW in all-red
letters, an executive who intimidated everyone he walked into a room with
in Knight, and a three-headed power dynamo in Dr. Dre, Snoop Dogg, and
Tupac—but almost as quickly as it came together, the label showed its first
signs of internal crumbling. In February 1996, Snoop Dogg was acquitted
of first-degree murder charges stemming from the 1993 shooting that left
Philip Woldemariam dead.

"Death Row respected you if they trusted you," said the former *VIBE*
editor in chief Alan Light. "It's not like our coverage of Death Row was
uncritical. [But] at that time in particular, how could you hurt them?"

No one needed to hurt Death Row. It could do bad all on its lonesome.
Beyond Snoop's legal victory and the immediate success of Shakur's *All Eyez*

on Me, Death Row was under a ton of pressure. A month earlier, Michael "Harry O" Harris filed a lawsuit saying that he had never been compensated for helping to get Death Row off the ground. And on March 22, 1996, Dr. Dre sent shock waves through the rap world when he announced his departure from the label he had helped create. Dre had grown weary of Death Row's direction. The label he and Suge had launched some four years earlier didn't feel like his anymore. There were people in the Death Row offices on any given day whom he'd never even met. So much had changed in such a short amount of time. The company was worth nine figures but lived on fear. Dre had helped create gangsta rap, but the overwhelming street mentality was affecting the way business was being done. Per *Newsweek*, Dre didn't even take his masters with him. That's how bad he wanted out.

Not that any of what was going on inside Death Row was any of Bad Boy's concern. Big was going up against pop megastars like TLC and Whitney Houston and Mary J. Blige and Method Man in the Best R&B/Best Rap Song of the Year category with his "One More Chance." Evans was up for two awards herself, including Best R&B/Soul Album of the Year. But the Bad Boy camp kept their heads on a swivel the entire time.

Combs granted a writer from *Details* magazine access while he was in L.A. A few days before the awards ceremony, Combs's rented Mercedes pulled up alongside none other than Knight and Shakur at a stoplight. That reporter witnessed Combs pass a gun to one of the members of his security. The two powerful Black CEOs looked at each other in the eye while Shakur appeared oblivious to the entire encounter. Combs made a point of saying to the writer that passing the gun was only a precautionary measure.

As the light turned green and both cars went their separate ways, Combs wasted no time explaining his reasoning to the writer. "I don't want you to be saying, 'We were driving by, the gats started coming from everywhere, they started taking aim, but the cops were there, so they can't do what they intended.' It don't be that type of vibe," Combs said. "Everybody around may want it to be—want the two powers against each other, almost like spiders in a jar. But Death Row is doing good, they paving the way for us to do good. He ain't my friend, but everything's cool."

The tense environment in L.A. was no different in the Shrine Auditorium for the awards show. Big nearly didn't perform because of a missing size 14EEE shoe, and while he, Combs, and Evans performed "One More Chance," that was the extent of his and his wife's communication that night. Both Tupac and Big took home awards that night with *Me Against the World* winning Best Rap Album and "One More Chance (Remix)" taking home Song of the Year. Big was accompanied by D-Roc, Lil' Cease, Mark Pitts, Un, and more on stage to accept the award. Per usual, he shouted out his mom, his daughter, and his record company—but when he, also per usual, sent love to Brooklyn, boos could be heard mixed in with cheers. It wasn't exactly the most welcoming environment. But it was outside the venue where the real fireworks took place.

Team Bad Boy was waiting on their transportation back to the hotel. That's when Team Death Row, led by Shakur and Knight, pulled up on them. Shakur was leaning out the window, screaming "West Side! Outlaws!" He was dressed in army fatigues as if he was ready for war. He'd been insinuating it for months, using Evans as bait to get Big's attention. Guns were drawn on both sides, though no shots were fired. But now there was no way to deny the tension. The two factions, with their two most visible talents in Big and Tupac, had come face-to-face.

"That was the first time I really looked into his face," Big said in one of the few interviews he gave at the time. "I looked into his eyes and I was like, 'Yo, this nigga is really buggin' the fuck out.'"

The *Hollywood Reporter* used an unnamed source who said Shakur pointed a gun at Big, but the latter denied that ever happened. "Nah, 'Pac didn't pull steel on me," he said. "He was on some tough shit, though. I can't knock them dudes for the way they go about their biz. They made everything seem so dramatic. I felt the darkness when he rolled up that night." Big had seen this side of his friend before, though only in the movies. "I was like, 'That's Bishop!' He played that shit to a tee. He had his little goons with him, and Suge was with him and they was like, 'We gonna settle this now.'"

It was the first time Biggie and Tupac, the two most dynamic names in rap, had seen each other in 486 days, the last time being when Shakur was giving Big, Chico Del Vec, and company the middle finger as he was wheeled on a stretcher out of Quad Studios. Following yelling between both sides, Big never said a word during the ruckus, maintaining his cool.

Eventually, both sides dispersed. There was bad blood in the air, but no one was harmed. Not this time, at least.

Throughout 1996, it was Tupac who would largely fan the flames of his fall-out with Big, Puffy, and the Bad Boy camp. For the most part, Big was doing exactly as Puff had advised him back when Shakur's jailhouse *VIBE* interview was on shelves. He was remaining quiet. But every now and then, Big would give a small glimpse of his thoughts on his personal life. The remix of Junior M.A.F.I.A.'s smash single "Get Money" dropped in '96 and featured a new beat, equipped with a sample of Dennis Edwards's 1984 hit "Don't Look Any Further." It also boasted three new verses from Lil' Cease, Lil' Kim and, of course, Big.

"Check it out, guns, I bust 'em," he rapped. "Problems with my wife, don't discuss 'em."

This was Big's way of acknowledging the rumors swirling about but managing to play things close to the chest. And it wouldn't be the only time he'd do so, either.

———

During the height of the crack era in New York City, Shawn "Jay-Z" Carter and Christopher Wallace attended Brooklyn's George Westinghouse Career and Technical Education High School together.

"We was like passing friends," Jay said in a 1997 MTV interview. "Just like wassup . . . we see each other and we acknowledge each other."

The two Brooklyn ships in the night crossed paths once again thanks to DJ Clark Kent in early spring 1996. Kent had known Big for years, long before even Matty C's *Source* column was written. He was from Crown Heights, Brooklyn, and along the way became cool with D-Roc, Un, and C-Gutta, too. Kent got his start as Dana Dane's DJ back in the late eighties, and from there made a name for himself via radio and rocking some of the hottest clubs all around New York City. Kent had been producing records for a while when he played Big what eventually became the "Player's Anthem" beat. Big came up with the hook on the tour bus on the spot.

But Kent also knew of Jay, another incredibly talented Brooklyn MC. Jay's Marcy Projects is only two miles away from where Big grew up at 226

St. James. Jay and Big were more alike than they realized. They were both products of the multigenerational war on drugs that led to selling crack both in Brooklyn and out of state, up and down Interstate 95. And they could both paint pictures with their words unlike anything Kent had ever heard. Kent was so adamant that Jay-Z take rapping seriously that he built a studio in his house just so he could come there and rap. Kent knew that as soon as Jay took making an album seriously, "it would be trouble for everybody."

"Yo, you said your rhymes better than anybody I've heard say their rhymes," Kent told Big of his display on "Who Shot Ya."

"What the fuck are you talking about?" he responded, super annoyed at this point. "So I'm the best?!"

"Nah, you're the best rapper I've ever heard."

"So what does that make your man?" Big followed up.

"My mans is the best MC I've heard."

Big paused for a moment, almost to do the math in his head. "What the fuck is the difference?!"

Big was sitting in on a session with Kent one day when he accidentally overheard a beat that Kent was cooking up for Jay. This was exactly what Kent didn't want to happen, but now it was too late. Big wanted it badly, but Kent was adamant he couldn't let that happen.

"You keep giving this mothafucka everything!" Big complained.

Kent's explanation was simple. He DJed for him, but Jay-Z was his artist. The answer was easy. Or as easy as it could get telling Biggie Smalls he couldn't have a beat. Big had grown annoyed with Kent telling him how good this guy Jay-Z was. But Jay-Z *had* to be on that record regardless of who was on the beat. In an act of spontaneity Kent would later admit he still couldn't explain, he told Big to come to the studio with him and wait in the car. Kent went in to make sure Jay was cool. He played the beat and Jay ripped the entire song on the solo. This is when Clark had to think on his feet.

"Yo, this shit is dope. You should put Big on the song," Kent said.

The Roc-A-Fella Records cofounder Damon Dash reportedly said no because he wasn't trying to deal with the hassle of going through Combs. Kent explained that he knew Big and could talk to him. Jay said if Kent could make it happen, then cool.

"But," Dash reiterated, "we ain't paying Puff no money."

Kent faked going to the bathroom, and, to everyone's surprise, walking back in with Kent was none other than Big. He and Jay nearly instantly burst out laughing upon seeing each other, and before long, both were vibing out to the beat that eventually became "Brooklyn's Finest." A half hour passed, and Jay hopped up to get in the booth. He knocked his verses out in one take.

"You ready?" he asked Big as he left the booth.

Big was floored. He looked at Clark in sheer amazement. As far as Big knew, he was the only artist who could sit and listen to a beat and then rip it to shreds off the top of the dome.

"Clark, that shit was crazy," Big said. Kent smiled in approval. After months of arguing with Biggie about Jay-Z's skills, he'd been proven right. Big wouldn't record then, but he'd come back weeks later and complete his verse. Big and Jay-Z went to see a Bernie Mac show in the city that night. During a time when Big's name was in the news about a former friendship gone awry with Shakur, away from the tabloids, a new friendship was formed. From the day that Kent brought them together in the studio, the self-proclaimed Marcy Projects hallway loiterer and the Mayor of Fulton Street reportedly spoke every day, until life had other plans.

"He pushed me because we both wanted to be the best. It was healthy," Jay later said. "It was like two competitors on the court that played basketball and then after the game's over be like, 'Yo, let's go to the movies or something.'"

When Big did finally record his verses for "Brooklyn's Finest," like most everything he did in the booth, it was worth the wait. In his verse, Big again poked fun at the current drama he was having with Shakur, claiming that if Faith was pregnant with twins, she'd likely have "two 'Pacs." The line, which the entire world heard when Jay's debut album *Reasonable Doubt* dropped on June 25, 1996, may have been a comical quip that most saw as Big attempting to downplay the escalating anxiety with Shakur. But to Mister Cee, it was an unnecessary verbal dart by Big at his own wife.

"If I was in the studio, or if I would've heard that record before it came, I would've told Big you can't say that," Cee told me. "Number one, you don't even know if she had sex with 'Pac. Number two, you don't know even know if that kid is 'Pac's kid. And number three, if the kid is your kid, this is something you're gonna have to live with for the rest of your life, saying this about the mother of your kid. Because Faith didn't do nothing to you, or it hasn't been proven that Faith did anything to you publicly for you to go back at her publicly."

—————

When Tupac Shakur was asked what he thought about the dispute that had been dubbed the East Coast/West Coast rivalry, his response was short, yet chilling.

"It's gonna get deep," he was quoted as saying the Death Row *VIBE* feature.

It was an ominous statement, and no one knew just how far this spat could go. There was already violence involved, and Shakur had been insinuating for months that he and Faith Evans were romantically involved. Shakur had the hottest album on shelves, with *All Eyez on Me* already five times platinum in just two months after its release, but all he could see was a target. Shakur had used Biggie and Bad Boy as visual muses before. He parodied Biggie and Puffy in the video for his and Snoop's "2 of Amerikaz Most Wanted." On "No More Pain," from *Eyez*, he dubbed himself a "Bad Boy killa" and referenced "cross-eyed, fat, Down syndrome motherfuckers" and "dancers turned fuckin' CEOs" on the song's outro. And he said that prison hadn't changed him at all. In 'Pac own words, "It made me worse." He wasn't lying, either.

On June 4, 1996, Shakur unleashed a ballistic missile in the form of his new record: "Hit 'Em Up." 'Pac left nothing to doubt, directly telling Big on the opening seconds of the song, "That's why I fucked your bitch, you fat motherfucker." The diss was set to the melody of Junior M.A.F.I.A.'s "Player's Anthem," not so ironically the same song Big and crew were working on the night Shakur was shot at Quad.

In the history of rap, there had been potent diss records like Ice Cube's "No Vaseline," Eazy-E's "Real Muthaphuckkin'G's," Roxanne Shante's "Have a Nice Day," and DJ Quik's "Dollaz + Sense." A line had been crossed, and Shakur was letting everyone know he was ready to go there. Innocent bystanders who were brought into the mix were just a casualty of a war, and Shakur was hell-bent on being its most valiant soldier.

"The first time we heard 'Hit 'Em Up' . . . hearing that record from 'Pac, it was like, 'Okay, we're in different territory here," said Alan Light. "These weren't little code words being dropped, or this wasn't something that if you know and you understand then you can read between the lines. That was beyond a diss track. It was a personal attack at a level we'd never heard before."

Light continued, "That, for me, felt like it was escalating into something else."

For the previous year, Shakur's life had been a living hell of court battles, prison cells, alleged unwarranted cavity searches by correctional officers, and paranoia-induced depression. "Hit 'Em Up" felt like all of that—with Knight goading him the entire time to carry out his personal vendetta against Combs as well. It is, without question, rap's most venomous battle record because it felt so personal. It felt like violence. Shakur took aim at a wide net of people: Biggie, Puffy, Lil' Cease and Lil' Kim, Mobb Deep (openly blasting Prodigy's sickle cell condition), rapper Chino XL, who insinuated Shakur was raped in prison, and anybody who wanted to be down with Bad Boy "as a staff, record label, and as a mothafuckin' crew."

Junior M.A.F.I.A. feverishly wanted to respond—and, in a way, did. In an unreleased version of Lil' Kim's "Big Momma Thang" set for her debut album, she made an obvious reference to Shakur's original shooting when she delivered the sharp line that maybe 'Pac should keep his head up next time, rapping it in the cadence of Shakur's 1993 hit single. That version wouldn't leak until it made its way to the internet years later, but in real time, everyone around Big took the silent approach, because that's what he demanded. If anyone responded in any way, he'd immediately cut them off.

"Even I was like, 'Yo, let's go. Do something,'" Jay-Z said. "He was like, 'Nah, I know where this is going. I'm not gon' feed into that energy . . . He saw something else for himself."

"Please, all you MCs out there, all you fans out there, please don't think Big gon' make a record dissing Tupac or the West Coast, because it's not going down like that," Big told Hot 97 radio personality Angie Martinez.

"I can't even see me wasting my time or wasting my talent to disrespect another Black man. He do his thing. I'ma continue to do my joints."

"Hit 'Em Up" was the talk of the industry, and Big knew it. Everywhere he went he heard the record. And according to Chico Del Vec, something weird happened.

"We heard it so much we began to like it," Chico said. "We heard it so much we started singing the song. It became funny."

It only became funny because it was a temporary distraction from how drastic the situation had become. As the summer of 1996 waged on, the obvious division became a rallying cry for fans. It split fan bases, and in a year where Clinton and Dole were vying for control of the White House, Tupac versus Biggie became the contest young Black America was locked in on. But only Shakur was campaigning. Big remained quiet for the most part. At a show in Atlanta, Big broke free from his set list to talk to the crowd and explain his side of the story. How he and 'Pac had once been as close as brothers, but a misunderstanding had driven a wedge between them, and how a certain record had been the catalyst for it all. Almost on cue, DJ Enuff had flipped "Big Poppa" over to its B side and dropped "Who Shot Ya." The crowd went bonkers. Big had tried for months to turn the other cheek. And he hadn't yet fully thrown his hat into the ring in an all-out battle. But Biggie Smalls had finally addressed Tupac Shakur.

That Atlanta concert was a turning of the corner. Yet it was Biggie and Puffy's *VIBE* cover story in September 1996 that fanned flames more than anything outside "Hit 'Em Up." It was meant to be a way to speak their piece and clear the air, but most people saw the now infamous cover of Bad Boy's top two honchos with "EAST vs. WEST: Biggie & Puffy Break Their Silence."

"What changed was that *VIBE* magazine cover. That's what changed everything," Mister Cee said. "That's what made everything become like now you're putting this in our face that it's a beef. So now it's a beef. Some people talk about it, but a lot of people don't even recognize it."

In actuality, they spoke about a wide range of issues. Combs questioned why, despite all he'd accomplished in music, it was always negativity that people knew him most for: the City College catastrophe, being fired from Uptown, the death in Atlanta, and now this friction with Death Row. He found it difficult to appreciate his success because there were too many other fires to try to put out.

If 1995 was a signature year for Big's career, when he became the biggest rapper in the game with the most infectious hits and hardest verses, then 1996 was a year of drama that he couldn't seem to escape. It was worse than being in the streets in a lot of ways. At least there he could lie low if he needed to. But there was no way Biggie Smalls could do that. The comfort in anonymity was gone.

"If the muthafucka really did fuck Fay, that's foul how he just be blowin' her like that," Big told *VIBE*. "Never once did he say that Fay did some foul shit to him. If honey was to give you that pussy, why would you disrespect her like that? If you had beef with me, you're like, 'Boom, I'ma fuck his wife,' would you be so harsh on her? Like you got beef with her? That shit doesn't make sense. That's why I don't believe it.

"Honestly, I don't have no problem with the nigga," he went on. "There's shit that mothafuckas don't know. I saw situations and how shit was going, and I tried to school the nigga. I was there when he bought his first Rolex, but I wasn't in the position to be rolling like that. I think Tupac felt more comfortable with the dudes he was hanging with because they had just as much money as him . . . He can't front on me. As much as he may come off as a Biggie hater, he knows. He knows when all that shit was going down, a nigga schooling him to certain things . . . But he chose to do the things he wanted to do. There was nothing I could do, but it wasn't like he wasn't my man."

Big had no plans to publicly respond to Shakur's threats against him, ever. He wasn't falling for the bait. People were already too divided. This wasn't what he got into rap for. If he wanted to beef and look over his shoulder all day, he could've stayed in the streets. But according to people closest to Big, he never gave up hope that he and Shakur could one day put all of this behind him.

Big and 'Pac were once again under the same roof at the 1996 MTV Video Music Awards, held at Radio City Music Hall in early September 1996. They never crossed paths, but Shakur's energy was felt in the city for days, touting a forthcoming Death Row East label coming soon and a harrowing encounter with Nas in Central Park over their war of words on wax. Tupac believed Nas's "Fake thug no love" line from "The Message." Though Nas said the bar was directed at 'Pac, he told Nas to his face that on his next album he'd be dissing him. The tension was thick and combustible, with both camps having several people strapped with guns in the event words weren't enough to quell the situation.

"[Nas] wasn't afraid . . . ever since that day, I respected Nas. It could have went either way," said Tupac affiliate and Outlawz member Napoleon. "We had so many guns that day, and I'm sure Nas and them did, too. That's why I thank God that Nas and 'Pac was able to come together and talk like men instead of being ignorant, because it would've probably been a bloodbath."

"Where I was coming from really wasn't an all love place 'cause there was a rumor *Makaveli* [was] coming out, so I really wanted to check the temperature with him," Nas recalled in a 2020 interview. "At that point we had to address the situation, because they was in the city and we had to step to our business."

Nas and 'Pac had plans to talk further and squash whatever bad blood remained in the coming days. Nevertheless, this was Death Row's first trip back to New York en masse since the Source Awards in 1995. And by then the tension had increased tenfold. Asked in a backstage interview if he could ever envision a day when he and Big recorded an album together, Shakur's answer was quintessentially complex. He didn't ever see the day when that would happen, but the idea of an east and west war—one he said would get "deep" months earlier—bothered him.

"The East Coast/West Coast thing is something that the journalists and people are making just to get paid," said Shakur, dripped in gold jewelry and seated beside Snoop Dogg. "They're perpetuating this so it could be drama, which I still love MTV. But when it all go down, don't look at me and Biggie and wonder why is there a Big East Coast/West Coast war when you're shooting this to three hundred countries about a 'war' that they would never know exist."

He ended with a pledge. "We'll try to be better role models, and y'all try to stop putting that drama out there. You got a lot of power and responsibility. We both do. We both need to exercise greater restraint."

If only Tupac Shakur had listened to his own words.

18
DEATH, NEAR DEATH, AND REBIRTH

BIG'S FIRST REACTION WHEN HE HEARD THAT TUPAC SHAKUR
WAS SHOT IN LAS VEGAS ON SEPTEMBER 7, 1996, WAS MUCH LIKE
A LOT OF PEOPLE'S.

"'Pac is a strong dude. I know dukes. *Real strong.* So when they was like,
he got shot, I was like, 'Again?'" he said. "He always getting shot or shot at.
He gon' pull through this one again, make a few records about it, and it's
gonna be over."

From the moment Tupac walked out of prison eleven months earlier,
it seemed he had made it his mission to make Big's life a living hell. It's not
that Big didn't do his own part to make sure his marriage hit some road-
blocks, but it was Shakur who seemed hell-bent on embarrassing the man
he'd once seen as a friend and mentee. Long gone were the days of them
rocking stages together at Bowie State University and Madison Square Garden. That had only been three years earlier, but it might as well have been a
lifetime ago. But as much as Tupac was making people's lives a living hell in
the summer of 1996, in particular Big's, there was another side.

Shakur was desperately attempting to get his own life in order. There
was never any doubt about how intelligent Tupac was, or how much he
valued wanting to be a leader within the Black community. He could get
onstage and perform the most gangsta of records and be the same guy

who could turn around and talk about wanting to build shelters for at-risk youth or battered women. He could spew graphic lyrics to his foes without a moment's notice and then give an interview on a movie set detailing why Black Jesus wanted him to be a light for ghetto boys and girls across the country. And he could also scream out Death Row all day while quietly planning his own exit from the label.

"I don't give a fuck if I don't get along with anyone else on the label. This is for Death Row," he said. "When it comes down to the point where I feel it can stand on its own, I'll move on. But me and Suge will always do business forever."

I will move on. Those were his own words.

Tupac's *All Eyez on Me* was the highest-selling album in Death Row history, eclipsing *The Chronic* and *Doggystyle* in a matter of months. But on the books, Tupac was reportedly in debt to Death Row for nearly $5 million for a litany of fees including cars, jewelry, studio sessions, and even his own bail. In the final days of his life, Tupac fired David Kenner as his lawyer. Kenner knew everything there was to know about Death Row, and firing him made people stop in their tracks and silently ask themselves if Shakur knew what he was doing.

Another part of Shakur's life that was in transition—this one in a direction he wanted—was his love life. His boasts about an affair with Evans may have been public fodder, but in private, Shakur was head over heels in love with Kidada Jones, the actress, model, designer, and daughter of music icon Quincy Jones. Shakur, by all accounts, was planning for a long future with Kidada. One with kids, too. The last thing he'd whisper to her every night, whether in bed together or on the phone, was always the same.

"I'd take a bullet for you."

———

"Fifty punches! I counted!" Shakur told a camera crew. "I knew he was gonna take him out. We bad like that. Come out of prison and now we running shit."

Tupac might not have wanted to come to Las Vegas for the Bruce Seldon–Mike Tyson fight on September 7, but he was a man of his word.

He'd just gotten back from the VMAs in New York and he was tired, but Tyson was one of his closest homeboys. And plus, the Baddest Man on the Planet was walking to the ring to a custom song Shakur had penned for him. Like most Tyson fights, it didn't last long, and Shakur was back in in the casino of the MGM Grand before he really had a chance to take a seat.

That testosterone and adrenaline that spiked from watching the fight was still running through Shakur's body when he was walking through the lobby of the MGM Grand. Travon "Tray" Lane, a Mob Piru Blood, informed Shakur there were rivals in the area. He pointed out Orlando Anderson, better known on the streets as Baby Lane, a Southside Crip from Los Angeles, who had gotten into a fight with Travon months earlier. Lane was said to have been jumped by multiple Southside Crips, and Anderson was the one who snatched his Death Row chain. There was a rumor spreading around the industry that Puffy had put a bounty out for the chain. Shakur had always been close with different members in different gangs across America. But now, since he had signed with Death Row and had aligned himself so closely with Knight, people around 'Pac had begun to wonder if he was aligning himself too closely with the Bloods. Shakur might have grown up in the streets and kept street dudes around him, but one thing he wasn't was a gangbanger. He could adapt to his surroundings and the energy around him. That's in part what Big was talking about when Shakur would be hanging with people like Haitian Jack and other high-rolling street cats who lived a lot of what Shakur rapped. 'Pac was a superstar in whatever he directed his energy toward. At only twenty-five, the potential of what he could he do in music and Hollywood was almost impossible to fathom. And if he kept his head on straight, who knew what lay in store for him as an activist and voice for Black America. But all that went up in smoke in the blink of an eye. Shakur bolted over to Anderson.

"You from the south?" Shakur asked.

Before Anderson could respond, Shakur decked him, knocking him on the ground. The rest of the Death Row entourage, including Knight, quickly stomped the hell out of Anderson. The fight itself only lasted seconds, but Shakur had done the unthinkable. Shakur had officially inserted himself in gang-related business in an extremely serious manner. Anderson soon left the MGM but refused to file a complaint against Shakur and Knight.

Back at the hotel, an animated Shakur was telling Kidada about both fights. He wanted her to stay at the hotel instead of coming to Knight's venue, Club 662, because they had just jumped a Crip and he was concerned for her safety. She wanted him to be safe, too, so she asked him to wear his bulletproof vest. Shakur refused, stating that it was too hot.

Just a short time later, on that night of September 7, 1996, Shakur sat in the passenger seat of Knight's BMW 750. Traffic on the Las Vegas Strip was thick, but that was to be expected the night of a Tyson fight. The two weren't thinking about the fight they had just gotten into. Instead, they were looking forward to linking up with Tyson at the after-party at 662. A group of women had noticed Tupac and called his name, saying they wanted to party as well. And a photographer, twenty-nine-year-old Leonard Jefferson, snapped a photo of Knight staring straight ahead in the driver's seat, and Tupac with a blank stare looking out of the window. Moments after Jefferson's photo, at the corner of Koval Lane and Flamingo Road, a white Cadillac pulled alongside Knight and Shakur. As the car came almost to a stop, a single hand holding a .40-caliber semiautomatic pistol emerged, aiming directly at Knight's BMW. In all, fourteen shots were fired into Knight's BMW. Four of those bullets pierced Shakur's body. The shooter's car sped off into the Las Vegas night while Knight did an immediate U-turn before crashing. The first cop on the scene was Metro Police Department lieutenant Chris Carroll. As Tupac was taken out of the car, Carroll said he held Tupac, bloodied and gasping for air, and asked him who did this to him.

Shakur's last words were "Fuck you."

For the next week, Shakur lay in the University Medical Center of Southern Nevada ICU. People like Kidada, Jada Pinkett, and Snoop Dogg rushed to be by his side. Across the country, Big had no clue of the extent of his former friend's injuries. He didn't know about the permanent coma. He didn't know about the right lung that had to be removed or the finger lost as a result of the shooting. He had no clue Shakur, who fought for his life inside that hospital, was still receiving death threats. He had no clue Shakur's head had swollen with fluid. Big had no clue that in the final moments of Tupac Shakur's life, his skin felt ice-cold. And he didn't know that 'Pac's mother, Afeni Shakur, witnessed her son being revived several times before she finally decided to let Tupac discover, firsthand, if heaven indeed had a ghetto. Throughout their entire friendship and its demise, Big had only known Shakur to be so full of vitality.

Shakur lived a life much like the revolutionary background he'd come from. He spoke forcefully, lived fast, fell hard, and died loudly. Tupac Amaru Shakur was pronounced dead on September 13, 1996, only a few months past his twenty-fifth birthday.

"Tupac was a person who was introspective, and who was trying to grow kinda like Malcolm X [who] was at an inflection point when he died," Drew Dixon said, who had recently begun a new job at Arista Records when Shakur died. "Martin Luther King was at an inflection point when he died. This missed opportunity for this really brilliant young Black man to evolve and have some introspection and the courage to be vulnerable and exposed about his growth and mistakes. I felt like he was emerging and then we lost him."

An entire hip-hop community mourned the loss of an artist so talented, yet so tormented, that there was really no singular way to define what the grief felt like. Back in New York, Big was stunned. More than that, Big was afraid. And how could he not be?

"When [Tupac] died," he said, "that shit fucked me up."

───────

Shakur's death came with far more questions than answers, and an overwhelming, suffocating cloud of grief. And it seemed like back east, everyone was finding out around the same time. Nas, who was having a concert in New York that evening, allowed radio personality Ed Lover to pause the show to announce the news to a stunned crowd. In the coming days, Treach, Flavor Flav, Kevin Powell, Roxanne Shante, Wendy Day, and Mobb Deep—the last of whom were beefing with Tupac up until his death—called in to Hot 97 to express their condolences. And many wondered exactly where rap was headed because the climate felt so cold and its outlook so dark. But now all attention focused on Big's reaction. Shakur had played a significant role in his life, good and bad. Big, perhaps more than anyone outside 'Pac's family or direct inner circle, was completely stunned. Everyone close to Big wanted to know where his head was. Just three years earlier, they had been running around with unloaded guns in 'Pac's backyard like little kids without a care in the world. Now, 'Pac was dead and they'd never have a chance to make right on where things went so wrong. Not in this lifetime, at least.

"Me and Big was together [when he found out 'Pac got shot]. Big was like, 'He gon' be a'ight. He's a good dude,'" Chico del Vec recalled. "But when he died, Big was in shock. He was really sad. 'Pac was his homie. He knew him like that through the music and hung out with him . . . Big kept saying, 'I can't imagine how his moms feel. I wanna do something to help.' He always wanted to be a peacemaker."

Big's manager, Mark Pitts, was at a *VIBE* party the night the news was delivered. He immediately called Big. For the last several years, the most reliable quality about Big was his ability to paint pictures with his words. On the phone with Pitts, try as he might, Big couldn't find the words.

"You could hear him crying. He was fucked up," Pitts told *VIBE* years later. "He didn't understand how it had come to that."

The night Shakur died, while all hell was breaking loose in Compton with retaliatory shootings and acts of violence, Big phoned Evans. She'd never heard him sound so down. He was in tears and sounded legitimately afraid for his own safety. If 'Pac could be touched, what made him any different? "Something ain't right, Faye. Shit got fucked up somewhere along the way," Big said. "But that was my nigga."

A day after Tupac's death, dream hampton lofted a question at Big. Would he attend Shakur's funeral? Like he told Chico, he wanted to do something to help, but he knew showing up at a memorial service would only incite hysteria. Big was hurting, but he'd also not forgotten the hell his former friend had forced him to endure.

"Nah, man. This nigga—he made my life miserable. Ever since he came home," he said. "He told lies, fucked with my marriage, turned fans against me. For what?"

For as much as Shakur's death was on his mind, Big had his own battles. In March 1996, roughly a week before the Soul Train Music Awards, he and D-Roc were leaving an Evans concert at the Palladium nightclub in New York around five in the morning. Two men in their twenties began talking disrespectfully to them. Could they have ignored the fans and gone about their early morning understanding that nothing good could come of this?

Sure, but they didn't. The two jumped in a taxi and Big and D-Roc followed them in hot pursuit. The caught up with them a few blocks later on West Sixteenth Street and smashed the windows of the taxi out with a baseball bat. The police hit them with an assault charge.

The hits kept coming, and not the ones that made Big rich. Bad Boy recording artist Mase stopped by Big's home in Teaneck, New Jersey, to pay a visit on July 23. Police noticed Mase's car illegally parked, and then noticed the scent of marijuana coming from the house. After a search of his home uncovered enlarged bullet clips and semiautomatic weapons with infrared beams, Big was again arrested on weapons and drugs charges.

Big was in and out of court so much in 1996 that it made him sleepy. Literally.

"I remember when we really had to go to court for him, for a situation that Biggie had," Lil' Kim reflected in a 2011 MTV interview. "I remember him falling asleep in front of the judge. And he was literally snoring in front of the judge. And the judge looked at his lawyer and was like, 'Excuse me, can you wake your client up?!'"

It seemed like for Big, for every step forward there were two steps back. And on top of all that, Evans was seven months pregnant when she burst into a studio and fought Lil' Kim. The clash between wife and mistress was but one of many—and was all Big's fault in the first place—but it coincided with a really rambunctious time in his life.

Life has an uncanny way of putting mortality into perspective. Less than a week after Shakur's death, Cease, Charli Baltimore, and Big went to go pick up their Lexus from the service department. The day before, Cease and Big were arrested for having weed in their car in Downtown Brooklyn. They were out within an hour, but when they were given their Lexus truck back, it wouldn't start. The next morning, they went to go pick up their temporary ride, much to the chagrin of Cease. It was a Chevy Lumina, not exactly the chariot of choice for a superstar of Big's caliber. Nonetheless, Big was adamant about taking the car and bouncing. Cease later said the brakes were faulty, which made him extremely uncomfortable to be driving in the rain.

"Big, I don't wanna drive this shit," Cease said.

"Fuck it, son," Big said. "Just drive. We just gon' ride low-key for awhile."

So Cease did, and moments later, as they got on the New Jersey Turnpike going north, the car spun out of control, crossed the other side of the road, and slammed into the rail. Everyone survived, but with some pretty nasty injuries. Baltimore's ankle was fractured, she had a gash on her forehead that required stitches, and she wound up in a neck brace after smashing into the windshield and passing out for a few seconds. Cease lost the top row of his teeth after hitting the steering wheel. And Big broke his leg badly; he had to be cut out of the car because he was stuck between the seat and dashboard.

Cease called the moment for everyone, but Big in particular, a "reality check."

For the next three months, Big would recover at the Kessler Institute for Rehabilitation in West Orange, New Jersey. Coincidentally, his room was the same exact room Christopher Reeve, who played Superman in the superhero movies Christopher Wallace watched as a kid, had stayed in after the horseback riding accident that left him paralyzed. Big thankfully would be able to walk again, though never the same. No going out to clubs, no smoking weed whenever he wanted to, no picking up women. He was often left alone with his thoughts. He'd been living life in the fast lane leading up to the fall of 1996, and like most twentysomethings, part of him felt untouchable. Lying on his back most of the day in a rehab hospital in suburban New Jersey, he had a chance to think about what Christopher Wallace's future, not just Biggie Smalls's, would really look like.

He was twenty-four years old and dealing with a lot, including the trauma of Shakur's passing and the rumors that he had been involved. He hadn't been able to shed the talk of him being involved in 'Pac's Quad shooting back in 1994, largely because of 'Pac's accusations. And now people actually believed he had him killed. Snoop Dogg saw firsthand how that weighed on Big. The two had squashed any ill feelings following the "New York, New York" video-set shooting less than a year earlier. Now he went to visit Big in rehab.

"Cease take me upstars, Biggie is upstairs in a walker, like what the old people walk around in," Snoop said. "He got the little walker sitting at the end of the bed. And when I walk in the room, we started talking. And then he looked me in the eyes and he say something that, you know what I'm saying, he's sad that Tupac is dead. But I could look in his eyes and I could see that he hurt. He didn't even have to say it. I could see that hurt."

"He had a lot of respect for Tupac as an artist. He was playing [Tupac's *The Don Killuminati: The 7 Day Theory*] in the car constantly," said Charli Baltimore in a 2009 interview. "When 'Pac died, I remember one of the first things Big said was, 'Damn, I just wish I would've had the chance to talk to him.'"

He had a new album he desperately wanted to complete. All year long he had heard the talks about how 'Pac was "winning" in their battle and that he'd fallen off. That the drama in his life would have a negative impact on the music. *Ready to Die* had given him everything he ever wanted out of a music career, and even some things he didn't. He'd proven he was as talented a rapper as the game had ever seen, but he knew the rap game and the streets had quick memories. He could have the best crack to sell in Brooklyn, but if it wasn't there the next week, then customers would move on to whoever the next dealer with a potent package was. With music, it was the same. His music still held permanent residency in clubs, but now there was so much to prove. The most important thing was that he was immune to a sophomore slump that had overtaken so many MCs before him.

"Only folks that be talking that shit is them niggas that be fucked up. They ain't got no money. They aggravated," an obviously annoyed Big said in a 1996 interview. "Artists just be aggravated talking that bullshit, 'He ain't keeping it real.' You broke. Fuck you telling me and you dead-ass broke?"

He wanted nothing more than to prove critics wrong. That not only could he do it again, but this time it would be even bigger. He also thought about the cases he caught back-to-back-to-back and how they were so embarrassing because they were all self-inflicted. Big could out-rap anyone he felt, and he could come up with hit records seemingly in his sleep, but he wasn't Teflon. There were reminders all around him, too. Like the wheelchair beside his bed that, thanks to his weight, was difficult to get into on his own. And the reality he was going to have to face—that he'd have to walk with a cane for the rest of his life.

Big experienced two life-changing conversations while rehabbing at Kessler. The first was with a therapist at the facility who helped patients cope with the overwhelming emotional weight of what they were dealing with. The older white man, per *Unbelievable*, didn't care about the stereotypes of what Big did for a living, and instead appealed directly to his emotional well-being. Looking at them side by side, they were opposites of each other in every way: appearance, upbringing, lifestyle—and perhaps that's why he got through to Big. He said that when Big was standing, he only looked forward. That could apply to anything in his life. The next show, the next session, the next woman. He never gave himself time to take full agency of where he was in his life.

"But when you're crippled, when you're on your back," the therapist said, "you're looking at the sky. You're looking at God. Why don't you talk to him?"

The therapist didn't know he was talking to a guy who rhymed his fair share of what could be considered blasphemous lines. But that's exactly what Christopher Wallace found himself doing as he lay in his bed in the dark. It wasn't just one conversation, either. These were constant communications. Christopher had always been expected to be the leader of those around him, dating back to his days as a kid with Hubert Sam and the Hawks. But even leaders have questions and doubts. Just four years earlier he was deciding if he wanted to stick to pursuing rapping or staying in the streets. Now he was one of the most recognizable rappers in the world, but it had nearly been stripped away from him.

"When you start making a whole lot of money and you start living too fast, it's up to you to slow yourself down," Big told Cheo Hodari Coker months later, in what would be the final interview of his life. "You can't be getting drunk, smoking two or three ounces of weed a day, and [having sex] with all these different females. Something's bound to happen. I was living like that for a second, but I had that car accident . . . I was in the hospital for two and three months, and it gave me a lot of time to think about my life and where it was headed."

Truthfully, Big had been having these moments of intense introspection even before his accident. In July 1996, Big, Junior M.A.F.I.A., Total, and Coolio all traveled to the Netherlands to perform at Feyenoord Stadium, the largest R&B concert Rotterdam had ever seen at the time. Traveling abroad was something Big wanted to do more of in his career.

"I remember he was like, 'Yo, we just gon' start traveling. We gon' start going to Africa. We just gonna' start moving all around,'" Groovey Lew,

Big's stylist, recalled of the Rotterdam trip. "He just had a taste of it and he knew what that felt like. He was ready for the world."

Big was his normal engaging, often hilarious self, but the European journalist Sonia Poulton saw a side of him she wasn't expecting. He wasn't necessarily sad, but he was in search of where all the fun had gone. It was never about people wondering what he was most excited about with so much of his career still in front of him. It was always about this drama or that controversy. The negative energy was taking its toll on him. His life wasn't even *his* life, he felt.

"It's hard. I don't even go out anymore," he admitted. "I'm not a security-type person. I don't want to have bodyguards around me. I'm not into all that. Now we just chill in the house. There are a lot of times when we want to go out, but we just don't. If it's not some drunks out on the street wanting to fuck with me, then there is some Faith shit or some Tupac shit. I just don't need it."

He continued, "I got feelings, too, you know."

And then there was Faith. He'd done more than his part to fracture that relationship. There would always be love between Faith and Big, but who knew if they would ever try to rekindle that initial flame that sparked in the summer of 1994. What Big did learn from their two years together was that he got married too fast, and they both were taken through an emotional ringer because of that. But they did have one positive that would connect them for the rest of their lives. Evans gave birth to their son on October 29, 1996, while Big was still in rehab. Faith, Christopher, and Voletta came up with his name. They decided Charles, Voletta's father's name, sounded too English.

"So, I finally said, 'You know what? I love the name Christopher!' And we all agreed," Voletta recounted in her memoir.

Big Christopher was a huge Michael Jordan fan, so they decided on Jordan being his middle name. And just like that, Christopher Jordan Wallace was in this world. Big was so happy to be a father again, but first Faith had to put him in his place. She reminded him of that line he spit on Jay-Z's "Brooklyn's Finest," his joke that if she had twins they'd be Tupac's babies. The bar truly hurt her. Faith was a platinum-selling recording artist and an extremely talented songwriter, but so much of her public persona had been wrapped up in a clash she had never asked to be in. Shakur had been spreading lies on her, she argued, and here was her husband making fun of the entire situation with her at the center. She had been holding this in since she heard the line over the summer. As it turns out, Faith actually was pregnant with twins.

"He was holding C.J. and I was just looking at him with that look of disgust like, 'What are you going to tell your child? That's on record,'" Faith revealed years later. "He just started crying like, 'I'm sorry. I was under pressure. People were talking shit' . . . C.J. was a twin, and the second one didn't develop. He knew that. Big would do stuff like that all the time, though . . . he would take stuff we'd talk about or personal jokes and put it in a rhyme and make it seem like something real. Although that wasn't a joke."

His lyrical mishap aside, the act of staying still and being present with himself was answering questions Big never knew he needed answers to. He'd never walk the same way again, but now he'd think about the purpose in every step. Reminded constantly of Shakur's death, the value of life was always near the front of his mind. His near-quarter-life crisis had given life-altering clarity. He began to see purpose in everything, even down to D-Roc and Cease sleeping in his room and taking him to and from therapy.

"I got two big-ass niggas . . . I'm rolling up in therapy and nothing but old people. And I'm running in there on some real Brooklyn shit," Big said. "They was feeling me, though. They gave me my love."

It wasn't just about the next check. Don't get it twisted; it was still about the money. But the money was building something for his kids that would live longer than he ever could. He didn't just want to be a father to T'yanna and C.J. He wanted to be a present dad. That guy who was in their lives picking them up from school, going to dance recitals and little league football and basketball games. He wanted all of that for them and himself. His idea of happiness had changed, and in large part it was dictated by the smiles on the two faces he was responsible for bringing into the world.

"He was always like, 'I wanna have another kid,'" said Chico. "When he realized he had a son, he was like, 'I'm blessed.' He was really becoming family orientated. Everything he had to do, if he had to step out the house, he had to get paid. If not, he always wanted to be around his kids. That's all he wanted."

"When I'm looking at my daughter or my son," Big said, "it's something to live for. When I finally realized it, at least it wasn't too late."

———

While Big was in New Jersey recovering and eager to get to work, Combs was ready to unleash the next phase of his Bad Boy takeover. Big was still a regular fixture on radio stations and clubs across the country thanks to the staying power of *Ready to Die* and his work with Junior M.A.F.I.A. Now the world deserved new Biggie Smalls music, and he was beyond anxious to give it to them. And, in an act that doubled down on Suge Knight's Source Awards proclamation, a Puff Daddy album, too. Combs had seen what was happening to Death Row, crumbling by the day, and he knew he didn't want that for Bad Boy. They had to get back in the studio, because if 1996 was defined by rumors, 1997 would be all about creating history.

Shortly after the Soul Train Music Awards incident in March, Combs organized a getaway to Maraval, Trinidad. Only this wasn't a vacation. This was part of Combs's master plan to, in his words, have radio on lock for the next two years. To enact this plan, Combs and his "Hitmen" producers—Ron "Amen-Ra" Lawrence, Stevie J, Nashiem Myrick, and Deric "D-Dot" Angelettie—and engineers Axel Niehaus and Tony Maserati, hunkered down in the quaint town and began working on the framework to the sound Combs was chasing. Big stayed back in the States. The atmosphere was comparable to a training camp, and every day more and more songs were produced. Future hit records like "Hypnotize," "Somebody's Gotta Die," "All About the Benjamins," "Been Around the World," and "Victory" were produced here.

Stevie J said during the assembly line process that no one got an ego. Everyone understood the greater good at stake. "Whatever it's gonna take to make this a number-one classic," he said in *Unbelievable*, "not a hit, but a classic, let's do it. We want to be remembered as a group of people who make classic material, not just hot beats for today."

What Combs and company were on the island plotting would soon prove fruitful. Bad Boy's franchise player was ready to come off injured reserve. He had a lot to get off his chest.

19

"I WANT MY SPOT BACK"

READY TO DIE WAS A SLOW COOKER, CREATED OVER THE COURSE OF A YEAR-PLUS AND TWO HOMES IN UPTOWN AND LATER BAD BOY. Big's new album, aptly titled *Life After Death*, was the complete opposite. He was motivated and recording quicker than anyone had ever seen him. He wasn't sacrificing the quality as a result, either.

During the late fall of 1996 into the early winter, as his recovery progressed and he could move around with assistance, whoever was in the studio with Big was bound to see some amazing shit go down. Making music was the reward for a day full of therapy. Groovey Lew was in the studio the night he recorded "Kick in the Door." Lew watched Big listen to the beat on loop for quite a while as he just sat down bobbing his head until it was showtime. Then Cease and Lew wheeled Big—still in his wheelchair—into the booth, and he took care of the rest.

"That man sat in that wheelchair and did that verse. In one take, Jake off the head! Genius shit!" said Lew. "I was like, 'Yo, you the illest.' He was like, 'Groove, get outta here, B!' I was like I'm good. I'm going home. I just left the studio. That was history."

Every day had the same routine. More Dutch Masters than anyone could count, an assortment of liquors and champagne—because Big loved playing in-studio bartender whenever he could—lots of delivered food, and the occasional lady friend chilling on the sofa. That's how it was in the Daddy's House studio, Puffy's four-room musical oasis in Midtown Manhattan. If the Knicks had Madison Square Garden two miles away, then this is where Bad Boy artists considered their home-court advantage. The goal for Puffy was to make his artists, producers, engineers, and people of the like feel as comfortable as possible. Because the more comfortable they were, the better the music. And the better the music meant the bigger the hit. All the studio time they needed was right there in that building. Video game consoles and VCRs were installed, and the best sound system known to man—or any of them, at least—was at their disposal.

"It was home," Angelettie said in *Unbelievable*. "You can take your shoes off, you can work as many hours as you want . . . We could do whatever we wanted to in there. And it was family in there, so like, you know, whatever we wanted to do stayed in there. Bitches coming there to freak out, you know what I'm saying? If somebody was in there doing something a little extra than weed, then that's what happened."

The only rule in the studio, especially at this time, was to keep Big working. He would come up with lyrics and hooks out of the blue, and everyone in the studio had to be ready on a moment's notice to get his vocals down. And under no circumstances could Combs be in the studio when Big laid his vocals. That's not because Big didn't trust Combs. It was quite the opposite. Big thoroughly respected him.

"You know, I used to think Puff was just one of them happy-go-lucky niggas, man. I knew so many niggas like that in the drug game, get-rich bitch niggas. Mostly that's what I always thought he was," Big said. "Like, one of them niggas in the hustling game that just knew a bunch of people, was mad cool, and that used to happen to be in a neighborhood where there were a lot of crackheads. He had a little bit of money, put it into the drug game, and quickly made a whole bunch of money. But he never went to war with no niggas. He never had problems with no niggas trying to take money from him, because he just was a cool nigga. That's how I always looked at Puff, like there's a cool nigga who just happened to be in the right position at the right time. Not really a fake nigga, but I knew he wasn't no street nigga. And at that time, when I first met him, street niggas meant everything to me."

Big didn't want Puffy in the studio when he was recording, though. He never wanted anyone, Puffy included, to disrupt his energy was. Lynn Montrose was one of the few women engineers in the industry and worked with Big on *Life After Death*. She described him as polite and said he put her at ease with his respectful and easygoing personality. Montrose understood exactly why Puffy being in the studio could be a distraction. Not many people work well with their boss standing over their shoulder micromanaging.

"You don't want to go in the vocal booth and as soon as you go in Puffy's like, 'I don't like your tone,'" she said. "That would be a large part of his waiting, waiting for Puffy to leave."

Big's real-life emotions went into making the songs on the album. Some days were more productive than others, and depending on Big's mood, multiple songs could get punched in a day, or one or none. Like with "Another" featuring Lil' Kim. The two weren't seeing eye to eye at all from both a business and a personal perspective. Kim was becoming a larger star by the day, it seemed, but Big still liked to assert control over her career when he could.

"Kim and him were really beefing, so you hear all that stuff at the beginning where she said, 'Fuck you,' and he said, 'Fuck you, bitch,'" Stevie J said. "They was really going back and forth at each other at the moment. That was real; it wasn't just ad-libs."

He was never short on inspiration—or frustration from a variety of sources that would soon serve as lyrical muses. There was a lot riding on this project, and Big knew it and felt it more than anyone. But he was far from hustling to make some money to feed T'yanna or wondering if his mom would let him in the house because she was tired of seeing him out on the streets wasting his life. He had to rap about what he knew.

"I call this album *Life After Death* because when I was writing stuff like, 'Fuck the world, fuck my mom and my girl,' I was dead, man," he said. "There was nothing but anger coming out about everything: about having to go out to sell crack, to hustle for a living. Nothing but anger. But now I can't do that."

Big's energy was undeniable. *Life After Death* was a body of work the game hadn't heard, with a combination of a robust budget and infectious anthems—with that patented Biggie Smalls flavor.

"I remember when he was doing *Life After Death* and he sent me four songs in the demo stage," Jay-Z said. "I was like, 'Oh my God! We got a problem!' I was happy for him and I was upset for myself. I was a little worried about myself as an artist."

Big knew the masses wanted to hear his thoughts on the Tupac beef and the east/west divide. Aside from subliminal disses on "Long Kiss Goodnight" and a slight mention on "Notorious Thugs," saying "So-called beef with you-know-who," Big steered clear of invoking his fallen former friend. But he did want to paint a classic for California, in particular Los Angeles. Big loved the West Coast; he wanted Californians' attention, and he wanted their respect.

Easy Mo Bee had flipped Zapp's "More Bounce to the Ounce" and gave it his own spin. He wasn't there when Big recorded his vocals, but what Mo Bee found out about the record troubled him. It wasn't the lyrics. Those were fine, but the title "Going Back to Cali" pissed off Mo Bee. Tensions were still too thick, and even if Big meant nothing but respect, the title could be misconstrued as a taunt. Mo Bee was traveling back and forth to L.A. He would be on full alert the entire time, and he was just a producer. He knew for Big it'd be worse, and in Mo Bee's eyes, this title wouldn't do anything to help.

Life After Death was almost near completion. But there was still one song missing. That one record Big could just "get his shit off" real quick on. Much like on *Ready to Die*, it was DJ Premier who'd give him that final moon shot over the center-field wall. That came in the form of the record "Ten Crack Commandments." Ever a student of the game, Big remembered an article in the July 1994 issue of *The Source*. It was called "The House that Crack Built," and the story's author, Khary Kimani Turner, listed ten practical steps to remember when selling rock. Big flipped it all into one of his catalog's defining records. Using a sample of Chuck D counting up the numbers (Chuck D would later sue Big's estate), Big was still rapping about the crack game. This time, though, it was from an OG's perspective. He was passing down game, sort of like what Michael Jordan was doing for that young Los Angeles Laker named Kobe Bryant at the time.

Big knew he had one. The one.

"'Preme, it's over! It's over," he yelled from the booth. "I'm the greatest! I did it!

"Those are exactly the last words I ever heard that man say," said Premier.

So now it was done. A double-disc behemoth of an album that would satisfy any and all cravings. Big may have been laid-back, but he was as maniacal a competitor as the genre had ever seen. He wanted to be the best, and he wanted fans to say he was the best, too. Most importantly, he didn't want to give them any choice in the matter, either. One disc wouldn't have been enough—not with everything he had to say. For those wanting to see if he could still make hits, there were records like "Hypnotize" and "Mo Money, Mo Problems." For those wanting to see if he could still paint a picture with the best of them, they'd have "Somebody's Gotta Die," "Niggas Bleed" and "Story to Tell"—the last of which was an account of sleeping with the girlfriend of a New York Knicks player, which rapper Fat Joe would later say was about Anthony Mason. Introspection? "Miss U"—when he'd eulogize his late friend Roland "O" Young on wax—and "Sky's the Limit." As best as he and Combs could, Big attempted to check all potential boxes.

Ready to Die told the story of a young Brooklyn kid who entered the drug game, hustled some crack, and lived to tell the story. Now *Life After Death* was attempting to tell the story of that former young crack dealer who found success beyond his wildest dreams, only to find that success came with a hefty price tag.

"I never did nothing wrong to nobody. I ain't never did anything wrong to Tupac. I ain't never do anything wrong to Faith, nothing wrong to Kim, nothing wrong to nobody. And I kept quiet. I kept my mouth shut. I figure if I had been sitting here riffin', it'd seem like I got a point to prove. I know I ain't do nothing, so it' don't make sense for me to say nothin'," he told journalist Chairman Mao. "On March 25, all answers gonna come out," Big proclaimed. "You gonna hear what Big got to say. And on top of hearing what I got to say, you gonna spend thirty dollars to hear it. Fuck it."

There was but one more thing Big had to do. It was time to do what the song title that Easy Mo Bee hated so much said. He was going back to Cali.

Between January 22 and 23, 1997, Big had two separate conversations with *ego trip* magazine. He spoke of how just three short years before, he had felt death was his best option for finding a "better place." Now he was singing a far different tune. Tupac's murder, the car crash, and talking to God—it had all helped him find peace and purpose, two values that were easy to lose track of in the music industry.

He didn't want the last thing people remembered him for was a bicoastal feud he wanted no part of in the first place. He realized the most powerful way to tell his story was to do just that—be the one to tell his story.

"With my mother finally being proud of me, finally saying, 'Damned police is not comin' to my house lookin' for my son no more,'" he said. "When she hear gunshots in the streets and wakes up out of her bed screamin' and I'm not in the house, she don't have to worry about, 'God, I hope that wasn't my son.' Now I got a life after that. I got a comfortable home. I'm safe. I'm with my family, and they got my best interest at heart."

Big felt he was in a good space and headed toward an even better one. His new album was dropping March 25, and he couldn't wait for his fans to devour *Life After Death*. Big wanted to master rapping. He wanted to put himself on a pedestal of consumer loyalty that had been reserved for pop megastars like Whitney Houston or TLC. When they dropped, selling millions of records was all but automatic. Big wanted that, and he felt he was well on his way.

But he also had plans beyond rap. He wanted to open a restaurant called Big Poppa's Chicken and Waffles and a clothing store with Heavy D called Big and Heavy. He was also in the process of getting his clothing line, Brooklyn Mint, off the ground. And he wanted to sign and develop more acts for his Undeas label. Like Cam'ron, whom he was introduced to through Mase. Cam had already written Lil' Cease's verses on Lil' Kim's blockbuster hit "Crush on You." But now Big wanted to see what he could spit in person.

"His leg was broke [from] the car accident. He had two bitches in the bed," Cam recalled in a 2021 *Drink Champs* episode. "He put on like fifteen beats, and every beat he put on I rapped to it. He was like, 'That's enough. I wanna sign you.' Then he called Un, and Un was like, 'Bet. Let's do it.'"

Though that particular deal wouldn't get done until later in the spring of 1997, Big's inspirations and goals knew no bounds. Even the supposed shots at his name, not just from Tupac, or insinuations that he'd brought tired clichés into the game like scantily clad women in bikinis dancing and popping endless amounts of champagne bottles—the Roots's "What They Do" video took aim at that. It was a move drummer Questlove would later say haunted him because he "never made it right" with Big. Even still, the perceived disrespect didn't bother him.

"I often have to say to myself, watch what you're doing, Big, 'cause you're not on Fulton Street anymore," he said. "If a nigga say, 'Fuck you,' you can't shoot at him. You just can't do it, Big."

Big spent much of the early part of 1997, large pockets of late January and February, in Los Angeles. He and Charli Baltimore had a falling-out after she found pictures of him with other women thanks to a mistake by Cease. He was pissed at Cease, the first and only time that ever happened, for the next day so.

Big's next order of business was to shoot the video for *Life After Death*'s lead single, "Hypnotize." The budget was more than $900,000 for a reason. It needed to be larger than life, and it needed to announce one thing: the Notorious B.I.G. was back, and anyone who ever doubted he could do it all again was gravely mistaken. The video took three days to film and featured scenes with Biggie and Puffy driving in reverse on a highway being chased by shadowy figures on motorcycles, and a giant black leopard that scared damn near everyone on the shoot except Big. It was outrageous, luxurious, and comical—everything Puffy wanted it to be.

The director, Paul Hunter, had already made the videos for Aaliyah's "One in a Million" and Combs's "Can't Nobody Hold Me Down," the latter of which shocked a ton of people into believing that maybe, just maybe, Puff Daddy the rapper might not be *that* bad. Yet with "Hypnotize," when Puffy asked him what ideas he had, Hunter came up with them on the spot. Thankfully, Puffy was rocking with the vision.

The boat they needed for the water scenes came with an owner who was petrified. For one, it was a rap entourage that wanted to rent his boat for a scene, and *they* wanted to pilot it. The owner, though, had already agreed to a deal. So there was Biggie, rapping on playback and actually maneuvering the boat himself—all after smoking a fat-ass blunt. The boat's owner was actually on the boat, too. Combs just made sure no one saw him.

"Puff put his hand on top of the guy's head, and he literally started strong-arming him to his knees," said Hunter in *Unbelievable*. "He was down on his knees driving the boat. You could see him pop his head over the steering wheel to see if we were gonna crash into somebody."

During a break from the marathon video shoot, Big received a call from the actor Christopher Walken at his hotel room. Walken had played the character Frank White in the 1990 film *King of New York*. "Big was like, 'Yeah, right,' and hung up the phone," said D-Roc. Big had been calling himself "the Black Frank White." "And then he called back like, 'No, I'm serious. I'm Christopher Walken, and I'd like to come meet you.' Big was so happy, but they never met."

When it came time to bring the black leopard out, everyone was on high alert. The idea was Combs's, but even he was apprehensive of it being out of its cage and seemingly a second away from mauling someone on set. But this was the type of extravagant stuff he wanted. Wallace seemed to enjoy the cat's presence.

"I'm about to call my barber and have him cut my initials into his fur," he joked. "I'm trying to sell five million albums this time out, nigga. If I need to, I'll ride that cat like a horse."

Big went back and forth with the trainer about the danger the cat presented. He believed the trainer, but he also needed the trainer to understand he wasn't scared. He was over three hundred pounds and had to walk with a cane. What was the point of being scared if he couldn't go anywhere, Big reasoned. When it came time to film again, he upped the ante, rapping with more force and energy than he had before the cat came onto the set. He had to prove who the boss was, and he did. The video wrapped on February 18, and thankfully no one was harmed by the leopard, though when Puffy scurried off-camera as soon as the scene was over, it brought an ovation of laughter from Big and the crew.

Big was the happiest people had seen him in quite some time. He was charting the course for the next chapter in his career, defined by a mammoth sophomore album and a looming supergroup, the Commission, with Jay-Z, Charli Baltimore, and Lil' Cease, and Lance "Un" Rivera as producer.

Not everyone in Bad Boy's crew made the trip to L.A., for a variety of reasons—one being the timing. Still, though, all the time he was spending in Los Angeles didn't sit well with everyone.

"I saw him in the mall. There were people kinda following him through the mall and bothering him. But just for some dumbass reason, we played it too cool to come and talk to each other," said Nas in a 2017 A&E documentary. "I hate that memory, because we could've talked. And I know I just wanted to tell him, you know, probably what a lot of people was telling him. He should go back home because it's not a good time to be in L.A. It's fresh off the war between these coasts. I never got to tell him."

Bad Boy was moving heavy in Los Angeles, and they could be seen almost anywhere in the city—clubs, restaurants, studios. This was still the home of Death Row Records, or what was left of it. And some allegiances weren't going to subside in the blink of an eye. It didn't matter that all Big wanted to do was enjoy California and do his part to show that the east/west rivalry wasn't something he was invested in or wanted to see continue. Or that he wanted to show, just like with Tupac's Quad Studios shooting, he had nothing to do with what had happened in Las Vegas less than six months earlier. Or that he was even looking for a house in the city. Some saw it as a taunt. It was possible to be *too* public *too* soon.

"You need to tell your boys to get the fuck out of here," a security guard who worked at many of the city's top nightclubs where Puffy and Big partied was quoted as saying in *Unbelievable*. "This is still Suge's fuckin' town."

———

The music industry is carnivorous, making friendships play second fiddle to bottom lines. Puffy and Snoop Dogg had appeared on the February 23, 1997, episode of *The Steve Harvey Show* in an effort to publicly denounce the so called East Coast/West Coast war. Though Tupac and Big's names weren't mentioned in the episode, and that bad blood involved countless more people than just them, they were still the stars with the most gravitational pull. With Tupac already gone, Big knew that part of that responsibility fell on his shoulders to move the game past that dark period. And more importantly, he couldn't let that be the defining chapter of his career.

But it's not as if he could stop living. He had too many people who depended on him. His Junior M.A.F.I.A. crew, whom he brought with him from the streets of Brooklyn to stages across the world, had always looked to him for the answers on what to do next. Lil' Kim was a bona fide star in her own right, and Cease was up next. Then there was Voletta. The mother who loved him even when he worked her last nerves, even when she kicked him out, and even when he veered off course, taking on a life she didn't quite understand or agree with. Then, of course, his kids: T'yanna and the recently born C.J. In them, he saw what his legacy looked like. Big knew imperfection was a part of life, but in that same vein, he knew he was changing for the better. Experiencing death, near-death, and the birth of life all in less than half a year does something to a man.

But on top of everything that had gone on in his life, and given how naturally private he was regarding matters in his personal life, the public needed to hear from Big again. And, quite honestly, Big needed them to hear him. His demeanor was always Brooklyn cool. Always that guy you'd want to party with, smoke with, drink with, and just be around. But make no mistake about it, Big heard all the talk.

"I just want my spot back," he told *Rap City*'s Joe Clair on February 24.

But this was L.A., a cultural mecca in its own regard, and, despite any of the drama, one of Big's favorite cities. Life in LaLa Land was treating him well. The weed was potent. The women were beautiful. And the weather? He could get used to seventy-degree weather in a month that normally left his Brooklyn streets filled with snow, ice, and slush. A day after that *Rap City* interview, Big's friend and then-Los Angeles Clippers guard Malik Sealy gifted him tickets to a game. Sealy and Big were cool based off the New York connection. Bronx to Brooklyn. New York's a large city, but still connected like a small town. They had a considerable number of mutual friends, too, like Jay-Z, for instance.

Biggie had come to see Sealy on February 25, 1997, when the Clippers hosted the Philadelphia 76ers. But he'd also come to see the NBA's most talked-about rookie in Allen Iverson. Much like how Big had described his own rise to superstardom as "ashy to classy," Iverson fit the same mold. It wasn't just the tattoos, or the cornrows, or the flashy clothes or jewelry. The connection was far deeper. Much like Big, so much in Iverson's life had changed drastically in such a short amount of time. In four years, he'd gone from a two-sport high school phenom in Virginia, to prison following a racially charged bowling alley brawl, to clemency granted by L. Douglas Wilder, the first elected Black governor in American history, to Georgetown University, to the number-one overall pick in the NBA draft. There was a refusal to lie down and accept the terms of America's one-sided agreement that lived in both Iverson and hip-hop.

So Iverson coming to L.A. was a significant deal, and definitely so for Big. That Friday night at the Los Angeles Memorial Sports Arena was a normal one. The Clippers, though they eventually made the playoffs that season, were still a below-average squad in a town that lived and breathed all things Lakers. And the fact that the Lakers, the offseason before, had signed Shaquille O'Neal and traded for a high school prodigy named Kobe Bryant didn't make their bid for local relevancy any easier. The Clippers charged less for tickets than their crosstown rivals, and constantly ran promotional packages and giveaways at schools and Boys & Girls Clubs of America. Still, except for whenever Michael Jordan and the Bulls came to town, the Sports Arena rarely sold out in those days.

That night, despite the less-than-sellout crowd, during the first quarter, a stir began to emerge from behind one of the baskets. Biggie Smalls had entered the arena.

"Somebody was at the free throw line, and the crowd had mixed emotions of booing and cheering," Iverson recalled the game to HYPEBEAST in 2017. "I'm like, 'What the fuck is going on?' I look up at the jumbotron and I see him. I'm like, 'Oh, shit.'"

"I just remember him coming in and it was a big fracas," said Gary Washburn, the national NBA writer for the *Boston Globe*. But in 1997, Washburn was a beat reporter for the *Los Angeles Daily News*. "Not fracas in a bad way, but just a lot of kids going crazy."

For all the talk of Big being in L.A. not being a good thing, the last people who seemed to be concerned with a bicoastal war were the kids in the arena. They flocked from all parts of the arena to zero in on Big, who attended the game with Cease and D-Roc. Big was unfazed. The kids were told to wait until halftime for their autographs, though Washburn wasn't sure Big would actually make the time.

"I'm thinking there's no way he was gonna sign all these autographs," said Washburn.

Around midway through the second quarter, kids began lining up on the stairwell near Biggie's seat. The line stretched up the stairwell all the way through the concourse.

"It was a massive line, and it was all kids. Basically all Black, from about six all the way to teenagers," Washburn said, the amazement still very much pure in his voice. "Nothing but kids. It had to be at least one hundred fifty kids."

As halftime began, Big made space for every kid one by one. With a pen in hand, he signed everything from pieces of paper to tickets to shirts. No kid was left behind. Each got their chance to interact with him. Decked out in a red velour suit, sunglasses, and cane, Big Poppa looked more like Black Santa Claus. This wasn't about proving to anyone that he had nothing to do with Tupac's killing or plugging his new album. It was about being a good person and giving a kid a moment they'd never forget.

Every kid went home happy that evening, and for Washburn, it was a moment that stuck to his ribs. The character exhibited that night mattered more than anything. Washburn wouldn't have blamed Big had he done a few autographs and then wanted to be left alone to watch the game.

"I was so impressed," Washburn said. "He got me there."

After the game, Big, Cease, and D-Roc waited for Iverson outside the locker room. In classic Big fashion, he played the cut. That million-watt smile infused with that Brooklyn charm was impossible to ignore. Fans came up to him and dapped him up until Iverson emerged.

"I came out and said, 'Yo, what are you doing here?'" Iverson remembered asking. Only five months had passed since Tupac's death. Big's answer surprised him.

"I've been out here for a month," Big said. "I'm looking for a crib."

"Then," said Iverson, "he continues to talk to me about the Questions sneakers and how he had my mom sending some of my shoes to him."

The entire exchange, from the outside looking in, was surreal. Here were two dudes in two different industries that, in many ways, had walked very similar paths to find success. And two young guys in Big and Iverson that, at that time only twenty-four and twenty-one, respectively, had their entire lives in front of them.

"That's always stayed with me. Because the whole perception is that he was hated in Los Angeles," said Washburn. "But that night was like Jesus had come to a game."

The thing about Jesus is that even He got crucified. Publicly, at that. And even He made it to thirty-three.

20
THE LAST WEEK

MONTHS EARLIER, ORLANDO ANDERSON HAD RECANTED HIS STATEMENT. In a bizarre twist of events, Anderson said the Death Row Records CEO didn't assault him and actually played peacemaker the night he was attacked by Tupac, despite video evidence saying the contrary. But not even that was enough to save Suge Knight.

"You blew it."

That's what Judge Stephen Czuleger had to say to Marion "Suge" Knight on March 1, 1997, the day of his sentencing.

For a while, it seemed as if Knight was untouchable by the long arm of the law. In a way, he was. He was already under investigation for possible improper ties to the district attorney Lawrence Longo, including Knight living in a Malibu condo owned by Longo, Knight signing Longo's eighteen-year-old daughter to a contract (making her the only white "artist" on Death Row), and working on Knight's 1992 assault with a deadly weapon case.

But that fateful night in Vegas changed everything. Not only was the label's top artist and money maker, Tupac Shakur, fatally wounded, but Knight was caught on camera stomping Orlando Anderson, too. In front of a wave of Knight's supporters who packed the courtroom, both Knight and his legal team argued that a kick shouldn't warrant him nine years in prison—a length that came from a nine-year suspended sentence that was part of his plea bargain from the 1992 case. Three nonprofit organizations pleaded with the judge to sentence Knight to probation rather than prison, saying that he would be active in their job training and community-based events and activities. Even C. Delores Tucker, the politician and civil rights activist who arguably became gangsta rap's most vocal critic in the nineties, expressed sympathy for Knight at his sentencing. Judge Czuleger was unfazed. He'd grown weary of Knight's antics and ability to avoid punishment for obvious punishable acts.

"I gave you every benefit of the doubt, and I have to say, you did blow it," the judge said. "You haven't accepted responsibility for your actions."

And just like that, Knight was off the streets for up to the next nine years. As Knight's career reached its nadir, Big's was preparing for his second apex.

Big was back in New York for a few days in early March 1997. Drew Dixon had recently left Def Jam and started a new job at Arista. Years later, Dixon publicly alleged that she had been raped by Def Jam founder Russell Simmons; she was one of the survivors featured in the critically acclaimed 2020 documentary *On the Record* about these horrific experiences. Big, Dixon says, never knew of that trauma she endured; nor does she not regret not telling him.

"There are two outcomes, and they're both heartbreaking. One outcome is that he would've confronted Russell and it would've been career-ending and destructive for him. And God knows that would've been a loss for all of us," Dixon reasoned to me. "The other is that he's a man at the end of the day, and he would've been upset for me personally, but he would've still had to smile in Russell's face because he's Russell Simmons . . . He's not a rap mogul—he's *the* rap mogul. So it would've either put Biggie in a terrible situation or it would've put me in a situation where he would've maybe let me down. I didn't want either of those outcomes."

All Big knew in March 1997 was that Dixon was now at Arista and that they were now label mates. A bond that was formed through a genuine love of hip-hop and smoking weed together back in Brooklyn when they were both just trying to make a name for themselves, had now led them to the same label. It was almost storybook. And there Big was to congratulate Dixon on the new gig, as he had always done.

Big called Dixon to come to Daddy's House. He wanted her to hear *Life After Death*. She felt she couldn't look the part—everyone there was so glamorous, she just didn't feel up to par in her sneakers, overalls, and royal blue bubblegoose coat—so she didn't pick up.

"We in the same family now, Drew," Big said on her voicemail. "I'm at Arista. You're at Arista. Why ain't you answering me? I'm leaving for L.A. I'm going to the Soul Train Music Awards. If you don't fuckin' come answer the damn phone and come to the studio and hear this fuckin' album, I'm gonna come get you!"

Dixon was sure glad she did. But one problem? She couldn't sit still in the room with Big as he attempted to play the album for her. Whenever the phone would ring, she'd jump up to answer it.

"Drew, I'm gonna go from the beginning to the end and I'ma need you to stop answering the phone, because you know what, Drew, you're a senior director of A&R at Arista," Dixon remembered Big commanding. "I just need you to understand. You're not an assistant anymore."

Dixon finally just sat there as he went through the entire album. She was floored by what she heard. She was super excited for "Notorious Thugs" with Bone Thugs-n-Harmony because she'd helped get them on *The Show* soundtrack. But more than anything, she was super proud of her friend. Then Big, according to Dixon, made her make a promise.

"I'm going to L.A., and when I come back we're gonna hang out for real. We've never hung out for real, Drew," Dixon said Big told her. "You got this big job now. I got this album that fire. I'm free. Let's hang the fuck out and figure out how we can win in this mothafucka."

"Yo, deal," she promised.

During the last week of his life, Big was making a ton of promises, all of which he intended to keep. Big changed his phone number often, so it was difficult for Hubert Sam to keep up. When he finally got the right one, Big was telling him about his West Coast trip, a move Sam wasn't too excited about. But it wasn't like he could stop his childhood friend, either.

"It was just really eerie, man," Sam said, sighing. "He apologized for not giving me the number, and he was telling me it was so much going on. I told him I was ready to make some beats and I knew what kinda machines I wanted to get."

"When I get back," Big told his childhood friend, "whatever you want, I got you."

"That was the last time," Sam said. "He never made it back."

Big had a flight to catch on March 6. He was heading back out to L.A. for the Soul Train Music Awards. But first, he had one last stop to make. It was a photo shoot with photographer Barron Claiborne. The assignment was brought to Claiborne by his friend Rob Marriott, who worked at *Rap Pages* at the time. The cover story would end up being written by dream hampton—an assignment that annoyed her because Big continuously avoided the piece's original author, Darnell Dawsey. Nevertheless, Claiborne liked shooting with Big and had done so a few years earlier.

"I always thought that Biggie looked like a big, Black king," Claiborne said. "So I was like I should make him a king. And I knew they were gonna think it was stupid. I knew that."

Claiborne picked up a couple of crowns from Gordon Novelty on Broadway. He set up red velvet for the background. Once Big, Puffy, Cease, and more arrived at the shoot, he broke down what his vision was. He'd always known Big to be a quiet, but at the same time, very nice guy, so it was no surprise when he didn't push back on the idea. Not everyone was so welcoming.

"Now Puffy's screaming in the background, 'Don't do that shit, nigga! You're gonna look like the Burger King!'" Claiborne recalled, unable to control his laughter. "This motherfucker."

The shoot lasted three to four hours, and the only thing really surprising to Claiborne was that Big didn't eat or smoke. He didn't talk much during the shoot, either, but he did tell Claiborne he was headed to Cali for an awards show. History rarely feels like history in the moment, and neither Claiborne nor Wallace understood how important the work they were creating together actually was. (In 2020, the crown sold at auction for $595,000.) It was a standard photo shoot. In and out.

Big was jet-setting all around the country in early March. He was in the Bay Area doing radio promo for the album. Then he was back in New York handling business, and now he was back in L.A. His album was dropping in less than twenty days, and he could feel the excitement and anxiousness that always came with the anticipation of a new project.

Those conversations he had with God in that rehab center in New Jersey never left him. So a day before the Soul Train Music Awards, he and D-Roc stopped to get tattooed on Sunset Boulevard. He inked Psalm 27 on his right forearm.

The Lord is my light and my salvation, whom shall I fear?

The Lord is the truth of my life, of whom shall I be afraid?

When the wicked, even my enemies and foes, came upon me to bite my

flesh, they stumbled and fell.

The tattoo artist had just finished inking the Los Angeles Lakers superstar and friend of Big's Shaquille O'Neal. The two giants in their respective worlds, who collaborated on 1996's "Can't Stop the Reign" from the NBA All-Star's third studio album, caught up again. Shaq was worried about his friend's presence in the city. Big just wanted to have a good time.

"Yo, be careful out here," Shaq said.

"Yeah, I hear you," Big said. "But come to my party."

The party he was referring to was going to be at the Petersen Automotive Museum on the evening of March 8. The night before was the actual Soul Train Music Awards. Before heading to the venue, Big spoke with one of his good friends, Robert "Don Pooh" Cummins, who was also in L.A. Don Pooh had miraculously survived being hit by a car, but it left him with a broken leg, and Big joked, in a warm and caring manner, that Pooh was trying to be like him with a broken leg and cane. He explained to Pooh that he really wanted this new album to be different. He was excited. But now he had to be off to the show.

It was wild. A year ago, Big had come face-to-face with Shakur for the final time. And now here he was with a new lease on life and a chance to do it all right. Introduced by Gladys Knight, he accompanied Brian McKnight, Puffy, and 112 onstage. But it was Big who was tasked with reading the winner for the Best R&B/Soul Single, Female.

"Wassup, Cali?" Wallace said before announcing the winner: "You're Making Me High" by Toni Braxton.

Big received mostly cheers from the Shrine Auditorium crowd, but there were boos coming from up top. A few hours later, in his suite at the Westwood Marquis, Big was watching the show on tape delay with his own brand of signature comedy while chopping it up with journalist Cheo Hodari Coker, who was working on a profile of him ahead of the new album.

Big felt comfortable with Coker. They'd spoken several times over the previous few years, and he respected Coker's approach to his craft and the care with which he asked questions. Questions that weren't always fun to answer, either. A sausage pizza had just been delivered to his room. He propped it on his belly and shot the shit with Coker. The next day Big was to fly to London to embark on an international press run, but even though he knew it would piss off some people at Arista, he had changed the plans.

"I canceled that shit," Big said. "I just ain't fucking with it."

He wasn't ready to leave L.A. He was having fun. Big, feeling comfortable, spoke candidly about several parts of his life.

"I asked him a lot of questions about his childhood and asked him a lot of questions about who was Christopher Wallace versus Biggie Smalls versus the Notorious B.I.G.," Coker recalled. "He was talking poignantly about how he wanted to give T'yanna away at her wedding and how he wanted to change his life, essentially. His whole dream was being a suburban soccer dad. He wanted to buy a house in Atlanta and be around his kids.

"The person I talked to was somebody striving for peace," Coker continued, "striving for maturity."

Big couldn't believe how much had changed from last year's Soul Train Music Awards—Tupac was dead, Suge was at the very beginning of a lengthy prison sentence—but he wasn't shocked, either. About his newfound relationship with God? He respected that the Lord would always steer him in the right direction even when he couldn't see. But he spoke about his first and only tattoo, still healing on his right forearm.

"That's how I feel sometimes. I want to feel like this all the time," he said. "That's why I went and got it, to reassure myself that no matter what goes wrong, no matter how bad shit is looking, God is right here . . . As long as you believe in Him and in His strength, all these jealous people, all these sharks, all these bitches that's out here to get niggas and expect you to fuck them and get on some real ghetto, grimy shit, and these haters—he'll stop all of that. He's gonna find you the road to take to avoid them."

It might not have been worded in the way most church folk would've preferred, but so what. Finding faith, however one chooses to express it, is a personal journey, and this was Christopher Wallace's. That faith came with a refueled sense of purpose and passion. He was proud of how he was supporting his family, and he was proud he was trusting in God to keep the right people around him to protect him. People like Hubert Sam, D-Roc, Chico, Cease, and, despite their contentious relationship, Kim—those who had known him long before life became so complicated. People like Puffy and Mark Pitts, who understood that making him a star was a labor of love and never gave up on him. People like Jan, who knew him back when he was Big Chris selling crack on the block.

"We spoke after the [Soul Train Music Awards]," Jan said in a 2012 Hot 97 interview. "'Friends' is not a strong enough word. We had a great relationship. It went beyond just us sharing a daughter."

And Faith, Coker asked?

They weren't really speaking, but Big was at peace with where they were. They'd always be in each other's lives because of the life they created in little C.J.

"I can treasure that forever, even if the relationship doesn't work out," he said. "I always wanted a son and I got one, and that's all that matters to me."

Coker and Big would speak for a bit longer, and that night Big, D-Roc, Cease, and his driver Gregory "G-Money" Young went to see the movie *Donnie Brasco*. Later they went to the studio, and the movie made it into his "All About the Benjamins" verse. He also recorded his verse for a song that would later become known as "Victory" during that same session. Big had spit a plethora of legendary verses in his career, but these two were different. His wordplay especially sharp. The pictures he was painting were crystal clear. "Real sick, brawl nights, I perform like Mike / Anyone, Tyson, Jordan, Jackson," he rapped. "Action, pack guns, ridiculous / And I'm quick to bust, if my ends you touch / Kids or girl you touch." Somehow, someway, the Notorious B.I.G. was getting *better* as an MC.

No one knows when their world is about to change. It just does. So when Big woke up the morning of Saturday, March 8, 1997, he treated it like any other in his life. Lance "Un" Rivera heard how excited Big was for

Life After Death's March 25 release date. He spoke to a litany of people that day, including Mark Pitts, his manager, who was heated that he had canceled his London flight. But Big played Pitts and D-Dot the two verses he had recorded the night before, and their jaws hit the floor. Pitts was still annoyed, but there was no way he could downplay what Big had just let him hear. These next several months promoting *Life After Death*, the tour, the videos, and the awards it would rake in, were going to be the time of their lives.

He spoke to his mother, who was surprised to hear he wasn't already halfway to London. Voletta wasn't some hip-hop expert, but even she knew about the tension in the industry, and she asked about his well-being. He told her not to worry; there was plenty of security around him to protect him from whatever foolishness the streets of Los Angeles could offer.

He spoke to Jan again, asking about T'yanna. They laughed and joked on the phone for quite a bit, and he told her he wanted to see his daughter. Jan promised they'd arrange it as soon as he got back around the way. Throughout the day—throughout his last weekend on Earth, really—Big's final conversations with a variety of people have all left their mark. Some were usual check-ins. Some were profound, like those with Jan, Drew Dixon, and even Matty C, who last saw him at Club Envy in Manhattan with D-Roc in January 1997. He frequently talked about spending time and creating agency with his time. But all were conversations that Big was totally invested in. Like with Lil' Kim. They had their disagreements about a litany of topics, including music. About Big wanting her to make certain decisions in her career and Kim bucking back, saying she wanted to do it another way. "I would never tell you to do something that would have you fucked up. I only do it the right way 'cause that's the only way I know how to do it. My track record is looking pretty good," he reflected to Coker in the final hours of his life. "She make it seem like I want to sabotage her shit." Yet, according to Kim, their last conversation was not only productive, it was an emotional breakthrough.

"We were going through some things for a long time, and it was major. But that weekend, I don't know, he must have had a change of heart," Lil' Kim said. "He was like, 'You know what, ma? I decided whatever it is you wanna do, I'ma support you because I love you.' He actually told me I'm a beautiful person inside and out. He never really would say things like that to me. He showed it, but that was the one time he really expressed from the heart how he felt about me."

According to Raekwon, he and Ghostface and Big made amends that weekend in L.A., too. It had been over a year and a half since he heard the "Shark Niggas" skit on Rae's *Cuban Linx* album. "We had an opportunity to catch him at the bar in the Roxy Club on Sunset. We just told him, 'You our brother, man.' He looked back like, 'C'mon, man. Have a drink.'"

At the hotel getting ready for the night's festivities, Groovey Lew called Big's room. The Bad Boy staff was assigned to different artists. Lew, who'd long had a great bond with the label's MVP, was assigned to Big. Lew asked if he needed anything.

"Nah," Big replied. "I'm good."

"I got some honies," Lew said.

"Yo, they fucking?" Big laughed—but still very serious in his questioning.

Lew's job was easy that night. He didn't have to arrange transportation, because Big was riding with Puffy.

"That was my last conversation with him," Lew said. "Just making sure he was good."

Big could've gone to the studio to lay more tracks, but he was in a good mood. His album was done, and he knew it was crazy. The video wasn't out yet, but he wanted to see how "Hypnotize" connected with the people that night, and he just wanted to have fun with Puffy. He hoped he could meet some people there who could help him do some more acting. He was going to have fun.

Big and company ended up jumping in the Suburban and heading to Andre Harrell's house, where Puffy was staying. The only soundtrack they needed came directly from the guy in the passenger seat. *Life After Death* pulsated out of the speakers. It had all the makings of a legendary night. In more ways than one.

———

Shaquille O'Neal had already picked out what he was going to wear to party with Big that night—a long white coat and a white top hat. The Petersen

Automotive Museum wasn't too far from the Wilshire Boulevard penthouse where he was staying. But a nap beforehand couldn't hurt, he figured. A second nap couldn't, either. Shaq ended up sleeping through the night and missing everything.

Meanwhile, another NBA All-Star and former Rookie of the Year was wide awake. Earlier that evening, Grant Hill dropped nineteen points and ten rebounds, and dished out eight assists in a 91–85 win over the Los Angeles Clippers. Hill was one of the NBA's brightest and most exciting young superstars. He was excited about having a mini-break between games—his Detroit Pistons didn't play again until March 11 in Seattle—and he planned on having a good time. His future wife, the R&B singer Tamia, came to the game with some people from her label, his good friend Kairi Brown, and more. After the game, Hill left with them in a stretch limo to go to Tamia's for a bit. Since he was with some music industry folks, they had the mixtape with advance copies of some of the songs on *Life After Death*.

"They had 'Hypnotize' and 'Another' with Lil' Kim. And the Dru Hill 'Sleeping in My Bed' remix," Hill recalls. "They were playing 'Hypnotize' over and over. So after that first verse, I kept rewinding it to the start to hear that lyric 'Pink gators, my Detroit players.'"

"We played the record for the one part, the Detroit players," said Kairi Brown, who was working at Qwest Records at the time. Qwest and *VIBE* magazine were the sponsors for the party that night at the Petersen. "We played that over and over from the time we left Bel Air until the time we got to the museum."

Hill had been with Tamia in L.A. when Tupac was killed six months earlier and he had seen the emotional fallout from that. "You know," Hill said, "I remember thinking that was a little weird that Biggie was out there partying."

Everyone was turning up, though. It felt like as many celebrities were in attendance as those who paid general admission. Stars like Whitney Houston and Bobby Brown, Marlon Wayans, Aaliyah, Missy Elliott, Ginuwine, Timbaland, DJ Quik, Salli Richardson, Jermaine Dupri, Da Brat, Jagged Edge, DJ Clark Kent, Ed Lover, Irv Gotti, and more were in the building. By all accounts, the event that night was one of the best they'd ever been to.

Anyone who was anyone was in there, with even more outside trying to get in. Puffy was his normal energetic self.

"I was aggressive Puff at that point," Combs recalled decades later. "I'm grabbing the mic and announcing that shit. 'Yeah, we up in this mothafucka! Love to L.A. Love to the Crips! Love to the Bloods!'"

Big sat taking in the scene from his section, smoking a blunt. Due to his cane, he didn't move around a lot—but he didn't need to; the party came to him. The bottles, the women, the people wanting to dap him up and give him congratulations on the new album. Big was feeling the love.

The music was thumping, asses were shaking, and everyone appeared to be having a great time. The venue was packed, people as far as the eye could see in every direction. Big had said he wanted to come party and hopefully meet some people who could help advance an acting career, but he was trying to mend some fences, too.

The group XScape was in the building, and the ladies still felt a way about Big calling them "ugly-ass XScape bitches" on his provocative "Just Playin' (Dreams)" from way back in the day. Big, in fact, had been trying to apologize to the group for years. They just weren't trying to hear him out. On that night at the *VIBE* party, Kandi Burruss still wasn't trying to entertain his apology, a decision she quickly came to regret. Meanwhile, Tameka "Tiny" Cottle went to go hear him out.

"He basically apologized for that. He said he thought we were beautiful," Tiny said. "He said, 'I'm an ugly mothafucka and I ain't have no business talking about anybody.'" Tiny and Big laughed about it all and then went their separate ways.

Three thousand miles and three time zones away, a groggy Jay-Z answered the phone around 2:30 in the morning at his place in New York. It was Big. He was excited, yelling into the phone over the top of the music in the background.

Big had plans for him and Jay that he couldn't stop talking about—which had been the case every day since that first studio meeting DJ Clark Kent set up. Big was excited for *Life After Death*, but he was geeked about the group he wanted to form with Jay called the Commission. He wanted the two of them to buy homes in Atlanta and live right beside each other. In Jay, he found a musical peer who was just as talented as him—in some ways—if not more. Instead of allowing that to form a level of animosity between them, it only brought them closer.

"Yo, where you at, playboy?! Where you at?" Big shouted. "You missin' this!"

Jay had intended to be in L.A. that night but had gotten caught up with work. And since Big had extended his trip, Jay planned on joining him out there in a few days. The two soon got off the phone. For Big, the party kept going. For Jay, though he didn't know it at the moment, his long night was just beginning.

Evans was also at the party, and though she didn't want to go looking for Big, him seeing her was part of her master plan. It was part of the game they always played. No matter how wrong he was in their relationship, and he was wrong a lot, there was still love there. They had fallen in love so quickly and had put each other through hell even quicker.

"Through the years, I've thought a lot about why I didn't go over and speak to Big that night," Evans wrote in her memoir. "Part of it had to be pride—I've got a lot of it. And I wasn't about to look like I was playing myself out. *Please.* Walking through a crowded party to see *him*? I don't think so. I needed him to see *me.* I never actually decided I wasn't going to talk to Big. I just figured I'd have all night to run into him and say a few words."

That's the thing about time. We always want to believe we have more of it.

21

LONG KISS GOODNIGHT

AT THAT VERY MOMENT, AS THE LATE-NIGHT HOURS OF MARCH 8 TURNED INTO THE EARLY-MORNING HOURS OF MARCH 9, THE NOTORIOUS B.I.G. CHERISHED THE ARTISTIC NIRVANA ALL AROUND HIM.

Every artist wants a record that makes the crowd lose its mind when they hear it. And that night in the Petersen Automotive Museum, "Hypnotize" was that record. There's no way of knowing how many times the single, which had been released just a week earlier, was played, but it was the unimpeachable song of the night. It was Big's first single as the lead artist since the "One More Chance (Remix)," and he'd proven one thing: there wasn't about to be a sophomore jinx.

His lyrics bounced off the walls all night long. Big surveyed the room and loved what he saw. He was back, and he was about to be larger than ever.

"I'm gonna make them love me," he told Combs at the party that night. "I can't wait until they hear 'Goin' Back to Cali' so they know I got nothing but love for them."

"That night, we felt like we turned the energy around," Combs reflected later. "Like everybody was in there, everybody just started to relax. You could see the players from the East Coast and the players from the West Coast, male and female, start to interact and talk with each other. We didn't take it serious enough. The only way we could've took it more serious was by living in fear. And we were too fearless and too young to live in fear at that point in time."

There were also a ton of street cats from both colors in the building, par for the course at big parties like this in L.A. Among them were Duane "Keefe D" Davis, who'd reportedly had ties to Combs for years. He was originally introduced to Combs by another Crip named Eric "Zip" Martin in 1993. Davis's '64 Chevy was said to be featured in Usher's "Can U Get Wit It" video. Davis's nephew, a man who had become infamous over the past six months, Orlando Anderson, was also in attendance at the party. Both men were rumored to be involved in the drive-by shooting that had killed Shakur, but they were chilling that night. The party never became a turf war, but it did become overcrowded. At approximately 12:35 A.M. on the morning of March 9, fire marshals shut the party down. People piled toward the exits, hoping to find the next party. Those in the know were already hip. Industry executive Steve Stoute was having a party in Hollywood Hills. Faith Evans and her friends were already en route.

Grant Hill, Tamia, and Kairi Brown saw Big and his crew riding around.

"While we waited for our limo to pick us up, they rolled through bumping music," remembered Brown. "We got in our limo right after that. And as we got in, it was some crazy stuff that went on."

It took a few minutes, thanks in part to Big being slowed down by his leg, but the Bad Boy entourage had already piled into their cars, GMC Chevy Suburbans from Budget Rent a Car in Beverly Hills. A few weeks earlier, they had stopped by Beverly Hills Motoring to check in on the progress of some custom-made bulletproof car armor. They ultimately decided not to buy it. In the white Suburban sat Combs and his three bodyguards. In the green Suburban were Big in the front passenger seat, D-Roc and Lil' Cease in back, and G, the driver. Paul Offord, another one of Puffy's bodyguards, pushed a black Chevy Blazer with an off-duty LAPD officer. Mark Pitts, D-Dot, and the rapper Tracey Lee were all in a white limo.

Inside Big's car, the energy was still high. The party may have been shut down, but the night was far from over. "Goin' Back to Cali" blasted through the Suburban speakers. All was right in the world. At the corner of Fairfax and Wilshire Boulevard, Puffy's vehicle made it through the intersection, but Big's got caught by a red light. That's when Lil' Cease, sitting behind Big, noticed a black Impala pull alongside their Suburban. Cease saw the driver clutching something in his right hand. It was a .40-caliber automatic handgun.

Pop. Pop. Pop. Pop. Before anyone in the car could react, the heinous deed was already done. Whoever had done this sped off like thieves in the night.

"Me and Cease were in the back seat when Biggie got shot," said D-Roc in *Unbelievable.* "He didn't say a word. He was just lookin' at me with this real shocked look on his face, like he couldn't believe it. He didn't even say, 'Ouch.' He didn't even say, 'Oh, shit.' Nothin.' All he was doing was breathing hard."

Panic instantly sat in. Cease hopped out to see if he'd been shot, but the only one hit was Big. D-Roc sat in the back seat, unable to move, unable to process what just happened. Puffy's Suburban doubled back after the four shots had been let off.

"Big!" Puffy yelled at the top of his lungs. "Big!"

"Where's the hospital?!" he yelled repeatedly.

The recording of the 911 call is harrowing: Puffy and others trying to piece together what just happened while on the phone with paramedics trying to find their way to the ambulance. The entourage didn't have time to wait. They went frantically searching for the hospital themselves. All the while still on the phone.

"He's hit, man! He's fuckin' hit!"

"If you want your friend to live, we're gonna send paramedics, so you need to pull over."

"I can't do that right now!"

As they pulled into Cedars-Sinai Medical Center, some ten minutes and less than two miles from the Petersen, they held onto Big, praying mightily that he'd show any sign of life. Something. Anything.

"Big, you hear me, baby?!"

Meanwhile, Evans had already gotten to the Hollywood Hills to hit the next party. Suddenly, Heavy D pulled up on her and gave her the news. She needed to get to the hospital immediately. Something bad had happened to Big. Evans hardly remembered the ride there. All she did was rock back and forth. When she got to Cedars-Sinai, she was taken inside to a small waiting room. It all seemed so surreal. Puffy, Mark Pitts, Stevie J, Paul Offord, and D-Roc were all in the room. Their faces were expressionless.

She approached Puffy first.

"Puff, what happened? What's going on? Where's Big? Is he okay?"

Puffy left the room and came right back with the doctor. He let him break the news to her. They'd tried to revive him, massaging his heart several times in the hope it would start beating again. Everything they tried proved unsuccessful. Faith was so delirious that she pleaded with the doctor to try again. There was nothing they could do. Christopher Wallace was dead. He was only twenty-four years old.

Next came the task that absolutely no one wanted. Someone had to call Voletta. Combs was given the phone, but he passed it off to Mark Pitts. Pitts passed and gave the phone to D-Roc.

"How am I gonna call this man's mom?" D-Roc pleaded. "I grew up with this kid."

He called Miss Wallace, who picked up. By then, it was nearly 4:00 A.M. back in Brooklyn. She quickly figured out it was D-Roc and could hear the chaos in the background. All he could get out was "Miss Wallace."

"What happened to my son?!" she yelled repeatedly.

The sheer ungodly pain of the situation couldn't let him finish the sentence. But she knew. Her only child was gone.

A short time later, D-Roc was at Faith's hotel when dream hampton called. They both agreed to meet at Big's hotel room. It was D-Roc who, in addition to breaking the news to Miss Wallace, had to call Un, Money L—one of BIG's good friends from Brooklyn who often went on the road with him—Lil' Kim, Charli Baltimore, and others. The thing D-Roc couldn't get over was that his friend had no last words.

"This nigga, who ain't never hurt nobody," D-Roc told hampton, trying to reason things out by speaking them only to realize they're even more outlandish when he hears them. He spoke through tears. "I could see if it was one of us . . . I been shot mad times—niggas get shot. This nigga died from one ass bullet."

In Big's hotel room were remnants of his final acts of life, like women's lingerie and weed. They wanted to clear the room before Voletta got there, not trying to hide anything from her, but out of respect. dream hampton brought several meals from Roscoe's Chicken and Waffles. No one really touched the food, because the feeling in the pit of their stomachs quashed anything resembling an appetite. On top of that, too, Big's crew were already receiving threatening messages from back east.

"From the very beginning they were getting calls from New York like, 'Y'all niggas ain't shit. Don't come back here. Y'all couldn't protect this nigga,'" hampton recalled in a 2011 interview. "Of course there were condolences, and that was the majority of the calls, but there were definitely some calls from Brooklyn that upset Cease in particular about the responsibility for being his safety and having failed at that."

Back in New York, Voletta, Money L, Jan, and Mann, one of Big's close friends from the neighborhood, boarded a flight to L.A. Voletta didn't say a word on the entire flight, drifting in and out of sleep. When she was awake, she couldn't help but think about her son's life and how they had practically grown up together, and now she'd have to live the rest of her life without him. By the time she got to L.A. and made her way to son's hotel room, the first thing she noticed was the silence. That and his tuxedo laid out. The rawness of it all and just how cold it was. The only thing she could hear was a faucet dripping and the air conditioner. Her son was a practical joker, and Voletta wanted nothing more than for him to scare her by jumping out from behind a door. But he didn't.

"I continued to just look around and listen, and in that total silence it hit me," Voletta wrote. "In my mind, I admitted for the first time that Christopher was dead . . . All I could do was sit down on the bed next to his things. It made me feel close to him."

The phone rang, breaking the silence. It was Faith. She told Voletta to come stay with her at her hotel. She didn't need to be alone in a city that had just taken her only child. Voletta agreed to, but not before she sat in her son's hotel room for just a little while longer.

"I felt that it was our last chance to be alone together without the world watching. It felt like it was our quiet time together the way it used to be when he was growing up and it was just me and Christopher."

The sun rose over Brooklyn on March 9, 1997, but it might as well have been complete darkness.

"I'm in the cab on my way to Hot 97, and I've never seen Brooklyn so quiet," Mister Cee says. "Nobody was outside."

By the time Cee arrived station, Lisa Evers and Angie Martinez were already there in tears.

"That's when it really hit me," said Cee, who started crying himself. Cee had helped get Big into *The Source*, which led to his meeting with Puffy—which led to his eventual superstardom. And now the young hustler from Brooklyn who trusted him with so much of his early career was already gone. For Cee, it couldn't be real. This couldn't be life.

But for Cee and the staff at Hot 97, their grieving process had to carry the city's. Program director Tracy Cloherty told Cee, Martinez, and Evers that they had to go on air. They had to be there for the people. If the city was going to heal, the city needed them to help it make sense of something so senseless.

"We had to be there to console them," Cee said. "If it wasn't for Tracy telling us that, we wouldn't have ever gone on the air and said anything. She said we needed to be there for the city."

Hot 97 and Power 106 in Los Angeles were both owned by Emmis Communications. The two stations did a live simulcast that was broadcast across the country. People called in to express their condolences. Some called in just to cry because that's all they could offer. But Hot 97 in particular took Big's murder very personally. Throughout his short life, and the even shorter existence of the twenty-four-hour hip-hop station, the two had become mutually responsible for each other's popularity in New York. This was about protecting the purity of that bond for the many people at the station who had gotten to know Big on a personal level.

"We lived there for an entire week, just breaking format," said Steve Smith. "Keeping all the newspapers at bay. MTV, too. They were all downstairs demanding to come up every day, threatening to use my name in their stories. The *New York Times*, *Daily News*, *Newsweek*, all of them. They wanted to get up here to film our control room. All of this shit, but there was no fucking way, man. No, no, no. Our audience was mourning. We were crying. There was no way we were going to sensationalize what had just happened."

A piece of Brooklyn's soul, a piece of its very identity, had been snatched away. Big, a first-generation American kid, *was* Brooklyn. The borough was responsible for so much in hip-hop culture, and Big represented so much of that in one body. One massive, beautiful body that bucked at normal standards for what beauty could look like artistically and spiritually. Throughout his career, the one thing that remained true always was the space he made in his soul for Brooklyn. The borough was with him in every studio session and every show.

Much like Tupac before him, Big was at an inflection point when he died. In the final weeks and months of his life, he couldn't stop talking about how much he was changing, that he was putting his faith in God, and where he wanted to take his life. As he'd say in song on the incredibly anticipated double LP *Life After Death*, released just two weeks later, the sky truly was the limit. And that meant for Brooklyn, too.

"I think we all had pagers then," said Drew Dixon, who took in the news along with close friend and Big collaborator the rapper/producer Daddy-O. "Our world is blowing up. If you were Black, and certainly if you were Black in hip-hop, the sky was falling."

"I broke down and started crying. I couldn't stop," said Chico Del Vec. He and Big—or Chris, as he makes it a point to say—had known each other since before they were teenagers. They went through street wars together. They made money together—lots of money. They toured the country together. "I didn't wanna come on the block after a while because that's all it was. Cameras in front of the door. You don't know who is pulling up and jumping out and showing love. It was just . . . a lot."

It was hard to fathom how it could all end so quickly. There Big was at the Soul Train Music Awards looking as confident as ever. Then, the *VIBE* party, which in a way, served as his pre-album release roll out. His future quite literally in front of him. And then, two months before his twenty-fifth birthday, it was over. Makeshift memorial sites popped up almost immediately near his old corner in Brooklyn and in L.A. by the Petersen Automotive Museum. The wound from Tupac's murder was still very much raw, open, and unsolved. Now it had to double the grief, double the pain, and double the anger.

But the overwhelming emotion was shock.

"I don't say I could've prevented it," Shaquille O'Neal told me. His mother called him to tell him the news after he had overslept and missed the whole party. "I was just saying . . . if I was out there by the car, would they still have fired? That's the only thing I would say to myself. I don't wanna make it seem like I could've saved him," he said again. "I don't wanna make it seem like if I was there, the shooters wouldn't have shot. If I was there by the truck, after we all left and I'm dapping him up, would they still have shot?"

Luther "Uncle Luke" Campbell of 2 Live Crew was in L.A. that night. He and Snoop Dogg had squashed their beef from years earlier and were in the studio together recording a song. Luke had been talking with Big throughout the day and planned on linking up with him that night after the party. The two had known each other for a few years, and there was a deep respect between them. Big for Luke as a hip-hop pioneer, and Luke for Big's talent on the mic and his overall laid-back demeanor. He saw Big as a friend.

"I'm on the plane," Luke told Coker about his flight back to Miami, "and the thought of him just goin' out there with the intentions of goin' to the awards, having a good time, and now he has to come back in a box up under the plane? That just stayed on my mind. Yo . . . he's coming back in a box up under the fucking plane."

As with most high-profile celebrity deaths, the rumor mill was in overdrive: this was retaliation for Tupac's murder six months earlier; the hit was actually meant for Combs; Suge Knight had ordered the execution from a prison cell; Big was killed by Crips over money that Bad Boy owed to the gang for protection when they were in L.A.; it was the government exacting the harshest punishment possible on a musical genre that it had been at odds with since its inception. The theories ranged from the impossible to the plausible, but there would be time for all of that. Years' and decades' and generations' worth of discussion about such theories still lives on.

Many could figure that Los Angeles would be, in the most inhumane way possible, celebrating. One of theirs, in Tupac, had been taken from them. Now one of the East Coast's, in Big, was gone, too. Los Angeles was no stranger to celebrity deaths, but Big's murder felt particularly sinister. His peace-treaty mission had been mistaken for reckless taunting. And now, with the deed done, the city had to live in the immediacy of it all.

"It was like *all* the wind had been let out of L.A. The whole city was depressed," former NBA All-Star point guard Baron Davis, a high school senior in Los Angeles at the time of Big's murder, recalled to me about the temperature of his city. "A lot of people felt the same way I did: 'How could we be responsible? . . . We killed their everything.'"

"Their everything" hit the nail on the head. All that mattered was that Christopher Wallace's body lay in a Los Angeles morgue. And all anyone wanted to do was to get him out of that city. D-Roc vowed not to sleep or shower until "I get my man out this motherfucker."

Looking back on the situation years later for the A&E documentary *Biggie: The Life of Notorious B.I.G.*, Voletta admitted, "I hated California. Hated it with a passion. It took something dear from me. I don't think there are words to express to tell you how much I miss him."

In Los Angeles, Voletta, Faith, and Jan were all experiencing profound grief together. Jan never had any beef with Faith, and likewise on the other end. But if there ever was a sense of bad blood or even the slightest sense of jealousy, it was gone then. On the ride to the morgue, Voletta began to ask questions. Where was the security that was supposed to be protecting her son? Where the hell was Puffy? The questions were already running through her head. It was already bad enough she'd lost her only child, but now no one had answers for her.

"Do you know if he was in any pain?" Faith remembered Jan asking in her memoir.

The doctor had told Faith that the bullet ricocheted throughout his body, so she could only imagine he had experienced some level of pain. But she couldn't tell them that.

After a few minutes of waiting at the morgue, a man came and laid out three extremely graphic photos of Wallace. The weight of the photos was enough to nearly knock them off their feet. The best way Faith could describe the photos was that her husband had been fighting for his life and had just passed away when the photos were taken. Voletta, however, wouldn't allow herself to accept the truth. And how could she? This was the life she'd brought into this world, and now she had to plan how to properly say goodbye.

"I can't identify my son this way!" she belted. "How do I know for sure that's my baby? I need to see him. Let. Me. See. My. Son!"

The entire scene was gutting. It was a mother's pain, her helpless cry, that made a heavy situation all that much heavier. Both Jan and Faith confirmed to her that it was Christopher. Because it was an active investigation, they weren't allowed to physically see his body, which made the situation even worse. On the day they were all going to fly back to New York, Voletta had a final request. She wanted to go to the corner of Wilshire and Fairfax. She wanted to be where he was when he took his final breaths. She placed a bouquet of white lilies by the museum.

———

Big's funeral was held at the Frank E. Campbell Funeral Chapel on the Upper East Side of Manhattan on March 18, 1997. The room where the service was held was intended to hold two hundred people, though more than 350 were in attendance. Jay-Z, Queen Latifah, all the members of Junior M.A.F.I.A., Heavy D, Foxy Brown, Busta Rhymes, Mary J. Blige, and more were in attendance. At the request of Clive Davis, former New York City mayor David Dinkins attended, though he did not know Big personally. All three of Big's kids—Chyna, whom he had unofficially adopted when he and Faith got together, T'yanna, and still-infant C.J.—wore white.

The program included a quote from Big: "I want to wake up with my kids. Get 'em ready for school and take 'em to school. I want to participate in all that. I want to see my kids get old." He had said this on March 8, 1997.

But it was seeing him in his white double-breasted suits made by 5001 Flavors and in that African mahogany casket that rocked everyone. Big had talked about finding God so much in the final months of his life. The peaceful look on his face suggested that maybe he had. But for everyone else at the service that day, heaven felt light-years away.

"They dressed him up like Big Poppa," DJ Premier said. "They dressed him up nice, but it was hard to look at him like that."

"To see him lying there, lifeless, I'll never forget touching his hand because it was cold and still," said Drew Dixon, who sat with Clive Davis.

"There's nobody in the world that is less capable of being lifeless and cold than Biggie. Biggie was this vitality and light and warmth."

To this day, Chico can't speak about that moment. "That's not something I wanna talk about, please. Is that okay?" he said to me, sniffling. "It's just real sad, man, you know what I mean?"

Lil' Kim was an emotional wreck, and by far the most vocal at the service. Some couldn't understand why she was so demonstrative, but that's the thing about grief. It's like a fingerprint. It looks different on everyone. And her grief was real. Voletta read scripture from the Book of Job while the Bad Boy R&B group 112 sang "Cry On." And Evans, who initially wasn't going to sing, ended up singing "Walk with Me, Jesus," which stood as the service's most beautiful moment.

From nearly the moment Big was pronounced dead, attention shifted toward Puffy. Questions swirled around why he and Big were moving around L.A. so freely so soon after Tupac's death—and a week after Suge's sentencing. Some believed that, like Knight six months earlier, Puffy may have been the actual target. First, the City College tragedy, and now Big's murder. Death seemed to be stalking Puffy. "Big made me feel like I could conquer the world," he eulogized. "Every day I wake up and pray that it's all just a bad dream. But it's not. Big's gone."

Once the funeral was over, it was time to head outside to a sea of crying fans and media all too eager to snap pictures of the celebrity mourners. A team of pallbearers carried Big's coffin. At the front was D-Roc. He'd known Big long before the music, before the hit singles and videos and before anyone knew him as Biggie. To D-Roc, Big would always be Chris. The friend he hustled with, laughed with, got arrested with, toured the country with, and dreamed with. Just nine days after having to make the hardest call of his life to Voletta, now he had to take the longest walk of his life—and the final one with Big.

Lil' Kim, as she had been at the service, was a complete wreck outside. Paparazzi snapped pictures as she cried and collapsed into Mary J. Blige's arms.

In the song he did with Shaquille O'Neal a year earlier, "Can't Stop the Reign," Big had one request of his neighborhood should something ever happen to him: "I rely on Bed-Stuy to shut it down if I die."

Man, did it ever.

As Big's family and friends drove through the city, the pain they were feeling at least temporarily gave way to the massive amount of love they were seeing. Men and women, boys and girls, elderly and youthful—they all came to say goodbye to their King of New York.

Pavement was almost impossible to make out. That's how many people were packed on the streets. The crowd on Fulton Street and St. James Place had been gathering since 10:00 A.M., listening to music and drinking beer. There was tension in the air, but it was more from the angst of the crowd feeling that outsiders were intruding on a sacred moment for the borough. Cops in riot gear drew the ire of local residents. And seeing members of the media descending on their block rubbed some in the crowd the wrong way. Big had been portrayed by some in the white press as a hardened criminal, a thug who cared only about his bank account and the violence he could spew in his rhymes. He wasn't a human to them; he was a headline. But to the people who lined those blocks, he was so much more than that. Biggie Smalls was everything to Brooklyn. He still is.

"Fuck these white mothafuckas! Get off my block! Y'all ain't allowed!" declared one Brooklyn resident from her stoop.

It wasn't until early in the afternoon that Big's procession rolled through. Out of nowhere, someone started blasting "Hypnotize." What happened next was a moment Big himself would be proud of.

"It was a riot. But, like, a love riot," veteran journalist Rob Marriott said. "A resurrection ritual."

People hung out of windows, danced on top of cars, and blew weed smoke to the heavens in honor of their slain neighborhood superstar. A day of intense mourning became a revival, if only for a pocket of time. Christopher Wallace's spirit was very much alive. From her limo, Voletta Wallace looked on in amazement.

"My God," she said. "I never knew my son was this famous."

The last stop was Fresh Pond Crematory in Queens, where Voletta would have her son cremated. The block was eventually cleared by New York's Finest. All in all, ten people were arrested, including a *New York Times* reporter. And that animosity between residents and police bled far into the evening. It was indeed that "Brooklyn bullshit" that Big opined about in "Hypnotize."

One week following his last dance through Brooklyn, *Life After Death* hit shelves, selling seven hundred thousand copies out of the gate and firmly supplanting itself atop the *Billboard* charts. The album was a culmination of everything Big had worked toward, the album he had envisioned while rehabbing from his car accident. He had monstrous records and anthems while still keeping his sense of graphic composure and ridiculously entertaining storytelling. Big didn't have any final words that fateful night in Los Angeles. So, in a way, *Life After Death* filled that void. Less than four years later, the record was certified diamond, with more than ten million copies sold. Months later, when Combs released his debut album, *No Way Out*, in it was a letter to Big. The man who partially convinced Combs to try being an artist, and the man who, in so many ways, saved Combs's career and viewed Big as a "gift from God."

"Not a second passes that you're not on my mind. I miss you so much. I still can't believe you're gone," Combs wrote. "I know you're at peace and definitely at a better place, but we still miss you terribly . . . I love you."

In 1997, Big's "Mo Money, Mo Problems" and "Hypnotize" both reached the top spot on the *Billboard*'s Hot 100. And by the start of 1998, Combs's "Been Around the World" nearly completed the trifecta, peaking at number two. Christopher Wallace blew up like he thought he would. It's just a damn shame he couldn't be here on his fiftieth birthday to see it all for himself.

22

THE LIFE AFTER HIS DEATH

A LONG TIME AGO, A FEW YEARS AFTER MY UNCLE DIED FROM COLON CANCER IN 1999, I HEARD THE QUOTE FOR THE FIRST TIME. I was talking to my mom and grandma about college and all these things I wanted to do when I got older. The career I wanted, the cities and countries I wanted to visit, and the money I said I would make that would buy them whatever they wanted. They had had similar conversations with my uncle in the past, and though he only lived to be forty-two, for the most part, he did everything he said he would do. But that's when my mom and grandma taught me the lesson that would completely change how I saw the world and my place in it.

"You know, when you look at your uncle's tombstone—anyone's, really—you see the same thing," my mom said.

"It's two dates on them," my grandma followed up, almost as if they'd rehearsed this routine. "The day you're born and the day you check out of here. But the story is in the dash. Your entire life and everything you are is in that dash."

Such was my approach to writing this book. Big's life and times, as I came to learn about them via books, including Cheo Hodari Coker's stellar 2003 biography *Unbelievable*, articles, podcasts, documentaries, movies, and, most important, his music, made the Notorious B.I.G. a tour de force so fascinating it's almost impossible to believe he accomplished so much in such an abbreviated fragment of time.

Yet during the process of writing this book, the great majority of which was done in the solitude of the pandemic, I came to know him for who he always was: Christopher Wallace. I'm far from the first person to note that Biggie Smalls and Christopher Wallace were two completely different people.

"I hear people talking about Biggie, and really, I can't get my mind around that," said Dr. Moises Smart. He knew him as Chris, one of his best friends in middle school. "The person that I knew was totally different than the character that's portrayed."

But the larger-than-life figure I discovered over the course of writing this book, through hours of original interviews, even more days of research, and my own spiritual journey, was far more complex, far more intentional, and far more human than I ever knew. Being in fifth grade when both Tupac and Big were murdered, I understood the weight of what happened. Or at least I believed I did. I knew their deaths were tragic. I remember being in Philadelphia when Tupac died and seeing grown women and men openly weeping. With Big, it was staying up way too late on a Saturday night knowing I was going to fall asleep in church the next morning—only to have an MTV news alert break the news. With both, I saw the weight it put on older cousins. Those same older cousins schooled me to game, and I was old enough to at least realize that those two losses in such a short amount of time left a hole that would be impossible to fill. With the blessing of growing older hopefully comes wisdom and perspective. It wasn't until I turned twenty-four, like Big, and twenty-five, like 'Pac, that I realized just how young they had been. The reality of just how much they accomplished in such a small window—and just how much responsibility sat on both of their shoulders—really hit me.

Big's loss, and the toll it's taken on those who loved him, has been apparent for the past twenty-five years. But working on this book, I learned just how deep that grief still lives inside people. It's one thing to know Biggie Smalls and to understand just how great an artist he was—or even understand just how much he had an impact on people while he was here. It's another thing to speak to so many who knew the man personally.

"In my mind, when he was out in L.A., I really pictured me and him arguing about putting a bulletproof vest on," said Hubert Sam, who is intentional about calling his friend by his birth name. "Back to when we was in elementary school and his attitude to passing a test would be like, 'Ehh, whatever.' Get a tailor-made flak jacket . . . ride in a bulletproof vehicle." Sam continued, "I figured he was gonna be protected. They needed to have a little more strategy. Being on the phone with you right now, man, I'm in a strange place with his whole legacy, because lately I've been seeing the holes and how things went left. I'm really starting to see more and more how senseless it was that he was lost. Even going back to what we going through in society now, how George Floyd's life got snuffed out on film for everyone to see. That didn't have to happen. He should easily still be alive. Same with Chris. His legacy is stronger than ever, but this doesn't get any easier. I lost my best friend."

This book was not written to answer the question that's been asked ad nauseum over the last quarter century: Who killed Christopher Wallace? But it's impossible not to turn over that leaf, either. The answer to that has been hiding in plain sight for years via YouTube rabbit holes and documentaries that have detailed the night of March 9 and the dizzying connections to the Los Angeles Police Department—whose history of violence against young Black men is extensive—gang politics, the detective Russell Poole's original investigation, and Death Row and Bad Boy Records in Zapruder film–like fashion.

Poole was brought into the case by happenstance. Kevin Gaines, an undercover Los Angeles Police Department officer, was killed by Frank Lyga, another undercover officer on March 18, 1997—coincidentally the same day as Christopher Wallace's funeral. As the lead investigator, Poole had no clue of the depths in which he'd find himself. Gaines's ties to Death Row Records led him to additional officers including David Mack and Rafael Perez. According to the *Los Angeles Times,* "When detectives searched Mack's house in connection with the bank robbery, they found what one police source called 'a shrine' to rapper Tupac Shakur," and a tipster said Mack owned a black Impala. Poole's investigation, which was the subject of the Johnny Depp and Forest Whitaker-led film *City of Lies,* opened the doors for the Rampart Scandal, which uncovered a longstanding culture of corruption within the LAPD. It also led to Voletta Wallace and Faith Evans suing the department for $400 million in a wrongful death lawsuit. The case was initially declared a mistrial because the U.S. district court judge Florence-Marie Cooper found the police had intentionally withheld statements that tied Mack and Perez to the shooting. She ordered the city to pay the family $1.1 million in legal costs. The larger case was ultimately dismissed in 2010. Poole died suddenly from a heart attack in 2015 while meeting with Los Angeles Sheriff's Department detectives.

In 2006, former LAPD detective Greg Kading was brought on to lead the investigation into Big's murder. Though their investigations would lead to starkly different findings, there was one common denominator at the center of it all: Suge Knight.

"If people are waiting on some sort of judicial resolution [in Biggie's murder], it's not gonna happen," said Greg Kading, who led the LAPD's special investigation unit to solve both Biggie's and Tupac's cases from 2006 to 2009. "There's too many complicating factors. So if a prosecution and conviction is how you evaluate justice, then you're gonna be unsatisfied." His theories about who killed both stars and the tangled web of corruption, greed, and fear were the source of his 2011 book *Murder Rap*. This led to the critically acclaimed USA miniseries *Unsolved*—a program that Voletta Wallace told *The Breakfast Club* was "98 percent" true.

"But if you perceive justice in a different way—more universal justice—and recognizing what happened to the people that were involved in Biggie's murder, what are their lives like? How have they suffered?" Kading said in our interview before breaking down the findings he and his team uncovered. "Well, you can't ask for anything more than a life for a life. And the individual that killed Christopher [Kading's team pointed to the longtime Suge Knight associate Wardell "Poochie" Fouse as the triggerman] was shot ten times in the back, basically executed the way Christopher was. So there's a sense of, 'That's perfect justice.'"

When Kading was brought on the case in the mid-2000s, his knowledge of Biggie Smalls was nonexistent. He wasn't a rap fan, and what he saw on the news was the extent of his familiarity. But his approach to the case was the same as it would have been on any murder case he took on throughout his career. If this were a family member or a friend of his, how would he want law enforcement to respond? After Voletta Wallace filed a lawsuit against the LAPD and the city of Los Angeles and demanded hundreds of millions of dollars, there was finally motivation to figure out who killed Big and why. That's when Kading was brought on. They never knew just how much Kading and his special task force would uncover. Over the course of three years, they secured two sworn confessions in not only the murder of Big, but that of Tupac as well. Just when Kading and his team had come within a stone's throw of breaking both cases wide open, he was relieved of his duties. Officially, he was under an LAPD Internal Affairs investigation for making a false statement on a nonrelated case—though he was ultimately cleared of that. Was it a case of Kading flying too close to the sun? Kading doesn't entertain that notion too much, but he's adamant on his and his team's findings.

"I do agree that if there's some type of ranking order, you've got Suge, who I think is the most sinister of them all. You've got Puffy, who was just extremely desperate and made some bad decisions associating with some people he probably shouldn't have been associated with. Then there's Tupac, who kinda begins to assume this kinda gangster persona, at least at the end, by making this decision and a fatal decision that he's going to step up for the gang. And then you've got Biggie, who really didn't take any affirmative action in everything other than maybe some lyrics."

Suge Knight, Kading says, ordered the hit on Big through the misunderstanding that Big had a role in Tupac's murder. Suge pleaded no-contest in a fatal hit-and-run case in 2018 and was sentenced to twenty-eight years. Kading said of Suge, "He's gonna die in prison and suffer the consequences for the choices in his life."

Suge's East Coast rival will, too, Kading says.

"Puffy's never going to sit down and be an open book with law enforcement, because why would he?" Kading said. "Those are skeletons that he has to live with. I think he probably in his deep, dark hours feels a lot of responsibility for what happened. There's just a lot of bad history and bad mojo that has followed that guy around. But not as bad as Suge."

As it relates to Big's murder, Kading says it largely involves three figures. One is Suge, who he alleges organized everything with a girlfriend whose alias was Theresa Swann. Kading says the two connected with Poochie Fouse, a thirty-six-year-old Mob Piru Blood who was extremely close with Suge, and paid him $13,000 for the hit. Fouse was killed in 2003 when he was shot ten times in the back while on his motorcycle. In a 2018 interview, Reggie Wright Jr., the former head of security for Death Row, said he believed Fouse was indeed the gunman.

With Suge in jail perhaps for the rest of his life and Fouse dead for almost twenty years, Kading says it's Swann who's left with the most emotional debt. "She's not faced justice and won't because of the conditions of the investigation. She's got prosecutorial immunity. I believe she has a responsibility to Miss Wallace to apologize and to admit her role in the whole thing."

And when he presented Voletta with the extent of his findings?

"She started crying. I started crying. My wife started crying, and it was this moment of just intimacy and honesty about her vulnerability. And how she may have not been completely informed as to what happened in the case in the prior investigation and potentially was misled.

"Those are the conditions. Those are the situations," Kading said, before asking a soul-stirring question. "So you have to ask yourself—what's just?"

A quarter century following Christopher Wallace's murder, the answer to that rhetorical question is as painful as the reality. The LAPD will not officially solve the case because the connection between many of its officers and many of the players involved runs deep. And the street operates on its own code—for those lucky enough to still be alive. But even then it's an emotional burden with no tangible sense of closure.

"I would love it if at some point everybody got in the same room at a conference and locked the doors, ordered food, and compared notes," Coker told me. "I think ultimately Greg probably got the closest. I've always thought, if we're being honest, that it was more of a Puffy and Suge having beef with each other and people around them taking it much further than it ever should've gotten than it was a Biggie trying to come at 'Pac–type shit. They were, to me, the collateral damage of the real street shit."

No matter how fascinating the story around his death is, Big represents so much more than what happened at the corner of Fairfax and Wilshire in Los Angeles a quarter century ago. His story was that of what America afforded Black people, or rather didn't afford. He's a product of post–civil rights movement America and the capitalistic bloodthirstiness the crack era and war on drugs left no other choice for so many Black folks to purse in the eighties.

Now, granted, Big had a choice. He didn't have to hit that corner and go from an honor-roll student who could've likely obtained a scholarship to his pick of schools. But how much could he have ever realized the choice he had? Outside his mother, the depth of role models with "traditional" career and life paths were few and far between. Also, Big was young when he finally stepped off the stoop. It's not uncommon for young people to make foolish short-term decisions. He made a bad choice, but it's hard to totally fault Big. That is one thing about Big I hope people appreciate and understand. He made a bad choice because that bad choice seemed like the only choice in the moment, and he stopped making that choice when he found a viable alternative.

"I can honestly tell you in a different environment that kid would've been Shakespeare. Obviously, we probably would've been deprived of Biggie and his wonderful works. But at the same time, the things he was exposed to really had consequences," said Smart. "I don't mean to be so dramatic, but it's just very close to my heart. I've seen so many kids that were gifted and just threw it away, you know?"

Travel through Big's journey and there are countless times you'll ask yourself why—or beg in your mind for him to take a different route. His success is a tale of ghetto triumph, but there are also sides to his personality that deserve further examination in a world where uncomfortable conversations are way more out in the open than they were when he walked this Earth.

In life, Big was like so many other Black men—misunderstood by society, beloved by his community, and wielding his talent to make space for himself in the wider world. The words he spoke with that one-of-a-kind flow and the stories he brought to life captured what it was like growing up Black in America and the horrors that experience brought. But also its countless beauties. And, somewhere in the middle, the uncomfortable complexities of it, too. His music was never monolithic because he wasn't, because none of us are.

His art has outlived him. In some ways, it makes it as if he never truly left. Walk into any party right now and turn on "Big Poppa," "One More Chance," "Player's Anthem," "Mo' Money, Mo' Problems," or almost any song from his brief-yet-incredibly-prolific catalog and gauge the reaction. Say "Spread love, it's the Brooklyn way" and try not to smile. Pull up on the corner of Fulton

Street and St. James Place, or, as it's known now, Christopher "Notorious B.I.G." Wallace Way. Or watch his *Martin* episode and try not to laugh. When we talk about the word "legacy," Christopher Wallace has just that.

"It is undeniable that when you hear the story of Brooklyn, that we have a story no other city in the world has: it is a story of triumph," said Laurie A. Cumbo, a New York City Council member, at the street naming in 2019. "During the time that Biggie created masterpieces, this neighborhood was redlined; people didn't want to live here, people moved out of the neighborhood, they left us to die. But there were people that struggled, people that fought—now everybody in the world wants to come to Brooklyn."

How Big lost his life will always be tragic, as painful an American fable there is. At the time of publication, he'll have been off this Earth for longer than he was on it. Life has gone on without Christopher Wallace in the physical sense, but that doesn't make it any easier. One of the most powerful moments in the course of writing this book came from DJ 50 Grand, the man who originally thought it would be a good idea if Big Chris recorded a demo tape. 50 Grand had no idea how far that demo tape would take his friend. These days, he celebrates his fallen comrade whenever he can: through block parties, Instagram posts, and clothing. He celebrates Big because he's come to accept that mourning is a lifelong process. In early 1997, 50 was on house arrest from a situation he got himself into previously, but he saw Big when he came to do a photo shoot for *Life After Death* on Bedford and Quincy.

Big was telling him he had to go to Los Angeles to promote the album.

"Do you really gotta go?" 50 asked. He already knew the answer to that, but he had to ask it anyway.

He begged Big not to go. He begged and begged and begged. The last words 50 ever said to him were "Don't go."

Big listened to 50 in the spiritual sense. Later in the interview, something else stuck with me. 50 says he still talks to Big all the time. The last quarter century hasn't gotten any easier for 50, but those conversations help.

"I talk to Biggie every day because they got a Big mural on Bedford and Quincy where the battle took place," he said. "I just start drinking and talk to him. People think I'm talking to myself, but that wall ain't there for nothing."

23
C.J.'S A MAN NOW

"I want him to be able to always feel, 'I can tell my pops anything 'cause that nigga's just the coolest nigga ever.' That's what I wanna be. I wanna be the nigga's best friend more than anything."
—CHRISTOPHER GEORGE LATORE WALLACE, JANUARY 1997

ON THE TWENTY-THIRD ANNIVERSARY OF CHRISTOPHER WAL-LACE'S PASSING, CHRISTOPHER WALLACE SAUNTERS THROUGH BROOKLYN ONCE MORE. Christopher Jordan, that is—the son of Christopher George Latore Wallace. Better known simply as C.J., the then twenty-three-year-old was back on the East Coast visiting family for a few days. Yet on March 9, 2020, C.J., a self-proclaimed L.A. native at heart, is in Brooklyn to support his older sister, T'yanna, for her first fashion show for her Notoriouss clothing line.

In a dark green Maison Margiela suit and shiny black Bottega Veneta shoes and, fittingly, a crisp New York Yankees fitted cap, C.J. hovers around T'yanna's show with the charisma, elegance, and swagger of the pops he was robbed of getting to know. Never the loudest in the room because his presence alone speaks volumes. Like father, like son.

The event, an invite-only affair, takes place at the Access Community Wellness Center on the 4000 block of Church Avenue, roughly three and a half miles from where Biggie grew up. Nearly two hundred people pack into the event as DJ Big Lou runs through a list of Big's greatest hits while never missing an opportunity to tell the crowd, "Twenty-three years later, he's still the best rapper!"

Shortly before the event started, C.J. and I cross paths. "Glad you could make it out, bro," he said, dapping me up with a drink in tow. As the music blared behind us, the deep, hypnotic voice of his biological father filled every corner of the room. With C.J., there's the ever-so-slight lazy eye. The measured poise in how he speaks. And a cool factor that can't be taught, but only passed down by hereditary measures, glows. "We gotta link up after this and chop it up."

The event goes off without a hitch that night, none of us thinking this would be our last time outside for months due to the pandemic. Lil' Cease gives the introduction for the event. C.J. and I sit on opposite white couches near the front of the makeshift runway. The models sport custom-made tank tops, shirts, shorts, and sweatpants all created with T'yanna's vision. She's the star of the evening, and she should be.

Roughly an hour and a half later, C.J. and his crew head back out into the Brooklyn night. And just like old times, Christopher Wallace is roaming those Brooklyn streets once more.

———

Christopher Jordan Wallace Jr. was born to Faith Evans and Christopher Wallace a few days before Halloween in 1996. "Lil' C.J.," as his dad called him, was the product of a brief reconciliation between the R&B starlet and hip-hop superstar. They were both young—Biggie was twenty-two and Faith was twenty-one—and famous. Biggie, by his own admission, was far from the model of fidelity in the marriage. And both involuntarily found themselves woven into a very public and disastrous entanglement with Tupac Shakur.

In the final weeks of his life, though, Biggie saw clarity in a failed public relationship. C.J. was the blessing.

"It's just the relationship ain't work out, but we gon' always be together because we got a lil' shorty together," Big said in February 1997. "That's gon' be the happy part of me and her. Lil' shorty."

C.J. was born in New York City, but Los Angeles is home.

"Along with Atlanta," he was quick to point out in our interview. "I can't forget about Atlanta."

Los Angeles, however, is where C.J. grew up. It's where he found himself, and it's where the bulk of his life experiences have taken place. He's not thinking about starting a family at this exact moment, but when that time does arrive, it's not really a question as to where he'd want to plant those roots.

"The more I think about it, the more I'm like, so in love with California," he told me. "I couldn't see myself raising a family anywhere else. Or living permanently anywhere else."

The thought has always been in the back of his mind. He doesn't think about it every day, or every week for that matter. But it's there. It's always been there for as long as he can remember. The city he calls home is the same city where his dad took his final breath. Make no mistake, though, Big adored Cali, so much so that in the final weeks of his life he openly contemplated moving out west.

"It's been kinda strange, because I'm so comfortable here. But there's always that thought in the back of my head like, this is the place that took him, if you will," C.J. said before going momentarily silent. "Man, I can't really pinpoint how I've been able to sort of almost block that out, because I don't really think about it that much . . . It's been a journey, man. Just being the West Coast kid with an East Coast foundation and roots. I take pride in that. I love all things Cali."

C.J. admits that in his younger years he grew up sheltered. All of his siblings were. The occasional album releases would come around, or his mom's video shoots, and C.J. would be seen out with his siblings, but for the most part, he wasn't a permanent fixture in the public eye.

"It wasn't like *Run's House*, where we had a camera in the house," C.J. laughed. "Or even having a lot of people around always at the house."

Mention the name Todd Russaw to C.J. and see where he takes the conversation. Or, as C.J. knights him, "the man who raised me." A long-time music industry producer, talent manager, and former A&R at Motown Records, Russaw married Evans in 1998. In C.J.'s voice when he speaks of Russaw lives a deep reverence.

"He's been everything," C.J. said. "He's always been that person to remind me, scream on me, and let me know when I'm doing something wrong or when I need to study this or look at that. He's everything to me. I can't put it any other way."

Russaw has also been the most important source in helping him understand who his biological father was. To suggest that his mother hasn't spoken about his father over the last twenty-five years would be inaccurate, but away from cameras, press runs, and interviews, C.J. and his mother didn't discuss his father nearly as much as C.J. and Russaw. "When it comes to talking about that relationship, I feel like there's still a lot of emotion for her that she hasn't really unpacked," C.J. said. "I'm definitely eager to ask her these questions, though."

In his early years, C.J. spent a lot of time in Atlanta, and prior to their permanent move out west in 2004, they would visit L.A. and stay in an apartment off Ocean Drive in Santa Monica a few months of the year. During one of those trips, when C.J. was about five or six, Russaw took him to the corner of Fairfax Avenue and Wilshire Boulevard. Though C.J. wasn't initially able to comprehend the totality of what was happening, he knew his dad, Russaw, was attempting to tell him more of his family's history.

"[My dad] would explain to me, 'Yeah, this is where it happened. Right here,'" C.J. said, reflecting on the first time Russaw explained what happened on March 9, 1997. "We'd always say a prayer. He'd always turn the music down, bow our heads, and say a prayer. I just continued to do that as I got older."

As C.J. has grown older and the gravity of his name came into clearer light, he has begun to understand just *why* the world could never let go of his memory. The first time it truly clicked for him was when he was filming his role in the 2009 biopic *Notorious*. C.J., then twelve years old, played the role of his father in his younger years. In the years before, friends who listened to rap would ask what it was like to be the son of an icon, but it didn't quite hit home until he was on a movie set with Angela Bassett, Derek Luke, and Anthony Mackie and getting points from director George Tillman Jr.

The respect that C.J. felt on set changed his life. He wasn't just a kid playing a role in a movie. He was the son of the man who had inspired an entire film. The experience went by quickly. In just a little over a month, C.J. felt the impact.

"It almost felt like looking at the pictures of the funeral," he says. "Just the amount of people that were on the streets and part of it. That was the first time I really got to feel his impact as a preteen, young adult."

That impact only became more and more refined as adolescence gave way to young adulthood. In late January 1997, just six weeks before his death, Biggie spoke to *ego trip* magazine of the recent birth of his son. And how excited he was to be part of his life. "I definitely want him to be able to learn from his mistakes," the elder Christopher Wallace said. "But at the same time, I would never want him to feel like he would have to sell a drug or do anything out of the ordinary, because I'm here."

When Big was eighteen, he still had one foot firmly in the crack game and the other tiptoeing into the music industry. By the time C.J. was eighteen, he was a California kid far removed from ever knowing that lifestyle. Able to pursue the life he wanted without having to look over his shoulder.

When he was eighteen, C.J. began working at a fashion boutique called Ssur. "The coolest job I ever had," he chuckled at the reflection. But the connections to his biological father were everywhere. The store's owner, with whom he quickly established a great rapport, was from Coney Island in Brooklyn. The job, too, was right off Fairfax Avenue.

"That became my daily route. I would always end up driving down Fairfax, so I would always pass by that spot," C.J. said. The same routine would occur every day for nearly two years. Stop. Cut the music down. And say a prayer.

"I'd remind myself that it's just so much more important than east versus west. Everything he was trying to accomplish, I'm continuing in that."

━━━━━━━━━

Words matter. It's a lesson C.J. has learned his entire life, from his own experiences but also from the man who shares his name. But intentions do, too. Talk to C.J. for five minutes and it's evident that he values both. He's been no stranger to the decades of analysis of his dad and Tupac Shakur's friendship and falling out. In many ways due to ill-timed words and intentions. Those principles? They go with him everywhere.

"I've always been really mindful of that. My dad named his album *Ready to Die*, and I believe whatever you put into the universe comes back to you," C.J. says. "I don't really think about 'Pac in any malice or regretful way or wishing things should've happened differently. Because if anything would've happened differently, truthfully, I might not be here . . . It's sad as hell. It's really fucked up to think about it that way. But it's the only way that kinda gives me peace."

Christopher Wallace's top priority when it came to fatherhood was simple. He wanted to be there. In the decade before C.J.'s birth in late 1996, Wallace's life had changed dramatically. He'd gone from honor roll middle school student to crack dealer to high school dropout working in New York and North Carolina to aspiring artist to the biggest name in the game alongside a man he once saw as a comrade. In 1996, in terms of stature in the game, Big was all alone.

Yet if there was a truth to Christopher Wallace (the father), it's that he understood his place in the world at all times. It didn't mean he always made the right decision—because which teenagers and young men in their early twenties always do? Nor does that absolve him of the mistakes he made. But there was an element of fatherhood that he cherished. In a way, it was a chance to begin anew, a rebirth.

"He was a dedicated father; not time-wise," Jan Jackson, mother of Big's daughter T'yanna, said in a 2008 oral history with *Blender*. "But in what he wanted for her future."

They grew up brother and sister. Not half brother and half sister. That was the way Voletta, Jan, and Faith always envisioned them growing up. There's a particular excited inflection in C.J.'s voice that arises whenever he gets to talk about T'yanna. About her own business ventures—not just the clothing line, but also things like Juicy Pizza, a restaurant she opened in L.A. in 2021 along with Tyra Myricks, the daughter of Jam Master Jay. But, really, how they've been on a particular journey only they understand for as long as they can remember.

"When we were younger and I was living in New Jersey, me and T'yanna were always tight all the time," C.J. said. "We're still the same, and it's always been that way. I don't know if it's because we have the same dad, but no matter how long we haven't seen each other it's like no time has been missed . . . distance doesn't change anything for us."

"When I had my daughter, it was like a little girl, so it was kinda like [I want to spoil her]," Big told *ego trip* in 1997. "But with a son . . . you wanna be able to school your son to the shit niggas was schooling niggas to. I want that to be my little partner right there. Put him on to everything. So nobody could ever get over on him."

A product of the internet era, C.J. has gotten to know his biological father in the same way that millions of others have over the last quarter century. Though his father only recorded two studio albums in his short lifetime, the internet holds a king's ransom of material, including interviews, music videos, documentaries, books, and even social media accounts dedicated to posting rare content.

But it's those sorts of comments—the "my little partner" comments—that both haunt and bless C.J.

"It makes me really sad that I don't have any memory of him," he said. "But it also makes me really excited to be a father as well. I wanna have that same passion for it . . . be that happy when that moment comes."

For C.J., there's also comfort in knowing that while his dad didn't have everything figured out at twenty-four, he was ready to take on the challenge of being a young Black man raising another young Black man in a world that has always viewed young Black men as expendable. Despite his growing fame in his final years, Big and his mother spoke constantly. Those deep conversations, C.J. says, revolved around fatherhood and wanting to change for the better. That's inspirational for C.J.

"[My dad's commitment to fatherhood] used to really kinda fuck with me. But now it's the biggest inspiration and drive for me," C.J. told me. He didn't really know how to speak about how missing his dad made him feel. Publicly, at least. "I just didn't know because I never talked to anybody about it. He's my guardian angel at the end of the day. Even when I'm somewhere I know I shouldn't be, I still feel like he's watching me and protecting me."

People are never just one thing, even if that's often how we register them in our minds. So while Christopher Jordan Wallace may be the son of Christopher Wallace and Faith Evans, while he may be "Biggie and Faith's kid," he is his own man.

"Whatever [C.J.] wants to do in life," his father said in early 1997, "it's completely his choice."

C.J. didn't attempt to follow in the patriarchal footsteps exactly, though it's hard to imagine Big wouldn't have approved of C.J.'s passion and career choice. C.J., a modern-day Renaissance man who already has acting and musical credits to his name, is a founder (with Todd Russaw and Willie Mack) of the appropriately titled Think BIG, a company dedicated to leading the "social movement that is fighting for global cannabis legalization, police and criminal justice reform and economic investment into communities most harmed by cannabis prohibition." The same war on drugs that introduced his father to the criminal justice system is the one C.J. is attempting to end, at least on one front.

As much as it is a dedication to societal change, Think BIG is personal. C.J. witnessed CBD's health benefits during his grandmother's fight against breast cancer and his younger brother Ryder's experience living with autism. There's this, too. Christopher Wallace, father and son, love their weed and even love the same strain: Lamb's Bread.

"My dad loved sativas, man. Chronic, sour, all that shit," C.J. said, unable to control his laughter. "Which means he needed to have an upper and probably worked best off those. It makes so much sense now that you think about it."

A junior outliving the senior who preceded him isn't uncommon. But when neither were afforded the opportunity to occupy the same airspace, to grow with each other, and to actually love each other, it's a reminder that life is never a fairy tale, and that horrible circumstances often dictate the course of a life. At the time this book was first published, C.J. was but months removed of his twenty-fifth birthday—the one his father missed by seventy-four days.

As for his father's final moments, he's done searching legal closure.

"[T'yanna and I] have both done enough research and watched enough documentaries to sort of draw our own conclusions," C.J. said. Does he feel like the Los Angeles Police Department could've done more to finding the assailants? "I'm not gonna go out and say the police were the murderers, but I will say it's too late at the end of the day."

He's been at more parties than he can count when any one of his dad's songs comes on and the crowd reacts. C.J. loves watching the room to see who knows what song, what lyric strikes the most nerves. He loves the debates over why Biggie Smalls is the greatest of all time. Or not. It doesn't matter. Those are the moments when junior and senior connect in the most heavenly way possible.

Living with regrets isn't the way C.J. was raised. It wouldn't do him any favors anyway. There are longings, though.

"I *really* wish I was alive through that time period. I don't have that same emotional connection to his music," said C.J. "I really wish I did."

He's like everyone else when they hear "Biggie Smalls at fifty." He's been gone longer than he was ever here, and even that just doesn't seem real. So what would he tell his dad on his fiftieth birthday?

"Fuck," he responded when asked this question. "I really don't know. I know I'd be smoking with him and we'd be joking about everything."

In a perfect world, C.J., his biological dad, and the man who raised him, Todd Russaw, would be thick as thieves. But even that comes with an alternate reality.

"It's so strange to think about if he were still here because if he was, I probably wouldn't have my two younger brothers. And they're like my best friends," he said, trying to weigh the totality of it all. "It's really hard to imagine what things would be like if things were different.

"Fifty years? Man, who knows the conversations we'd be having," C.J. said with a laugh. "I'd probably just give him a pound of weed and be like, 'Let's see who knocks out first.'"

ACKNOWLEDGMENTS

SEEING AS HOW THIS IS THE CLOSEST I'LL EVER COME TO GIVING A GRAMMY SPEECH, LET'S GO AHEAD AND START.
There's absolutely no way this book would have ever been completed without my beautiful wife, Jade, who was there for quite literally every step of the process. From telling her, "I think I got some spam from this guy named Jamison who wants me to write a book on Biggie" to her being there when I signed the contract to do this; to her suffering through my panic attacks about not being able to get enough interviews and wondering how I would come up with 100,000 words; to sending in my first draft last spring. She's been a life force that I couldn't ask God for a better version of. Jade, thank you. *For everything.*

To my mom and grandma, thank you. Ma, you taught me the value of research and understanding that each step of the process was all for realizing a blessing I couldn't even imagine. Grandma, those stories we shared over the years about everything have motivated me—and will always motivate me. You wanted to work in nutrition when you graduated from Xavier University in New Orleans in the early '50s, but Black women couldn't participate in that line of work. Having the opportunity to do what I love, and to see the pride in your face, knowing you were never given that chance, means the world to me.

To my in-laws, Jackie and Laurence, thank you for allowing me to use your house as a means to work on this book. I did my first interview during quarantine and worked on so many hours of outlines, notes, and additional interviews there. Ernest and Stephanie, thank you for your excitement about this from day one. This is you all's book, just as much as it is mine.

There are also a ton of people I want to give individual shout-outs to, the great majority of whom took the time to speak with me for this book, and some of whom were beacons of inspiration and light when I needed it the most. To C.J. Wallace, thank you so much for your patience and your trust. Hubert Sam, I consider you a friend and your friendship means the world to me. I'll never forget that. To Chico Del Vic, I know how much Chris—that's what you called him throughout our interview—will always mean to you, and those hours we spent talking was life-altering. DJ 50 Grand and Mister Cee, without you, this book simply wouldn't have happened. To Matty C, thank you for challenging me on every question I asked. Drew Dixon, your strength and your personality gave me so much courage to keep writing. Donald Harrison, your attention to detail is second to none. Stacy Carmichael, I—as a Hampton grad—have got mad love for Howard, and you're another reason why. Grant Hill, all love for the hour-long conversation we had about Big. Jessica Chong and Moises Smart, those intimate details about young Christopher Wallace were incredible. Greg Dent, those stories of Big in Raleigh were dope as hell! Rob Stone, where would this book be without you—thankfully, I'll never know! Barron Claiborne, it was a true honor to speak with the man behind one of Big's most iconic photos. Groovey Lew, thank you so much for your candid transparency. Naima Cochrane, the way you put our culture in proper perspective is breathtaking. Kierna Mayo, your honesty and vividness kept me going. Alan Light, you were part of the front line covering rap in the '90s and that position was critical to this book. Steve Smith, it's impossible to talk about hip-hop and not mention Hot 97—you're part of the reason for that.

There are so many more people I would love to thank, but I have to specially thank Cheo Hodari Coker and Rob Kenner. You two were the minds behind the original Biggie biography, *Unbelievable*. In a way, I'll always be chasing the quality of such a phenomenal piece of work. Rob, thank you so much for your support and just always being willing to ride for me even though we've technically never met in person. Cheo, I've got so much love in my heart for you. You're a real-life superhero. From the moment I told you about this, you've been in my corner 100 percent. To have you cosign for me is an honor I'll cherish for the rest of my life. Thank you.

I also want to thank some of my closest confidants who held me down throughout this process, like my brother Anthony, Aunt Cynt, Kim, Angela, Terry, Alana, Kaden, Brad, Sophia, Danielle, Jon, Trevon, B.P., Dax, Momo, Kevon, Coy, Shannon, Elliott, Danyel, Kateri, Vaughan, Gotty, David, Kelley Carter, Kelley Evans, Jason Reid, Marc Spears, Kevin Merida, Stephen Reiss, Mirin Fader, Yoh Phillips, Max, Will, Jean, Dawan, Joanne and so many more. Rest in peace to my Uncle John, Aunt Alexis, and my grandmother-in-law Angelia. I love all of y'all.

I want to thank the family and loved ones of Christopher Wallace. This book isn't officially stamped by the Wallace estate, nor did I get the opportunity to speak with Miss Wallace, Faith Evans, Jan, T'yanna, Diddy, D-Roc, Lil' Cease, Lil' Kim, Wayne Barrow, Mark Pitts, and so many more. But hopefully, you find this book a fitting testament to someone who will always represent such an important part of who you are. I only mean for this book to be a true, honest, accurate—even if harsh, at times—and beautiful embodiment of who Christopher was and what he means to the world he changed. In Miss Wallace's memoir, I read about a journalist who years ago took her kindness and grief for weakness and how that soured her trust. Lord knows I couldn't blame her for that. I do hope you see the pure intention in this book. Thank you for being you. And thank you for your courage and commitment to keeping Chris/Big's name so alive over the last quarter century.

To the team at Abrams, I appreciate you all, more than you know. I'd never written a book before, and to write about someone of the magnitude of Big, it seemed fake. Salute to Jamison Stoltz, who is one of the most laid-back people I've ever met and one hell of an editor. To my agent, Charita Johnson, I love having a Black woman in my corner, and I love that our bond will always run deeper than business. Randall Williams, I appreciate you bossing up and knocking out so much archival research for me in the early stages.

I could keep going, but I'm sure this is already too long. It's impossible to describe just how taxing writing a book is. But it's also the same trying to describe just how fulfilling it is. I'm so blessed and I'm so honored to share this space with you. Hopefully you've gotten as much out of the book as I did writing it. Your time is deeply valued. Thank you so much. And, who knows, we just might end up running this entire process back again sometime in the future.